ARTFUL DODGERS

ARTFUL DODGERS

Reconceiving the Golden Age of Children's Literature

MARAH GUBAR

Oxford University Press, Inc., publishes works that further
Oxford University's objective of excellence
in research, scholarship, and education.

Oxford New York
Auckland Cape Town Dar es Salaam Hong Kong Karachi
Kuala Lumpur Madrid Melbourne Mexico City Nairobi
New Delhi Shanghai Taipei Toronto

With offices in
Argentina Austria Brazil Chile Czech Republic France Greece
Guatemala Hungary Italy Japan Poland Portugal Singapore
South Korea Switzerland Thailand Turkey Ukraine Vietnam

First issued as an Oxford University Press paperback, 2010

Published by Oxford University Press, Inc.
198 Madison Avenue, New York, New York 10016
www.oup.com

Library of Congress Cataloging-in-Publication Data
Gubar, Marah, 1973–
Artful dodgers : reconceiving the golden age of children's literature / Marah Gubar.
p. cm.
Includes bibliographical references and index.
ISBN 978-0-19-975674-2
1. Children's literature, English—History and criticism.
2. English literature—19th century—History and criticism.
3. Children in literature. 4. Childhood in literature.
5. Adolescence in literature. I. Title.
PR990.G83 2008
820.9'928209034—dc22 2008024308

Printed in the United States of America
on acid-free paper

To Kieran, with all my love

PREFACE

There is something odd about the way scholars treat the Golden Age of children's literature. On the one hand, the unprecedented explosion of children's literature that took place from the mid-nineteenth to the early twentieth century has been accorded immense respect, as the "Golden Age" moniker indicates. Indeed, it would be difficult to deny the importance of an era when writers such as Lewis Carroll and J. M. Barrie penned famous fantasies that continue to be read and recycled into new forms to this day. Yet the same authors who have been given the most credit for making the Golden Age golden have simultaneously been censured for producing escapist literature that failed to engage with the complexities of contemporary life and promoted a static, highly idealized picture of childhood as a time of primitive simplicity.

This familiar (and still circulating) critical account underestimates the richness and complexity of Golden Age children's literature. To be sure, like Charles Dickens, George Eliot, and other Victorians writing primarily for adult audiences, children's writers from this era sometimes invoke an ideal of innocence inherited from the Romantics. But far from being the worst offenders in this regard, they frequently complicate, challenge, ironize, or interrogate the artless "Child of Nature" paradigm. It is time, in other words, to let go of the idea that Carroll and company failed to conceive of children as complex, acculturated human beings in their own right by regarding them either as lost selves or alien Others. On the contrary, celebrated children's authors from this era frequently characterize the child as a collaborator who is caught up in the constraints of the culture he inhabits—just as older people are—and yet not inevitably victimized as a result of this contact with adults and their world. By entertaining the idea that children might have the ability to cope with, deflect, or even evade adults' efforts to control or oppress them, these authors react against Dickensian plots that imply that youngsters who work and play alongside adults (including the so-called Artful Dodger) are not in fact inventive or ingenious enough to avoid a sad fate.

Part of my goal here is to insist that we accord the Victorians the same kind of respect the Romantics have recently received by recognizing that their representations of children are just as diverse and dynamic as their predecessors'. Much good work has been done recently that acknowledges there is no such thing as a singular Romantic Child, since authors such as William Wordsworth vacillated quite dramatically in their stance toward youth. Yet the notion that the Victorians avidly latched onto, simplified, and sentimentalized Romantic discourse about childhood continues to enjoy widespread support. In an effort to illustrate how much nuance and variation there was in the Victorians' stance toward children, this book contends that two concurrent, intertwined phenomena—Golden Age children's literature and the cult of the child—must be reconceived to reflect the fact that many of the male and female artists who participated in them were *conflicted* about the issue of how to conceive of children rather than fully committed to a particular ideal of innocence. Moreover, far from being oblivious to the possibility that adult fantasies about childhood might impinge on children, the Victorians and Edwardians frequently manifested a high level of critical self-consciousness about the whole problem of representing, writing for, looking at, interacting with, and worshipping children.

One difficulty I ran into in the process of trying to make this argument was that the nineteenth-century cult of the child has often been referred to but rarely described in any detail. While articles on individual authors such as Carroll and John Ruskin sometimes identify their subjects as members of the cult, I could not find a single study that fully defined the parameters of this phenomenon. Going back to what I assumed was the foundational scholarly account, George Boas's *The Cult of Childhood* (1966), I was amazed to discover that he spends fewer than three pages discussing the Victorians and Edwardians, never mentioning Carroll, Ruskin, and many other artists who are now commonly associated with the cult. Boas does not linger on this period because he treats the cult not as a social trend that originated in a particular historical moment but as a doctrinal group to which anyone at any time or in any place can belong, as long as they subscribe to a form of cultural primitivism whereby the child replaces the noble savage as a paradigm of the human ideal. Indeed, reading *The Cult of Childhood* is a pleasure precisely because Boas so effortlessly accesses a diverse range of sources, from French and German texts to English and American ones, from Plato to Norman O. Brown.

Yet Boas's theory of a transnational, transhistorical cult of childhood does not adequately account for the particularity and complexities of the newly intense obsession with childhood that numerous scholars assert originated with the Victorians (even though they decline to fully articulate this argument or provide a detailed list of participants). Thus, even the brief catalogue of nineteenth-century writers that Boas generates—Dickens, Eliot, Algernon Charles Swinburne, Frances Hodgson Burnett, and Henry James—complicates his characterization of the cultists as united in their adherence to the notion that contact with adult civilization will despoil the child's primitive purity, since several of these authors were at best ambivalent about the idea of exalting the innocent otherness of children. Sensitive to such waverings and distinctions, the most brilliant and influential theorist of Victorian child-loving, James R. Kincaid, has proposed that we drop the whole concept of the cult from our critical conversation: "The image [of the innocent child] does not seem to me all that common in the nineteenth century, propaganda about 'the cult of the child' notwithstanding" (*Child-Loving* 73).

I strongly agree with Kincaid's point that the Victorians did not wholeheartedly embrace the ideal of childhood purity, but I want to resist his suggestion that we should therefore dismiss the cult as an unhelpful category—an injunction that has surely contributed to the critical silence surrounding the term. For one thing, the cult is one of the very few literary–historical categories that absolutely demands that we consider children's literature alongside mainstream "adult" texts, a valuable and still underutilized strategy that enriches our understanding of both fields. Moreover, it seems crucial to recognize that this term is not a label critics have retroactively imposed on the past but rather a phrase the Victorians themselves invented to make sense of their own culture, as I will demonstrate. Rather than dismissing the term because the strand of cultural primitivism Boas traces does not match up perfectly with the late Victorian moment, we should grant Boas his "cult of childhood" for that transhistorical trend, and use "the cult of the child" to refer specifically to the Victorians and Edwardians. After all, this is the phrase the poet and essayist Ernest Dowson used as a title for his 1889 essay in which he boldly claimed: "There is no more distinctive feature of the age than the enormous importance which children have assumed" ("Cult of the Child" 434).

Such statements by Victorians provide support for my claim that we ought to conceive of the cult of the child as a phenomenon generated by inhabitants of a specific cultural moment, who were in contact with and influencing one another. As a group, they shared a tendency to set up the child as the epitome of attractiveness for a *variety* of reasons, often while pondering the question of what the implications of this radical shift in regard were for both children and adults. As I will show, the artwork and actions of many key members of the cult were informed not simply (or even mainly) by primitivism but by a habit of extolling the child's innocent simplicity while simultaneously indulging a profound fascination with youthful sharpness and precocity. Reconceived in this way, the term "the cult of the child" can be redeployed to help us appreciate the work of a wide range of creative Victorians, including visual artists (John Everett Millais, Julia Margaret Cameron, Frederic Harrison, Philip Wilson Steer, Walter Sickert); religious authorities (Frances Kilvert, Edward White Benson); children's authors (Carroll, Burnett, Barrie, Kenneth Grahame, Stella Austin, Amy Le Feuvre); and a variety of other kinds of writers (Dickens, Eliot, Ruskin, Ernest Dowson, Marie Corelli, Joseph Ashby-Sterry, Henry James).

Let me hasten to add that this book represents only the first step of my ongoing effort to delineate and redefine the cult of the child. A full account of this phenomenon would need to examine in greater depth the representation of children in visual art and literary texts aimed at adults, as well as exploring the possibility that it was a transatlantic trend. After all, there was a great deal of contact between England and North America at this time, with popular books and plays featuring child characters travelling freely back and forth across the ocean. Burnett's life and work illustrates this point; born in England, raised in America, her literary and dramatic productions were popular on both sides of the Atlantic. While I do discuss the hard-to-categorize Burnett here, in general this study focuses exclusively on British authors, not because Americans did not participate in the cult and the Golden Age of children's literature, but simply because my overarching argument here is so bound up in trying to bring out the complexities of the English attitude toward childhood during this period. I do however believe that my central argument can be extended outward to apply to American children's classics such as *Little Women* and *Adventures of Huckleberry Finn*, so I refer occasionally to these and other major American texts.

I cannot possibly mention by name all of the people who have helped me in what has often seemed like an impossible task. But I must thank the brilliant teachers and mentors who made my undergraduate experience at the University of Michigan so wonderful, especially Bert Cardullo, James Winn, and Patsy Yaeger. I was also very lucky to have a series of superb interlocutors at Princeton, including U. C. Knoepflmacher, who nurtured this project from its origins as a two-page response paper and supported me even when I was at my most anxious and defensive. Claudia L. Johnson, Jeff Nunokawa, Esther Schor, and Carolyn Williams also deserve special mention for helping me survive graduate school, as does the Jacob K. Javits Fellowship Program for supporting me very generously during my time at Princeton.

Thanks, too, to all of my colleagues at the University of Pittsburgh, who have been so universally encouraging that I cannot name everyone who has helped me, although Troy Boone must get special credit for reading and commenting on so many drafts, and Dave Bartholomae and Jim Knapp for all the support they have given me since I first arrived at Pitt. I am also profoundly grateful to the knowledgeable and obliging staff at Hillman Library, especially Eugene M. Sawa, Elizabeth Mahoney, and Robert Hallead. A University of Pittsburgh

Faculty of Arts and Sciences Third Term Research Grant enabled me to finish the manuscript more quickly, while a generous gift from the Richard D. and Mary Jane Edwards Endowed Publication Fund paid for the pictures.

An earlier version of my fourth chapter appeared under the same title in *Style* 35.3 (Fall 2001): 410-29. Chapters 5 and 6 draw on several passages from "The Drama of Precocity: Child Performers on the Victorian Stage," my contribution to *The Nineteenth-Century Child and Consumer Culture* (Ashgate 2008). Together, these chapters offer a more carefully qualified version of the argument I made there about the appeal of nineteenth-century child actors. Thanks, then, to *Style* and Ashgate, and of course to everyone at Oxford University Press, especially Shannon McLachlan, Christina Gibson, Brendan O'Neill, and Karla Pace. I am also deeply grateful to Martha Ramsey for her phenomenally accurate and intelligent copyediting.

In the past few years, I have been extremely blessed to have had wonderful female mentors at my own institution and elsewhere, especially Mary Briscoe, Karen Coats, Nancy Glazener, Laurie Langbauer, Michelle Martin, Julia Mickenberg, Claudia Nelson, Roberta Seelinger Trites, and the late and much-missed Mitzi Myers. My gratitude to them is beyond words. Similarly, I have drawn enormous amounts of support from dear friends from each period of my life, including Liz Zirker, Allison Garner, and Eva Sanders in high school, Kate Guyton and Susan Welch at Michigan, and Jennifer Trainor and Amanda Godley at Pittsburgh. My time in graduate school was marked by an embarrassment of riches where friends were concerned; I cannot mention everyone, but I must convey my deep affection and thanks to Elissa Bell, Peter Betjemann, Lorna Brittan, Erik Gray, Zena Hitz, Jessica Richard, and Amada Sandoval, as well as Andy Miller and Emma Bell.

Most people I meet look unconvinced when I say that I have not found it difficult or debilitating to forge a career in academia with a mother as well-known as mine is. (Yes, I am related to Susan Gubar!) She has always been so unbelievably loving and supportive that I have only ever experienced her as a deeply enabling force in my life. From the time I was scribbling my first efforts at prose in grade school all the way up though grad school, I remember her telling me, "You're a much better writer than I was when I was your age!" Nevertheless, the process of writing this book was protracted and full of discouraging moments. I feel profoundly grateful to my father Edward Gubar, an endlessly patient and kindhearted person, who coached and cheered me from childhood onward (on the softball diamond and elsewhere). Among other things, he taught me the importance of gumption, relaxation, and not throwing bats.

Thanks, too, to my beloved sister Simone, who shares my unreasonable affection for any form of pop culture related to ice skating or gymnastics; the marvelous Mary Jo Weaver, my dear godmother; and the (also) endlessly patient Don Gray, who has read countless drafts not only of this book but of virtually everything I have written over the past few years. I would also like to express my love and thanks to Luise David; all the English Davids; the Setiyas; Leonard, Sandy, and Justine Gubar; and my son Elliot, known (in true "cult of the child" style) as "The Adorable One" and "The Most Obliging Baby" for reasons that no one, surely, wants to hear about.

Finally, I must try to express my boundless love and gratitude to my husband, Kieran Setiya, for aiding and abetting me in all kinds of crazy schemes, including parenthood and book-writing. He, too, has read a ridiculous amount of my stuff, and helped me so much as I struggled to sharpen my thinking and express myself clearly. It is a sign of how much I depend on him in this last regard that I actually tried to get him to write this acknowledgment for me; I knew he would write something incredibly moving and beautiful. I'm not up to the task. But this book is dedicated to him, because I never could have written it without his love, help, criticism, and encouragement.

CONTENTS

Introduction	"Six Impossible Things Before Breakfast"	3
Chapter One	"Our Field": The Rise of the Child Narrator	39
Chapter Two	Collaborating with the Enemy: *Treasure Island* as Anti–Adventure Story	69
Chapter Three	Reciprocal Aggression: Un-Romantic Agency in the Art of Lewis Carroll	93
Chapter Four	Partners in Crime: E. Nesbit and the Art of Thieving	125
Chapter Five	The Cult of the Child and the Controversy over Child Actors	149
Chapter Six	Burnett, Barrie, and the Emergence of Children's Theatre	180
Notes		211
Works Cited		233
Index		253

ARTFUL DODGERS

INTRODUCTION

"Six Impossible Things Before Breakfast"

Given the sad fate suffered by so many of Charles Dickens's child characters, it is perhaps unsurprising that the "Artful Dodger" fails to live up to his jaunty nickname. Proving himself the *least* artful in dodging punishment, young Jack Dawkins is caught before any of the other thieves, a full one hundred pages before *Oliver Twist* (1837–39) concludes. As Dickens's description of his trial reveals, the Dodger's skill with language does not enable him to resist the power of the adults who surround him. Transported for life, he disappears entirely from the narrative, thus belying Fagin's assertion that we should not consider him "a victim" because he establishes for himself "a glorious reputation" at his trial (391, 396). In fact, neither the narrator nor a single one of the novel's characters ever mentions him again. For Dickens, even an Artful Dodger cannot function as an escape artist: though ostensibly a shrewd collaborator whose collusion with adult thieves leads him to adopt "all the airs and manners of a man" (100), the Dodger's dismal fate proves that we should instead regard him as yet another casualty of a corrupt society that starves orphan boys and ruins their female counterparts. Here and elsewhere in Dickens's work, precocity is presented as a problem: to the extent that the Dodger and other "sharp" little youngsters like Jenny Wren interact with and come to resemble adults, they are stunted, damaged, and often doomed (*Our Mutual Friend* 402).

To be disturbed by precocity, as Dickens and many other socially conscious Victorians were, indicates one's commitment to the idea that there ought to be a strict dividing line separating child from adult. Scholars such as Peter Coveney, Hugh Cunningham, and Judith Plotz have ably shown that Victorians committed to this position embraced a strand of Romantic thinking that posits children as a race apart, associating them with "primitive" people and insisting that their health and happiness depend on remaining detached from and unaffected by contemporary culture. Rather than conceiving of children as savvy collaborators, capable of working and playing alongside adults, many nineteenth-century artists and activists were eager to establish and preserve the child's difference, whether by passing laws aimed at marking off childhood from adulthood or by constructing fictions that fix the child in place as an isolated emblem of innocence. Attentive to such efforts, many commentators suggest that this era witnessed a complete polarization of adult from child (Andrews 22), culminating in the late nineteenth-century cult of the child, a movement whose members have been criticized for objectifying and eroticizing the innocent child, whose very remoteness from adults renders him (or her) "exotic and heartbreakingly attractive" (Kincaid, "Dickens" 30).

Since children's authors such as Lewis Carroll and J. M. Barrie were among the most famous members of this cult, it is unsurprising that the genre of children's literature has been held especially accountable for promoting this paralyzing form of primitivism. In her influential book *The Case of Peter Pan: or, The Impossibility of Children's Fiction* (1984), Jacqueline Rose contends that the desire to compose literature "for" children is in fact driven by the adult's yearning to conceive of the child as "a pure point of origin in relation to language, sexuality, and the state" (8). Particularly during the Golden Age of children's literature, a host of critics agree, political, social, and religious crises led Victorian and Edwardian authors to construct childhood itself as a golden age, a refuge from the painful complexities of modern life.[1] According to this line of thinking, when children's authors whisk child characters away to Wonderlands, secret gardens, or uninhabited islands, it attests to their "regressive desire for a preindustrial, rural world," as well as their longing to believe in the existence of a natural, autonomous self, free from the imprint of culture (Wullschläger 17). "Essentializing Romantic discourse" of this kind, we are told, invariably casts the child as a solitary figure who exists "outside of the context . . . of schools, of the state, and especially of their families" (Plotz, *Romanticism* 13, 24). While such stories comfort adults by offering a luxuriously nostalgic brand of escapism, they are problematic for children, because they attempt to seduce young people into identifying with—and conforming to—a static, anti-intellectual ideal of naïve simplicity.

This book contends that Golden Age children's authors were far more skeptical about Romantic primitivism than this account suggests. Even when they detach child characters from home and school, classic Victorian and Edwardian children's books do not represent young people as untouched Others, magically free from adult influence. On the contrary, they generally conceive of child characters and child readers as socially saturated beings, profoundly shaped by the culture, manners, and morals of their time, precisely in order to explore the vexed issue of the child's agency: given their status as dependent, acculturated beings, how much power and autonomy can young people actually have? In addressing this question, Golden Age authors often take a strikingly nuanced position, acknowledging the pervasive and potentially coercive power of adult influence while nevertheless entertaining the possibility that children can be enabled and inspired by their inevitable inheritance. In doing so, they resist the Child of Nature paradigm, which holds that contact with civilized society is necessarily stifling, in favor of the idea that young people have the capacity to exploit and capitalize on the resources of adult culture (rather than simply being subjugated and oppressed). To find the real artful dodgers of the Victorian period, then, we must turn to children's literature, a genre that celebrates the canny resourcefulness of child characters without claiming that they enjoy unlimited power and autonomy.

The conviction that Golden Age authors represent children as free from the shaping force of social, familial, and scholastic institutions arises out of a long-standing tradition of ignoring or denigrating the contributions of influential female authors of this era, who routinely locate child characters firmly within the domestic realm. Catherine Sinclair, Mary Howitt, Harriet Mozley, Juliana Ewing, Charlotte Yonge, Mary Louisa Molesworth, and Dinah Mulock Craik often embed child characters in extensive networks of family members, friends, servants, and teachers, extolling the importance of moral and intellectual education while simultaneously acknowledging the painful aspects of this process. Although Sinclair's *Holiday House* (1839) often receives lip service as a harbinger of the Golden Age, and Yonge's *The Daisy Chain; or, Aspirations, a Family Chronicle* (1856) is sometimes recognized as an important precursor to Louisa May Alcott's *Little Women* (1868), the popular genre of the family story still tends to get left out when commentators commend the accomplishments of children's authors from this era.[2] This type of tale does not indulge in the fantasy that children are self-sufficient figures but instead weighs the benefits and drawbacks of various modes of discipline, often by exposing child protagonists to a variety of caretakers who have very different styles of parenting.[3] Moreover, the Victorian and Edwardian period also witnessed the proliferation of the school story, a genre that likewise dwells on the good and bad influence exercised on children by peers, parents, and various kinds of teachers.

The fact that family and school stories do not generally celebrate the isolated Child of Nature is hardly startling. More surprising, however, is the fact that celebrated fantasy authors such as Lewis Carroll, Robert Louis Stevenson, and J. M. Barrie also refuse to characterize child protagonists as miraculously autonomous agents. Even when child characters set out to explore family-free space in classics such as *Alice's Adventures in Wonderland* (1865) and *Peter Pan* (1904), they never manage to extricate themselves from the formative effects of their upbringing. Alice's adventures may take place in a realm outside the middle-class nursery and schoolroom, but she herself is and remains firmly enmeshed in that milieu. Indeed, her sense of her own identity entirely depends on it: unable to recall correctly the content of her lessons, deprived of contact with her sister, governess, pals, and pets, Alice loses any sense of "who in the world" she is (Carroll, *Complete Works* 24). A drawing-room child rather than a Child of Nature, Alice is much more self-assured during her second adventure, when Carroll allows her unproblematic access to her own sociocultural archive (which includes nursery rhymes and didactic literature as well as the rules of polite discourse and popular parlor games like chess). Similarly, when the Darling children follow Peter Pan to Never Land, they immediately reconstruct and reenact the domestic routine they have just left behind, revealing in the process their thorough acceptance of the bourgeois mores and conventional gender roles embraced by their parents.

Such moments remind us that the physical absence of adults in a story does not necessarily imply the absence of adult influence. Golden Age authors often represent child characters as fully socialized subjects, even as they assume that child readers are highly acculturated as well, and thus capable of appreciating sophisticated language and wordplay and a wide array of literary, educational, theatrical, religious, and scientific references. Indeed, as I will demonstrate, Victorian commentators often objected to "modern" children's books for precisely this reason: they complained that authors such as Carroll, William Makepeace Thackeray, Charles Kingsley, and Tom Hood conceived of children as fellow inhabitants of contemporary culture who could be addressed in the same terms as adults. In their own time, in other words, famous Golden Age fantasy authors were often faulted for *failing* to endorse the new ideology of innocence, which aimed to erect a firm barrier between adult and child. Rather than promoting the idea that young people are primitive naïfs, these authors more often characterize the child inside and outside the book as a literate, educated subject who is fully conversant with the values, conventions, and cultural artifacts of the civilized world. And whereas the Child of Nature paradigm insists that such precocious knowledge is enfeebling and even deadly, children's stories frequently suggest that young people have enough resourcefulness or recalcitrance to deal with (and even profit from) worldly influences.

By characterizing the child in this way, Golden Age writers acknowledged the *belated* nature of the child's subjectivity—the fact that young people are born into a world in which stories about who they are (and what they should become) are already in circulation before they can speak for themselves. More than that, though, the popular and influential authors studied here recognized that their own genre was a prime source of such prescriptive narratives. Self-conscious about the fact that adult-produced stories shape children, they represented children as capable of reshaping stories, conceiving of them as artful collaborators in the hope that—while a complete escape from adult influence is impossible—young people might dodge the fate of functioning as passive parrots. By giving writers such as Carroll and Barrie credit for recognizing the ideological nature of their own genre, I aim to counteract the still common assumption that these authors were themselves childlike, naïve "writers who could not grow up" (Wullschläger 3). Far from being oblivious to the ways fantasies about childhood impinge on children, Golden Age children's authors grappled with this very problem, constructing narratives that raise the question of whether and to what extent young people can rewrite the scripts handed to them by adults, taking a hand in the production of stories and their own self-fashioning.

Their groundbreaking decision to employ child narrators, I contend, provides the best concrete illustration of this tendency. When it is discussed at all, the development of this new technique receives a few lines in historical surveys of children's literature or articles about E. Nesbit, who used it with great success in *The Story of the Treasure Seekers* (1899). These abbreviated accounts invariably credit Dickens and Nesbit for pioneering this form of writing and suggest that the act of employing a child narrator allows adult authors to obscure their own presence in order to secure the child reader's unreflective identification with an ideal of innocence.[4] This book challenges both of these claims, tracing the important role that critically neglected children's writers such as Craik and Ewing played in developing this technique, and showing how they and their colleagues (up to and including Nesbit) use the trope of collaboration to dwell explicitly on the issue of influence. Rather than characterize child storytellers in Romantic terms, as visionary beings who effortlessly produce original work, they depict child narrators as highly socialized, hyperliterate subjects who work *with* grown-ups, peers, and preexisting texts in composing their stories. The fact that these juvenile narrators habitually employ the first person plural—"we" rather than "I"—indicates how deeply they are embedded in communities, surrounded by other children, adults, and adult-produced texts that inspire (and sometimes impede) their own forays into fiction.

The child narrator thus provides Golden Age authors with a vehicle to explore how young people enmeshed in ideology might nevertheless deviate from rather than ventriloquize various social, cultural, and literary protocols. Rather than pretending that children can or ought to function as autonomous Others, early experimenters with this technique frequently represented identity itself as collaborative: children develop a sense of self not in a vacuum but in reaction to the directives of the society they inhabit and the texts they read. Besides tracing how a range of female writers used the trope of adult–child collaboration to explore this idea, I also show how a preoccupation with the problem of whether children can enter into productive alliances with adults pervades the work of male authors such as Stevenson, Carroll, and Barrie. Like their female counterparts, these writers were invested in blurring rather than policing the subject positions of child and adult, reader and writer. Yet even as they represent the child as a potential collaborator, they also recognize that the idea of reciprocity can itself function as a seductive mirage that curtails the agency of children. Collaborating with an equal is all very well, their stories warn, but entering into a partnership with a stronger party raises the specter of coercion: perhaps the younger, weaker party is not acting as a self-motivated colleague but instead merely collaborating with the enemy.

My use of the term "collaboration" requires some explanation, since in common discourse it tends to carry very positive connotations, evoking the image of an uncomplicated partnership between equals. Here, however, it is employed to evoke a range of relationships of coproduction. That is to say, while I do mean the term to imply something more upbeat than out-and-out coercion in which a stronger party oppresses a weaker one, it need not (and rarely does) refer to a perfectly reciprocal bond between equals. Given how attuned these authors are to the child's belatedness, a phrase like "collaborator-after-the-fact" might better capture how they represent young people: less like founding partners than like Hollywood script doctors who arrive midway through the creative process and struggle to transform preexisting narratives. But this term is too unwieldy to use. Moreover, it muddies the point that literal acts of collaboration in these stories (among children themselves or between children and adults) provide a metaphor for Golden Age authors as they ponder the issue of agency. Their decision to represent young people as coproducers of texts attests to their (sometimes quite tenuous) hope that the undeniable primacy and power of adults does not doom the young to the unfulfilling role of puppet, parrot, or pawn.[5]

By entertaining the possibility that children might have (or attain) the ability to deflect adult efforts to control or oppress them, children's authors reacted against Dickensian plots that implied that youngsters immersed in adult society too soon were doomed to suffer a sad fate. Moved by a profound anxiety about the child's vulnerability to adult exploitation, Dickens and others writing primarily for adults often reified the young by portraying them as untouched innocents whose purity is either destroyed by contact with adult culture or helps to regenerate it (though sometimes at the cost of the child's own life).[6] While children's authors followed this pattern, too, at times, something about the act of writing with young people as an intended audience seems to have allowed them to create more nuanced, individualized characterizations of child characters than we see in popular novels such as *Oliver Twist*, *The Old Curiosity Shop* (1841), *Silas Marner* (1861), and *East Lynne* (1861).[7] Dickens's own *Holiday Romance* (1868) provides striking support for this claim; one of the only fictions he wrote aimed specifically at child readers, it features canny child protagonists who function as artful dodgers rather than hapless victims, as I will demonstrate in chapter 1.

Generally speaking, though, Dickens's strong sense of the child's vulnerability to adult exploitation led him to align himself with those authors and activists who were committed to erecting a barrier between adult and child. Like

Mary Carpenter, Ellen Barlee, and others opposed to child labor, he presented precocity as a horrifying offense against the true nature of childhood, which he often associated—as in the case of Little Nell and Paul Dombey—with a pastoral purity diametrically opposed to the industrialization and commercialization of contemporary society. As George Boas notes, glorifying childhood in this way entails the elevation of nature and intuitive wisdom over art and acquired knowledge. Education, acculturation, and even growth itself take on negative connotations; the child is valued for his or her very blankness or lack of experience, for remaining "unspoiled by the artifices of civilization" (Boas 11).

Boas termed this anti-intellectual, anti-artistic stance "the cult of childhood," and ended his landmark study on this subject by gesturing at what it lacked: "The history [of the cult] would not be complete without at least a long chapter on literature written for children" (102). Since then, there has been no shortage of critical studies that explore how this obsession with the primitive manifests itself in children's fiction.[8] Yet, I contend, children's literature was also the genre that offered the most serious and sustained *resistance* to this way of conceiving of the child. Indeed, these two impulses often coexist in the work of the same author, as when Carroll frames his unconventional *Alice* books with sentimental musings on the simplicity of childhood that many readers find jarring, or Frances Hodgson Burnett portrays the girlchild as a wide-eyed naïf in *Editha's Burglar* (1888) and a penetratingly observant and erudite author figure in *A Little Princess* (1905). Recognizing how regularly these and other children's authors deviated from the static ideal of innocence that infused Victorian novels, poetry, painting, and drama forces us to reconsider the critical commonplace that Golden Age children's authors latched onto and popularized the most sentimental and disabling strand of Romantic discourse about childhood.

More than that, though, taking into account Carroll and his colleagues' treatment of child characters and actual children also calls into question whether Boas's account of a transnational, transhistorical cult of childhood actually applies to late Victorian child-loving. For as I will show, the artwork and actions of key members of the cult were informed not by undiluted primitivism but rather by a habit of extolling the child's natural simplicity while simultaneously indulging a profound fascination with youthful sharpness and precocity. Fascinated by the idea of premature development, cultists such as Carroll, Burnett, and Barrie frequently conceived of children as knowing, acculturated, and accomplished beings. In other words, the late Victorian cult of the child is better characterized as a cultural phenomenon that reflected *competing* conceptions of childhood. More specifically, it was the site where the idea of the child as an innocent Other clashed most dramatically with an older vision of the child as a competent collaborator, capable of working and playing alongside adults.

Indeed, even as they paid lip service to the child's appealing difference from adults, members of the cult frequently *opposed* new attempts to segregate the young from adult society and shield them from the pleasures and exigencies of civilized life. Their efforts in this regard sometimes seem unobjectionable, and even enabling to young people. For example, far from embracing the notion that acquired knowledge would spoil the child's primitive purity, notorious child-lovers such as Carroll and John Ruskin championed early exposure to the arts and sciences, including logic, mathematics, mineralogy, architecture, foreign languages, painting, photography, even theatre. Yet their willingness to treat the child as a partner in artistic, intellectual, and even amorous matters often arouses our discomfort, as when we learn that Ruskin fell in love with a precocious ten-year-old whom he was tutoring, and Carroll campaigned against child labor legislation because he enjoyed seeing skilled child actors perform alongside adults on the professional stage. Clearly, conceiving of the young as artful collaborators rather than primitive Others does not magically release them from adult desires and control—although we should not assume that Carroll and his contemporaries were unaware of this fact. Just as many children's fictions from this era acknowledge the aggression inherent in the act of addressing the child, so, too, cultural artifacts associated with the cult of the child are often marked by a profound anxiety that the power imbalance that complicates any adult–child relationship precludes mutual pleasure and genuine reciprocity.

Thus, just as we must reconceive the Golden Age of children's literature to account for its practitioners' frequent refusal to align child characters with a static ideal of innocence, so, too, we must reconceive the cult of the child for precisely the same reason: far from being in the vanguard of efforts to establish and police a strict barrier between childhood and adulthood, the cultists frequently ignored, denied, or attempted to blur this line. Moreover, participants in both of these (often overlapping) phenomena manifested a high level of critical self-consciousness about the whole problem of representing, writing for, looking at, interacting with, and adoring children. A rarely acknowledged sign of this self-reflectiveness is that the Victorians themselves coined the term "the cult of the child" and spilled a lot of ink mulling over their own propensity to "worship our children" (Filon 44). Dowson defended this trend in his article "The Cult of the Child," which appeared in the *Critic* in 1889. And he was by no means the only commentator to weigh in on it; articles with titles such as "Babyolatry" (1846), "The Worship of Children" (1869), "The New Hero" (1883), "Child-Worship" (1901), and "The Literary Cult of the Child" (1901) appeared throughout the nineteenth and early twentieth centuries.[9]

As the title of this last essay hints, many who identified "this fanatical cultus of children" linked it explicitly to the explosion of children's literature as a popular genre (Worship 1299), thus confirming Boas's hunch that the two phenomena were closely intertwined. Yet in a move that supports my argument that neither is most usefully read as an expression of cultural primitivism, many of these commentators complained that the cultists as a group were not protective *enough* of the child's otherness. Thus, the anonymous author of "Babyolatry" begins by quoting Wordsworth's Immortality Ode, then complains that the new "child-worshipping" undermines this Romantic ideal of childhood innocence (129). Rather than being sequestered in the nursery or allowed to roam free in nature, he grumbles, modern children are brought in to mingle with adults in the social space of the drawing room, to flaunt their fancy clothes and display their many "acquirements" (130). As he waxes eloquent about the horror of being forced to endure "Norval-spouting boys and Rossini-strumming girls" (129),[10] it becomes clear that his main objection to the cult is that it immerses children in adult culture too soon, turning them into precocious performers. He thus goes on to recount he and his companions' sadness at seeing a radical change in a child whose home they recently visited: watching little Miss Wilhemina dance, sing, speak French, and show off her ability to write and draw elegantly, "we could not refrain from contrasting, in our own mind, the vain little creature thus burdened with tinsel and finery, and the laughing child whom we had often seen happily and innocently occupied with her playthings, seeking for no one's applause, and unconscious of any admirers" (130).

Just as the author of "Babyolatry" suggests that overly cultivated children such as Miss Wilhemina have nothing in common with Wordsworth's artless "little Actor" in the Immortality Ode (line 104), so too the professional child performers beloved by Carroll and other cultists were publicly attacked throughout the nineteenth century for presenting a threat to a Romantic ideal of innocence. Chapter 5 makes the case that the cultists' fascination with and support of highly accomplished child actors provides strong proof that they were at best ambivalent and often hostile to the growing cultural pressure to view children as innocent, incompetent Others. Chapter 6 then offers a new story about the emergence of drama aimed squarely (though not only) at a juvenile audience, arguing that many of these shows blurred the line between child and adult by celebrating precocity, addressing a mixed audience, and interrogating rather than affirming Romantic notions about childhood innocence. As a result, dramas by child-loving authors such as Burnett and Barrie were attacked for undermining the innocent simplicity of young people both in the audience and up on stage.

Indeed, those who disliked the escalating tendency to make children "the centre of attention" frequently lamented that the effect of this trend was to transform young people into artful, acculturated, self-conscious beings (West 1154). "The worship of children has increased, is increasing, and ought to be diminished," the *Spectator* complained in 1869: "It . . . has seriously injured the children of this generation. When artlessness gets to know its power, it is very near to art. Children are too much consulted in our generation. Their pleasures are far too numerous and elaborate" ("Worship" 1299). As primary examples of such "horrible and profligate" amusements, this commentator cites two celebrated Golden Age children's periodicals, George MacDonald's *Good Words for the Young* and Margaret Gatty's *Aunt Judy's Magazine*, which he dismisses as "too luxurious, elaborate, and refined" for young people: "Simplicity, and we may almost say monotony, are of the essence of a true child's amusements" (1299). Turning now to other contemporary reactions to Golden Age children's literature, we can see that this complaint cropped up fairly often: ironically, the very authors faulted by recent critics for portraying childhood as "an impossibly sanitized and Edenic time and space" were censured in their own time for failing to promote a Romantic ideal of primitive simplicity (Hemmings 55).

THAT THOROUGH CHILD-ABOUT-TOWN AIR

Historians and critics of children's literature have often suggested that Charles Lamb, Samuel Taylor Coleridge, and William Wordsworth helped initiate the Golden Age of children's literature by celebrating the importance of fairy tale and fantasy and insisting that the focus of the genre should shift from instruction to delight.[11] Such accounts follow the lead of the Romantics themselves, who declared themselves opposed to "the cursed Barbauld Crew" of rationalist writers such as Maria Edgeworth, whom they accused of indoctrinating children with facts rather than liberating their imaginations (Lamb, *Letters* 82). Recently, however, Mitzi Myers and Alan Richardson have productively troubled this stock opposition of didactic and fantastic by demonstrating that late eighteenth- and early nineteenth-century children's books do not neatly divide along this line.[12] At the same time, Richardson points out that the Romantic valorization of the realm of "Faerie" can be viewed as a deeply conservative and controlling move, since (among other reasons) it went hand in hand with a stultifying tendency to arrest the child in place as a primitive Other: close to nature, uncorrupted by civilization, animalistic in his or her rustic simplicity.[13] Fairy tales were deemed appropriate reading by virtue of their ostensible status "as a natural, rather than cultural product" arising organically from ancient, folk sources—an anti-literary origin myth that obscures the role that individual authors played in transmitting these stories to the page (Richardson, *Literature* 124).

This cult of rusticity—and concomitant suspicion of the literary—originates in large part from the work of Jean-Jacques Rousseau, who condemned reading as "the plague of childhood" and argued that virtually all books should be banned from the child's universe (116). In *Emile: or, On Education* (1762), Rousseau outlined his "purely negative" plan of education, whereby those in charge of children should "do nothing and let nothing be done" for the first twelve years (93), other than allowing their charges to build up their physical strength by romping around the countryside, "far from the black morals of cities which are covered with a veneer seductive and contagious for children" (95). Children are fundamentally different from adults, Rousseau maintains, and this difference should be preserved by delaying formal education and all other contact with the civilized world for as long as possible, since "learned" children are not only distasteful but doomed: "Nature wants children to be children before being men. If we want to pervert this order, we shall produce precocious fruits which will be immature and insipid and will not be long in rotting" (102, 90). Rousseau's decision to ensure that his pupil Emile "gets his lessons from nature and not from men" or books is tied to a glorification of savage folk whose "subtlety of mind" comes from being forced to fend for themselves both physically and mentally (119, 118).

English Romantic writers who weighed in on the issue of what children should read often echoed Rousseau's aversion to the literate, worldly child. Thus, in an 1813 lecture on education, Coleridge declared that "It was a great error to cram the young mind with so much knowledge as made the child talk much and fluently: what was more ridiculous that to hear a child questioned, what it thought of the last poem of Walter Scott?" (S. T. Coleridge 85). Similarly, in *The Prelude* (1805, 1850), Wordsworth famously contrasted the monstrous "dwarf man" produced by modern children's authors and educators to the far more appealing Boy of Winander, a solitary figure who revels in the woodland lore that leaves his precocious counterpart cold (V.295).[14] Stuffed to the gills with useless bits of acquired knowledge, the Infant Prodigy has also internalized social norms to such a degree that he worships "worldly seemliness" and can laugh knowingly at "the broad follies of the licensed world" (V.298, 311). In contrast, the Boy of Winander exists apart from adult influence and particularly from an educational system that would purchase knowledge by the loss of power. Rather than interacting with teachers, parents, or peers, he instead communicates in hoots with the owls, an act that attests to his instinctual, innate wisdom.

Yet despite his success in evading the shades of the prison-house of civilized life, the Boy of Winander nevertheless comes to a sad end, dying before he reaches his tenth birthday. Indeed, as numerous critics have noted, Romantic literature is littered with spectral children who never get to grow up, including Lamb's dream-children, the dead child-friends who haunt Thomas De Quincey's prose, and Wordsworth's Lucy Gray. Explaining the presence of these and other ill-fated youngsters, Richardson suggests that the very impermeability and otherness that makes them prized also seals their doom:

> These noble savages are naturally resistant to the adult attempts to form (or deform) them; their mentalities are rooted in a transcendentalized nature rather than being culturally produced. Wordsworth protests against the ideological construction of childhood by envisioning an ideology-proof,

> organic sensibility, a move which tends to leave the child unsocialized and frozen in a state of eternal innocence. (*Literature* 71–72)

Still, even as Richardson and other critics such as Plotz and Catherine Robson trace how a range of Romantic writers endorsed the Child of Nature paradigm, they are careful to acknowledge that there is no such thing as a singular Romantic Child: not only are there important differences between, say, William Blake's and William Wordsworth's treatment of childhood, there are inconsistencies within the work of individual authors as well. For instance, Robson persuasively argues that Wordsworth's glorification of a static state of innocence in the Immortality Ode should be viewed as a departure from his more nuanced treatment of childhood in other poems.

The Victorians, on the other hand, are frequently taken to task for wholeheartedly embracing the image of the child as an innocent Other and drenching it in nostalgic desire.[15] Coveney set this critical movement in motion in 1957 by tracing what he saw as a "continuous deterioration" of the literary image of childhood (33), whereby the Victorians appropriated what had been a rich, multivalent Romantic symbol and "negated its power" by sentimentalizing it (193). Identifying the deeply nostalgic Immortality Ode as the "*locus classicus* . . . for the whole literature of childhood in the nineteenth century" (78), Coveney faults children's authors such as Carroll and Barrie for turning to childhood as

> an habitual means of escape, a way of withdrawal from spiritual and emotional confusion in a tired culture. In an age when it became increasingly difficult to grow up, to find valid bearings in an adult world, the temptation seems to have been for certain authors to take the line of least emotional resistance, and to regress, quite literally, into a world of fantasy and nostalgia for childhood. (32)

In the five decades since *The Image of Childhood* appeared, numerous critics have followed Coveney's lead, arguing that the Romantic habit of figuring childhood as an idyllic separate sphere triggered the Golden Age of children's literature, and particularly the work of male fantasy writers.[16] Indeed, this notion is now so widely accepted that many critics simply announce that Carroll and his contemporaries participated in "the cult of childhood innocence which the Victorians inherited from the Romantics" rather than actually arguing for this claim (Cohen, "Lewis Carroll and Victorian Morality" 12).

Yet I would contend that Golden Age authors were not only as inconsistent as the Romantics in their adherence to this sort of primitivism, they also regularly situated themselves in opposition to it. Contemporary critical reaction to their work bears out this point, since nineteenth-century commentators who hewed most closely to Rousseau's line often objected to the work of Golden Age fantasists on the grounds that they failed to erect a cordon sanitaire between child and adult. In an 1855 essay entitled "Fictions for Children," for example, William Caldwell Roscoe criticizes John Ruskin's *The King of the Golden River* (described by Stephen Prickett as "the first original English fairy story") for being insufficiently attuned to the child's "unconscious simplicity" (Prickett 64; Roscoe 27). Throughout this piece, Roscoe expresses his support for the primitivist position, noting his agreement with what he describes as the "common" gesture of comparing the child to "a nation in its early stage" and to the rural poor (26). *The King of the Golden River* is not ideal for children, he explains, because Ruskin does not tell it simply and directly, as an illiterate nurse might do, but in finely wrought prose that contains "conceptions and descriptions . . . too much in advance of [the child's] stage of development" (41). Unhappy in general with the way "modern" children's literature is developing, Roscoe urges children's authors to eschew complex characters, ambiguity, and intellectual humor because "subtleties are lost upon a child" and "you must be quaint, not witty, to please him" (25). This condescending attitude is fully in keeping with Rousseau's habit of characterizing children as blankly incompetent beings; in the space of few pages of *Emile*, Rousseau suggests that young people have no ideas, no feeling for others, and no ability to acquire more than one language, learn history, or comprehend even the simplest fiction.[17]

Roscoe was right to suspect that Ruskin's attitude toward young people did not align neatly with this stance. Himself a highly precocious child, Ruskin was drawn to similarly accomplished youngsters, such as Rose La Touche, who from an early age "had chosen all knowledge for her province, and was an admirable scholar. She was very brilliant in conversation, and had an encyclopaedic memory."[18] Acting as the ten-year-old Rose's tutor, Ruskin exulted in her "quick intelligence" and goaded her into learning trigonometry, geology, and Greek as well as art and art history (*Works* 35:529). He also considered her emotionally mature enough to engage in a romantic relationship, lauding her perfect "sympathy" with and "power" over him (533). Just like the ideal wives he described in his essay "Of Queens' Gardens" (1864, 1865)—which he dedicated to her—little Rose "knows exactly what *I* am feeling, and thinks only of that. . . . Her one thought always is, 'Can I help him, or give him any joy?' " (533). Realizing at some level that this description of Rose did not fit with the untrammeled Child of Nature paradigm, Ruskin simultaneously insisted that there was "no precocity" in her, a claim that his biographers dismiss as unconvincing (533).

Such inconsistency is a defining characteristic of late Victorian child-loving; members of the self-proclaimed cult of the child expressed their allegiance to the ideal of unconscious innocence even as they demonstrated a profound fascination with knowledgeable, experienced, and remarkably competent children. An equivalent tension manifests itself in Ruskin's stance toward fairy tales.

In his introduction to an 1869 reissue of *German Popular Stories* by the Brothers Grimm, Ruskin echoes the obligatory Romantic line on the naturalness of fairy tales, complaining that modern children's authors mar the pristine simplicity of the genre by inserting moral messages and satiric references to contemporary fashions into their fairy tales. In objecting to these "more polished legends" (*Works* 19:233), Ruskin is often held to be attacking the work of Thackeray, Carroll, and George MacDonald, though his barbs also seem targeted specifically at the interpolated tall tale that graces Sinclair's *Holiday House*.

At the same time, however, virtually every criticism Ruskin makes of these stories also applies to his own fairy tale. Written in 1841, before Ruskin had graduated from Oxford (and not published until ten years later), *The King of Golden River; or, the Black Brothers: A Legend of Stiria* features an unmistakable moral about capitalist greed and a magical character whose calling card reads "South West Wind, Esquire" and who wears a "doublet [that] was prolonged behind into something resembling a violent exaggeration of what is now termed a 'swallow-tail'" (*Works* 1:324, 316). With its lushly detailed descriptive passages, it certainly does not partake in the "rude and more or less illiterate tone" Ruskin praises "all the best fairy tales" for having (*Works* 19:237). Indeed, Ruskin himself clearly agreed with Roscoe that the tale was not innocent enough, since he felt compelled to censor various aspects of the manuscript before allowing it to be published, and repeatedly tried to distance himself from it afterward, even going so far as to dismiss it as "totally valueless" in his autobiography (*Works* 35:304).

Besides objecting to Ruskin's witty, sophisticated fairy tale, Roscoe attacks another foundational Golden Age fantasy, Thackeray's popular Christmas book *The Rose and the Ring* (1854). Indeed, he finds this story far more problematic than Ruskin's, because it assumes the existence of children who are not just literate and intelligent but also—like Wordsworth's Infant Prodigy—are capable of enjoying satire. Rather than recognizing and inculcating primitive purity, Roscoe complains, Thackeray's story provides "stimulative diet for jaded appetites" by sending up "the slang language and slang habits of modern society" and making knowing references to pantomime, Shakespeare, and popular novelists such as G. P. R. James (45). In other words, Thackeray's fairy tale presupposes the presence of well-read, socialized, and sophisticated child readers. Indeed, as U. C. Knoepflmacher observes, the mocking humor that pervades *The Rose and the Ring* makes it tonally quite similar to *Vanity Fair*: in keeping with his practice of regarding "children and grown-ups as travelers on different stretches of the selfsame road," Thackeray explicitly aims his Christmas book at a mixed audience of children and adults, treating the young as "incipient fellow-ironists" (*Ventures* 86–87).

Interestingly, Roscoe doesn't deny the existence of such precocious readers so much as decry it. Children who enjoy a story like *The Rose and the Ring*, he declares,

> have little of the bloom of childhood to be impaired. They are weary of balls, of theatres, of puppet-shows; they have waltzed, they have flirted, they have supped; they are *blasés* at four years old, and satiated with literature at seven, and may lay Mr. Thackeray's book down with a yawn of approval like that of the weary novel-grinder of fifty, when she declares that the *Heir of Redclyffe* is "a pretty book." (42)

This description strongly recalls the troops of precocious children who appeared in John Leech's *Punch* cartoons during this very period, world-weary tykes who are thoroughly versed in social, scholastic, and romantic matters. From the mid-1840s to the mid-1860s, Leech routinely depicted well-to-do children drinking, gambling, flirting, using slang, and showing up adults with their knowledge of history and foreign languages. These "Very Acute" youngsters flip through books and newspapers and attend dances, parties, pantomimes, and exhibitions (Leech, *Pictures* 20). For instance, in one of many sketches entitled "The Rising Generation" (figure I.1), a jaded juvenile reader declares Shakespeare "over-rated," while "The Disappointed One" (figure I.2) features a miniature "lover" who complains that his wooing has been interrupted by the arrival of his nurse, even as two luckier children in the background lock lips. Similarly, poor children in Leech's cartoons exhibit prematurely developed street smarts, class consciousness, and a propensity to drown their troubles in drink (see figure I.3).

As Albert Wertheim notes, "one sees in Leech's cartoons . . . a society which serves relentlessly to shape children into the image of their parents" (76). Leech's habitual treatment of this theme should prompt us to reconsider the confident critical assertion that "the old view of the child as miniature adult . . . had largely receded" by the mid-nineteenth century (Carpenter 9). On the contrary, Victorians were constantly confronted with young people behaving like adults, whether it was poor children who were already "old hands" at whatever form of labor they practiced or wealthy children accompanying their elders out to various social, scientific, artistic, or religious events, not to mention participating in a wide array of intergenerational domestic activities, including private theatricals, novel reading, the production of family magazines, "botanizing," church work, and so on.

What is new at midcentury is that precocity begins to gain a more negative association, thanks in part to the efforts of author–activists such as Dickens, Lord Shaftesbury, and Mary Carpenter, who were fighting to persuade the general public that all children should enjoy a protected period of dependence and development before experiencing the cares and pleasures of adult life—a battle that was not won until the early twentieth century, as Cunningham and other historians of English childhood have demonstrated.[19] Leech's cartoons illustrate the slowness of this shift, both because of their content, which reminds

FIGURE 1.1 "The Rising Generation" (1847) by John Leech. *Punch*. Journal Collection, University Library System, University of Pittsburgh.

us that mid-Victorian children continued to engage in activities we consider "adult," and because his attitude toward precocious children fluctuates. Sometimes, he seems aggravated (by academic prodigies who show off their learning, for instance) or anxious (principally about the plight of poor children prematurely aged by poverty or parental neglect). At other times, he seems amused by the wittiness of knowing youngsters who advise their elders on how to conduct their love affairs, demand claret with their dessert, or make fun of the class pretensions of their social superiors.

Roscoe, by contrast, is altogether revolted by the idea that children exist who are worldly enough to "appreciate [Thackeray's] satire and his parodies, pronounce judgment on the appropriateness of his footmen's dialect, and enjoy the thorough child-about-town air of which the whole is redolent" (42). And

THE DISAPPOINTED ONE.

Lover. "WHAT A BORE! JUST AS I WAS GOING TO POP THE QUESTION TO JENNY JONES, HERE'S MY NURSE COME FOR ME!"

FIGURE I.2 "The Disappointed One" (1858) by John Leech. *Punch.* Journal Collection, University Library System, University of Pittsburgh.

once again, he is correct in assuming that the author in question did not share his absolute commitment to treating children as a race apart. In *Vanity Fair* (1848), to be sure, Thackeray seems repulsed by the precocious posturing of spoiled Georgy Sedley, who drinks, dresses, and circulates around London "just like a grown-up man" even though he is "scarcely eleven years of age" (654, 651). "Half tipsy" on wine and champagne, Georgy rudely cuts into the conversation at his grandfather's dinner parties, swears like a trouper, and visits "all the principal theatres of the metropolis" so regularly that he knows "the names of all the actors from Drury Lane to Sadler's Wells" (652–53).

Yet, like Leech, Thackeray was ambivalent about the issue of children engaging in "adult" activities, as indicated by his treatment of his own daughters. Far from sequestering little Anny and Minnie in a nursery to shield them from

FIGURE 1.3 Detail from "The Pious Public-House. (Where You May Get Adulterated Beer and Gin.) A place in which the Great Brewers DON'T see any Particular Harm!" (1860) by John Leech. *Punch*. Journal Collection, University Library System, University of Pittsburgh.

contact with the civilized world, Thackeray made them his companions on trips to the theatre, the opera, fancy dress balls, dinner parties, lectures, long walks, and excursions abroad. In the absence of their mentally unstable mother, "My dearest little women" dined with Thackeray and entered "freely and unsnubbed into the general talk" when acquaintances such as Alfred Tennyson and Charlotte Brontë visited their home (*Letters* 4:49; Gérin 31). Moreover, these "little Misses" also assisted their father in his writing and drawing work and served as trusted confidants; his long letters to them relate his hopes and fears about various social, professional, and domestic matters, including the problem of finding a governess clever enough to cope with and further stimulate the precocious Anny's "genius" intellect (*Letters* 2:605, 292). Nor did Thackeray shield them from risqué romantic matters; in 1853, he admitted to two friends that his teenage daughters knew "all about" his forbidden love for a married woman, much like the well-informed youngsters in Leech's cartoons (*Letters* 4:437).

Given that *The Rose and the Ring* was inspired when these socially saturated children asked their father to help them prepare a traditional Twelfth Night game for a holiday party, it is unsurprising that the narrative does not dilate on the primitive otherness of children. Recent critics such as Richardson and Rose have suggested that Thackeray's Christmas book is exceptional in its refusal to posit an innocent child reader.[20] In fact, *The Rose and the Ring* was one of many famous fantasies attacked by commentators who shared Roscoe's sense that contemporary children's authors were insufficiently appreciative and protective of the child's difference from adults. Thus, when Alfred Ainger complained that "burlesque, and satire, and humour (of the intellectual sort) are inestimable things, but their proper place is later than the nursery and the schoolroom" (75), his examples were three more Golden Age classics: Kingsley's *The Water-Babies* (1863), Carroll's *Alice's Adventures in Wonderland* (1865), and Stevenson's *A Child's Garden of Verses* (1885). Like Roscoe, who contends that children's books are "spoiled" when authors attempt to address a mixed audience (40), Ainger opines: "The fault of some of the most famous children's books of our time is that their clever authors have written with one eye on the *child* and the other on the *grown-up person*. . . . They may contain elements fitted to engage the attention of the child, [but] it is the *grown-up intellect* and the *grown-up sense of humour* that alone is capable of enjoying them to the full, or any degree near it" (74). Similarly, in "Literature for the Little Ones" (1887), Edward Salmon protests that the allegorical complexity of stories such as *At the Back of the North Wind* (1871) ensures that George MacDonald's work "soars above the intelligence of children of tender years" (572), just as the "undercurrent of satire" in Tom Hood's children's books disqualifies him from being regarded as a successful writer for children (570).

Much more could be said here about works such as MacDonald's "The Light Princess" (which was so full of sexual imagery that Ruskin felt compelled to try to censor it, as he had his own fairy tale) or Kingsley's *The Water-Babies* (which is crammed with references to contemporary literary, political, and scientific controversies, and written in the digressive, aggregative style of Rabelais).[21] *The Water-Babies* in particular offers a case study of how little attention has been paid to the original reception of even the most well-known Golden Age texts. Numerous accounts of Kingsley's life and work declare that the contemporary reaction to it was uniformly positive, without citing a single specific source for this claim.[22] In fact, the book puzzled and even offended early reviewers, one of whom complained that "it consists of a farrago of crude ideas and jesting allusions, either to science or to the economy of human life, which could neither be understood by children, nor afford them . . . amusement" (review of *Water-Babies* 257).[23] But I shall focus instead on the work of Tom Hood—for two reasons. First, although his children's stories and poems were "deservedly popular" during his own lifetime, they are virtually unknown today (Salmon, "Literature" 571). Second, they provide some of the most amusing proof that Golden Age fantasists often resisted the pressure to construct a barrier between innocence and experience, viewing Romantic primitivism as a target for humor rather than a cherished creed.

Son of a Romantic poet of the same name, Thomas Hood junior self-consciously attempted to address a mixed audience of children and adults, as the dedications and prefaces to his books reveal. Introducing his novel *From Nowhere to the North Pole* (1875), for instance, he states that he is determined "to avoid the Scylla of a narrative suitable simply for the little ones, and the Charybdis of a work that would be fitted only for the grown-up" (iii–iv). In keeping with this goal, he pokes fun not only at the childish faults of his boy hero but also at legalese, bad poetry, political corruption, the idiocy of school board inspectors, and the craze for inventing things and exhibiting them. Drawing attention to these parodic moments, Salmon complains: "It requires an older intellect than one of eight or ten years to appreciate the fun of [these] shots at human failings and weaknesses" ("Literature" 571). My point is not to insist that children (then or now) *could* be amused by these gags but merely to note that Hood feels no need to establish or preserve the primitive otherness of young people by avoiding certain topics.

More than that, though, I would suggest that when Hood and other Golden Age children's authors explicitly aim to address a mixed audience, this decision often attests to a desire to resist the strand of Romantic rhetoric that sets the child up as an uncivilized Other. Indeed, in *Petsetilla's Posy: A Fairy Tale for Young and Old* (1870), Hood makes Rousseau's child-rearing philosophy the butt of one of his extended jokes when he describes the educational practices of a kingdom in which all the royal daughters are turned outdoors at birth into "a park for the rearing of wild princesses" (55):

> There they were allowed to grow up without being taught their own language even. On reaching a marriageable age, they were duly catalogued, and a description of their beauties was sent to all surrounding and single potentates. As soon as one of them was selected for marriage by one of these princes she was transferred to the Royal Nursery Palace, where masters and governesses duly qualified speedily taught her the language of her future country, and the accomplishments and manners in vogue there. (10–11)

In contrast to credulous souls such as Thomas Day, who actually attempted to raise children using Rousseau's guidelines, Hood slyly sends up the philosopher's habit of conceiving of young people as mindless plants rather than sentient individuals, not to mention his sexism and suspicion of language.

Furthermore, when Hood turned his hand to retelling classic fairy tales, he did so in a way that humorously undermined Romantic notions about the genre's archaic authenticity. Articulating this reverential position, Coleridge's son Hartley asserted that the ideal literature of the nursery has "every mark of extreme antiquity" and no sign of having been written by an individual author: "it is not without effort we remember that [fairy tales and nursery rhymes] must all have been made at some time by somebody. We rather deem them like the song of birds, 'a natural product of the air'" ("Nursery Lecture" 303–4). Hood's *Fairy Realm: A Collection of the Famous Old Tales* (1865) subverts such mythologizing in a number of ways. To begin with, rather than adopting the "quaint simplicity of phrase" recommended by Hartley (303), Hood relates famous fairy tales like "Little Red Riding Hood" in elaborate comic verse that refuses to settle down into a regular meter or rhyme scheme and is dotted throughout with amusing footnotes and parenthetical asides that draw attention to his own authorial presence. For example, after rudely suggesting that Little Red's frantic love for nature makes her "mad as a hatter," he muses,

[It's not clear to me
Why a hatter should be
Proverbially called a fit subject for *De*
Lunatico—so runs the writ—*inquirendo*;
But I fancy the hatter this harsh innuendo
Must, in the first place, to a humorous friend owe,
Who fain in the sneer would his gratitude smother
For a man who's invariably *felt* for another.] (37)

As this passage indicates, many of Hood's jokes emphasize the strangeness or slipperiness of language. Besides pointing up the oddness of common expressions and using puns to remind readers that words can have more than one meaning, he frequently employs snippets of foreign languages (French, Latin, Greek), highlighting the arbitrary relationship between signifier and signified. He also reminds readers that rhyme depends on pronunciation and pronunciation depends on class, as when he rhymes "harass" with "what Jane Housemaid calls the tarrace" (24).

Sophisticated wordplay of this sort undermines Rose's claim that Golden Age children's authors insisted on defining childhood as "something which exists outside the culture in which it is produced" in order to deny their own anxieties about class division, the instability of sexual identity, and the ambiguity of language (44). Refusing to play along with the Romantic custom of aligning the child with a primitive past, Hood shakes up these "Old" tales by mixing in repeated references to newfangled things. Throughout *Fairy Realm*, for instance, archaic expressions such as "I ween" and "o'er" jostle against slang that sounds so modern it is hard to believe the Victorians used it (10, 3), such as "snooze" (24), "dad" (42), and "peepers" (16). Similarly, after situating his Little Red Riding Hood in a traditional rural setting, Hood describes her famous garment as "a red opera cloak"—and then proceeds to highlight the ludicrousness of this choice: "But operas ne'er, that I am aware, / Had been heard of by anyone dwelling round there" (29). While his characters remain ignorant of the fashions and foibles of civilized life, Hood assumes that his readers are immersed in modern consumer culture, as indicated by his description of what was sitting next to the cake intended for Little Red's grandmother:

> And beside it a pot
> Whose equal could not
> At Fortnum and Mason's be easily got;
> For, as every one tells me, fine fragrant fresh honey
> Is not always obtainable, even for money. (32)

Like Thackeray and Kingsley, Hood frequently refers to contemporary customs, celebrities, and texts, presuming the existence of highly acculturated readers who are capable of appreciating his departures from familiar plots and his digs at modern manners.

As one might expect, such a stance was not calculated to please everyone. Echoing the reviews already cited, a critic for the *Nation* sniffed that Hood's verse version of "Sleeping Beauty" could "hardly" be considered a children's poem, because of its length and "ever-changing metres, which no nurse and few mammas could manage, but more because of the forced jokes and rather elaborate puns with which it bristles, and which to children would be words without meaning" ("Old Fairy Tale" 309). Once again, it is the commentator rather than the children's author who adopts a condescending attitude toward the young, characterizing them as "unconscious" Others incapable of enjoying topical references and linguistic play ("Old Fairy Tale" 309).

At times, it is embarrassingly evident that such confident critical assertions about the cluelessness of children are based on nothing but the reviewer's own desire to pressure young people into conforming to an ideal of innocence. Alexander Innes Shand's nostalgic essay "Children Yesterday and Today" (1896) provides a prime example of this tendency. Objecting to the inclusion of "bankers and bill-brokers among the members of the adventurous expedition" chronicled in *The Hunting of the Snark* (1876), Shand thunders, "We thank Heaven that many a year must pass before any of our darlings in brief petticoats know anything of pecuniary worries, and we hope it may be long ere our boys of the preparatory school are tempted by usurers and versed in accommodation bills" (91). Yet in the same breath, Shand laments that contemporary children are too "*blasé*" and "well-informed" to appreciate the simple pathos of less worldly texts than Carroll's (91). Nevertheless, he declares, parents should at least *try* giving their offspring more innocent books from an earlier era: "we are optimists enough," he concludes, "to believe that the experiment will be a success" (91). More a matter of hope than certainty, ingenuousness must be inculcated into children through texts.

Ignoring complaints like Shand's, Golden Age authors continued to include references to impure topics such as money in their narratives, even as they resisted the call to simplify their language and avoid satire. Writing at the turn of the century, Nesbit, Barrie, and Kenneth Grahame constructed formally complex narratives that featured jokes about moneylenders, household bills, and checkbooks, as well as parodic references to a wide variety of literary genres that late Victorian children were likely to have read, including religious tracts and adventure stories. In contrast to condescending critics who insisted on the child reader's incompetence, these writers produced texts that presuppose the existence of socialized, literate, and sophisticated child readers. Moreover, their cheerful representation of child characters as fully domesticated beings suggests that they did not indulge in the Rousseauvian fantasy that young people can be shielded from acculturation. "Do you want an adventure now," Peter Pan asks the Darling siblings, just after they fly away from the nursery, "or would you like to have your tea first?" (*Peter and Wendy* 107). The children unanimously opt for tea. And no wonder: throughout the story, Barrie makes the delights of home—its coziness, the comfort of established routines, the presence of a deeply desirable mother figure who tells entrancing stories—as vivid as the often discomfiting excitement of autonomy in the wild. Taking issue with precisely this aspect of *Peter Pan*, Barrie's contemporary Saki (H. H. Munro) questioned the playwright's knowledge of boys and even his masculinity, demanding, "Can you imagine a lot of British boys, or boys of any country that one knows of, who would stay contentedly playing children's games in an underground cave when there were wolves and pirates and Red Indians to be had for the asking on the other side of the trap door?" (21).[24]

Indeed, it is ironic that critics so often characterize Golden Age fantasies as driven by an intense longing to escape from social strictures, since even animal stories such as *The Wind in the Willows* (1908) are infused with a deep regard for the pleasures of civilized life, as well as a resigned though by no means despairing recognition of its drawbacks. Early reviewers of Grahame's story recognized this. Rather than describing the landscape Mole and Ratty inhabit as "an innocent pastoral milieu," as contemporary critics do (Poss 84),[25] *Punch* noted in 1908 that "the chief characters are woodland animals, who are represented as enjoying most of the advantages of civilisation—shopping, caravanning, motoring, traveling by train, and so on" (review of *Wind* 360). True, cars can cause havoc, and "hired lodgings" can be "uncomfortable, inconveniently situated, and horribly expensive" (as Mr. Badger complains), but on balance Grahame comes down firmly in favor of amenities like black velvet smoking jackets and hot buttered toast (47). Such a stance caused E. V. Lucas to grouse that "ordinary life is depicted more or less closely" in *The Wind in the Willows* (362).[26] Similarly, Arthur Ransome opined in the *Bookman* that the story boasted too much "knowledge of the world" to be appropriate for children (190).

Rather than regret the bars of the prison-house that close down on educated, town-dwelling types, *The Wind in the Willows* elaborates on the pleasures of the cage. When Ratty and Mole journey home from the terrifying Wild Wood in the chapter "Dulce Domum," civilized domesticity emerges as a locus of intense desire. Traveling through a town, they are transfixed by the sight of a bird cage and its contented occupant: "it was [there] that the sense of home and the little curtained world within walls—the larger stressful world of outside Nature shut out and forgotten—most pulsated" (52). Here Grahame pointedly resists Romantic notions about the importance of unconstrained autonomy, such as Blake's impassioned claim in "Auguries of Innocence" (c. 1805, 1863) that "A Robin Red breast in a Cage / Puts all Heaven in a Rage" (490). Tender male fellowship is one of the greatest pleasures of the cage;[27] another is literature. Thus, we learn that Rat spends a great deal of time scribbling poetry or doing "other small domestic jobs about the house," while Grahame's narrative is characterized by a "rich alluvial deposit of parody and imitation" of authors ranging from Homer to William Morris (*Wind* 28; P. Green 261). Although Grahame declared that his intended audience for *The Wind in the Willows* was mainly children, he nevertheless did not feel the need to cleanse his prose of contemporary and classical allusions; stylistically, *The Wind in the Willows* has a great deal in common with *The Golden Age* (1895), his earlier attempt to write about childhood for an adult audience.

No wonder, then, that reviewers committed to conceiving of the child as an unpolluted origin strenuously objected to Grahame's work; not only does he refuse to address young people in specially simplified prose that would make his work instantly identifiable as "children's" literature, his representation of child characters likewise blurs the line between child and adult, innocence and experience. Surprisingly, this is particularly true of the youngsters represented in *The Golden Age*, the book that helped give this era of children's literature its name. Critics intent on reading classic children's texts as imbued with nostalgic primitivism invariably point to the prologue of *The Golden Age*, in which the narrator describes how, as a child, he and his four siblings conceived of adults as a race apart, distant "Olympians" enslaved to social conventions and deaf to the call of the wild that the nature-loving, imaginative children felt so strongly. Here and elsewhere, the narrator certainly does suggest that children perceive grown-ups as "hopelessly different" than themselves (67).

Yet everything from the narrator's own uncertain position to the behavior he and his siblings engage in as children blurs this line, making the childish conviction of adults' otherness one of many subjects Grahame treats ironically. Although the narrator of *The Golden Age* speaks of childhood as "those days of old" (3), his own status somehow remains ambiguous; as Peter Green observes, he seems to be constantly "fluctuating in viewpoint between child and adult" (161). Trying to capture this shifty quality, the dubious reviewer for the *Spectator* noted in 1896 that Grahame "writes as a small boy with the knowledge and experience of a man" (review of *Golden Age* 140). In other words, rather than evoking the effect of an adult reflecting back on childhood from a safe distance, Grahame's narrator sounds like a precocious child whose discourse—like that of Wordsworth's Infant Prodigy—"moves slow,/ . . . Tremendously embossed with terms of art" (*Prelude* V.320, 322).

Why should this be so, given that the narrator of *The Golden Age* reiterates at the end of the prologue that many years have passed since he was a child? The reason is that in the loosely connected stories that follow, the narrator recounts how he and his siblings—*as children*—speak, think, and act in a preternaturally knowing way, which effectively undermines the notion that a significant gap separates child from adult. In "The Child in Recent English Literature" (1897), J. Sully vehemently objected to precisely this feature of *The Golden Age*, complaining that although the child hero cannot be older than ten, he "not only gives himself now and again an air of superiority to the others' play, wandering forth into the fields alone to indulge in precocious poetic raptures, but shows himself capable of reading into a scene in which figure his little sister and her two dolls, a significance which surely could only have occurred to an experienced adult" (226–27). This incident occurs in the chapter "Sawdust and Sin," which chronicles how the narrator *as a child* interprets the movements of his sister's dolls in sexual terms, attributing lust not just to the male doll who is "overmastered by his passion" and throws himself into the lap of his beloved but also to the "(apparently) unconscious" female doll, who willingly "yield[s], crushing his slight frame under the weight of her full-bodied surrender" (84, 81).

Sully, who felt that this scene was "a dishonour done to the sacred cause of childhood" (227), was not alone in recognizing that *The Golden Age* subverted Romantic notions about the purity of young people. In her 1895 review in the *Bookman*, Virginia Yeaman Remnits likewise felt compelled to reiterate conventional sentiments about childish naïveté in order to counter Grahame's insufficiently reverential stance. Criticizing the lines just quoted from "Sawdust and Sin," she insisted that while "children do indeed have ideas about love and love affairs . . . they are so deliciously, so alarmingly innocent and quaint in their conception of such matters! There is nothing innocent about this passage" (50). And such impiety, it should be noted, is not exceptional: Grahame included erotic content in virtually every chapter of *The Golden Age*. Like Leech's children, his youngsters are as familiar with the conventions of courtship as they are with literary figures and tropes. Indeed, sexual and textual knowingness tend to go hand in hand, as indicated by the fact that during the scene in which the narrator and his little sister Charlotte condemn the "wicked" behavior of the randy dolls, Charlotte is recounting the story of Alice's adventures in Wonderland to her sawdust friends (83).

The chapter "The Burglars" provides a still more striking example of this tendency. Having picked up on the fact that the curate and their Aunt Maria are romantically involved, the narrator and his older brother Edward send out little Harold as a scout to eavesdrop on the two lovers. When he is caught, Harold artfully covers for himself by telling a wild story about burglars lifted from "the last Penny Dreadful lent us by the knife-and-boot boy" (116). This choice of reading material is itself telling; whereas contemporary commentators such as Salmon inveighed against penny dreadfuls on the grounds that they would corrupt the purity of young people, Grahame seems utterly unconcerned by the promiscuous reading habits of the five siblings, who routinely build their play around—and borrow the "lofty diction" of—a variety of texts from both high and low culture (116). Such behavior suggests that far from inhabiting a separate sphere, the children are greedy sponges who have absorbed a huge amount from the culture at large and the educational process they only pretend to despise. Their pronounced artiness further undermines the notion that a significant distance separates them from the narrator, who also adopts a highly allusive and self-consciously literary style.

The Golden Age was not written with child readers in mind, but its portrayal of young people as highly acculturated beings prompts us to notice a key characteristic of Golden Age texts that were: despite a growing cultural unease with the idea of precocious, worldly youngsters, children's stories from this era are packed with hyperliterate child heroes. As I will show, Juliana Ewing's artful child narrators improvise on old fairy tales, as well as modern stories such as *The Rose and the Ring*; Stevenson's Jim Hawkins has a working knowledge of adventure stories; Carroll's Alice has absorbed the cruel logic of cautionary tales; and Barrie's Wendy is on intimate terms with "Dear Hans Christian Andersen, Dear Charles Lamb, Dear Robert Louis Stevenson, Dear Lewis Carroll."[28] Perhaps the most voracious consumers of modern fiction are Nesbit's Bastable siblings, who have read Hesba Stretton's religious tracts, Rudyard Kipling's *Jungle Books* (1894, 1895), and S. R. Crockett's *Sir Toady Lion* (1897), not to mention "adult" literature such as Dickens's *David Copperfield* (1849–50) and Grahame's *Golden Age*. North American children's literature from the same period offers still more examples of well-read child protagonists: the March girls in *Little Women* (1868), for instance, and the eponymous main characters of *The Story of a Bad Boy* (1869), *What Katy Did* (1872), *The Adventures of Tom Sawyer* (1876), and *Anne of Green Gables* (1909).

What explains the prevalence of prodigious child readers? Given the current climate of cynicism about the genre of children's literature (which I will discuss in a moment), our first inclination might be to say that Golden Age authors were motivated by a craven desire to drum up business and create docile readers. That is to say, they represent child characters as avid consumers of books in order to encourage child readers to invest in literature in a double sense: by buying (or requesting) it, and by internalizing without question the messages contained within it. But this explanation is inadequate, since the influence books have on children in these stories is not always good. Literacy tends to function not as a wholly admirable attribute but rather as a sign of the child's status as a culturally inscribed being. Thus, as I will show, Ewing, Craik, and Nesbit represent young people as enmeshed in a literary, cultural, and social scene that influences them in both positive and negative ways. Even as many of their child protagonists glean intellectual inspiration from art and emotional support from beloved family members and friends, they also soak up negative qualities such as class prejudice, sexism, and blind nationalism, often from the very same sources.

The reason Golden Age authors chose to link literacy and acculturation was that they recognized that their own genre had historically functioned as a tool for socialization and even indoctrination. In essays, autobiographies, and especially in their children's fiction, Carroll, Kingsley, Stevenson, Nesbit, and others poked fun at their predecessors and peers for aggressively attempting to inculcate particular beliefs, behavioral norms, and bodies of information into the minds of child readers.[29] Like the Romantic poets before them, Golden Age authors objected to the catechistic mode that informed some early children's books and that aimed to persuade child readers that their role was not to engage in any creative way with texts but simply to absorb, parrot back, and obey them.[30] Of course, it could be argued that when Carroll parodies didactic poems, or Stevenson slyly subverts the rah-rah ethos of adventure stories, or Nesbit makes fun of Burnett's more angelic child characters, it is part of a sneaky campaign to seduce child readers into believing that *their* stories are different, utterly unedifying texts that aim only to delight, never to mold or manipulate. But as I will show, these authors actively entertain the possibility that their own fictions are just as pushy and controlling as those penned by their more overtly preachy counterparts. Their books are pervaded by anxiety about the issue of influence: given that children are born into a world in which stories about who they are and what they should be like are already in circulation before they can speak for themselves, how can they develop their own voices, their own desires, their own distinctive identities?

In other words, Golden Age authors do not ignore or repress what Rose terms the "problem of address": the complex issues raised by a literary genre whose recipients inhabit a less powerful subject position than its practitioners (21). In *The Case of Peter Pan*, Rose contends that whereas early children's authors made no effort to hide their own authorial presence and aims, over time "the adult intention has more and more been absorbed into the story" as writers increasingly have tried to elide the question of "who is talking to whom, and why" (60, 2). Indeed, children's fiction has had no choice but to downplay the issue of address, Rose suggests, because it committed itself to a characterization of the child that ensured that it could not acknowledge the conditions of its own production: if you are determined to conceive of the child as a totally separate species whose purity depends on avoiding contact with adult civilization, you cannot admit that your chosen medium is one in which adults address and influence children. This is (in part) what Rose means when she declares that "children's fiction is impossible, not in the sense that it cannot be written (that would be nonsense), but in that it hangs on an impossibility, one which it rarely ventures to speak. This is the impossible relationship between adult and child. Children's fiction is clearly about that relation, but it has the remarkable characteristic of being about something which it hardly ever talks of" (1).

The (ostensible) innocence of childhood, Rose argues, licenses adult authors to pretend that language can be innocent, too, an unmediated reflection of the real world rather than a shaping force in its own right. To this end, children's writers eagerly embraced a "form of writing which attempts to reduce to an absolute minimum our awareness of the language in which a story is written in order that we will take it for real (the very meaning of 'identification')" (65). The adoption of this "realist aesthetic" provides further proof for Rose that "children's fiction has never completely severed its links with a philosophy which sets up the child as a pure point of origin," an unpolluted link to the prelapsarian world (60, 8).

Rose's incisive intervention into the field of children's literature criticism has been extremely invigorating, as the constant stream of scholarly citations to *The Case of Peter Pan* indicates. In particular, she has persuasively demonstrated how problematic it is to presume that children's books are simply written "for" children: this assumption allows us to avoid acknowledging how adult needs and desires shape the genre, while simultaneously essentializing the child, since "the very idea of speaking to *all* children" ignores the socioeconomic, historical, and cultural divisions in which children (as well as adults) are necessarily caught (7). Yet perhaps the time has come, a few years past the twentieth anniversary of its publication, to adopt a more critical stance toward a text that has taken on a sort of totemic power—invoked at the start of so many recent essays and books focused on children's literature. As should be evident by now, I disagree with the sweeping statements Rose makes about the *content* of children's fiction: I think that the habit of defining childhood in terms of primitive purity is not nearly as widespread as she implies, and that the complicated relationship between adult author and child reader often emerges as a key theme in children's fiction, particularly during the Golden Age.

More fundamentally, though, I am troubled by Rose's characterization of the *process* of the creation and consumption of children's books. Using metaphors of physical, sexual, and imperial aggression, Rose maintains that children's fiction builds up an image of the child inside the book in order to seduce the child outside the book—"the one who does not come so easily within its grasp"—into molding himself to match his fictional counterpart (2). Such an account assumes that the production of children's fiction is driven by the adult author's desire to ensure the child reader's absolute, unreflective identification with a particular child protagonist, a generalization that is surely worth challenging. Moreover, while Rose is right to react against excessively cheery representations of reading as an arena of undiluted pleasure and enrichment for children, she veers to the opposite extreme by characterizing young readers as the victims of an invasive and overpowering form of colonization, as Perry Nodelman has shown.[31]

To be sure, Rose maintains at the start of her study that she considers it "more or less impossible to gauge" how books actually affect children (9), adding that she will not comment on this topic. And yet, rather than arguing that children's stories *attempt* to entrance, colonize, and reify young readers, Rose makes statements which presuppose the *success* of such efforts, as when she declares that "children's fiction draws in the child, it secures, places and frames the child" (2). Similarly, she suggests that we interpret *Peter Pan* not as merely a proffered representation of the child but rather as a coercive "demand made by the adult on the child . . . which fixes the child and then holds it in place. . . . the child is used (and abused) to represent the whole problem of what sexuality is, or can be, and to hold that problem at bay" (3–4). Because this passage is directly preceded by a discussion of Barrie's desire for the real "little boy (or boys)" who inspired *Peter Pan* (3), it is unclear whether Rose is referring here to the child inside or outside of the book, an elision in line with her habit of implying that the latter has no recourse against the former.

While I certainly don't wish to deny that children's texts function ideologically, as tools often employed by adults in an effort to socialize, shape, or even indoctrinate children, my concern is that such highly charged rhetoric resurrects the very image of childhood to which Rose herself so cogently objects. That is to say, by implying that child readers invariably succumb to adult efforts to regulate and exploit them, such discourse itself "others" children by characterizing them as innocent naïfs whose literacy skills are too primitive to enable them to cope with the aggressive textual overtures of adults. Indeed, even though Rose vows that she will not say anything about "the child's own experience of the book" (9), she does not abide by this ground rule. We consider *Peter Pan* "a classic for children," she declares, "despite the fact that they could not read it" (6).

Rose's evidence for this dubious claim is that early versions of Barrie's story appeared in expensive books aimed at an adult market (true, though not conclusive),[32] and that when a retelling geared toward children finally appeared, it was written in complex, extremely allusive prose: *Peter and Wendy* (1911), she alleges, "was a failure, almost incomprehensible, and later had to be completely rewritten along the lines of a new state educational policy on language" (6). By making a priori assertions about the inability of child readers to understand Barrie's novella, Rose unwittingly aligns herself not only with the British educational officials who censored and revised it but also with the long tradition of critics quoted earlier who complained that Golden Age texts were insufficiently attuned to the primitive simplicity of children. Indeed, her description of *Peter and Wendy* precisely matches Ransome's of *The Wind in the Willows*: as a children's book, Ransome contends, Grahame's story "is a failure, like a speech to Hottentots made in Chinese" (190). Just as Rose deems Barrie's prose too difficult for child readers to comprehend, Ransome complains that *The Wind in the Willows* is written in the "wrong language": in a sophisticated, allusive style that only adults could appreciate (190).

In Rose's case, this unfortunate tendency to characterize young people as artless beings devoid of agency carries over into descriptions of other activities besides reading, as when she refers to photography as "the seizing of the child by an image" or performances featuring child actors as events that involve adults "setting the child up as a spectacle, shining a light on it and giving it up to our gaze" (31, 29). Given her provocative and persistent use of such rhetoric, which suggests that children are invariably exploited and oppressed by adult attention, it is no wonder that Rose *twice* feels compelled to assert in her conclusion that she does not consider "what carries on in the name of children's literature" to be "the perpetration of a crime" (137). But no brief disclaimers about the import or scope of her argument can cancel out the effects of the generalizations she makes about children's fiction, which repeatedly characterize children as helpless pawns in the hands of all-powerful adults. As a result, the critics who adhere most closely to her argument routinely represent young people as voiceless victims, as David Rudd has demonstrated (30).[33]

Like Nodelman, Rudd, and Myers, I believe that it is too reductive to view "representations of children only as unproblematic socialization narratives which 'Other,' smother, and colonize the child subject" (Myers, "Reading Children" 50). We might contest this dark vision of the genre—which I refer to as "the colonization paradigm"—by trying to make the case that classic children's texts are subversive, undermining rather than promoting the status quo.[34] But because this move constitutes a simple binary reversal of the colonization paradigm, its effect would be to impose yet another totalizing metanarrative on a defiantly diverse set of texts. A better alternative, I would suggest, is to follow in the footsteps of the Golden Age authors who so carefully acknowledge the tremendous power that adults and their texts have over young people, while still allowing for the possibility that children—immersed from birth in a sea of discourse—can nevertheless navigate though this arena of competing currents in diverse and unexpected ways. Such a stance does not deny that children's fiction (like all literature) is ideological or that actual children are culturally inscribed by adult discourse. Rather, it involves acknowledging what Nodelman has helpfully characterized as "the complex weaves that form individual subjectivities and the complex and often conflicting range of discourses and ideologies available to each of us as we go about living our lives" ("Precarious" 4).

Although this complicated balancing act is harder to sustain than the more clear-cut colonization paradigm, I believe it is worth attempting, not only because it avoids essentializing child readers as passive victims but also because it opens up new vistas in the study of children's literature and culture. In 1984, Rose performed an invaluable service in shifting the focus of criticism from children to adults, rightly insisting that more attention needed to be paid to the issue of "what the adult desires—desires in the very act of construing the child as the object of its speech" (2). But it is not productive, now, to continue to insist that we limit ourselves entirely to the discussion of adult ideas, practices, and discourse.[35] The case of children's theatre provides a perfect example of how this tactic tends to obscure rather than illuminate the history of children's culture. The story of how this genre emerged as a discrete dramatic category in its own right has never been fully told, precisely because once you insist (as Rose did) that such shows were created by and for adults (102), there is no way to isolate children's theatre as a distinct subgenre, and thus it evaporates from our field of vision. In order to trace its development, we must be willing to explore the issue of what children were actually doing, both onstage and in the audience.

Admittedly, making this move raises thorny epistemological problems about what counts as evidence when we are talking about child playgoers and their reactions to particular shows. Nevertheless, the fact that we cannot speak in certitudes about this topic does not mean that we should throw up our hands and simply ignore the impressive amount of evidence related to the child's presence in the theatre that we have, ranging from journalistic and autobiographical accounts of how young people reacted to various shows to fan letters written by child audience members.[36] Viewing children's theatre solely in terms of voyeuristic adult desire has led us to ignore the mountain of evidence that suggests that the mixed audiences of children and adults who flocked to these productions valued the child actors who frequently appeared in them not merely for their physical appearance but also for their abilities, artfulness, and professional proficiency. In other words, even as precocity began to take on a more negative connotation in the culture at large, the theatre seems to have provided an arena for celebrating the prematurely developed abilities of youngsters whose performances blurred the line between innocence and experience. Considering how interested Golden Age authors were in the issue of the child's agency, it is no wonder that so many of them were drawn to drama; an inherently collaborative art form, children's theatre set before the public child performers who at once embodied script-following conformity *and* creative self-expression.

Given my resistance to the notion that the Victorians were fully committed to conceiving of the child as an innocent Other, this book might appear to be a departure from (or rebuttal to) the influential work of James R. Kincaid. After all, in *Child-Loving: The Erotic Child and Victorian Culture* (1992), Kincaid contends that the dividing line between child and adult was "constructed, and . . . often constructed sexually" by the Victorians (70), thereby making the child "available to desire [by] making it different, a strange and alien species" (198). But although this point has been repeatedly cited by other critics as Kincaid's main idea, his argument about nineteenth-century culture is actually more nuanced than this particular formulation suggests. True, *Child-Loving* traces how some Victorians anticipated our contemporary habit of characterizing the child as a bastion of "purity, innocence, emptiness, Otherness" (5). But Kincaid also insists that "we vastly overstate the dominance of this view of the child in the Victorian period" (72), failing to acknowledge that nineteenth-century constructions of childhood were hardly uniform, but "shifting, various, and mysterious" (63).

Kincaid even entertains the idea that "the notion of the sentimentally fixed, 'innocent' child" may be a "modern imposition" (77, 73). Because our own culture has so thoroughly embraced this image, he explains, critics have tended to focus disproportionately on Victorian texts that feature it, even as they misrepresent Philippe Ariès's famous point about the separation between adult and child. Whereas Ariès is careful to argue that the emergence of the desire to distinguish childhood from adulthood "was quite gradual," Kincaid observes, his followers attempt to "seize control of the past by erasing distance, turning Ariès's gradualism into Noah's flood: 'The point in cultural history when childhood and adulthood became separate and opposing worlds is clearly the late eighteenth century'; or 'Whatever its origins, the separateness of childhood was axiomatic in Victorian ideology' " (*Child-Loving* 62-3).[37] To refute such generalizations, Kincaid points readers toward a host of nineteenth-century texts that conceive of the child in more complicated, adventurous, and unexpected ways. But his real attention is focused elsewhere: not on nineteenth-century culture but on contemporary attitudes toward children. Or, as he puts it, "the Victorians are employed here to assist in exposing our discourse and its compulsions . . . I am, that is, less interested in reconstructing the past than in examining what our methods of reconstruction might tell us about our own policies" (4).[38]

It would therefore be churlish to criticize Kincaid for spending so little time analyzing these surprising stories. More worrying, however, is the fact that even when he acknowledges the presence of texts that do not erect a binary opposition between adult and child, he quickly closes down the possibility that they could be setting up the child as anything other than an Other. For example, after citing the children's fiction of the popular didactic author Hesba Stretton, whose characterization of the child does not fit the expected mold, he adds, "But . . . does a celebration of the child's freedom really manifest a concern for health or a concern for distancing. . . ? The encouragement of individualism, even of naughtiness . . . can be read as a way to maintain the gap, to formulate the category of 'child' so as to make it safely other" (65). There is no way out; authors *must* be constructing the child as an embodiment of difference whether they portray young people as obedient or resistant, naïve or sophisticated, mature or childish. Thus, even as Kincaid mounts a very convincing argument that Alice functions as an unattractive adult figure in Wonderland, he simultaneously tries to claim that she is an icon of "erotic Otherness" (275). This convoluted argument is far less convincing than his suggestion—which has been, so far as I can tell, completely ignored—that the Victorians were less obsessed with the image of the innocent child than we are—that "most of their discourse was more aware and honest than our own" (261).

Taking Kincaid at his word, I contend that, far from adhering religiously to a Romantic conception of childhood innocence, children's authors and participants in the cult of the child vacillated quite dramatically in their stance toward young people. Like the culture around them, which only gradually committed itself to erecting a firm barrier between innocence and experience, they remained fascinated by an older paradigm that held that children were capable of working and playing alongside adults. Thus, rather than equating precocity with death and decay, children's authors frequently characterized it in positive terms, rejecting the notion that education and contact with the civilized world was necessarily damaging.

Consider for example the case of Burnett's Sara Crewe, a truly artful orphan whose ability to dodge a Dickensian doom is inextricably linked to her social, intellectual, and linguistic competence. Sara's precocity is evident from the opening scene of *A Little Princess* (1905). Like the equally "precocious" Paul Dombey, who has "a strange, old-fashioned, thoughtful way" about him (Dickens 151), Sara regards the world "with a queer old-fashioned thoughtfulness in her big eyes":

> She was such a little girl that one did not expect to see such a look on her small face. It would have been an old look for a child of twelve, and Sara Crewe was only seven. The fact was, however, that she was always dreaming and thinking odd things and could not herself remember any time when she had not been thinking things about grown-up people and the world they belonged to. She felt as if she had lived a long, long time. (5)

Preternaturally advanced in emotional as well as academic matters, Sara acts as an "adopted mother" to her younger classmates at Miss Minchin's school and longs to be a wife to her father (34); at age five, her ambition is "To keep the house for [him] and sit at the head of his table when he had dinner-parties; to talk to him and read his books" (7).

Such statements would have prompted Burnett's more literate readers to fear for Sara's life, since British novelists, scientists, and journalists had all begun to pound home the message that "precocious children usually die early" ("Precocious Children," *Lady's Newspaper*).[39] Moreover, Burnett emphasizes the fact that she wants to evoke the convention of the doomed child by linking Sara to two more notoriously pathetic child characters: Smike, the sickly schoolboy who staggers through Dickens's *Nicholas Nickleby* (1837–39), and little William Carlyle, the saintly soul who succumbs to a sad fate in Mrs. Henry Wood's phenomenally popular *East Lynne* (1861).

Indeed, Sara's position at Miss Minchin's female academy precisely matches Smike's at Mr. Squeers's Dotheboys Hall: in both cases, the adult who previously paid for the child's education suddenly disappears, leaving neither money "nor no clue to be got" regarding the existence of other relatives or friends who might care for the child (Dickens, *Nicholas* 144). Although the chores they are given differ, both Sara and Smike are kept on in order to be exploited by their stingy, cruel teachers. Both eventually manage to escape, but whereas the "drooping" Smike cannot recover from this experience and dies of a broken heart (857), Sara stubbornly perseveres, survives, and thrives. As for Wood's William, he famously rhapsodizes on the beauties of heaven just before he dies: "a beautiful city, with its gates of pearl, and its shining precious stones, and its streets of gold . . . and the lovely flowers" (588). As readers of *A Little Princess* will recall, Sara makes a strikingly similar speech about heaven's "shining" streets, "fields of flowers," and "walls made of pearl and gold all round the city" (33). Yet it occurs in a completely different context: Burnett replaces a scene in which a child embraces the idea of dying as a positive pleasure with one in which an older child persuades a younger one to stop dwelling on her mother's death and embrace the pleasures of life instead.

In contrast to her Dickensian counterparts, Sara's knowledge of the world is not purchased by the loss of power. Her precocity does not enfeeble her; on the contrary, it quickly emerges as an enabling quality that helps ensure her survival. A voracious reader who is fluent in four languages by the time she is seven years old, Sara uses her phenomenal storytelling and communication skills to connect with adults and children around her who later come to her aid. "Of course the greatest power Sara possessed," Burnett stresses, "was her power of telling stories" to provide solace for herself and others (35). Ultimately, her skill as a storyteller even allows her to help script her own happy ending; after hearing Sara spin out a fantasy about how beautiful her miserable existence could be if she had access to various comforts, the servant who overhears this narrative persuades his master to undertake the project of "making her visions real things" (128). Like other child storytellers from this era, Sara's creativity is portrayed not in Romantic terms—as the original freshness of an untutored mind—but rather as a sign of her impressive ability to work *with* grown-ups and the material they give her. The countless books she consumes inspire her own forays into fiction, as when she rewrites Hans Christian Andersen's "The Little Mermaid" to give it a happy ending; or uses the *Arabian Nights* as inspiration in creating stories about diamond mines; or steals material from her French history books in order to weave her comforting fantasy that she is a noble prisoner in the Bastille.

Just as Sara enjoys an extremely intimate relationship with adults and their texts, *A Little Princess* engages with pressing contemporary issues relevant to adults as well as children. For instance, when Burnett punishes the English men who race after foreign riches, she calls into question the ethics of empire-building. Sara's father dies and her future guardian Mr. Carrisford becomes gravely ill as a direct result of their quest to reap a huge profit from Indian diamond mines. Mr. Carrisford later admits that he and Captain Crewe "half lost our heads" with greed for this great prize (113). Perhaps to make amends for the problematic origins of her fortune, Sara decides at the end of the novel to commit herself to helping the underprivileged in England. As in *The Secret Garden*, then, Burnett suggests that venturing abroad is unhealthy for English families, who would be better advised to invest their energy in healing their own far-from-perfect society rather than taking over someone else's.[40] Both of these stories also raise the question of what effect class has on character. Early on in *A Little Princess*, Sara wonders whether her father's wealth has made it impossible for her to know whether she is truly a good person: "if you have everything you want and every one is kind to you, how can you help but be good-tempered? . . . Perhaps I'm a *hideous* child, and no one will ever know, just because I never have any trials" (28). Similarly, in chronicling Sara's relationship with two lower-class girls, Burnett repeatedly raises the question of whether girls who inhabit such different worlds are "just the same—only two little girls" or so radically different that they can never truly be equals (70).

Like Roderick McGillis, we may feel that Burnett's attitude toward Empire and class is conflicted and her ultimate message ambiguous. But it would certainly be wrong to suggest that she and her colleagues produced "escapist" texts that failed to grapple with such topics (Carpenter 19), including the double-barreled issue of how much agency one can have as an acculturated subject, and how children ought to respond to literature, that premier vehicle for the transmission of ideology. In her autobiography, Burnett makes fun of children's stories that portray the ideal child as a parrot who mindlessly absorbs and echoes back the texts fed to her by adults (*One I Knew* 188–89). In *A Little*

Princess, she posits a very different model for her young audience. A major source of Sara's power, as noted above, is that she views texts not as marching orders but as blueprints for creative activity, a stance other child readers are invited to embrace as well.

Indeed, Burnett articulates this vision of active literacy explicitly in "The Whole of the Story," the preface she composed for *A Little Princess*. Written in part to justify her decision to publish an expanded version of Sara's story, which she had already presented as a novella and as a play, this essay also encourages young people to follow in her (and Sara's) footsteps: to retell, revise, and renew the stories they find in books like *A Little Princess*. In it, Burnett encourages her readers to "realize how much more than is ever written there really is in a story—how many parts of it are never told—how much more really happened than there is in the book one holds in one's hand" (3). Other people's stories, she points out, can serve as infinitely rich sources of material: "Between the lines of every story there is another story, and that is one that is never heard and that can only be guessed at by people who are good at guessing" (3).

Similarly, Dinah Craik ends *The Little Lame Prince* (1875) with the words "I have related, as well as I could, the history of Prince Dolor, but with the history of Nomansland I am as yet unacquainted. If anybody knows it, perhaps he or she will kindly write it all down in another book. But mine is done" (124). Characterizing creativity more in terms of intervention than pure invention, such gestures attest to a desire to encourage young people to view literature not as the undisputed domain of all-powerful adults but as a sort of no-man's-land, a shared field of play. "Stories belong to everybody," Sara asserts (37); and by characterizing children as capable of taking up the pen themselves, these writers encourage their readers to own and renovate the stories told for and about them by adults. Rather than embracing a realist aesthetic that "denies . . . the fact that language does not simply reflect the world but is active in its constitution of the world" (Rose 60), these writers imply that we are all scripted beings who can at best only collaborate on our life stories. Or as Sara explains to a more innocent friend, "*Everything's* a story. You are a story—I am a story. Miss Minchin is a story" (89). "And since it is all a story," as Lynne Sharon Schwartz has observed in an appreciative afterword to *A Little Princess*, "how much better to make it up for ourselves rather than to let the world make it up for us" (225). Hopeful but not naïve, Burnett and other Golden Age authors entertain the possibility that children can resist and reconceive the scripts handed to them by adults, participating not only in the production of narrative, but in the drafting of their own life stories.

1

"OUR FIELD"

The Rise of the Child Narrator

The Victorian age was marked by a new interest in the child's perspective and voice. For the first time, as Hugh Cunningham notes, children's testimony was sought out and recorded; disseminated in government reports and journalistic accounts of city life; it helped drive reform on a variety of fronts and affected literary representations of children.[1] *Oliver Twist* (1837–39), which Peter Coveney identifies as the first English novel centered around a child (127), was followed by a host of fictions, such as *Jane Eyre* (1847) and *David Copperfield* (1849–50), in which characters reflect back on their earliest memories, as well as books like *The Mill on the Floss* (1860) and *What Maisie Knew* (1897), in which omniscient narrators describe a young protagonist's reaction to the surrounding world. For their part, authors of children's fiction began routinely to employ child narrators. The use of this technique is now so ubiquitous in literature for children and young adults that it is difficult to imagine a time when it was not utterly conventional. But in the 1850s and 1860s, the act of chronicling events from a child's point of view was still daringly experimental.

Early efforts on the part of Victorian children's authors to speak from the position of childhood or early adolescence have received virtually no critical attention. In part, this is because commentators are working with a radically incomplete genealogy. On the infrequent occasions that literary critics and historians discuss the rise of the child narrator, they generally identify Dickens's *Holiday Romance* (1868) as the first piece of prose to employ this technique, and then jump directly to Nesbit, who has young Oswald Bastable chronicle *The Story of the Treasure Seekers* (1899) and its sequels. Thus, as Anita Moss notes, Nesbit is often "given credit for creating one of the first child narrators in children's literature" ("Story" 189).[2] Occasionally, Mark Twain gets a mention for allowing Huckleberry Finn to describe his own adventures in 1884, though not always. Why would this most famous example be left out? Perhaps because Twain was American, but more likely because, as Beverly Lyon Clark has recently argued, the canonization of *Huckleberry Finn* involved a campaign to recategorize it as adult literature rather than exploring its ties to the children's literature tradition (77–101).[3]

These three authors undoubtedly helped to popularize and perfect this new way of writing, but a chorus of critically neglected women writers actually played the biggest role in developing it. Dickens was not the first to experiment with using a child narrator. Dinah Maria Mulock Craik tested this technique out over a decade before he did in *The Little Lychetts: A Piece of Autobiography* (1855) and again in *Our Year: A Child's Book, In Prose and Verse* (1860).[4] Years before Huck Finn or Oswald Bastable appeared on the scene, Hesba Stretton let *Max Krömer* (1871) tell his own tale, and Juliana Horatia Ewing used child narrators in a plethora of stories, including *A Great Emergency* (1874), *A Very Ill-Tempered Family* (1874–75), "Our Field" (1876), "A Bad Habit" (1877), *We and the World* (1877–78), "A Happy Family" (1883), and *Mary's Meadow* (1883–84). Mary Louisa Molesworth also experimented with this technique in *The Boys and I* (1883) and *The Girls and I* (1892), as did Frances E. Crompton in *The Gentle Heritage* (1893).[5]

Some of these stories are more successful than others, but Ewing in particular excelled at this kind of writing, and as I will demonstrate, her work exerted a major influence over Nesbit and thus, indirectly, on a vast array of contemporary authors. Because of her consummate skill as an artist and the key role she played in popularizing this technique, Ewing's name should be included on any list of key figures from the Golden Age of children's literature, alongside writers like Carroll and Stevenson. The Victorians certainly recognized her power and prominence in the field. John Ruskin admired Ewing's writing so much that he offered to help her bring out a volume of her stories independently when she became dissatisfied with her publisher. He called "Our Field" a poem (Avery, *Mrs. Ewing* 66), while Henry James enthused that Ewing's story *Jackanapes* (1883) was "a genuine masterpiece" (quoted in Laski 11). Referring to Ewing's *Six to Sixteen* (1872), Rudyard Kipling remarked, "I owe more in circuitous ways to that tale than I can tell. I knew it as I know it still, almost by heart" (quoted in Maxwell 189). Thirty years after Ewing's death, Lord Baden-Powell used her story *The Brownies* (1865) as the basis for the junior branch of the Girl Guide movement, just as he mined Kipling's *Jungle Books* (1894–95) in forming the Cub Scouts.[6] Craik's impact is more difficult to measure, but striking similarities between *The Little Lychetts* and Burnett's *A Little Princess* (1905) and *The Secret Garden* (1911) suggest that she, too, was read and imitated.[7]

Early efforts to employ a child narrator demand our attention not only because of their literary merit and influence but also because critics have leveled some serious charges against this technique, and it seems important to determine whether these neglected examples shore up or undercut such criticism. Victorian attempts to speak from a child's perspective are "rarely satisfactory," Penny Brown contends, "for they are often coloured by the author's subjective and idiosyncratic view of childhood and may be merely cute or embarrassing" (9–10). But the charge of sickly sentimentalism is mild compared to the allegations made against this technique by Rose and other critics committed to the notion that children's fiction functions as a form of colonization. Of all the techniques that authors employ to mold and manipulate the child, they contend, using a child narrator is the most sneakily seductive, since this move enables an author to obscure her own presence and purpose(s) in addressing the child, thus smoothing the path of identification. In other words, writers set up the child as a surrogate storyteller in order to trick young audience members into identifying with an adult-produced picture of what children should be like.[8]

Thus, Mavis Reimer argues that the act of using of a child narrator is "not simply a coercive domination, but rather a domination that also manufactures consent" (51). Quoting Pierre Bourdieu, she maintains that "instead of telling the child what he must do" such texts tell "him what he is, and thus lead him to become durably what he has to be" (50). And what the child has to be, according to this line of argument, is innocent. Stories featuring child narrators set up a strict division between child and adult, and use the purity of their youthful speakers to persuade readers of the absolute veracity of the tales they tell: as Rose puts it, "seeing with their own eyes, telling the truth and documenting without falsehood—what characterises the child's vision is its innocence in both senses of the term (moral purity and the undistorted registering of the surrounding world)" (79). Rose identifies *Treasure Island* (1883) as the exemplary specimen of this kind of writing, a choice that enables her to claim that "autobiographical" children's fiction is "fully colonialist" in content as well as form (57).

In the abstract, the decision to use a child narrator does seem like an obvious ploy on the part of the adult author to repress the issue of "who is talking to whom, and why"—the key question Rose claims children's literature ignores (2). But the fictions themselves tell a different story. Far from downplaying the presence and power of grown-ups, these stories grapple directly with the issue of adult influence. Child narrators are represented not as innocent naïfs but as fully socialized beings who have already been profoundly shaped by the culture they inhabit, often as a result of their extensive reading. Young audience members are encouraged to recognize the conventions and prejudices the child speaker has absorbed, rather than indulging in unreflective identification. At the same time, the representation of what it means to be an author in these stories reinforces the importance of deviating from rather than ventriloquizing familiar social, cultural, and literary protocols. Craik, Ewing, Molesworth, and Nesbit all characterize artistic agency not in terms of innocence and unproblematic autonomy but as a struggle that involves recycling, resisting, and revising preexisting narratives.

Thus, these writers rarely characterize child authors as independent agents who effortlessly produce original work. Instead, child storytellers function as ingenious collaborators, who are far more likely than traditional narrators to describe their experiences in first person plural ("we"). Many of these stories chronicle how *groups* of children—often but not always siblings—collectively engage in creative play, including the act of drafting stories. Such activity almost always involves appropriating elements from their favorite storybooks. The use of a communal voice therefore reflects how deeply the child narrator draws not just on the help of her peers but also on the creative property of adults. According to the Child of Nature paradigm, everything that the young soak up from the civilized world is bad, since it corrupts their natural purity. But in these stories, adults and their texts serve as a crucial source of inspiration and support. The adult's primacy and power—both in the child's daily life and in the field of fiction—are undeniable and sometimes overwhelming, but child characters cope with this pressure in creative ways, treating even the most didactic text as a "potential space" that they can annex and imaginatively transform.[9]

In doing so, these artful dodgers function as models for child readers, inviting them to view fiction not as a set of marching orders from an omnipotent author but as a shared playing field. Showing by example how this process might work, authors who employ child narrators themselves often revise popular stories. For instance, as I will demonstrate, Craik rewrites *Jane Eyre* as a children's book, allowing her orphaned female heroine to shun marriage in favor of embarking on a career as an artist. Similarly, Ewing recasts one of W. H. G. Kingston's imperialist adventure stories to suggest that the project of seeking out excitement overseas is misguided and ethically suspect.[10]

As these examples indicate, it is untenable to claim, as Daphne Kutzer does, that Victorian children's fiction was a "highly conservative" genre that "unquestioningly celebrated" imperialism and other patriarchal systems (xvi). Following Rose and other proponents of the colonization paradigm, Kutzer takes this argument a step further and argues that the children's novel *as a genre* shares this reactionary bias: "whereas adult fiction may—indeed, often does—question the reigning cultural code of behavior, children's fiction rarely does so" (xv). Setting aside the question of whether it makes sense to generalize about a genre as large, flexible, and varied as children's fiction, it seems crucial to note that even the subgroup of texts that Rose and company consider most suspect—the "autobiographical" children's story—fails to conform to this picture: early efforts to employ a child narrator, condemned for attempting to seduce children into unthinking compliance with adult desires, in fact encourage young readers to become more aware of the societal pressures that affect their lives.

OSWALD'S ANCESTORS

Texts featuring child narrators, we are told, attempt to "draw the [child] reader into the text in such a way that the reader accepts the role offered and enters into the demands of the book" (Chambers 254). Yet readers are clearly meant to notice that Oswald Bastable, one of the most celebrated child narrators from this period, is conceited and prone to condescension; as Julia Briggs observes, "Oswald is the Victorian patriarch in short pants, and his sense of superiority to anyone except another gentleman borders on the outrageous" (*Woman of Passion* 187). Juliana Ewing's boy narrator Bayard, who appeared on the scene over a decade before Oswald, exhibits similar qualities. Indeed, Bayard sounds so much like Oswald that perusing the opening of "A Happy Family" (1883) is an eerie experience for Nesbit fans:

> I am the eldest, as I remind my brothers; and of the more worthy gender, which my sisters sometimes forget. Though we live in the village, my father is a gentleman, as I shall be when I am grown up. I have told the village boys so more than once. One feels mean in boasting that one is better born than they are; but if I did not tell them, I am not sure that they would always know. (197).

Though Bayard complains about his "swaggering, ridiculous name," it fits him nicely (199); besides looking down on girls and poor people, he is also rude about the Irish, even though his mother is from Ireland. Yet both he and Oswald are appealing as well as appalling; inventive and energetic, they take the lead in creating games based on "all kinds of things" that they and their siblings have read or seen, including books, magazines, paintings, advertisements, concerts, circuses, theatricals, magic shows, and so on ("Happy Family" 201). For good and for ill, these child protagonists are enmeshed in and affected by the culture they inhabit.

Rather than striving to secure the child reader's unreflective identification, Ewing and Nesbit invite their audience both to sympathize with and separate themselves from these child narrators—to appreciate their finer qualities while recognizing their limitations and prejudices. For in both cases, the boy narrator's complacency is amusingly undermined by run-ins with girls and members of the working class, as well as the failure of ambitious projects that he insists on directing himself. Thus, in "A Happy Family," Bayard appoints himself "Showman" and orchestrates an entertainment featuring live animals that goes disastrously (and comically) wrong, partly because he gets into a fight with a "village-boy" whom he tries to order around (202). Similarly, in *The Wouldbegoods* (1901), Oswald elects himself "captain" of a reenactment of Kipling's *Jungle Books* that spirals out of control (9), and he and his siblings frequently interfere in the lives of the less privileged. Inspired by texts like *Ministering Children* (1854) and the "*All the Year Round* Christmas numbers," the young Bastables assume that "the poor grateful creatures" will "bless the names" of their wise, kindly benefactors (*Wouldbegoods* 214, 93). The spectacular failure of such schemes suggests that fiction cannot always be trusted to provide a guide for living, a recurring theme in stories featuring child narrators. Books do not transparently reflect the reality of the world, even (and perhaps especially) when they feature child narrators. Thus, in a memorable scene that I discuss in chapter 4, Nesbit inserts herself as a character in the Bastable books to remind readers of the presence of the adult author behind the scenes. Similarly, *Adventures of Huckleberry Finn* (1884) opens by outing the actual author and emphasizing the unreliability of *all* narrators. Huck famously declares,

> You don't know about me, without you have read a book by the name of 'The Adventures of Tom Sawyer,' but that ain't no matter. That book was made by Mr. Mark Twain, and he told the truth, mainly. There was things which he stretched, but mainly he told the truth. That is nothing. I never seen anybody but lied, one time or another. (1)

Huck included, we presume. Indeed, he proves just as adept at lying and adopting false identities as those famous frauds the King and the Duke. Huck's painfully long struggle to extricate himself from the company of these two hucksters symbolizes how hard it is for him to escape the effects of inhabiting a corrupt society. As a resident of the pre–Civil War South, Twain suggests, Huck has been absorbing lessons in hypocrisy, selfishness, and cruelty since his birth.

As these examples reveal, nineteenth-century authors who employ child narrators do not insist on the primitive purity of their juvenile raconteurs and the absolute veracity of the words they utter. Instead, they take it for granted that children are shaped by the culture they inhabit, and suggest that their development into creative and ethical individuals depends on their willingness to resist and revise the conventions of adult society and adult-produced texts. This theme is already present in one of the earliest English children's novels to feature a child narrator: *The Little Lychetts: A Piece of Autobiography* (1855), by Craik.[11] Thirteen-year-old Eunice Lychett, who narrates the tale, and her little brother Bion, eight, are snobbish and spoiled; their deeply felt sense of their own gentility is shocked when the death of their parents forces them to move into the "poor, mean, dirty little house" of their undistinguished cousin Reuben (39).[12]

As in the case of Oswald and Huck, no miraculous transformation occurs whereby the child protagonists become paragons of virtue. Instead, all of these characters are caught up in the slow, unsteady process of struggling to reform their own elitist worldview. Such development depends on differentiation rather than identification: as far as they are able, these child narrators evade the pressure to comply with prevailing cultural norms. Thus, Huck refuses to turn Jim in, though in many ways he remains a racist in both word and deed.[13] Similarly, Eunice's pride continues to "linger" on and influence her actions even after she renounces her "contemptuous" attitude toward the lower ranks of society (116, 23). For instance, although she declares that she has put aside the pride that made it hard for her to accept the idea of becoming a governess, she clearly continues to regard this job as beneath her, since she refuses to narrate any portion of her time in service.

This focus on the importance of deviating from convention is infused into the very fabric of Eunice's narrative. Describing her own character, she declares, "I do not set myself up as a pattern of perfection—the 'good child' of young folk's storybooks, which 'good child' I don't believe in—not a bit of it!" (80). Books often twist the truth, and creative self-expression depends on twisting back, a move Craik models by revising Charlotte Brontë's *Jane Eyre* (1847), a book whose ignored subtitle is *An Autobiography*, and whose opening chapters furnish the closest thing to a child narrator that we get in the early Victorian novel.[14] Like Jane, Eunice is an orphan whose parents' death sends her sliding down the social scale and eventually lands her at a new home with a forbidding name: Stonyhide rather than Thornfield. Wandering along a muddy road soon after she arrives, she (too) meets "a gentleman, on a tall black horse," whom she quickly learns to call "Master," eventually becoming governess to his children and worshipping the ground he walks on (Craik 53). Moreover, both girls long for affection but worry that their physical plainness will prevent them from getting it; staring into a "cruel looking-glass" in the opening scene of *The Little Lychetts* (4), Eunice regrets that her appearance is not likely to please others and, just like Jane, dons simple gray and black attire, hoping at least to look neat.

In both cases, however, the heroine's sober exterior in no way disguises her fiery inner self. Like the young Jane Eyre, Eunice describes herself as a fierce, "savage" creature, "seething and boiling" with "all sorts of erring passions" (85, 89). Treated coldly by hard-hearted schoolteachers after she becomes an orphan, Eunice "burn[s] with wrath" and violently rejects their suggestions for her future life, which she finds demeaning (12). Tellingly, her besetting sin of pride is precisely the failing that Brontë's heroine was sharply criticized for exhibiting; in her damning 1848 review, Elizabeth Rigby complained that "Jane

Eyre is proud" and ungrateful: "she looks upon all that has been done for her not only as her undoubted right, but as falling far short of it" (173). The ferociously discontented Eunice deserves this criticism far more than Jane, but both girls are indisputably hungry for more of everything, from food to love. However shocking the act of demanding more was when a boy orphan did it, it was immeasurably more so when performed by a Victorian girl, since they were expected not to seek self-fulfillment but to renounce their own desires and confine themselves to caring for others.

For this reason, as Sandra M. Gilbert and Susan Gubar have argued (336–71), Brontë creates a double for her heroine, Bertha Mason, who personifies all the passion and rage that Jane cannot ultimately be allowed to feel or express. Craik, by contrast, allows her heroine to exhibit and even eventually revel in the "virile force" that Brontë transposes onto Bertha (*Jane Eyre* 328). Like the madwoman, Eunice is extremely large and strong; for this reason, she explains, "I was the sort of girl of whom people say from her cradle, 'What a pity she wasn't a boy!' " (4). Trapped in society that does not value powerful women, Eunice often feels miserable, angry, and oppressed; seeking relief, she takes "a wild pleasure in pacing up and down" (26), either inside or out, in order to work off "that choking passion which made me feel as if I hated . . . everybody" (79). Jane likewise takes a "wild pleasure" in pacing, but as Gilbert and Gubar note, her restlessness is transferred onto Bertha, who runs "backwards and forwards . . . on all fours," groveling and growling "like some strange wild animal" (Brontë 309, 327–28). Thus, Brontë uses the climactic occasion of Jane's first glimpse of Bertha to emphasize the dissimilarity between Jane's calm purity and Bertha's frantic fury.

In contrast, Craik's revision of this scene reveals her determination to acknowledge her heroine's sense of enraged oppression, rather than denying or displacing it. Accompanying the Master and his family to "a wild-beast show" (58), Eunice hears a "premonitory savage growl," then sees some "perpetually-moving, low-growling forms in the cages" (61). More than once, she openly expresses her strong sense of identification with these unhappy fellow pacers, as when she declares, "I being myself a free, wild creature at heart, felt a certain pity for the poor captive animals, and would rather have seen the tigers and leopards bounding over their native jungle than pacing to and fro in those wretched cramped cages" (61–62).[15] Eunice's characterization of herself here echoes Mr. Rochester's description of Jane as "wild, free thing" who, though caged, manages to elude his grasp (357). But Jane cannot acknowledge this ferocity within herself: twice, she gazes into a looking-glass and sees a feral apparition that she does not recognize. Eunice, on the other hand, begins her story by spending half an hour "contemplating my own likeness" in the mirror, an act of self-examination she declares to be "excusable" (2), presumably because it does not engender vanity but rather reinforces her conviction that she is "a great, ugly, awkward girl," unladylike and unrefined (3).

As feminist critics have noted, female writers from this period often signal their anxiety that assuming the role of author requires a level of self-absorption and assertiveness not in keeping with culturally enshrined ideal of selfless womanhood.[16] As Eunice's lengthy communion with her own reflection indicates, Craik aims to legitimate the egotism that enables female artistic expression. Indeed, Eunice explicitly characterizes her story as an attempt to comfort and encourage other young women who do not match the angelic ideal: "I tell all this," she declares, "for the benefit of ugly people, especially young people. . . . My dear ugly girl, take heart!" (66–67). And, hearteningly, Eunice's eccentric otherness is never fully tamed or transformed, but rather fuels her career as an artist. Like Jane, Eunice loves to draw. In fact, her declaration that "I was happy, absorbingly happy" while wielding her pencil precisely echoes Jane's answer to Mr. Rochester about whether she enjoyed the process of creating art: " 'I was absorbed, sir: yes, and I was happy' "(Craik 114; Brontë 143).

But although Jane experiences "one of the keenest pleasures I have ever known" while composing these pictures, Brontë never seriously entertains the idea of her heroine making a career out of painting, and permits Rochester to dismiss her as a dabbler; looking at her work, he observes, " 'You had not enough of the artist's skill and science to give [your vision] full being' " (144). Eunice's talent is treated very differently. Near the end of her story, she explains that "last year, a stranger, an artist, staying at the Master's house, saw my poor drawings, and said that I had absolute 'genius;' that, if I studied properly abroad, at Munich especially, I might soon earn a living and in time become a real artist!" (127). Although such encouragement is inspiring, Eunice in fact already considers herself a serious artist. A few chapters earlier, describing the afternoon when she returned to drawing after a long hiatus, she proudly declares, "From that day I was—from the depth of my heart, however feebly and unworthily my hand worked out its conceptions—wholly an artist" (114).

While sketching, Eunice lapses into "selfish unconsciousness" of the world around her, "never once" noticing what Bion or Reuben are doing while she works (114). Rather than punishing her heroine for this indulgence, Craik rewards her; Eunice's "frantic" desire for more freedom and fulfillment is granted when she inherits enough money to give up governessing (79), an occupation that makes her feel like a "wild zebra in harness" (122). When Jane receives a similar competency, she gives most of it away and uses the rest to settle down into domesticity. In contrast, Eunice exults that she is now "free to wander" the globe and pursue her artistic ambitions (127). Thus, although Craik's heroine often pays lip service to the need to "conquer" her unruly passions and faults (83), there is no question what message the story ultimately sends about confining powerful creatures such as herself to a stiflingly narrow existence; as the Master says, referring to the caged beasts, "It's a bad thing! a bad thing" (62).

In a period when—as Elaine Showalter notes—women writers generally "punished assertive heroines" because they could not cope with "the guilt of self-centered ambition," Eunice's triumphant escape to Europe represents a truly radical departure (28, 23). It is enabled, in many ways, by Craik's manipulation of male characters. To begin with, she transforms the domineering Mr. Rochester—who, by his own admission, is old enough to be Jane's father—into a nurturing parental figure. A doting husband and dad, this selfless master acts as a "kind, and good, and fatherly" friend to Eunice, giving her food and books and caring for her when she is ill (55). The circumstances of their first meeting reveal Craik's determination to transform Brontë's overweening hero into a figure who dispenses aid rather than demanding it: whereas Rochester asks Jane to help him up when his horse slips, Craik's master stops his steed in order to rescue Eunice and Bion from a mudslide on the moors. Eunice loves him for his kindness, but she is not in love with him.

Nevertheless, there is a male figure in *The Little Lychetts* who takes on many of Rochester's unpleasant characteristics—who treats Eunice quite cruelly, yet wins her passionate love, and who inspires raging jealousy in her heart by espousing his affection for another young woman. This adored yet "hated" figure is Eunice's little brother, Bion (79). Her ferocious desire to be first in his affections seems not just "exaggerated and foolish," as she terms it, but disturbingly incestuous (89). Inscribing a book that she has gotten him as a birthday gift, for example, Eunice declares that "many a happy maiden [has signed] her marriage settlement, with less of emotion" (76). When Bion dallies with another woman during an afternoon walk, Eunice pretends not to notice, but she gives away her feelings of rage and pain by pulling roses from the hedge and "playing nervously with the thorny stems, pricking finger after finger, till they were marked with blood" (68).

The extreme intensity of this relationship makes sense when we recognize that Craik involves her heroine in a tortured relationship with her closest relative in order to dwell on the unspeakable issue of the need for female self-love: the difficulty Eunice faces in loving Bion symbolizes how hard it is for her to cherish and accept herself. Just as she regards her mirror image with "melancholy" dissatisfaction at the start of the story (4), Eunice also looks unfavorably on Bion, who is just as "peevish and discontented" as she is: "I did not love him then" she admits (20, 11). Over and over again, he nastily reminds her that she is ugly, which is just what she is always telling herself. After her parents die, Eunice has no choice but to take care of Bion, and, as she gradually begins to love him, she likewise learns to value her own competence and power. During an outing on the moors, for example, she hugs him to keep him warm and observes, "I was now glad I was such a big, strong girl, and forgot that my coarseness of appearance had ever been a trouble" (50).

During this process, it becomes evident that Bion functions as Eunice's double, since he, too, turns out to be an artistic genius, excelling in music rather than visual art (121). In caring for this delicate, "girlish" boy, Eunice nurtures her own talent, her own ambition, her own inner self (16). Thus, explaining her decision to pursue an artistic career, she declares that although such a choice "may seem very ridiculous and altogether impossible," she is galvanized by the fact that "Bion has, I find, likewise made up *his* mind to be a great musician and composer.... He must study, and Germany is the best place for musical instruction. So we shall try our fortunes together" (127). So whereas Brontë uses a female double in order to funnel off her heroine's fiery rebelliousness, Craik employs a masculine double in order to license Eunice's burning desire for liberty and self-expression. The fire imagery that David Lodge notices in *Jane Eyre* is just as present in *The Little Lychetts*, but rather than associating conflagration with destructive rage, as Brontë does, Craik reclaims fire as a positive symbol of artistic inspiration. Thus, in a rapturous account of her visit to a blacksmith's forge, Eunice observes, "It was so beautiful to see the red-glowing iron beat out into form as easily as clay—so grand to see the sparks flying, and hear the measured musical fall of the hammers, which gave Handel the first idea of the tune that Bion thinks so fine, 'The Harmonious Blacksmith'" (57).

Bion's ambition not only enables his sister's career, it also allows Craik to entertain and dismiss the idea of selflessly sacrificing one's artistic dreams in order to care for one's family (which Victorian girls were generally expected to do). When Eunice falls ill, Bion gives away his beloved piano because she has never liked music and he wants to aid her recovery and make her happy. But when Eunice realizes what he has done, she emphatically refuses to accept his sacrifice, buying him a better instrument so that he can continue to improve.

Unlike other child narrators whose stories I will turn to next, Eunice does not characterize the act of writing her story as a joint endeavor. Yet collaboration nevertheless functions as a key enabler of artistic expression in this novel. Just as teaming up with Bion facilitates Eunice's self-assertion, the work of male artists directly inspires her drawing. Indeed, Eunice comes to the conclusion that she is "wholly an artist" after spending a blissful afternoon studying and sketching from three books: Shakespeare's plays, Homer's *Iliad*, and *Flaxman's Illustrations of the Iliad of Homer* (114). As she explains, the experience of copying Flaxman's images and attempting "pencilled portraits" of Shakespeare's heroines "coloured all the rest of my life" (114); the volume of Shakespeare in particular furnishes her with "as much treasure for future fishing-up as the mysterious bottom of the sea" (113). Thus, even as Craik builds on Brontë to construct her story, she suggests that female artists must exploit and elaborate on the work of male artists as well. In keeping with this focus on a two-parent tradition, Eunice thrives at Stonyhide because, despite being an orphan, she receives both paternal and maternal affection, as indicated by the fact that although these books are given to her as a gift "out of the Master's library," they are "chosen by his wife's own hand" (113).

Despite her status as a child narrator, we know that Eunice succeeds in later life because although she speaks as a thirteen-year-old for most of the story, Craik breaks this illusion at various points. Halfway though the novel, for example, the heroine who has characterized herself as a child suddenly prefaces some advice to readers with the startling words "I, now a grown woman, say to you, 'My children' " (65). Thus, at the very moment when Eunice reaches out directly to child readers, any sense of identification that may have developed between child character and child reader is unceremoniously extinguished. It is possible that such moments merely attest to the difficulty of adjusting to an unfamiliar literary technique: Craik simply slipped up in allowing Eunice's adult self to intrude onto the scene. But when we turn to other examples of this kind of writing, including one by Craik, such an explanation seems inadequate, since undermining the illusion of the autonomous child narrator turns out to be a common feature of the genre. Committed to the idea that the child's creativity depends on adult support—and that artistry in general involves coping with one's forebears—Craik and her successors characterize the writing process in terms of adult–child collaboration.

Thus, the opening of Craik's *Our Year: A Child's Book, In Prose and Verse* (1860) proclaims that the volume is a result of the collective effort of an adult and two children. "We have gathered together our recollections and experiences," the first chapter explains, "and combined them so as to make this 'Our Year's History' " (26). Craik makes no attempt to hide the fact that she has taken the upper hand in this process—that an adult functions as the actual author: "We have not thought it necessary to particularize what each one has remembered or communicated; the general 'we' includes the three; but the author of this book has been collector, arranger, and writer of this 'History' " (26). In chronicling a year's worth of activities, Craik breaks the book up into months, including two poems and a prose chapter in each section. The latter segments are the ones that conform most closely to the children's point of view, as the narrator describes in detail how "we" build snowmen in January, gather wildflowers in June, go blackberrying in September, and so on.

As narrative unfolds, however, Craik's willingness to acknowledge her own presence continues to manifest itself. Thus, she frequently shifts from "we" to "I" at moments when she wants to impart a bit of motherly advice or instruction. This move, which sometimes occurs in the middle of a sentence, unquestionably complicates the process of identification. Meanwhile, the poems sandwiched in between each chapter engender similar disorientation, since some feature child narrators, and others adult or omniscient narrators. As a result, readers must pay close attention to the issue of address in order to figure out what is going on in the various verses. In terms of content, both poems and prose strongly emphasize the pleasures of interacting with the natural world. But by alternating back and forth between the two, Craik draws attention to the fun of playing with language, and the complex ways shifts in genre and meter affect the act of storytelling. Indeed, she experiments with a truly astonishing variety of different meters in her verses, hardly ever using the same one twice.

Dickens's *Holiday Romance: In Four Parts* (1868) does not formally introduce readers to the adult author lurking behind the scenes, but it too represents itself as a collaborative effort. Dickens's only fictional work aimed specifically at children consists of a quartet of tales, each narrated by a different child character—two boy cousins (aged eight and nine) and the two girls they have chosen as their "brides" (aged seven and six). As their eager aping of adult courtship rituals indicates, these children have absorbed the conventions of their culture like thirsty sponges; besides imitating the behavior of their elders, they also mimic their storytelling style. The boys borrow the high-flown rhetoric of adventure stories in order to characterize their clashes with real-life authority figures as epic battles. "Vain were my endeavors," eight-year-old William complains, describing his efforts to free the girls from the company of their headmistress as a military engagement that ends in a court-martial (329). Similarly, his cousin Bob recasts his battle with the Latin-grammar master using plot devices and phrases lifted from imperialist island narratives, while the girls playfully recycle the conventions of the fairy tale and the domestic romance.

Holiday Romance thus characterizes authorship as a collaborative act not only by having four separate child characters contribute material but also by stressing how indebted these offerings are to preexisting texts. When William declares that an event occurs "ere yet the silver beams of Luna touched the earth" (331), it is clear that Dickens does not portray the child narrator as a naïve reporter of the unadorned truth, completely innocent of adult influence. If anything, as seven-year-old Alice points out, "'the grown-up people are too strong for us'" (332). Far from denying the authoritative clout of adults, *Holiday Romance* chronicles the children's efforts to usurp, deflect, or reverse that power. For instance, six-year-old Nettie pens a domestic drama set in "a country . . . where the children have everything their own way [and] the grown-up people are obliged to obey" (354). Moreover, just as each separate story is a revenge fantasy in which the child exerts power over the previously dominant adult, *Holiday Romance* as a whole represents a combined effort on the part of the children to turn the tables on their elders by appropriating for themselves the role of sneakily didactic author. Near the start of the story, Alice proposes, "'Let us in these next holidays . . . throw our thoughts into something educational for the grown-up people, hinting to them how things ought to be. Let us veil our meaning under a mask of romance'" (333).

Since adults have already established their primacy and power as the producers of fiction, the children must use the tools of the master to dismantle the master's house. Thus, Alice borrows the basic framework of the fairy tale for her story but comically subverts it by unexpectedly juxtaposing realistic and fantastic elements, as Claudia Bacile di Castiglione has noted. At the same time, the heroine of Alice's story—seven-year-old Princess Alicia—revises the prejudiced opinion of her father the King, who wrongly assumes that "we children never have a reason or a meaning" (338). Alicia quickly proves more competent at coping with a crisis than the King, and her creative ingenuity is linked to her talent at "snipping, stitching, cutting, and contriving"; when a family member gets into trouble, Alicia fixes the problem by weaving together items from the "royal rag-bag," in much the same way Alice constructs her story by selecting and rearranging bits from other people's fairy tales (339).

In focusing on child characters who contrive to rescue themselves and others from various kinds of oppression, *Holiday Romance* lends credence to my claim that producing children's literature often enables Victorian authors to move away from the image of the passive, victimized child. For as Bacile di Castiglioni points out, the children in *this* Dickens story "are not at all like those in his social novels who have been abandoned, abused or mortified in a variety of melodramatic ways. He finally creates young people who . . . decide with great enterprise and creativity to challenge the adult world, exploiting and overturning the literary patterns and modes of behavior that they had learned in their 'stultifying' books" (154). In other words, the children in *Holiday Romance* function as artful dodgers: subjected to the undeniable force of adult influence, they nevertheless manage to cope with this pressure in creative, subversive ways. Similarly, in *The Little Lychetts*, Eunice secures for herself more freedom and power than the heroines of Craik's "adult" novels. Her closest counterpart, the "crippled" *Olive* (1850), has a far more ambivalent attitude toward her own artistic talent, only pursuing a career as a painter when forced to by financial necessity (6). Haunted by the sense that her "art-life" constitutes a poor substitute for a more traditional and self-sacrificing mode of existence (263), Olive ends up marrying a difficult man who was recognized by Victorian critics as a reworking of Mr. Rochester.

Part of the reason child narrators succeed in functioning as empowered subjects rather than pathetic objects may be that there is strength in numbers. In Romantic poetry and Victorian novels, children often function as isolated, alienated figures. But child narrators are almost always enmeshed in extended families and networks of friends. The titles of these texts reflect this sense of collective identity: Craik's *Our Year* was followed by Ewing's "Our Field" and Molesworth's *The Boys and I* (1883) and *The Girls and I* (1892). In the latter two tales, the child narrators speak not only for themselves but for their opposite-sex siblings; and even as they chronicle their interaction with a complex community of family members, servants, and acquaintances, they also attest to their embeddedness within a community of authors. Thus, fourteen-year-old Audrey models her story of what happens to herself and "the boys" around suspenseful books that she has enjoyed as a reader. After revealing that she sent a letter to the family's former nursemaid, for example, she adds,

> I am not going to tell you just yet what I wrote. . . . You will know afterwards. You see I want to make my story as like a proper one as I can. . . . I have noticed that in what I call proper stories, real book, printed ones, though it all seems to come quite smooth and straight, it is really arranged quite plannedly—you are told just a bit, and then you are quietly taken away to another bit, and though you never think of it at the time, you find it all out afterwards. (132)

Far from insisting on the transparency of language, Molesworth here encourages child readers to pay more attention to the constructedness of texts, to notice that authors employ certain conventions in order to hoodwink their audience. Moreover, both Audrey and her eleven-year-old counterpart Jack—who narrates *The Girls and I*—acknowledge that even when they aim to give a perfectly truthful account of "simple things that really happened," they cannot (*Girls* 56). Thus, even as Jack vows to provide a "veracious history" of a series of events that affect his family, he admits that such a task is impossibly difficult; he cannot simply use language to reflect the reality of the world, because all the different "bits" of his story "get so mixed. It's like a tangle of thread—the ends you don't want keep coming up the wrong way, and putting themselves in front of the others. I must just go on as well as I can, and put down the things as straight as they'll come" (8, 56).

The notion that writing inevitably shapes, stretches, or distorts the reality of everyday experience is a central theme in many of these stories. Nesbit's child characters often complain that life is not like books, a sentiment expressed by earlier child narrators as well. Indeed, the principal grievance that motivates the quartet of children in *Holiday Romance* to rebel against adult control is that no king, queen, or wicked fairy attended the christening of William's baby brother, as their storybooks had led them to expect. Similarly, the child narrator of Ewing's "Our Field" (1876) begins her story by expressing her and her siblings' annoyance that fairy tale conventions have failed to come true in their family: "There were four of us, and three of us had godfathers and godmothers. Three each. Three times three makes nine, and not a fairy godmother in the lot. That was what vexed us" (228).

Once again, even as the child narrator is embedded in a large extended family, she is also characterized as a latecomer to an already crowded literary scene. This opening instantly associates the act of writing not with autonomous invention but with collaborative intervention; having read lots of fantastic fiction, a group of children take over the role of storyteller, giving a new twist to an old genre. Fairy tales, newspaper stories, and the *Arabian Nights* all provide grist for their imaginative mill, which may help explain why the child narrator of this tale remains unnamed: "Our Field" is simply not a story that represents the creation of narrative as the act of a single individual—as indicated, once again, by the narrator's frequent use of the first person plural.

The siblings in Hesba Stretton's *Max Krömer: A Story of the Siege of Strasbourg* (1871) likewise inhabit a crowded domestic scene, but this more somber story is also intent on emphasizing how children get caught up in large scale economic, political, and military affairs. Describing why she chose to set her story during the Franco-Prussian War, Stretton (whose real name was Sarah Smith) explains in a preface that during her travels through Europe the previous summer, "At every stage I saw how children were involved in the keen sufferings of the war" (5). More specifically, the story of how fourteen-year-old Max and his little sister Sylvie manage to survive the Siege of Strasbourg exposes how social class colors one's attitude toward—and chances for survival in—war. Before the fighting starts, the wealthy, well-bred Max anticipates it gleefully, since " 'War brings glory!' " (19). In contrast, two of his more humbly born (adult) friends explain to him that " 'the peasants hate war' " (59). When the King of France and the Emperor of Germany refuse to negotiate with each other, they point out, it is " 'we poor' " who starve at home and die on the battlefield (20).

The outcome of Stretton's story underscores the truth of this claim. Witnessing the miserable procession of peasants driven from their homes by the impending fight, Max realizes that "there was not much of glory in that dismal procession" (38). One of these refugees, a girl named Louise who has lost both her parents, awakens his sympathy so much that he invites her to stay with him and his family. Still, "poor Louise" eventually dies in the rubble (86), while rich Sylvie manages to escape and survive precisely because her family is so well-connected: a friend of Max's from the exclusive school he attends arranges for his colonel's wife to smuggle her out with her own children, which she can do because she is friends with government and military officials on both sides of the conflict.

Like a number of the young narrators discussed here, Max emphasizes the inadequacy of language. In his case, literary representation proves problematic because of the traumatic nature of his experiences. In the midst of a chapter entitled "Our Night of Terror," he declares that "a boy like me could never describe" the experience of "that first terrible night of the bombardment" (77, 89). Similarly, he maintains that "I could never describe to you in any words" the look in the eyes of a starving street child (108), and calls the sight of a dying friend "more horrible . . . to me than I can tell" (118). Once again, we see an emphasis on the importance of community and adult–child collaboration: everyone trapped in the building where Max's family lives must help each other in the quest to survive. More broadly speaking, this text—which was published by the Religious Tract Society—thematizes the importance of fellowship and cooperation by repeatedly stressing that all men are brothers in the eyes of God. Stretton therefore characterizes the French and German people not as utterly alien and opposed groups, but rather as two "children quarrelling in the same mother's lap" (52).

Indeed, before the bombardment begins, Max observes that the "troops that surrounded us . . . had been our friends and neighbours for many a quiet year. Even now we did not feel any hatred towards them; everybody said they were only doing what the Emperor and his army had intended to do to them" (47). Not "with" them but "to" them: with her choice of preposition, Stretton again characterizes the common soldier as a victim of class oppression. Unapologetically instructive, Stretton's narrative occasionally veers into sentimentality, as when it focuses on an angelic child neighbor of the Krömers who spends most of her time knitting a birthday present for the baby Jesus. Yet neither its didacticism nor its schmaltz should prevent us from appreciating how brave and unsparing this story is in its denunciation of economic injustice and the horrors of war.

Though it too contains religious content, Frances E. Crompton's *The Gentle Heritage* (1893) follows more in the tradition of Ewing's "Our Field" by cheerfully chronicling the adventures of a group of siblings—Patricia, Helen, Bobby, Annis, and Paul Scrope—who indulge in "imagining games that we have taken from books" or stories that their adult caretakers have told them (71). Helen narrates, but we do not learn her name until thirty pages into the story, since creativity is once again represented as a collective endeavor; besides the fact that the narrative of *The Gentle Heritage* is something that "we" produce, other acts of collaborative composition likewise absorb the attention of the Scrope children. For example, after their nursery maid scares them with stories about a "Bogy" man who has recently moved in next door, Patricia says to her siblings, "Let us each get a piece of paper, and write our imaginings about Bogy, now we know where he really is; and then let us have a meeting and read them"—which they do, eventually weaving together an elaborate fantasy about this figure (46). (The real Bogy turns out to be a kind soul who teaches the children about the "gentle heritage" that is Christian humilty and kindness.)

Like Stretton, Crompton occasionally lapses into sentimentality, particularly in her representation of the saintly Paul. Yet the Scropes children are deeply engaged with adults and their texts in a way that precludes any simple characterization of them as untouched innocents. Besides basing their play on popular fiction, they also discuss a lengthy Bible excerpt with Bogy, and their intense relationship with him turns out to be the catalyst that transforms them into better people. In other words, the children need the help of adults to inspire and improve themselves. At the same time, Crompton bends to the influence of the child narrator genre by allowing her young speaker to model the art of resistant reading. Admitting that she cannot fully accept a tale her nurse has told her, Helen declares, "I only believe it in the way I believe that Don't-care fell into the pond, and that the child who played with fire was burnt to death, and all those things, which are also warnings to us, but yet do not seem to make us very uneasy in our minds" (9). Crompton surely did not intend readers to notice that the revelation about Bogy's past history that occurs at the end of *The Gentle Heritage* bears an uncomfortably close resemblance to such cautionary tales, or to treat her own didactic tale in this dismissive way.[17] Still, by floating this possibility, she, too, participates in the lively tradition that paves the way for Dora, Oswald, Dicky, Alice, Noël, and H. O. Bastable, Nesbit's hyperliterate child protagonists, who borrow and improvise on whatever interests them in other people's stories and cheerfully ignore the rest.

WE AND THE WORLD

Over and over again in her children's stories, Nesbit suggests that since adults have already colonized the field of fiction, children wishing to wrest away the role of author are trespassers in someone else's domain, "treasure seekers" who lift language and ideas from other people's stories. In focusing on the issue of influence in this way, Nesbit follows directly in the footsteps of Ewing. In both "Our Field" and *Mary's Meadow*, Ewing links her child narrator's foray into fiction with the act of annexing areas owned by grown-ups. Even as the siblings in "Our Field" reenact and revise adult-produced texts, they literally encroach on a piece of land that does not belong to them, invading a neighboring field and playing a variety of games there. Similarly, in *Mary's Meadow* (1883–84), the eponymous heroine chronicles how she and her four siblings appropriate ideas from beloved books in order to create a gardening game that itself involves infringing on other people's territory. Drawing inspiration from a variety of sources, including John Parkinson's *Paradisi in sole Paradisus terrestris*, a French storybook entitled *A Tour Round My Garden*, fairy tales, and a Van Dyke painting, the siblings compose first a story and then a game based around the act of taking "seeds and cuttings, and off-shoots" from one place and replanting them in another (35).

Here and elsewhere in Golden Age children's literature, gardening provides a rich metaphor for creativity and the development of selfhood. Neither wholly organic nor wholly constructed, gardens hold out the promise that cultivation and contact with civilization can enhance rather than destroy nature. They can therefore be used to symbolize a mode of being in which the authentic and the imposed coexist. In Ewing's case, her focus on transplanting ensures that creativity emerges not as an autonomous act of originality but as a process of selection and rearrangement of elements lifted from other people's property. Of course, the ability to reject certain aspects of preexisting texts matters as well. In order to collectively fashion new narratives for themselves, the children in *Mary's Meadow* must exercise their critical capacity, as Mary's brother Arthur does when he exclaims, "'I'm sick of books for young people, there's so much *stuff* in them'" (19).

The episode that follows, in which Arthur helps his younger brother Christopher rewrite an especially disappointing children's book, vividly demonstrates that child readers are not limited to passively accepting the plots proffered to them by adults; rather, they can fill up texts with other "stuff" that is more to their own taste. Chris is reduced to tears when he discovers that his enticing new book, which features a picture of a toad on the cover, is actually "about the silliest little girl you can imagine—a regular mawk of a girl—*and a Frog*. Not a toad, but a F. R. O. G. frog!" (20). But Arthur counsels action, not lamentation: "Don't cry, old chap. I'll tell you what I'll do. You get Mary to cut out a lot of the leaves of your book that have no pictures, and that will make it like a real scrap-book; and then I'll give you a lot of my scraps and pictures to paste over what's left of the stories, and you'll have such a painting-book as you never had in all your life before" (20–21). Working together, the siblings creatively transform the offending text. Scenes like this one—coupled with Ewing's decision to employ a child narrator—encourage child readers to view literature not as an inviolable domain owned by authoritative adults but rather as a "potential space" that they can take over and renovate to suit themselves.

But Ewing does not suggest that encroaching on the field of fiction is an easy task. On the contrary, shifting from consumer to producer proves extremely challenging, as indicated by the difficulties the children in *Mary's Meadow* experience when they try to make up an original tale. Describing the day when she and her siblings begin composing their gardening story, Mary notes, "That afternoon the others could not amuse themselves, and wanted me to tell them a story. They do not like old stories too often, and it is rather difficult to invent new ones" (26). Called on to produce a fresh tale, Mary finds that she is paralyzed by her recollection of Parkinson's text: "My head was so full of the Book of Paradise that afternoon that I could not think of a story" (26). Thus, the central act of creativity in this story is framed in terms of Mary's struggle to cope with the problem of influence: since Parkinson's text has taken over her imagination, she must find a way to be enabled rather than silenced by it.

Once again, the solution to coping with the indisputable power and primacy of adult authors involves collaboration: multiple child characters participate in the production of a new gardening story, culling their ideas from a variety of sources. Building on the fact that Parkinson dedicated his book to Queen Henrietta, and borrowing her phrasing from the fairy tales she loves, Mary begins,

> "Once upon a time there was a Queen—"
> "How was she dressed?" asked Adela, who thinks a good deal about dress.
> "She had on a beautiful dark-blue satin robe. . . . And a high hat, with plumes, on her head, and—"
> "A very low dwarf at her heels," added Arthur. . . .

"Had he a hump, or was he only a plain dwarf?"
"He was a very plain dwarf," said Arthur. (26)

Although Mary complains about constant interruptions, it quickly becomes clear that these interjections are crucially enabling. After Harry and Adela begin arguing a point, Mary admits that she is "glad of the diversion, for I could not think how to go on with the story" (27). "Luckily," though, Harry asks a question that suggests a whole new character and plotline: "Was there a Weeding Woman in the [Queen's garden]?" he inquires, and Mary quickly seizes on this idea and elaborates on it (27). As this query reveals, the siblings often steal material from real life as well as books; Harry has this thought because he knows a real "Weeding Woman" who works for the wealthy Squire who owns the meadow that Mary invades after the children turn their story into a game.

The fact that the children in *Mary's Meadow* and "Our Field" actively occupy land that does not belong to them has led some critics to accuse Ewing of participating in the transmission of imperialist ideology. In " 'We and the World': Juliana Horatia Ewing and Victorian Colonialism for Children" (1991), Donald E. Hall links both of these stories to *Robinson Crusoe* (1719), a book widely regarded as a "classic text of imperialism and imperial masculinity" (Richards 9). Like Defoe, Hall argues, Ewing depicts English subjects achieving absolute sovereignty over a wild landscape by invading and investing their labor in it. Hall's reading is firmly in keeping with Rose's vision of the child narrator tradition as "fully colonialist" (57); she, too, views *Robinson Crusoe* as a founding text that inspired a generation of first-person accounts of young people exploring the world around them. The plots of such stories, she claims, imply that "discovering, or seeing, the world is equivalent to controlling, or subduing, it" (58),[18] a message underscored by their format: just as the child protagonist's actions demonstrate his autonomy and mastery over the landscape he inhabits, his position as narrator attests to his self-sufficiency and uncontested control over his own life story.

There is no denying that the children in *Mary's Meadow* and "Our Field" enrich themselves by planting, tending, and harvesting land that does not belong to them. In "Our Field," for example, the siblings win a monetary prize at a flower show by displaying a collection of flora and fauna they have gathered from the eponymous field. But these are hardly narratives that portray children as autonomous masters of the universe. Rather, they are stories about collaboration, in which the weaker party (the child, who owns nothing) must learn to deal with the more powerful party (the adult, who owns everything). In "Our Field," for example, Ewing emphasizes in no uncertain terms that the meadow belongs to someone else; the children will never gain complete control over it. Thus, even as the narrator's brother Sandy boldly declares, "This is our field," the narrator admits that she knows immediately that this fantasy of ownership is nothing but a "fairy-tale" (232), a point she reiterates at the end of the story: "I know that Our Field does not exactly belong to us" (239).

Like their counterparts in *Holiday Romance*, the children in "Our Field" dream of sovereignty not because they have a chance to achieve it but because they, too, suffer from a sense of powerlessness, a fear that "the grown-up people are too strong for us" (Dickens, *Holiday* 332). Indeed, feeling crowded out by adults is what leads the children to seek out the field in the first place. Everywhere they go, "there were a lot of grown-up people, and it was very hard work getting along among them" (238). Even the field, which at first seems to offer the siblings the privacy they crave, proves vulnerable to adult intrusion. The old gentleman who sponsors the flower show insists on attending the celebratory feast they hold there after they win, literally inserting himself into their most prized secret space: although they do not wish him to join them, the narrator notes, "he would come, and he brought a lot of nuts, and he did get inside the [hollow] oak, though it is really too small for him" (239). Ewing's message is clear: there is no escaping the influence of adults, so children must learn to cope with it, to cohabitate the field and the field of fiction. Working together, the siblings create a work of art—the flower arrangement—out of materials they annex from an adult's domain, just as they build their imaginative play around preexisting texts, as when they decide to act out "Aladdin in the store-closet" (230). Ewing's choice of *Arabian Nights* as a source text is apt, as this narrative revolves around a character who tells stories in order to defuse an authority's lethal power.

Therefore, the "Our" in the title "Our Field" refers not simply to the siblings but also to the adults around them who serve as a crucial source of aggravation, inspiration, and support. In other words, a phrase that seems to insist on absolute ownership actually attests to mutuality and communality, as indicated by the resolution of the plot involving the children's dog, Perronet. Although "Our Field" appears to celebrate how the siblings single-handedly save their dog's life, rescuing Perronet in fact requires the collective action of children *and* adults. True, Sandy prevents him from drowning, and the children earn the money for "the tax and his keep" by giving up sugar and constructing their prize-winning flower arrangement (229). But it is their mother who allows them to keep him at all, despite her worries that they cannot afford it; and the old gentleman who organizes and funds the flower show; and the owner of the field who supplies the materials for their contest entry. Rather than establishing the siblings as undisputed masters of their domain, "Our Field" celebrates the productive possibilities of shared space and adult-child collaboration.[19]

In the case of *Mary's Meadow*, the imperialist reading strikes me as even more deaf to the ethical tenor of Ewing's tale, since the driving desire to own space absolutely is precisely what causes conflict in this story. The trouble begins when the selfish Old Squire takes Mary's father to court to prevent him from cutting across his meadow to reach his own fields. It is clear from the opening line of Mary's narrative that we are meant to disapprove of this parsimonious patriarch, and that a maternal ethos of unselfishness is being promoted instead: "Mother is always trying to make us love our neighbours as ourselves. She does so despise us for greediness, or grudging, or snatching, or not sharing what we have got, or taking the best and leaving the rest, or helping ourselves first, or pushing forward, or praising Number One . . . or anything selfish" (11). A central theme of this story is how difficult it is to avoid behaving in a greedy way, especially "when you want a thing very much" (11). The Squire embodies this sort of stubborn covetousness; besides refusing to share his space, he prefers to destroy the extra food his fields and trees yield rather than share it with others. And Ewing associates this determination to exert absolute dominion over natural resources not just with class privilege but with nationalist pride and militarism. Thus, as the Squire embarks on various missions to defend his territory, he exults in the ferociousness of his dog, whom he has named "Saxon."

All of these qualities link the Squire to other hypermasculine characters in Ewing's books, bullying figures who believe that their position as upper-class, Anglo-Saxon males gives them the right to rule the world. Often, these characters explicitly spout imperialist ideology, only to learn the error of their ways. In *We and the World*, for example, the "purely masculine" patriarch who bosses around his family and brags that "every Briton has a natural tendency to rule the waves" is proven wrong by the failure of his own son to succeed in a seafaring career (115, 261). Similarly, the boy narrator of *A Great Emergency* (1874), who has "always boasted" about "the noble sentiments and conspicuous bravery which have marked our family from Saxon times" (12, 13–14), eventually realizes that he has actually been behaving obnoxiously to his sister, schoolmates, and servants. Rather than endorse young Charlie's hero worship of male ancestors who participated in the imperialist project, Ewing undermines it by characterizing colonization as a form of freeloading: when Charlie and his friend Fred run away to sea for the crass purpose of discovering uninhabited islands "on which we could live without paying for our living," they are caught embarrassingly quickly and brought home in disgrace (44).

Like Craik before her and Nesbit afterward, Ewing employs a child narrator here not to ensure the child reader's absolute identification with her young protagonist, but to highlight the issue of influence: although Charlie is an engagingly frank and enterprising character, he has also absorbed a lot of bigoted notions from the culture he inhabits, and *A Great Emergency* chronicles his dawning recognition that it might be best to adopt a less patronizing attitude toward women, the working class, and other outsiders. As the story opens, for example, Ewing shows how Charlie has learned to mimic his older brother Rupert's condescending attitude toward females. In order to exclude their sister Henrietta from a series of lectures he plans to give his siblings on "How to act in an emergency," Rupert declares that " 'women are not expected to do things when there's danger,'" whereupon Charlie—hoping that "my mouth looked like Rupert's when I spoke"—quickly adds, "'*We* take care of *them*'" (4). Tomboy Henrietta disproves the truth of this maxim over and over again; most dramatically, at the end of the story she heroically helps rescue her baby brother Cecil from a house fire, proving that she can cope admirably with an emergency.

Born into a sexist culture, Charlie gradually realizes that he should resist rather than reiterate dictums like "girls oughtn't to dispute or discuss" (9). Child readers are likewise encouraged to become more skeptical readers and subjects: to challenge conventional wisdom and differentiate themselves from prescribed ways of being. Indeed, the humor of Ewing's tale often depends on child readers picking up on the limitations or blind spots of her child narrator, rather than accepting whatever he says as the gospel truth. A particularly amusing example of this occurs when Charlie, trying to defend Rupert's behavior toward Henrietta, unwittingly attests to his brother's imperiousness and his sister's competence: "I am sure [Rupert] would have been *very* kind to [Henrietta] if she would have agreed with him, and done what he wanted. He often told me that the gentlemen of our family had always been courteous to women, and I think he would have done anything for Henrietta if it had not been that she would do everything for herself" (9). Furthermore, even though Charlie develops into a less prejudiced person by the end of the story, readers are *still* not meant to identify with him absolutely. To begin with, as in the cases of Eunice and Huck, it is not clear how much wisdom and self-knowledge Charlie has really gained, since he remains committed to joining the navy, even though the story's moral is that "really great" heroes concentrate on "doing their duty at home" (100).

Then, too, Ewing allows Henrietta to narrate a large portion of the ending; she, not Charlie, gets to recount the climactic scene of the house fire. This move, which transforms the narrative of *A Great Emergency* into a collaborative effort, inhibits Ewing's audience from simply aligning themselves with Charlie. At the same time, it reminds child readers that people who have formerly functioned only as the *subjects* of stories can evolve into creative agents in their own right. By picking up the pen herself, Henrietta asserts her own selfhood, independent of her brother's efforts to represent her (sympathetically or not). This is a key subtext of many early stories featuring child narrators: we are all born into a world in which stories about who we are—or what we should be like—are already in circulation before we can speak for ourselves. But that should not prevent us from trying to wrest away control over our own life stories, to challenge rather than simply enact these limiting scripts.

Yet Charlie's reeducation into a less sexist subject raises the question of whether Ewing, in criticizing cultural indoctrination, does not simply reiterate this process. After all, she clearly has a pedagogic agenda of her own that manifests itself in most of her stories. Crucially, though, part of what she wants to teach is the value of questioning received wisdom—a lesson that, if absorbed fully, readers could apply when perusing her own work. In other words, the act of opposing passive literacy can set into motion a sort of domino effect: once an author introduces the possibility that readers can rewrite or reject textual elements that do not appeal to them, nothing is sacred. Moreover, Ewing's didacticism is not hypocritical, since she never denies that adults and their texts wield a profound influence over children. Clearly they do, and the child's identity is constructed in reference to all of these competing forces (which would include her own tales). Like many other Golden Age children's authors, Ewing refuses to portray children as untouched Others, pristine beings who are unaffected by the values, customs, and cultural artifacts of the civilized world. Instead, she embraces a collaborative model of agency, whereby the child is shaped in both positive and negative ways by these outside influences, while at the same time retaining some ability to dodge or deviate from the status quo.

Thus, just as she often acknowledges the difficulty of coming up with fresh tales when inundated by old ones, Ewing also dwells on how hard it is to resist prevailing cultural pressures. To return to *Mary's Meadow*, the ending of this story suggests that adults as well as children struggle in their efforts to renounce the driving desire to assert sovereignty over space. To make amends for wrongly accusing Mary of stealing flowers from his land when in fact she was planting them, the Squire grants Mary ownership of the field she invaded. (Hall is right about that.) Crucially, though, this is *his* solution, not the one Ewing endorses. Mary proposes a different plan: since they are now friends, the Squire should simply allow her family free access to the space. In other words, they should share it. But the Squire cannot let go of the idea of absolute ownership, thus proving that he has not really learned his lesson. As Mary notes, he remains just as stubborn and dictatorial as he was at the start of the story:

> He cannot tolerate the idea that he might be supposed to have yielded to Father the point about which they went to law, in giving Mary's Meadow to me. He is always lecturing me on encroachments, and the abuse of privileges, and warning me to be very strict about trespassers on the path through Mary's Meadow; and now that the field is mine, nothing will induce him to walk in it without asking my leave. (73)

Rather than renouncing the kind of behavior that caused all the trouble in the first place, the Squire tries to persuade Mary to follow in his footsteps and rule the territory with a rod of iron. But Mary, bemused by his fervor, decides not to listen to him. She betrays no interest at all in patrolling the space to prevent intruders. Instead, she freely shares it with all of her siblings.

Tellingly, it is not Mary but her *brothers* who get excited about the prospect of owning the field and all of its contents. On hearing the Squire's decision,

Chris excitedly asks, "'Is everything hers? Is the grass hers, and the trees hers, and the hedges hers . . . and if she could dig through to the other side of the world, would there be a field the same size in Australia that would be hers, and are the sheep hers...?'" (74). According to Hall, "the story clearly implies that the answer is 'yes'" (53). In fact, the only response Chris receives is strongly negative; Mary's father snaps, "'For mercy's sake stop that catalogue, Chris. . . . Of course the sheep are not hers; they were moved yesterday'" (72). Like the Squire, however, Chris does not learn his lesson. "Looking very peevish," he confronts Mary in the final scene, declaring, "'Mary, if a hedgehog should come and live in one of your hedges, Michael says he would be yours, he's sure. If Michael finds him, will you give him to me? . . . I feel discontented without a hedgehog'" (73). Throughout *Mary's Meadow*, "discontented" functions as a code word marking the moments when the siblings give in to selfish desire. Because this incident is no exception, Mary responds by chiding Chris. Thus, the last moments of the story reiterate the opening warning about how easy it is to become grasping and greedy. If Chris goes on as he has begun, he runs the risk of turning into another Squire.

It is no wonder that the boys prove especially vulnerable to the desire to assert absolute authority over the land and its inhabitants, given that many of the storybooks they enjoy trumpet the thrills of empire-building. Whereas Mary favors fairy tales like Thackeray's *The Rose and the Ring*, her brothers prefer reading adventure stories, including one "about the West Coast of Africa, and niggers, and tom-toms, and 'going Fantee'" (16). Hall argues that by having the siblings act out the events chronicled in this unnamed novel, Ewing indicates her endorsement of imperialist ideology. But this book is simply one of many texts the siblings use as the basis for their games; there is no evidence that its worldview is privileged above Thackeray's or Parkinson's. If anything, the fact that Ewing refuses to name it suggests that she would prefer her child readers not to seek out such fiction. Indeed, as I have tried to show, there is strong proof that she intends her own story to work against the "profoundly masculinist" ethos that permeates adventure stories (M. Green, "Robinson Crusoe Story" 36).

Further evidence of Ewing's distaste for this genre appears when we take a closer look at the two adventure stories she produced. Both *A Great Emergency* and *We and the World: A Book for Boys* (1877–78) characterize imperialism as a morally suspect form of masculine overreaching. The young narrators, Charlie and Jack, run away in search of adventure and the opportunity to perform heroic deeds, but instead of enjoying triumphant experiences abroad, they are overwhelmed and return home thoroughly chastened. "I should never have run away," Jack flatly declares (144). "I . . . made a fool of myself," Charlie admits (100), describing his abortive flight as a "vain, jealous wild-goose chase after adventures" (103). As these lines suggest, these tales are not so much adventure as anti-adventure stories. In his influential study

Dreams of Adventure, Deeds of Empire (1979), Martin Green points out that traditional male quest romances like R. M. Ballantyne's *The Coral Island* (1858) and W. H. G. Kingston's *The Three Midshipmen* (1873) portray roving as an exciting and empowering experience in order to stimulate boy readers with the desire "to go out into the world and explore, conquer, and rule" (3). In contrast, the moral of Ewing's tales—explicitly articulated by the man who brings Charlie back to his family—is " 'There's no place like Home' " (91).

Ewing's desire to discourage roving is built into the very structure of *We and the World*. Since its first appearance, readers have noticed that this novel is unlike typical adventure stories in that it gets off to an astonishingly slow start: although it begins with Jack voicing his determination to go to sea, more than half the book goes by before he manages to leave home. Critics, including Ewing's sister Horatia Gatty, have assumed that Ewing simply made a mistake, failing to realize that " 'The World' could not properly be squeezed into a space only equal in size to that which had been devoted to 'Home' " (55). But this decision is actually one of many moves Ewing makes in her campaign to validate domesticity over roving. However many times Dorothy repeats "There is no place like home" (45), readers know that this endorsement is specious, since L. Frank Baum's apportioning of the story makes it clear that Oz is far more exciting than Kansas; he spends only a few paragraphs at the beginning and end of his tale in the sterile Dustbowl, while elaborating on Oz in luscious and lengthy detail. Ewing, on the other hand, puts the weight of her narrative behind her assertion that home life beats adventuring abroad, portraying the private realm as a far more loving and hospitable environment than a world that does not welcome the intrusion of Jack and his colleagues. In doing so, she situated herself in opposition to the growing numbers of fiction and nonfiction writers who, as John Tosh observes, represented imperial careers as offering a glorious "escape . . . from the routines of domesticity" (175).

Indeed, Ewing suggests in *We and the World* that such books cannot be trusted. Thus, Jack's desire to rove is whetted by reading adventure stories "full of dangers and discoveries, the mightiness of manhood, and the wonders of the world" (134). But the moment he sets out on his journey, this fantasy of power and pleasure is shattered. On his arrival in London, he finds the chaotic scene that confronts him at the docks "utterly bewildering" (149). Duped, robbed, and stymied in his efforts to join a ship's crew, he is reduced to tearfully imploring an old Irishwoman to tell him how to stow away. She does, but expresses disapproval of whole idea, warning him "Many's the one that leaves [England] in the highest of expictations [*sic*], and is glad enough to get back to it in a tattered shirt and a whole skin, and with an increase of contintment [*sic*] under the ways of home" (154). Of course, Jack ignores her good advice and stows away, whereupon his condition becomes even more abject. He suffers from an intense and unromantic case of seasickness, and the other members of the crew tease him unmercifully, playing practical jokes on him and referring to him sarcastically as an "accomplished young gentleman of fortune" and a "pea-green beauty" (175, 177). Far from accomplishing mighty feats of manliness, Jack cannot even master the trick of walking steadily on the heaving deck or of getting into his hammock at night.

By focusing on Jack's vulnerability and disillusionment with shipboard life, *We and the World* provides further evidence against the claim that "autobiographical" children's stories from this period are colonialist in terms of both content and form. According to this argument, even as the boy narrator's masterful actions establish his status as a self-determining agent who easily dominates the world around him, his (seemingly) uncontested control over his own story tricks child readers into forgetting that the story was actually written by an adult hoping to indoctrinate them into embracing nationalist and imperialist ideals. *We and the World* utterly fails to conform to this paradigm. To begin with, Jack is far more affected by the outside world than it is by him. Whereas he leaves no discernible mark on any of the foreign lands he visits, the "hard buffetings" he endures abroad awake in him a new appreciation of the tenderness and quiet courage of friends and family members at home (143), and even prompt him to let go of some of his (well-justified) resentment toward his domineering father.

Moreover, Ewing's novel sets out to expose how sea stories constructed by Empire enthusiasts like Ballantyne and Kingston aim to seduce boys into committing themselves to the project of imperialist expansion. To this end, she precisely reproduces the setup of one of Kingston's most popular adventure yarns in order to counter its message that the navy offers boys the most exciting and fulfilling existence imaginable. Like *The Three Midshipmen*, *We and the World* chronicles the adventures of an English boy named Jack, who goes to sea at a young age and forms a close friendship with two other young mates, one of whom is Irish and the other Scotch. (Kingston's Jack, Alick, and Terrence become Jack, Alister, and Dennis in Ewing's version.)

From the moment they arrive at the dock, Kingston's triumvirate enjoy themselves hugely: playing pranks and practical jokes, embarking on excursions to exotic locales, chasing pirates, and triumphantly defeating various other enemies of Empire. Their heroic feats instantly earn them the respect of their superior officers, who entrust them with all kinds of important tasks, such as saving a mate from drowning or helping to cut off a train loaded with gunpowder. Referring to this last assignment, Alick proudly reports that his commanding officer has specially requested his presence: "'He said he wanted a midshipman who would be calm and collected whatever might occur, and yet one on whose courage and resolution he could perfectly rely, and he has selected me. It is that he has spoken of me in such flattering terms that has given me so much pleasure'" (91). Indeed, flattery is the dominant mode of adult–child interaction in Kingstonian romances; even as grown-up characters praise young ones, the adult author ingratiates himself with child readers by painting a highly complimentary picture of boys as spectacularly powerful and autonomous figures.

Yet even this obviously pro-imperialist novel does not fit perfectly into Rose's paradigm, since none of the boys in *The Three Midshipmen* enjoy the privilege of narrating the novel. In revising Kingston's story, Ewing allows her boy protagonist to tell his own tale, and the decision to employ the first person coincides not with an insistence on pumping up the prowess of the boy adventurer but with a determination to deflate such puffery—to show how the fantasy of male potency that writers like Kingston peddle is a snare and a delusion. Thus, when *Ewing's* trio arrive onboard ship, they are given the most menial jobs imaginable: sewing sails, polishing brass, cleaning pots and pans for the cook, and other "miscellaneous and very dirty work . . . down below" (181). Most of the time, Jack admits, nothing happens onboard ship but hard, uninteresting labor. When exciting events do occur, the boys are not important enough to be selected as participants. Indeed, they are generally ignored by their superior officers, though they are occasionally "harangued . . . in very unflattering phrases" for their incompetence, or made the object of practical jokes (172).[20] Awful weather and irresponsible and cruel commanders exacerbate the unpleasantness of life at sea, leading Jack to conclude that "a ship . . . is not to be beaten (if approached) for the deadliness of the despondency to be experienced therein" (170).

But Ewing does not simply portray imperialist adventuring as dull and difficult work; she also implies that the whole endeavor is an ethically bankrupt form of bullying whereby the strong dominate and exploit the weak. The most explicit articulation of this concern occurs when Jack describes his experience at a boarding school, that traditional breeding ground of future imperialists. Kingston, in keeping with his habit of portraying masculine institutions and authority figures in glowing terms, has his boys attend a "capital" academy run by a "first-rate schoolmaster" (5). In contrast, Ewing portrays Jack's school as a factory that churns out tyrants. Because parents like Jack's father believe that tough methods are necessary to produce manly men who will keep Great Britain great, headmaster Mr. Crayshaw operates just as he pleases, with "no check whatever upon his cruelty" (102). Later, Jack links the headmaster's viciousness to the behavior of others he meets onboard ship, including a "wicked brute" of a first mate who tortures a mixed-race cabin boy (252).

Reflecting back on his experiences at Crayshaw's prompts Jack to voice a diatribe on the evils of "irresponsible power," which he calls an "opportunity in all hands and a direct temptation in some to cruelty. . . . It affords horrible development to those morbid cases in which cruelty becomes a passion" (100–101). In an impassioned monologue—suggestive of Joseph Conrad's later meditation on the darkness hidden in men's hearts—Jack declares that "human nature cannot, even in the very service of charity, be safely trusted with the secret exercise of irresponsible power, and . . . no light can be too fierce to beat upon and purify every spot where the weak are committed to the tender mercies of the consciences of the strong" (102). Kingston, too, introduces a bully into his tale, but only in order to stress that such unpleasant characters are exceptional, unpopular figures who tend to fail quickly "when they get into the world, and have their measures properly taken" (69). In contrast, Ewing sees such swaggering types everywhere, the natural result of a system whose goal is world domination.

Thus, whereas Kingston's bully is a mere boy, the blustering, cruel characters in *We and the World* are key male authority figures: Jack's father, his schoolmaster, and a number of his commanding officers, including a drunken captain and a second mate who is driven by "a burning desire to trip up his fellow-creatures at their weak points and jump upon them accordingly" (180–81). Hoping to counteract the disdainful indifference toward women, domesticity, and "feminine" virtues like empathy and tenderness that is so apparent in adventure stories by Kingston and others, Ewing routinely rates "womanly" men who exhibit a "delicate tenderness" over hypermasculine ones and refuses to represent shipboard life as an appealing environment (115, 59). Unlike Kingston's trio, who are promoted and go on to enjoy many further adventures abroad in *The Three Lieutenants* (1875), Ewing's boys choose not to pursue military careers; as the novel ends, they joyfully return home.

As their shared focus on a threesome of boys indicates, both of these novels thematize collaboration—but in radically different ways. In general, when pro-imperialist adventure stories feature teamwork, it involves fully formed young men banding together with each other or adults to subdue foreign people and territories. In keeping with this tradition, *The Three Midshipmen* offers readers almost no information about the boys' early childhood and home life. They may work with others to accomplish their goals, but nothing in the text suggests that their identity is shaped in reference or response to other people or the outside world. By contrast, Ewing's Jack engages in extensive reminiscence and self-analysis; in passage after passage, he contemplates how his personal development and life choices have been affected by his relationship with his parents, friends, and mentors, as well as his experiences abroad. Once again, shifting into the first person corresponds with an authorial willingness to delve into the issue of subject formation, and to entertain the idea that identity itself is collaborative. The title *We and the World* reflects Jack's embeddedness and engagement with outside influences; rather than leaping into action as a fully formed agent, he is still caught up in the process of deciding what to absorb and what to reject as he interacts with various people, places, and things.

In reference to this question, *We and the World*—like so many of these early "autobiographies"—warns child readers not to believe everything they read. For

Ewing is not content to allow her critique of pro-imperialist adventure stories to remain implicit. She attacks such yarns directly, by having Jack describe these books as "dirty," "greasy," and extremely unreliable (134). "Reading sea-novels had not really taught me much" our hero admits after arriving onboard (197), and even his father acknowledges that such stories twist the truth in dangerous ways. Praising *Robinson Crusoe* as novel beloved by all boys, Jack's father nevertheless describes Defoe's tale as "a book which my [brother] remembered had nearly cost him his life on a badly-made raft on the mill-dam, when he was a lad" (262). This moment confirms that Ewing aims to subvert the Crusoe tradition, since a key aspect of this genre—as Rose notes—is an insistence on the absolute reliability of what is being related. Robinsonades portray themselves (and other imperialist texts) as completely trustworthy instruction manuals for aspiring colonists: " 'I once read that the green nuts contain [drinkable liquid],' " exclaims a young explorer in *The Coral Island*, "and you see it is true!' " (Ballantyne 42). Ewing chips away at the idea that such stories provide undistorted records of reality, suggesting instead that they are romantic fantasies. Boys who listen to their siren call will garner not glory but misery, humiliation, even death.[21]

Like many of the other stories discussed in this chapter, *We and the World* encourages children to become more canny critical readers of the stories handed to them by adults. These tales also send a cautionary message to children's literature critics, reminding us that we cannot assume that all stories featuring child narrators aim to seduce their audience into a state of unreflective identification, or that all stories featuring boy adventurers and exotic islands are necessarily pro-Empire.[22] Indeed, I argue in the next chapter that Robert Louis Stevenson's *Treasure Island*, a text that we assume *must* be sending an imperialist message, is as much an anti–adventure story as *We and the World*. Like Ewing, Stevenson warns young audience members to beware of silver-tongued storytellers who set out to seduce and deceive them. He, too, hopes to encourage child readers to resist manipulation, to dodge rather than succumb to the powerful force of adult influence.

2

COLLABORATING WITH THE ENEMY

Treasure Island as Anti–Adventure Story

Nineteenth-century adventure stories often invite their audience to admire and emulate the figure George Santayana has dubbed "the schoolboy master of the world" (quoted in Richards 74). The Victorians themselves recognized that *Robinson Crusoe* (1719) inspired a cascade of texts that set authoritative boys loose on unsuspecting islands. In his 1888 survey *Juvenile Literature as It Is*, Edward Salmon opens his chapter on boys' books by mentioning Defoe's tale, and attempts to unpack the secret of its appeal in his conclusion. "The chief charm of a supreme figure, like that of Robinson Crusoe," he opines, "is that it constitutes an ideal. Unless the hero dominates every situation, the story loses for boys its directness. . . . The whole body of successful boys' literature cannot be more concisely described than as a vast system of hero-worship" (217). Anticipating Rose, Salmon suggests that the appealing autonomy of the plucky boy adventurer is often enhanced by the fact that he is allowed to tell his own tale. Master of his fate, unchallenged narrator of his own life story: the spectacular potency of characters like R. M. Ballantyne's Ralph Rover and W. H. G. Kingston's Mark Seaworth encourages boy readers to believe that a juvenile crewmate—however young and inexperienced he may be—can function as an invaluable collaborator in the important work of taming the unruly world outside England.

It has long been taken for granted that *Treasure Island* stands as an exemplar of this sort of story. For those who admire the genre, *Treasure Island* is not just a typical boys' book but "the best of boys' books" (Meredith 730), not just an adventure yarn but "one of the most satisfying adventure stories ever told" (Kiely 68). Those who object to the imperialistic tendencies of the Robinsonade likewise consider *Treasure Island* a classic specimen. Joseph Bristow asserts that

Stevenson's story brings this "tried-and-tested genre" to perfection by presenting its young hero as a masterful figure who performs the lion's share both of the narration and of the daring deeds that ensure the success of the gentlemen's quest (95).[1] This argument is enabled by the fact that the prefatory poem Stevenson affixes to *Treasure Island*—addressed "To the Hesitating Purchaser"—promises that the tale that follows will offer "all the old romance, retold / Exactly in the ancient way" of "Kingston, or Ballantyne the brave, / Or Cooper of the wood and wave" (xxx). And indeed, as numerous critics have demonstrated, Stevenson borrows many incidents from the work of these unabashedly imperialist authors, including the triumphant scene in which Jim Hawkins manages to pilot the ship back into the island harbor almost single-handedly.[2] This episode, which is lifted directly out of *The Coral Island*, seems to exemplify the urge to characterize the boy hero as a supremely commanding figure.

But although *Treasure Island*'s status as an energizing myth of empire has become a critical commonplace, the novel can more plausibly be read as an anti–adventure story. Rather than encouraging youngsters to seek out wealth and glory overseas, Stevenson depicts the project of draining foreign lands of riches as terrifying, traumatizing, and ethically problematic, a move that is fully in keeping with the "anti-imperialist sentiment" that critics have begun to discern in his later work (Rothstein 12). As I will demonstrate, the classic elements of the Robinsonade remain in place, but only to be parodied, deflated, or subversively transformed. Moreover, Stevenson's critique extends past content to form; he exposes flattery as the key narrative technique adult storytellers employ to seduce boys into going along with imperialist schemes. Whereas typical desert island romances curry favor with child readers by portraying their young protagonists as the monarchs of all they survey, Stevenson gives the lie to such fantasies of potency. Moments in which Jim triumphs in the traditional way are inevitably followed by ones that undermine the idea that he functions as an autonomous agent and empowered colleague. Over and over again, the reader is forced to recognize Jim's essential passivity and vulnerability, and thus to distrust the moments when the narrative shifts back into its sycophantic, adulatory mode.

The opening poem, then, represents the first of many moments when the reader is suckered into believing that he is reading a classic adventure story, only to realize afterward that he—like Jim—has been seduced and betrayed by a silver-tongued stranger who is out to make a profit. Hoping to ensnare the "Hesitating Purchaser," Stevenson delicately flatters his potential readers by wondering in the first stanza whether the traditional trappings of the quest romance "Can please, as me they pleased of old / The wiser youngsters of to-day" (xxx). Glib, greedy adults who compliment children cannot be trusted, a lesson Jim learns in his encounters with the "obsequious" Long John (186). Tellingly, Silver and other sly adults take Jim in by addressing him as an equal, promising to tell him the truth, and portraying him as a hero, the very strategies authors of boys' adventure stories routinely employed in their effort to appeal to child readers. *Treasure Island* thus warns children to beware of the treachery of adult storytellers, especially those who court children by pretending to treat them as powerful allies. Jim's most upsetting experiences attest to the pain of realizing that you are not a collaborator but a pawn in someone else's game: rather than functioning as a self-determining agent, you have been co-opted into complying with the plans of a "partner" who turns out to be stronger, smarter, and far more cunning than you are.

Treasure Island thus grapples with the very problem that proponents of the colonization paradigm claim children's fiction ignores: the power imbalance that complicates the adult author–child reader relationship. As the Victorians themselves recognized, the act of addressing children often entails a desire to influence, mold, or manipulate them, and the difference in age and status that divides writer from addressee(s)—a unique feature of the genre—raises the possibility that narrative might exert a coercive force. Knowing that Empire enthusiasts were making a play for the hearts and minds of young readers, Stevenson presents the cautionary tale of a boy whose cooperation is conscripted by a parade of grasping grown-ups who "speak like . . . book[s]" (54). Like Craik and company, he does not employ a youthful narrator in order to deny the presence and power of adults and secure the child reader's unreflective identification with his hero. On the contrary, he presents his audience with the negative example of a boy who fails to evade the pressure of adult influence: his child protagonist ultimately functions as a helpless parrot, whose pained passivity incites child *readers* to act as artful dodgers—to see through the seductive propaganda of books that urge them to take part in the project of imperialist expansion.

DEROMANTICIZING THE DESERT ISLAND ROMANCE

A key feature of the desert island romance is that it glamorizes the act of exploration. Ralph Rover, the aptly (nick)named hero of *The Coral Island*, opens his story by declaring:

> Roving has always been, and still is, my ruling passion, the joy of my heart, the very sunshine of my existence. In childhood, in boyhood, and in man's estate, I have been a rover; not a mere rambler among the woody glens and upon the hill-tops of my own native land, but an enthusiastic rover throughout the length and breadth of the wide, wide world. (9)

"Enthusiastic" is an understatement. Before setting out on his journey, Ralph relates, "my heart glowed ardently within me as [the seamen I knew] recounted their wild adventures in foreign lands"—exciting yarns that inspire him to go to sea as well (12). After boarding the vessel that is to carry him to the South Seas, Ralph exclaims, "Oh, how my heart bounded with delight!" (15). Even being shipwrecked cannot quench his cheerfulness; as he looks around the eponymous island, he observes, "my heart expanded more and more with an exulting gladness, the like of which I had never felt before" (47–48). It is no wonder that Ralph compares his life abroad to "a delightful dream" (15). During his sojourn on the island, he and his two young mates mount successful expeditions, make discoveries, solve problems, and rescue themselves from sharks, savages, and pirates. Eventually they commandeer a ship and sail home, none the worse for their hair-raising experiences. Indeed, Ralph concludes that he has spent "the happiest months [of] my life on that Coral Island" (272).

Ralph's exciting chronicle seems calculated to produce the same effect on boy readers that the sailors' stories had on him: to inspire them to venture out into the world that has afforded him such intense and various pleasures. In contrast, *Treasure Island* recasts roving as the stuff of nightmare. Rather than dwelling happily on the hero's bounding, glowing heart, the early chapters attest to Jim's rapidly escalating anxiety as a parade of fierce, mutilated seamen intrudes on his father's inn: "I was very uneasy and alarmed" (9); "I was in mortal fear" (15); "I was so utterly terrified" (17); "I jumped in my skin for terror" (19). Indeed, as Harold Frances Watson notes, *Treasure Island* "opens with one nightmare and closes with another" (129), and both these moments attest to the horror of being conscripted as a pawn in someone else's game. Whereas the typical hero of the desert island romance feels an inner compulsion to go to sea—often against the wishes of his family—Jim expresses no such desire. Instead, he is co-opted into participating in an adult's affair when the scarred old sailor Billy Bones takes him aside and instructs him to look out for "a seafaring man with one leg" (3).

Far from expressing any excitement or pleasure about being included in Bones's business, Jim is "so terrified" of the thought of the one-legged man that he begins having terrible nightmares, which he famously describes at some length (3).[3] Like his jolly counterparts in *The Coral Island*, Bones recounts his various adventures at sea, but these "dreadful stories" do not inflame Jim with a longing to follow in the sailor's footsteps (4). Thus, when the treasure map surfaces, it is Dr. Livesey and Squire Trelawney who are "filled . . . with delight" at the prospect of setting out in search of the prize (34). Standing by silently as the adults enthuse, Jim once again finds himself drafted into someone else's scheme: " 'Hawkins shall come as cabin-boy,' " the squire decrees, and the doctor accepts for Jim, declaring, " 'I'll go with you; and . . . so will Jim' " (34).

Moreover, it soon becomes clear that Jim was right to be cautious, because his adventures abroad prove just as upsetting as the "abominable fancies" that disturb his sleep (3). Whereas Ralph's happy experiences on the Coral Island encourage him to continue roving for the rest of his life, Jim is so traumatized by his excursion that he decides never to roam again. In the final lines of the novel, he admits that although the island still holds hidden treasure, "oxen and wain-ropes would not bring me back again to that accursed island; and the worst dreams that ever I have are when I hear the surf booming about its coasts, or start upright in bed, with the sharp voice of Captain Flint still ringing in my ears: 'Pieces of eight! pieces of eight!'" (191). This is hardly a conclusion that encourages young people to journey out into the world to make their fortunes. Of the twenty-six men who set out on the quest, Jim reminds us, only five have returned alive—hardly encouraging odds. One might expect that this drastic reduction would make each surviving crewmate fabulously rich. But Stevenson resolutely undercuts the squire's exultant prediction that the quest will bring the men "money to eat—to roll in—to play duck and drake with ever after" (34). Ben Gunn, the man who discovers the cache, manages to fritter his share away "in three weeks, or, to be more exact, in nineteen days, for he was back begging on the twentieth" (191). As for the rest, the cursory account Jim gives of how his shipmates dispose of their money does not suggest that their lives have been radically transformed. Abraham Gray, for example, manages to become part-owner of a ship—but only after he "saved his money [and] studied his profession" (191).

In other words, rather than romanticizing the quest for money, Stevenson suggests that it is simply not worthwhile to engage in such dangerous, greed-driven forays. His portrayal of the treasure itself drives home this point. To begin with, he organizes his narrative in such as way as to *deprive* readers of the pleasure of discovery. The frenzied scene in which Jim and the pirates follow the map to the treasure site ends in "horrid disappointment" (184); the gold is gone, having been discovered months earlier by Ben Gunn. It is hard to imagine a more anticlimactic end to a novel built around a treasure hunt. Moreover, when Jim finally gets to see the cache that has been squirreled away by Gunn, the description he gives of it attests not to the romance of money but to the terrible human cost involved in its accumulation:

> I beheld great heaps of coin and quadrilaterals built of bars of gold. That was Flint's treasure that we had come so far to seek, and that had cost already the lives of seventeen men from the *Hispaniola*. How many it had cost in the amassing, what blood and sorrow, what good ships scuttled on the deep, what brave men walking the plank blindfold, what shot of cannon, what shame and lies and cruelty, perhaps no man alive could tell. (185)[4]

Just as the silver fourpenny Billy Bones pays Jim to look out for the one-legged man does not make up for the nightmares this task triggers, the treasure in no way mitigates the widespread misery it engenders. Indeed, the trauma Jim has undergone seems to have rendered him incapable of enjoying his prize; as a number of critics have noted, he says nothing whatever about how he spends his share. Rather than representing the act of roaming the world as the surest path to pleasure and profit, Stevenson strongly implies that roving damages and depletes young men. Venturing abroad has put Jim into the same category as the scarred souls who arrive at the inn at the start of the story: maimed men, haunted by their violent pasts.

I have begun by discussing the beginning and end of *Treasure Island*, but these are not the only sections of the novel that broadcast Stevenson's determination to depart from the traditional Robinsonade formula. After the doctor and squire begin to make arrangements for the journey, it is true, Stevenson allows his hero a period of "charming anticipation" during which he fantasizes about the classic pleasures of imperial adventuring: "I approached that island in my fancy, from every possible direction; I explored every acre of its surface; I climbed a thousand times to that tall hill they call the Spy-glass, and from the top enjoyed the most wonderful and changing prospects. Sometimes the isle thick with savages, with whom we fought; sometimes full of dangerous animals that hunted us" (36). Immediately afterward, however, Jim admits that his "actual adventures" bore no resemblance to these pleasant fancies; they were not exhilarating but "tragic" and terrifying (36).[5] The long-anticipated act of approaching the island proves sickening rather than exciting. Having just overheard Silver's murderous plan to take over the ship, Jim admits "my heart sank . . . into my boots; and from that first look onward, I hated the very thought of Treasure Island" (69).

Moreover, as the novel unfolds, every single aspect of Jim's fantasy fails to come true, thus invalidating the common critical claim that *Treasure Island* "fulfill[s] the 'sea-dreams' of its boy hero, Jim Hawkins" (K. Blake, "Sea-Dream" 165).[6] To begin with, Jim never gets a chance to perform an exhaustive inspection of the island, and therefore misses out on the sense of mastery this act inevitably engenders. After making his "Survey of the Island," for example, Robinson Crusoe confidently declares, "I was King and Lord of all this Country indefeasibly, and had a Right of Possession" (Defoe 78, 80). When Jim first lands on the island, he seems poised to follow in his predecessor's footsteps; having eluded the pirates, he begins to look around, noting, "I now felt for the first time the joy of exploration" (73). But moments later his progress is arrested when he stumbles on Silver murdering another crew member. Horrified by this sight, Jim falls into a swoon, the first of several fainting fits in which he loses "possession of myself" (143). Such moments indicate that Jim does not function as a "supreme figure" who asserts dominion over the territory he surveys (Salmon, *Juvenile* 217). Rather, the landscape he dreams of conquering overpowers him: "the whole world swam away from me in a whirling mist; Silver and the birds, and the tall Spy-glass hill-top, going round and round and topsy-turvy before my eyes" (76).

To reinforce this point, Stevenson denies Jim the moment of mountaintop mastery he dreams about, no doubt as a result of having read stories like *The Coral Island.* The rapturous chapters in which Ralph chronicles the boys' exploration of "our island" culminate with a long description of clambering up hills that afford them one "new, and . . . grander prospect" after another (55, 62). When they finally reach the highest point of the island, Ralph's account of this moment indicates his firm belief that the mere act of traversing this terrain grants the boys jurisdiction over it: "we saw our kingdom lying, as it were, like a map around us" (65). In contrast, when Jim finally gets to mount Spy-glass Hill, it is not as a masterful adventurer but as a pathetic prisoner. Having been caught by the pirates, he is dragged along as they race to find the treasure, tethered to Long John Silver: "I had a line about my waist, and followed obediently after the sea-cook. . . . For all the world, I was led like a dancing bear" (171). Stumbling along in a "wretched" state of alarm (179), Jim never gets to enjoy a moment of monarchic mastery; he remains a helpless hostage until he is rescued by the gentleman.

Moreover, Stevenson's characterization of the terrain of Treasure Island decisively departs from the deserted isle prototype. As Diana Loxley notes, one major way Victorian writers glamorize imperial roving is by describing islands as "idyllic space" characterized by "fertility and abundance" (3, 2). From *Robinson Crusoe* onward, such stories contain purple passages in which the adventurer breathlessly compares the island to a paradise, as when one excited member of *The Welsh Family Crusoes* (1857) exclaims, "'How exquisite! How lovely! What rocks! What trees! Look, a gushing stream, a lovely water-fall! I see birds, bright birds, and beauteous flowers, I am sure! What colors! What a lovely bay! What blue water! What golden sands! Was ever such a scene beheld by mortal eyes!'" (quoted in H. Watson 85). All that is missing from this example is the characteristic use of the word "luxuriant" to describe the varied vegetation and the traditional long list of natural resources that provide food and shelter to the resourceful visitors. Such descriptions form a crucial part of the "rising curve of achievement and accumulation" that Martin Green identifies as a key aspect of the Robinsonade ("Robinson Crusoe Story" 36).

It is impossible to overemphasize Stevenson's determination to undermine this vision of the island as an inviting, enriching environment. Instead of celebrating profusion, Jim's first description of Treasure Island stresses its stark sterility: "Grey-coloured woods covered a large part of the surface. . . . The general colouring was uniform and sad. The hills ran up clear about the vegetation in spires of naked rock. . . . There was not a breath of air moving. . . . A peculiar stagnant smell hung over the anchorage—a smell of sodden leaves and rotting tree trunks" (68, 70).[7] Rather than portray the island as an Edenic haven, Stevenson represents it as a lethal swamp that threatens to engulf Jim in its "poisonous" embrace (69). As Dr. Livesey instantly recognizes, this type of environment is more likely to deplete than to enrich visitors: "'I don't know about treasure,' he said, 'but I'll stake my wig there's fever here'" (70). Indeed, a few chapters later the doctor notes that "the nasty stench of the place turned me sick," and the pirates soon begin to succumb to malaria (84). Here again, Stevenson intimates that pursuing treasure is a dangerous sport that may well lead to death rather than pleasure and profit. To underline this point, he twins Treasure Island with another body of land called Skeleton Island.[8]

Just as the landscape of Treasure Island fails to conform to the imperialist's playground paradigm, its inhabitants also prove disappointing. Indeed, Stevenson not only refuses to provide the requisite predatory beasts and savages, he comically deflates his hero's expectations. When Jim beholds "huge slimy monsters" crawling on the craggy shore of the island and "making the rocks . . . echo with their barkings" (126), it seems that his fantasy about being hunted by dangerous animals may be about to come true. Instead, it is doubly undermined. Far from relishing this encounter with the animal kingdom, Jim decides to avoid it, declaring himself "willing rather to starve at sea than to confront such perils" (126). This is especially funny because, as Jim sheepishly admits, these creatures in fact pose no threat at all: "I have understood since that they were sea lions, and entirely harmless" (126). Instead of wrestling with lions, Jim is petrified by sea lions. His evasive action stands in stark contrast to Crusoe's bold attacks on various ravenous beasts, including leopards and "a terrible great Lyon" he hunts for fun (Defoe 24). Thus, when *Crusoe* encounters a group of barking sea creatures, he naturally views himself as the aggressor, recounting how the seals "got into the Sea and escap'd me for that time" (58).

Jim's long-anticipated encounter with savage folk does not fit the Robinsonade mold either. Fleeing from Silver in a "frenzy" of fear (77), Jim suddenly spies a "dark and shaggy" creature "unlike any man that I had ever seen" trailing him though the woods (78). Like any reader familiar with the conventions of the desert island romance, Jim knows what to expect: "I began to recall what I had heard of cannibals" (78). Once again, though, Stevenson subverts our expectations. His hero does not grapple with a fierce, benighted Other but instead finds himself face to face with "a white man like myself": Ben Gunn, who is hungry not for human flesh but for a nice piece of cheese (79). The comic aspect of this revelation is enhanced by the fact that Gunn prefaces it with a bit of Robinsonian rhetoric: "'Wherever a man is, says I, a man can do for himself. But, mate, my heart is sore for Christian diet. . . . Many's the long night I've dreamed of cheese—toasted, mostly'" (79). Here Stevenson parodies what Rousseau celebrates as the moral of Defoe's story: the reassuring idea that "each man suffices unto himself" (*Emile* 185). Like Crusoe, Gunn has access to wild goats—yet he never produces his own cheese. Perhaps, Stevenson hints, it is silly to assume that a man marooned on an island could reproduce all the products of the civilized world. How likely is it, after all, that although Crusoe "had never milk'd a Cow, much less a Goat, or seen Butter or Cheese made," he nevertheless manages to produce both in unlimited quantities (Defoe 116)?

Besides dispensing with the fantasy of masculine self-sufficiency, Stevenson also refuses to champion the civilizing power of Christianity, another central theme of the desert island romance. Whereas writers such as Ballantyne enthusiastically extol the missionary efforts of British rovers, whose noble presence brings "inestimable blessings to these islands of dark and bloody idolatry," Stevenson declines to include any pro-Empire propaganda in his story (384). Critics have dealt with this notable absence in two ways. The first wave of respondents, which included John Rowe Townsend and Maurice Rooke Kingsford, celebrated the novel for its lack of didacticism, claiming that it "represents almost a complete break from the traditions of the past" because it "was not designed to teach anything at all, but . . . to provide untrammeled hours of spontaneous refreshment and delight" (Kingsford 205). More recently, commentators like Rose and Loxley have rejected the idea that *Treasure Island* offers "pure" fun. By dropping "the most obvious trappings of the colonialist ethos," they argue, Stevenson produces a novel that can indoctrinate readers far more effectively than its preachy predecessors (Rose 79).

The problem with this reading is that evangelical and imperialist rhetoric is not just absent from Stevenson's story; it is parodied and subversively undercut. For example, as William Hardesty and David Mann point out, Stevenson sends up his precursors' penchant for miraculous conversion scenes, since Jim's encounter with the wounded pirate Israel Hands is a comic reworking of Ralph Rover's interaction with a dying buccaneer named Bloody Bill (189). Whereas Ralph easily convinces the wily old sea dog to repent and save his soul, Jim's pompous moralizing has no effect whatsoever on Hands; when Jim intones "'You can kill the body, Mr. Hands, but not the spirit,'" Hands cheerfully replies, "'Well, that's unfort'nate—appears as if killing parties was a waste of time. Howsomever, sperrits don't reckon for much, by what I've seen. I'll chance it with the sperrits, Jim'" (136). Here Stevenson prompts readers to recognize the absurdity inherent in the idea that a boy could convert a lifelong criminal to Christianity with a few well-chosen words.

Working in a more serious vein, Stevenson takes up the damning adjectives Ballantyne and company use to denigrate "savages" and applies them to his white characters. On their journey home, the gentlemen stop at a port where they encounter "negroes, and Mexican Indians, and half-bloods" (190). Far from requiring enlightenment at the hands of the whites, these hospitable people are associated with civilization and illumination; Jim observes that their kind faces, delicious food, and "above all, the lights that began to shine in the town, made a most charming contrast to our dark and bloody sojourn on the island" (190). Rather than bringing blessings to "islands of dark and bloody idolatry" (Ballantyne 384), Stevenson's rovers are themselves the source of violence and brutality. This authorial choice links *Treasure Island* to Stevenson's later work, which often "subverts European assumptions of superiority" by refusing to align whiteness with wisdom, culture, and progress (Jolly xiv). "Will you please to observe," Stevenson urged his friend and literary advisor Sidney Colvin, "that almost all that is ugly is in the whites?" (*Letters* 7:282). He was referring here to the action that takes place in his South Seas story "The Beach of Falesá" (1892); he could just as easily have been talking about *Treasure Island*.

By refusing to promote a strong sense of religious and racial superiority in his adventure story, Stevenson drains imperialist roving of its primary claim to moral legitimacy. His skepticism about the true motivations of Englishmen who spout religious rhetoric is evident in his portrayal of Ben Gunn. Critics have noticed that the maroon functions as a Crusoe figure but have failed to pick up that in shaping his character, Stevenson exaggerates the least attractive qualities of Defoe's iconic empire-builder. Thus, although Gunn echoes Crusoe when he asserts that "it were Providence that put me here" (80), the terms in which he does so underscore his predecessor's religious fickleness, a quality most Victorian readers preferred to ignore.[9] " 'I've thought it all out in this here lonely island,' " Ben announces, " 'and I'm back on piety' " (80). His phrasing suggests that piousness is a superficial adornment one can slip on and off as easily as a goatskin garment. Similarly, when Ben insists that he was a very religious child, the proof he gives reveals that he does not know the meaning of deep devotion: " '[I] could rattle off my catechism that fast, as you couldn't tell one word from another' " (80). Moreover, Gunn's name and murderous behavior remind us of Crusoe's fascination with firearms, while his actions on the island attest to a tremendous lust for money, a motivation that Crusoe explicitly disowns, even as he ends up earning a fortune by exploiting the resources of various foreign lands.

Viewed in light of these unpleasant character traits, the narrative logic behind Gunn's entrance comes into sharper focus. By having the bestial "creature" Jim mistakes for a savage turn out to be British (78), Stevenson once again suggests that *whites* occupy the position of moral depravity when action takes place on islands. Indeed, rather than encouraging Anglo-Saxon chauvinism, Stevenson repeatedly undermines the idea that Englishness and godliness are synonymous. As Naomi J. Wood has persuasively demonstrated, "the pirates and the official representatives of English society are difficult to distinguish": both the "gentlemen born" and the "gentlemen of fortune" are greedy men who commit acts of awful violence solely in order to enrich themselves (69). Such blurring undercuts the nationalistic pride that pervades imperialist adventure stories by suggesting that British rovers are nothing more than common pirates.

Thus, as Wood notes, various characters in the novel identify bloodthirsty buccaneers as exemplary British citizens, as when the squire admits that he often felt "proud [that Flint] was an Englishman" when he considered how thoroughly the pirate had terrified the Spanish (32). Such admiration links the squire to Silver, who names his parrot after Flint. Even more striking is the moment when Long John recounts why his bird has "seen more wickedness" than the devil: "She's sailed with England," he explains (54). To be sure, Silver immediately clarifies his meaning; the parrot traveled with "the great Cap'n England, the pirate" (54). And Stevenson did not create a dastardly buccaneer called England out of whole cloth. As Emma Letley points out, the exploits of Edward England were chronicled in Defoe's book *A General History of the Robberies and Murders of the Most Notorious Pirates* (1724), which Stevenson used as a source for his story. Still, it is telling that he chose to mention this particular pirate—and that the structure of Silver's sentence invites us to mistake his meaning: to assume that the bird witnessed untold evils while accompanying English military missions.

Indeed, although Dr. Livesey seems proud of having served under the duke of Cumberland, Alan Sandison reminds us that this fearfully effective general earned the sobriquet "Butcher" Cumberland for "his brutal tactics in the battle of Culloden which ensured the decimation of the Jacobite forces and the disfavor of romantic nationalists like Stevenson" (59). It is also striking that Stevenson chooses to call the gentlemen's ship the *Hispaniola*, thus linking his rovers to the Spanish, a people whose imperialist forays the British had historically condemned as tyrannical efforts to extort massive amounts of money and minerals from their colonies.[10] English commentators routinely contrasted the rapacious actions of Spanish explorers—whom they blamed for destroying the New World and its inhabitants in their relentless pursuit of gold and silver—with their own determination to cultivate the land of colonies and improve the lives of natives. Clearly, Stevenson's portrayal of the gentlemen's quest undercuts this differentiation; no one cares about cultivating Treasure Island. Critics have suggested that Stevenson's decision to set the novel in the eighteenth century represents a nostalgic return to the early years of British colonialism.[11] Yet the fact that he names the ship after England's most hated imperial rival from those years—a rival whose empire eventually fell apart—suggests skepticism about both the morality and the durability of empires.

Critics who study Stevenson have acknowledged that anti-imperialist sentiments inform his later work. Following the lead of Patrick Brantlinger, who shows how "The Beach of Falesá" (1892) and *The Ebb-Tide* (1894) undercut the conventions of the classic imperial adventure story (39–42, 239), Katherine Linehan, Rosalyn Jolly, and Rod Edmond argue that Stevenson, having witnessed the devastating effects of white rule during his travels in the South Seas, produced narratives pervaded by a Conradian pessimism about what he saw as the "folly and injustice and unconscious rapacity" of an ethically problematic system (quoted in Jolly xiii). Similarly, Julia Reid notes that Stevenson's Scottishness made him particularly prone to ambivalence about English efforts to domineer over other countries and contends that his Scottish and Polynesian writings are pervaded by a profound "skepticism about a confident evolutionary narrative" that asserts the superiority of the "civilized" over the "savage" (55).[12]

Given that Stevenson's later romances have been described as "psychological and moral attacks on empire" (D. Jackson 31), why do commentators shy away from the possibility that *Treasure Island* subverts rather than participates in the Robinsonade tradition?[13] One probable cause is that the novel's status as children's literature—it first appeared as a serial in the magazine *Young Folks*—leads critics to assume that it follows a familiar formula, since many of the boys' adventure stories that appeared in journals like this one celebrated Empire unreservedly. Then, too, critics have been misled by Stevenson's own account of his work in the essays "A Gossip on Romance" (1882) and "A Humble Remonstrance" (1884). Indeed, the argument that we should read *Treasure Island* as a boy's daydream is lifted directly out of Stevenson's own account of the novel's genesis in "A Humble Remonstrance." Assuming that his audience had indulged in "youthful day-dreams" about going to sea, Stevenson explains, "the author, counting upon that, and well aware (cunning and low-minded man!) that this class of interest, having been frequently treated, finds a readily accessible and beaten road to the sympathies of the reader, addressed himself throughout to the building up and circumstantiation of this boyish dream" ("Humble Remonstrance" 197).

Stevenson's characterization of himself as "Humble" is no empty boast; besides suggesting that his "little book about a quest for buried treasure" is merely an "elementary" exercise in giving the public what it wants, he goes on to characterize the protagonists of *Treasure Island* as one-dimensional "puppets" who exhibit "but one class of qualities" (196–97). As a romancer, he explains, he does not aim to engage the intellect: "To add more traits, to be too clever, to start the hare of moral or intellectual interest while we are running the fox of material interest, is not to enrich but to stultify your tale" (197).

Stevenson's intensely self-deprecating stance has had a chilling effect on critical accounts of *Treasure Island*. Choosing to take Stevenson at his word when he insists that we should not analyze romances but allow ourselves "to be submerged by the tale as by a billow" ("Humble" 196), critics have insisted that "an adult can get nothing more from *Treasure Island* than a boy does" (Aldington 143); that "*Treasure Island* is a very simple book" (Kiely 68); that Stevenson's "artistic maturation" did not occur until after writing *Treasure Island* (K. Blake, "Sea-Dream" 175). Similarly, Alastair Fowler warns that "every critic of *Treasure Island* has to begin by noticing the limitations of kind and Stevenson's zestful acceptance of them" (109). To scrutinize the story too much, he concludes, would be "to break a butterfly on the wheel" (115). Even Sandison, who resists such dismissive accounts and characterizes Stevenson as an innovative and intensely self-conscious writer, twice worries that he will be criticized for "taking a spade to a soufflé" (16, 50).

Stevenson himself often expressed concern that he was a literary lightweight, as when he declared, "I cannot take myself seriously, as an artist; the limitations are so obvious" and "There must be something wrong in me, or I would not be popular" (quoted in J. Smith 44, 28). But surely we should not echo such sentiments or accept Stevenson's excessively modest claims for his "little book" at face value. Henry James, who condescendingly praised *Treasure Island* for being excellent "in its way," nevertheless knew better than to listen to its author: "the figures are not puppets with vague faces," he insisted in his 1888 essay "Robert Louis Stevenson" (154). Following the lead of recent critics who locate a profound ambivalence about imperialism in Stevenson's later writings, we should recognize that *Treasure Island* does not deny or repress late Victorian anxieties about empire; it reflects and amplifies them.

PUNCTURING THE MYTH OF POTENCY

Another critical commonplace reviewers have stolen from Stevenson is the idea that *Treasure Island* encourages readers to identify themselves closely with Jim Hawkins. In "A Gossip on Romance," Stevenson declares that the great "triumph of romantic story-telling" comes when the reader "plays at being the hero," submerging himself uncritically in the story (179). But like the other stories featuring young narrators that I discussed in chapter 1, *Treasure Island* simultaneously invites and disrupts identification. To begin with, Stevenson's habit of parodying other popular books reminds readers of the artificiality of his narrative. But more than this, the novel dramatizes the danger of being duped by silver-tongued storytellers. Thus, even as imperialist roving is associated with piracy, so, too, is the act of telling tales aimed at seducing children to involve themselves in the act of exploration. From the start, duplicitous pirates like Bones and Silver are the ones who relate exciting sea yarns. And crucially, it is Silver—the archvillain—who invites Jim to view Treasure Island as an alluring environment to explore and master: "'Ah,'" he exclaims when they first spot land, "'this here is a sweet spot, this island—a sweet spot for a lad to get ashore on. You'll bathe, and you'll climb trees, and you'll hunt goats, you will; and you'll get aloft on them hills like a goat yourself'" (64).

Here again, Stevenson marks his story's distance from the traditional Robinsonade, in which boy heroes do indeed indulge in such pleasures. Jim does not: having just overheard Silver's murderous plans, he can only "shudder" in "horror" at the pirate's inviting overture (64). *Treasure Island* prods its audience to share this response, to recognize that the flattering fantasy of potency such storytellers peddle ("you'll climb trees," "you'll hunt goats") is a dangerous delusion (you'll actually be "a goat yourself"). The pirates are not just storytellers but shameless child flatterers, and this deluge of admiration mimics—and thus draws attention to—the way the narrative itself repeatedly shifts into an obsequious, adulatory mode. As Hayden W. Ward notes, Jim "is made a collaborator in grown-up enterprises" (310), and his inclusion, prominence, and conspicuous achievements combine to paint a highly complimentary picture of what boys can do. Yet this pleasing vision of juvenile power and potency is constantly punctured; each time Jim gets established as a heroic figure, his agency is quickly shown to be chimerical; his collaboration compelled; his actions circumscribed.

This dynamic is evident from the start of the story; pressured into helping Billy Bones, Jim becomes an unwilling "sharer in his alarms" (3). Tellingly, Bones is at his most coercive when he adopts the role of raconteur; on evenings when he would "force all the trembling company" at the inn "to listen to his stories or bear a chorus to his singing," the pirate was, according to Jim, "the most overriding companion ever known": "Often I have heard the house shaking with 'Yo-ho-ho, and a bottle of rum'; all the neighbors joining in for dear life, with the fear of death upon them" (3). Bones also employs more subtle tactics to ensure cooperation. Indeed, he is the first in a parade of adult storytellers who flatter Jim in an effort to manipulate the boy into satisfying various greedy desires of their own. "'You're the only one here that's worth anything,'" Bones tells the boy, hoping to cajole Jim into bringing him rum despite the doctor's orders (13).

Meanwhile, the narrative itself is busy confirming this gratifying statement. Jim's pathetic father never musters up the strength to confront Bones about the money he owes him, and dies soon after the pirate arrives. Terrified by the reputation of the buccaneers, the townspeople likewise prove useless and cowardly; not one of them will agree to help Jim and his mother defend the inn when the barbaric crew returns to find the treasure map. Thus, the narrative neatly aligns itself with piratical praise; Jim's bravery earns him the right to disparage more mature members of the community with the words "You would have thought men would have been ashamed of themselves—no soul would consent to return with us to the 'Admiral Benbow'" (20). Right from the start, *Treasure Island* floats the complimentary idea that a mere child is more manly than an entire town of grown-ups.

At the same time, however, the arrival of two more sycophantic criminals reminds readers to beware the cost of succumbing to such flattery. Requesting rum, the buccaneer Black Dog echoes Bones by referring to Jim as "this dear child here, as I've took such a liking to" (9), and a few scenes later the blind pirate Pew likewise addresses the boy as "my kind, young friend" in order to lure him into taking his hand and leading him into the inn (16). In both cases, sweet words do little to mask the utter ruthlessness of these men. Waiting with Black Dog for Bones to return to the inn, Jim relates:

> Once I stepped out myself into the road, but he immediately called me back, and, as I did not obey quick enough for his fancy, a most horrible change came over his tallowy face, and he ordered me in, with an oath that made me jump. As soon as I was back again he returned to his former manner, half fawning, half sneering, patted me on the shoulder, told me I was a good boy, and he had taken quite a fancy to me. (8)

Pew quickly proves equally hypocritical; as soon as Jim proffers his arm, the ostensibly amiable old man startles him, he says, when he "gripped it in a moment like a vice," causing the boy to cry out in pain (16). Like Black Dog's metamorphosis, this physical transformation is coupled with a sudden change in tone of voice; the blind man begins by speaking in an ingratiating, obsequious "sing-song" (16), and then switches over to "a voice so cruel, and cold, and ugly" that it "cowed me more than the pain" (17).

These radical shifts echo and alert us to the endless rocking of Stevenson's sea story. Like the "half-fawning, half-sneering" pirates who use flattery to manipulate Jim, *Treasure Island* is a two-faced text that alternately exalts Jim to heroic status and undermines his achievements. Even as Stevenson characterizes his hero as an indispensable partner in the adults' enterprise, he suggests that Jim is not so much collaborating as collaborating with the enemy, functioning as a helpless pawn rather than a genuine colleague. First enlisted to help Billy Bones, Jim quickly finds himself coerced into abetting the man who is out to *trap* Bones: pushing Jim along, Black Dog declares, " 'You and me'll just go back into the parlour, sonny, and get behind the door, and we'll give Bill a little surprise' " (8–9). Scenes involving the gentlemen likewise convey the sense that Jim is strong-armed into compliance with their wishes. As I have already noted, this oddly passive hero does not volunteer to join the adults' treasure quest—he is drafted. His limited agency is made evident by the fact that after the discovery of the map, the doctor is so set on "keeping [Jim] beside him" that he arranges for the boy to be held captive, kept "almost [as] a prisoner" at the squire's house (36).

This dynamic even extends to Jim's interactions with his mother. Indeed, the most striking way Jim's agency is undermined in these early chapters is that he discovers the treasure map as a result of his mother's plucky heroism, not his own. Mrs. Hawkins is the one who takes action after the townspeople decline to come to her assistance, boldly declaring that she refuses to "lose money that belong[s] to her fatherless boy": " 'If none of the rest of you dare,' she said, 'Jim and I dare. Back we will go, the way we came, and small thanks to you big, hulking, chicken-hearted men. We'll have that chest open, if we die for it' " (20). Once again, Jim is exposed as a reactive recruit rather than an autonomous agent; rather lamely, he adds, "Of course, I said I would go with my mother" (20). Noting that Mrs. Hawkins fusses over the money and faints when the pirates arrive, commentators typically dismiss her as a silly woman, apt to lose her head in a crisis. This seems unfair, given that male characters in *Treasure Island* are also prone to foolish utterances and blackouts. Moreover, when Jim tells the story to the gentlemen, they instantly recognize that Mrs. Hawkins is the real hero: "When they heard how my mother went back to the inn, Dr. Livesey fairly slapped his thigh, and the squire cried 'Bravo!' " (31).

Perhaps because he senses that he is not the undisputed star of his own story, Jim quickly succumbs to the solicitations of the next pirate bearing praise who appears on the scene: Long John Silver, the greatest child-flatterer of them all. When Jim arrives at Silver's inn, he has every reason to suspect that the one-legged landlord is the dreaded pirate Bones feared. Not only is Silver missing the appropriate limb, he has christened his inn the "Spy-glass" after the tallest hill on Treasure Island. Moreover, Jim sees Black Dog sneaking out of the tavern, which ought to confirm beyond question his suspicion that Silver is another member of Flint's old crew. Yet Jim ignores all of this evidence, in part because he is fooled by Silver's pleasant appearance, but mostly because the "obsequious" Silver massages his ego by treating him as if he is more mature than a grown man (186). After questioning an elderly sailor named Morgan about his relationship to Black Dog, Long John remarks to Jim "in a confidential whisper, that was very flattering, as I thought:—'He's quite an honest man, Tom Morgan, on'y stupid' " (44). Thrilled to be treated as a superior specimen of manhood, Jim ignores the overwhelming evidence of Silver's guilt and drinks in his praise: " 'You're a lad, you are, but you're as smart as paint. I see that when you first came in' " (45).

Silver also stokes Jim's sense of self-worth by choosing him as the favored audience for his sea stories, seeking him out once they are onboard the *Hispaniola*: " 'Come away, Hawkins,' he would say; 'come and have a yarn with John. Nobody more welcome than yourself, my son' " (54). From the start, Stevenson links Silver's seductiveness to his ability to purvey fascinating tales and tidbits of information about life at sea. Describing one of their earliest conversations, Jim recollects how the sea-cook "made himself the most interesting companion, telling me about the different ships that we passed by, their rig, tonnage, and nationality, explaining the work that was going forward . . . and every now and then telling me some little anecdote of ships or seamen, or repeating a nautical phrase till I had learned it perfectly" (45–46). As Israel Hands observes, Silver "can speak like a book" (54), and the nonfictional nature of his narration links him to tellers of boys' adventure stories, who frequently adopted an encyclopedic style in order to educate their young audience about the world around them. Desert island romances like *The Swiss Family Robinson* (1814, 1818) and *Masterman Ready* (1841) are full of lengthy explanations of phenomena like typhoons and the Gulf Stream, mini-lectures on the habits of African birds, or the way coral islands form. Child readers are intended to react just as Jim does in this scene with Silver: to absorb and parrot back the information offered.[14] In fact, authors are so intent on encouraging this sort of response that they often have their boy protagonists model it. For example, faced with task of trying to herd antelope, one of the sons in *The Swiss Family Robinson* recalls a Hottentot technique he read about in a book, prompting his father to exclaim, "'Well done . . . I am glad to see that you remember what you have read'" (Wyss 291).[15]

As this compliment suggests, an encyclopedic style is not only thing Silver has in common with authors such as Marryat, Ballantyne, and Wyss. Like Long John, these storytellers routinely ingratiate themselves with boy readers by suggesting that young people are smarter, braver, and more powerful than grown men. When shipwrecks occur in their stories, experienced sailors sink into a watery grave, while amateur cabin boys survive and thrive. Or, if adult authority figures live, they spend most of their time lavishing extravagant praise on juveniles. "'Well done, Franz!'" booms the patriarch of the Swiss Family Robinson, "'these fish hooks, which you the youngest have found, may contribute more than anything else . . . to save our lives'" (6–7). Similarly, when experienced seaman Masterman Ready finds himself wrecked on an island with the Seagrave family, he soon begins to depend on the steadiness of the boy rather than his parents. "I will not at present say anything to Mr. and Mrs. Seagrave," he muses in the midst of one crisis, "And yet I cannot do without help—I must trust Master William—he is a noble boy that, and clever beyond his years" (Marryat 209).

As the narrative of *Treasure Island* unfolds, Stevenson himself seems to indulge more and more in this sort of puffery. Out of all the crew members, Jim is the one who salvages the gentlemen's mission by discovering the mutiny and commandeering the ship. And even as he basks in the glow of adult appreciation—"'Every step, it's you that saves our lives,'" the doctor marvels (168)—he enjoys the privilege of scoffing at the "silly," "childish" behavior of much older men (71, 79). Yet while Stevenson fawns in the typical fashion, he repeatedly warns readers about the dangers of placing their trust in pandering adults who pretend to worship youthful prowess. The first such cautionary moment occurs onboard the *Hispaniola*, when a horrified Jim overhears Silver buttering up another juvenile victim:

> "You're young, you are, but you're as smart as paint. I see that when I set my eyes on you, and I'll talk to you like a man."
>
> You may imagine how I felt when I heard this abominable old rogue addressing another in the very same words of flattery as he had used on myself. I think, if I had been able, that I would have killed him. (57–58)

In a narrative full of traumatizing events, this scene stands out as the one in which Jim expresses the most extreme emotional distress. His feelings of rage and pain result from being forced to recognize the falseness of adult flattery, to doubt his own status as a uniquely intelligent and manly colleague.

Jim's habit of viewing the buccaneers, the squire, and Ben Gunn as simple-minded children receives similar treatment: even as Stevenson lays this form of narrative flattery on rather thickly, he undermines it at the same time, since none of these grown-ups turns out to be as moronic as he seems. Ultimately, Jim has to admit that the man he refers to as "the half-idiot maroon . . . was the hero from beginning to end" (183). In fact, Gunn functions as yet another adult who successfully coerces Jim into cooperating with his self-promoting plan. Having hidden the treasure away, he uses the boy as a go-between to align himself with the squire, putting words into Jim's mouth and pinching him hard every few minutes to punctuate his points. The squire also proves far less flighty than he originally seems; after injudiciously blabbing news of the treasure map while on land, he grows "silent" and "cool as steel" when the bloody battle commences at sea (93, 91).

But the best example of how Stevenson undercuts the idea that Jim's adult companions are infantile idiots comes when the boy faces off against Israel Hands aboard the *Hispaniola*. This is the scene that seems to indulge most fully in the fantasy that a boy can effortlessly become "the master of his fate and the captain of his soul" (Bristow 95). Working alone, Jim quickly wrests away control of the ship from the pirates, who fail to notice his approach because they are fighting among themselves. Locked in a one-on-one struggle with Hands, Jim deftly evades his opponent's knife thrusts by climbing up into the crosstrees and chortles as he considers how "densely stupid" the pirate is: "I could see by the working of his face that he was trying to think, and the process was so slow and laborious that . . . I laughed aloud" (137, 142). In a moment that may well have inspired J. M. Barrie to make cockiness Peter Pan's primary characteristic, Hands bemoans how hard it is for a "master mariner" like himself to lose to a mere youth—flattery Jim swallows greedily: "I was drinking in his words and smiling away, as conceited as a cock upon a wall . . . " (142). But note how this sentence ends:

> when, all in a breath, back went his right hand over his shoulder. Something sang like an arrow through the air; I felt a blow and then a sharp pang, and there I was pinned by the shoulder to the mast. In the horrid pain and surprise of the moment—I can scarce say it was by my own volition, and I am sure it was without a conscious aim—both my pistols went off, and both escaped out of my hands. (142)

Like the scene in which Jim overhears Silver sweet-talking another boy, this incident vividly illustrates that adults who curry favor with children by praising their superior potency cannot be trusted. Boys who succumb to such solicitations put their lives at risk. Only dumb luck enables Jim to triumph over Hands, who is clearly not as stupid as he seems.

Thinking back, we realize that this was evident from the start of the story, since Israel Hands is introduced as "a careful, wily, old, experienced seaman, who could be trusted at a pinch with almost anything" (53). Indeed, *Jim* is the one who makes rookie mistakes during their fight. Even though he knows that Hands plans to kill him, Jim forgets to keep him under surveillance; excited to witness the moment when the ship finally touches the shore, Jim fails to notice that Hands has begun his attack. When Jim then tries to shoot Hands, his gun refuses to fire because he has forgotten to reprime and reload it. Here and elsewhere, Jim wins the day not because he is especially intelligent or brave but simply because his opponents—as Hands repeatedly complains—"don't have no luck" (142).[16] Indeed, only considerable "good fortune" with regard to wind and tide enables Jim to reach the *Hispaniola* in the first place (121). Rather than ingeniously piloting his coracle to the ship, Jim can only sit there and hope for the best: "I could in no way influence her course" (127). A similar combination of passivity and luck enables Jim to kill Hands; it is amazing that he hits his target, given that he fires accidentally, without even aiming his weapons.

By attributing Jim's triumphs to fickle chance, Stevenson again departs from the traditional desert island romance formula, since such stories pound home the message that success depends on continual hard work that *earns* men the blessing of a benevolent providence. "'There is nothing to be had in this world without labour,'" Masterman Ready observes (Marryat 205), an opinion backed up by the basic plot of the Robinsonade, which compulsively chronicles the endless tasks that must be done in order to improve the productivity of already fertile space. Luck plays no part in the carefully controlled, hierarchical universe posited by writers like Marryat, Ballantyne, and Wyss; instead "everything is governed by fixed laws" (Marryat 153). Of these, perhaps the most sacred is "'God helps those who help themselves!'" (Wyss 2), a credo perfectly in keeping with the imperialist mindset. *Treasure Island*, by contrast, declines to promote the reassuring idea that man can shape his destiny through faith and hard work. Instead, this novel reads like "a record of queer chances," as Henry James observed ("Robert Louis Stevenson" 154). Jim succeeds only because "fortune . . . particularly favoured me," while "the dice [keep] going against" his enemies (*Treasure Island* 121, 142). He is not the master of his fate but fortune's fool, as Captain Smollett realizes. As the quest draws to a close, the captain remarks, "'You're a good boy in your line, Jim, but I don't think you and me'll go to sea again. You're too much the born favourite for me'" (185).

Other adult characters also chime in to remind Jim of his youthful inadequacy, and their comments further undermine the flattering idea that boys can routinely expect to best men. "'You're a good boy,'" Ben Gunn tells Jim, "'but you're on'y a boy, all told'" (98). In contrast, as the maroon himself observes,

" 'Benn Gunn's the man' " who can and does save the day (81). Similarly, although Hands agrees to call the boy "Cap'n Hawkins" when he unexpectedly appears onboard the *Hispaniola*, the pirate nevertheless remains firmly in control of the vessel. Noting that Jim cannot sail to shore without his help, Hands wryly remarks, " 'Without I gives you a hint, you ain't that man,' " and Jim, recognizing truth when he hears it, meekly agrees to follow orders: "I think I was a good, prompt subaltern, and I am very sure that Hands was an excellent pilot" (134, 139). Thus, the scene that attests most strongly to Jim's independence and self-sufficiency—"I was greatly elated with my new command," he proudly reports (135)—simultaneously reveals that he is still subject to adult supervision: Hands "issued his commands, which I breathlessly obeyed" (140).

The overarching structure of the narrative likewise reflects Stevenson's determination to oscillate back and forth between setting Jim up as a heroic figure and cutting him down to size. In the grandly titled sections "My Shore Adventure" and "My Sea Adventure," Jim gets a chance to chronicle his adventures as a free-ranging troubleshooter who strikes out on his own. Yet in between these stirring segments, the doctor takes over the narration for three chapters, a fact that has puzzled generations of critics. Rightly so, because Jim's inability to maintain control over his own story presents a major challenge to the idea that he functions as the undisputed master of his fate. According to Salmon and Rose, the use of the first person functions as a crucial signifier of the alluring autonomy of fictional boy adventurers. On the flimsiest of pretexts, Stevenson deprives Jim of this privilege, thus puncturing our sense of him as an independent agent.

Of course, it could be argued that the doctor's participation merely attests to Jim's position as a valued collaborator who works *with* the gentlemen to achieve his glorious success. But the problem with this reading is that, once again, Stevenson manages to suggest that Jim's adult partners wield much more power than he does. Despite the fact that Jim narrates the lion's share of the story, Stevenson makes it clear from the start that his hero's authority over the act of storytelling is minimal. In his opening sentence, Jim informs us that he picks up the pen not on his own behalf but because adults have roped him into it: "Squire Trelawney, Dr. Livesey, and the rest of these gentlemen having asked me to write down the whole particulars about Treasure Island, from the beginning to the end . . . I take up my pen" (1). Although the memory of this adventure gives him terrible nightmares, Jim nevertheless complies with the adults' demand that he "go back" and recount all the details of this terrifying time (1). When Jim interrupts a description of their journey to the island with the words "I am not allowed to be more plain" (56), it reinforces our impression that the gentlemen are looking over his shoulder and exercising control over his story. The very act of narration is haunted by a sense of coercion.

Acknowledging that Jim starts off as a relatively passive figure, a number of commentators have suggested that *Treasure Island* is a bildungsroman that eventually promotes its boy protagonist to heroic status.[17] But in fact, Stevenson never stops seesawing back and forth between flattery and insistent, undercutting irony. Thus, Jim's climactic encounter with Silver at the stockade—the scene in which he makes his famous speech advertising his own valor—runs precisely parallel to his earlier altercation with Hands. Here, too, Jim's inflated self-regard leads him to make a foolish mistake that almost costs him his life. Returning from the newly recovered *Hispaniola* "in famous spirits," Jim notices that none of the gentlemen have stayed up to guard the stockade (145). Mentally chastising his elders for keeping "an infamous bad watch," Jim enjoys "a silent chuckle" at their expense, imagining how surprised they will be when they wake up to find him back among them (147). Yet once again, the laugh (and the surprise) is on him. Though he knows that his companions are not in the habit of building large fires or failing to keep watch—those are things that the pirates do, and the gentlemen scorn them for it—Jim disregards the deserted, smoldering bonfire and enters the stockade, only to discover that he has stumbled right into the arms of the enemy.[18]

Shortly after making this enormous error, Jim launches into his declaration of superiority. After taunting the pirates that their "whole business [has] gone to wreck," he exults: "and if you want to know who did it—it was I! I was in the apple barrel the night we sighted land, and I heard you, John . . . and told every word you said before the hour was out. And as for the schooner, it was I who cut her cable, and it was I that killed the men you had aboard of her, and it was I who brought her where you'll never see her more, not one of you. The laugh's on my side; I've had the top of this business from the first" (152). *Treasure Island*'s status as a two-faced text is nowhere more clear than at this instant. Jim's proclamation of supremacy can (and has) been read as a straightforward statement of truth. But given that it occurs at the precise moment in the narrative when Jim wields the least power, it is hard to take this assertion of strength at face value. Helpless in the hands of his enemy, his "worst . . . apprehensions realised" (149), Jim himself hints that his bravado is a façade when he describes how he presents himself to Silver "pluckily enough, I hope, to all outward appearance, but with black despair in my heart" (150).

Silver's response to Jim's speech illustrates the ambiguity Stevenson builds in to this moment. When Jim dramatically winds up his monologue by asking the pirates to inform the doctor that he took his death like a man, Long John replies to this defiant entreaty "with an accent so curious that I could not, for the life of me, decide whether he were laughing at my request, or had been favourably affected by my courage" (152). Should we consider Jim heroic or ridiculous, powerful or puny? Silver's immediate reaction gives us no clue. Admittedly, the next wave of responses suggests that Jim really does function as the hero of the story. Rather than losing their tempers and attacking Jim, as one might expect, the pirates first regard him in awed silence—"staring at me like as many sheep"—and then begin affirming his claims and admiring his other achievements (152). For example, Tom Morgan marvels, "'It was him that knowed Black Dog,'" while Silver adds, "'I'll put another again to that, by thunder! for it was this same boy that faked the chart from Billy Bones. First and last, we've split upon Jim Hawkins!'" (152).

But given that this sycophantic frenzy takes place after countless other incidents attest to the dangers of being beguiled by adult adulation, it seems evident that we are meant to follow Jim's lead in learning to distrust such discourse. Still playing his old game, Silver continues to pile compliments onto Jim, remarking loudly to his crew, "'I never seen a better boy than that. He's more a man than any pair of rats of you'" (153). But now that Jim has overheard Silver seducing a series of juvenile victims with the same move, he knows better than to trust him. Reading this scene, avid consumers of boys' adventure stories would have experienced a similar sense of déjà vu, since this incident is closely patterned on the moment in *The Coral Island* when Ralph Rover boldly confronts the pirate captain who has captured him, wrapping up his defiant speech with the words "'I am made of such stuff as the like of you shall never tame, though you should do your worst'" (Ballantyne 263). "Instead of flying into a rage," the buccaneers regard Ralph with looks of amazement and sing his praises: "'Well done, lad! you're a brick'" (262–63). Ballantyne expects his audience to agree with this sentiment and place complete trust in books that trumpet boyish vigor. But Stevenson prods his readers to become suspicious of textual overtures of this sort.

This commitment to creating skeptical readers sets *Treasure Island* even further apart from the typical Robinsonade, which insists on being taken as the gospel truth. As I have already noted, such stories celebrate and encourage the act of echoing back information that one has gleaned from books of travel and adventure, whereas Stevenson aims to deter such behavior by sending up the conventions of the genre and by presenting the negative example of Silver's parrot. If Jim's suspicious stance at the end of the novel represents the best attitude to take toward silver-tongued storytellers, the bird's habit of mindless reiteration signifies the worst. The parrot serves as a haunting symbol of voicelessness and an utter lack of autonomy, and the fact that he gets the last word confirms that *Treasure Island* is not a story about achieving maturity and mastery. For Jim, skepticism comes too late; he has already played the parrot's part.

Thus, in his first encounter with Silver, Jim begins repeating back information fed to him by the one-legged pirate, just as he reiterates the story to suit the gentlemen. Like "Cap'n Flint," "Cap'n Hawkins" frequently acts in a clueless, compliant way, as when he finds the gentlemen's excitement about the map "incomprehensible" yet participates in their quest (34); or when he cannot help laughing along with Silver "though I did not see the joke" (45); or when he agrees to follow Gunn's directions while admitting " 'I don't understand one word that you've been saying' " (83). Tellingly, the sea-cook lavishes the same sort of sweet talk on the bird that he does on the boy: " 'Ah, she's a handsome craft, she is,' the cook would say, and give her sugar from his pocket" (55). The sharp cries of Silver's ancient yet innocent "babby" haunt Jim's dreams because he represents the terrifying possibility that one may age yet never acquire any real power, authority, or agency (55). Indeed, Jim fails to gain command over himself or the world around him: Silver escapes; the rest of the treasure remains on the island; and our hero is too immobilized by the horrors he has seen to seek out any more trouble.

Still, it is odd that Jim's worst nightmares after his adventure ends are not about Silver or any of the brutal scenes of physical violence that he has witnessed but instead involve "the sharp voice of Captain Flint still ringing in my ears: 'Pieces of eight! pieces of eight!' " (191). Stevenson clearly intends us to interpret this dream as a flashback to the horrible surprise Jim suffers in the stockade; that chapter is entitled "Pieces of Eight" because the boy realizes he has made a terrible mistake when he hears the parrot's cry. This moment attests to the trauma of recognizing that the people you thought were your friends are actually your most dangerous enemies—the very message *Treasure Island* sends about manipulative storytellers who cozy up to boys by championing their superior prowess. Whereas the fantasized audience for this sort of story is profoundly passive and parrot-like, readers of *Treasure Island* are invited to take a more active stance. Committed to creating a more truly collaborative reader–writer relationship, Stevenson does not merely present the cautionary tale of a boy who is seduced and betrayed by adult raconteurs, he also employs a range of literary techniques that challenge his readers to draw their own conclusions, including understated satire, ambiguity, and incomplete closure.

Indeed, it is a sign of how much leeway he gives to his audience to exercise their own judgment that generations of readers have missed his critique of Empire completely, interpreting the novel as a simplistic, humorless, and pro-imperialist text.[19] That is the risk of moving away from an autocratic authorial stance: people have the freedom to construe your tale in a variety of ways. In writing *Treasure Island*, Stevenson did not merely aim to accommodate active, skeptical readers, but to create them. Yet precisely because the text is informed by this desire, it too constitutes an effort to produce a particular kind of young person. Hoping to mold juvenile readers into becoming less moldable does not magically erase the power imbalance built in to the adult author–child reader relationship. Nothing can do that, and the overarching message of *Treasure Island* is that getting involved in the plots of people more powerful than you are can profoundly endanger your mental, physical, and emotional well-being. As I will show, the same anxiety pervades the work of Lewis Carroll; he, too, dwells on the difficulties that ensue when young and old beings interact, including the danger that the child will function as a pawn who parrots back adult propaganda. Even as Carroll self-consciously tries to create children's fiction that invites audience members to operate as active collaborators in the production of meaning, he remains keenly aware that nonsense itself can be experienced as a form of coercion, a brand of "fun" that pushy adults foist on profoundly uninterested children.

3

RECIPROCAL AGGRESSION

Un-Romantic Agency in the Art of Lewis Carroll

When he was eighteen years old, the young man who would soon begin signing himself "Lewis Carroll" contributed a caricature of Joshua Reynolds's *The Age of Innocence* (figure 3.1) to one of his family's domestic magazines. Reynolds's famous painting gave pictorial shape to the Romantic ideal of childhood; his white-clad figure, set apart from the civilized world in an Edenic natural landscape, seems "socially, sexually, and psychically" pure (Higonnet 24). Carroll faithfully reproduces the countryside setting but replaces the child ensconced in nature's lap with a gently smiling hippopotamus (see figure 3.2). In a tongue-in-cheek editor's note, he pompously announces that his reproduction of Reynolds's masterpiece "presents to the contemplative mind a charming union of youth and innocence" (*Rectory Umbrella* 8). Whereas Reynolds's decision to establish a visual link between the whiteness of his central figure and that of the heavens beyond imbues his cherubic little girl with the aura of Wordsworthian clouds of glory, Carroll's dehumanized and desexed "child" seems an earthbound, lumbering blank.

What exactly does Carroll want to caricature here? One possibility is that he means to send up the whole idea of yoking youth with innocence. In that case, the parody reveals his sly determination to take the Romantic conception of the child as primitive Other and push it to an amusing extreme, literally turning the young sitter into a "noble savage": a mild, wild animal. Then again, perhaps he means to lampoon not childhood purity per se but merely Reynolds's mode of representation, the way his close focus on the child lends an elephantine enormity to a figure that is (and thus ought to appear) small.

FIGURE 3.1 *The Age of Innocence* (c. 1788) by Sir Joshua Reynolds. Oil on canvas. Reprinted by permission of Plymouth City Museum and Art Gallery (Plympton St. Maurice Guildhall).

FIGURE 3.2 "The Age of Innocence. From the picture in the Vernon Gallery" by Lewis Carroll. *The Rectory Umbrella* (c. 1850–53). Harcourt Amory Collection of Lewis Carroll Materials (MS Eng 718). Reprinted by permission of the Houghton Library, Harvard University.

Most Carroll commentators, I think, would gravitate toward the second interpretation, since it is generally assumed that Carroll fetishized littleness and wholeheartedly embraced Romantic notions about childhood. According to this line of thinking, Carroll conceived of children as categorically different from (and superior to) adults; desperate to maintain this primal purity, he used his camera and his children's fiction to freeze his child-friends in place like flies fixed in amber. Thus, Douglas R. Nickel argues that photography allowed Carroll "to suspend his child subjects in a state of innocence forever" (66), while many critics of the *Alice* books, including Morton N. Cohen and Jackie Wullschläger, suggest that Carroll shares Humpty Dumpty's wish that Alice had stopped growing at age seven.

My own sense is that Carroll, like many other members of the cult of the child, was both drawn to and dismissive of Romantic figurations of childhood innocence, and that this conflicted attitude manifested itself not just in this equivocal caricature but also in his fiction, photographs, and commentary on child actors. Thus, as Nina Auerbach points out (131–42), the prefatory poems affixed to the *Alice* books that depict children as "Gentle" and "pure" contrast sharply with the representation of childhood within the books (Carroll, *Complete Works* 13, 123). Similarly, some of Carroll's photographs celebrate the innocent unconsciousness of children by featuring sleeping child subjects garbed entirely in white, while others (as I will show) present the child as a precocious partner, a knowing participant in artistic and erotic affairs. Then, too, the standard Romantic sentiments Carroll employed in correspondence with the parents of child sitters conflicts sharply with some of the images that he produced. Although he frequently raved to mothers about the beautiful naïveté of their daughters—as when he described one potential sitter as a "perfectly simple-minded child of Nature" (*Letters* 1:338)—many of his photographs subvert such rhetoric by characterizing girls in particular as wily, aggressive, artful beings who have more in common with the chameleonic child actresses Carroll and other cultists flocked to see than with flowerlike Wordsworthian waifs such as Lucy Gray.

Because so much work has already been done that attests to the allure innocence held for Carroll, I concentrate here on tracing how an opposing impulse also emerges in his art: a willingness to jettison the solitary Child of Nature paradigm and explore instead the complex, fraught relationship that links children to adults, himself to his beloved child-friends. Rather than single-mindedly insisting that a firm barrier separates—and ought to separate—young from old, Carroll frequently blurs this line, characterizing the child not as an untouched Other but as a collaborator enmeshed in a complicated relationship with the adults who surround her. Like the work of the female children's authors discussed in chapter 1, Carroll's art reveals a keen awareness of the fact that children are always already involved with (and influenced by) adults. But whereas those authors seem comfortably certain that children can nevertheless develop into creative agents who help shape their own life stories, Carroll remains unsure. He hopes that children can function as empowered collaborators, but—like Stevenson—he fears that the power imbalance inherent in the adult–child relationship ensures that all adults can offer children is a fraudulent illusion of reciprocity.

This tension is evident in the prefatory poem Carroll affixes to *Alice's Adventures in Wonderland* (1865), which chronicles how he composed the tale while boating with the three Liddell girls. By itself, Carroll's decision to publicize the story's origins bespeaks a desire to share credit with his child-friends, to alert readers to the fact that actual children inspired and were involved in the creation of *Alice*. Moreover, his description of the trip vividly attests to the pleasures of adult–child collaboration. "All in the golden afternoon / Full leisurely we glide," he begins (11); "And home we steer, a merry crew," he concludes in the penultimate stanza (12).[1] This emphasis on communal activity carries over into the representation of story-making, since Carroll depicts the Liddell sisters as active participants in the production of narrative:

> Imperious Prima flashes forth
> Her edict "to begin it":
> In gentler tones Secunda hopes
> "There will be nonsense in it!"
> While Tertia interrupts the tale
> Not *more* than once a minute. (11)

Just as the afternoon is golden because they are "all in" it together (all in the same boat), the story's specialness is crucially linked to its status as a collective effort: it is not simply the result of his "one poor voice," Carroll emphasizes, but rather springs from the joyous cacophony of many "tongues together" (11). Indeed, Carroll portrays himself as a faint, "weary" figure who quickly runs out of ideas, only managing to produce a full-length narrative because the girls goad him on: "'The rest next time—' 'It *is* next time!' / The happy voices cry" (11). Besides commingling his voice with theirs in this line, Carroll also uses the first person plural throughout the poem; he never once says "I" or "me," only "we."

As his representation of the feisty Liddell girls indicates, Carroll's "dream-child" is not an angelic Other who inhabits a separate sphere but a close companion capable of engaging in an unintimidated way with anyone she meets. Thus, when he sums up the plot of the story that will follow this prefatory poem, Carroll emphasizes his heroine's unflustered willingness to interact with the world around her; far from being arrested and isolated, Alice is constantly "moving through a land / Of wonders wild and new," chatting freely to every creature she encounters (11). Indeed, the Wonderland books are built around conversations and games, a fact that signals Carroll's desire to envision an adult–child relationship based on interaction and reciprocity. Yet as a number of critics have noticed, these opportunities for mutual engagement almost invariably result in antagonistic, unproductive encounters. Recent explanations of why this is so tend to place the blame squarely on Alice. For example, Auerbach and Kincaid both suggest that an unimaginative Alice tries to coerce the playful Wonderland creatures into conforming "to the absurd rules of civilization, which seem to revolve largely around eating and being eaten" (Auerbach 139). Whereas the creatures are "oblivious to the rules of power [and] entirely at home with play," they contend, Alice has internalized the stifling conventions and "predatory hierarchies" of Victorian society (Kincaid, *Child-Loving* 289, 291).

These readings are exciting in that they resist the idea that Alice embodies untouched innocence. But they are unconvincing insofar as they jump to the opposite extreme, portraying the often-autocratic creatures as "victims" of the machinations of a power-hungry, cruel, and "cannibalistic" Alice (Auerbach 137). Carroll blames neither Alice nor the creatures for the aggression floating around in Wonderland. Instead, he represents it as a *relational* problem that dogs interaction between two unequal parties. The Wonderland books are full of what Kathleen Blake dubs "cat and mouse games": lopsided engagements in which the stronger partner dominates over the weaker one, thus ruining the possibility for mutual pleasure (*Play, Games* 115). Because of her many size changes, Alice alternates between the roles of cat and the mouse, providing Carroll with multiple opportunities to dwell on this problem, which preoccupies him partly because of his concerns about the adult author–child reader relationship. As the opening poem intimates, he longs to conceptualize this liaison as dialogic and pleasurable for both parties. Yet he cannot disregard his own pessimistic conviction that the power differential between adult and child ensures that *all* children's literature functions as coercively as the didactic poetry and sadistic cautionary tales he parodies so brilliantly.

Thus, even as the first two lines of the prefatory poem float a vision of perfect mutuality in which "we" control the boat, the rest of the stanza undermines the idea that adult and child are genuine collaborators:

> For both our oars, with little skill,
> By little arms are plied,
> While little hands make vain pretense
> Our wanderings to guide. (11)

Reciprocity stands revealed here as a sham; the girls are too small to exert any real influence over the course of the boat. Their control over the story, moreover, proves equally illusory. Carroll begins by characterizing the girls as "Imperious," Fate-like figures ("Ah, cruel Three!") who dictate the course and content of the narrative (11). But he subverts this image in the final stanza when he declares "Alice! A childish story take" (12). This classic dedicatory move not only outs Carroll as the author and Alice as a mere audience member, it also suggests that *he* is the truly imperious figure, the one who issues commands and inflicts his story on the child. Self-conscious about the constraints his own vision imposes, Carroll later allows his "dream-child" to exclaim, "'I don't like belonging to another person's dream'" and fight her way out of it, not once but twice (11, 214). Similarly, his photographs of children actively entertain the idea that child sitters function as victims compelled into cooperation rather than willing cocreators of an artistic scene.

Arguing for Carroll's critical self-awareness involves resisting a long tradition of conceiving of the author of *Alice* as an innocent himself, a man wholly unmindful of the possibility that adult attention might impinge on the well-being of the child.[2] Yet the problem of undue influence pervades his work. Consider Alice, who—as Kincaid notes—enters Wonderland having already absorbed so many cultural imperatives that she functions as a parrot, a slave to scripts not of her own making. Given that adults and their texts wield so much power over children's lives, how can they ever develop into creative agents in their own right? Reciprocal aggression, Carroll suggests, provides the only hope: yes, adults impose their maxims, morals, and fantasies onto the child, but the child can rudely reject some of these overtures. In other words, he often represents children as social, socialized beings whose autonomy is limited to saying no to other people's stories about them. In this way, Carroll conceives of identity itself as a collaborative affair, in that it is inevitably *reactive*, formed in reference to the commands and desires of the community one inhabits. His insistent focus on the drawing-room child and his habit of parodying the ideal of primitive simplicity that he elsewhere endorsed have not yet been fully recognized.

SUBVERTING THE IDEAL OF INNOCENCE

Drawing-room children are on prominent display in Carroll's short story "A Photographer's Day Out" (1860), which chronicles what transpires when a bachelor cameraman is invited to capture on film "Father, mother, two sons from school, a host of children from the nursery and the inevitable BABY" (980). One shot forever preserves the image of the bucking baby giving its nurse a nosebleed. Another immortalizes "the three younger girls, as they would have appeared, if by any possibility a black dose could have been administered to each of them at the same moment, and the three tied together by the hair before the expression produced by the medicine had subsided from any of their faces"

(981–82). The final shot, designed by the fond parents, "was to have been the great artistic triumph of the day": an allegorical tableau of "Victory transferring her laurel crown to Innocence, [with] Faith, Hope, and Charity looking on" (982). But the baby (Innocence) has a fit, prompting the mother (Victory) to squeeze it viciously into a ball while two of the girls (Faith and Hope, perhaps?) begin "strangling the third" (982).

Far from prostrating himself at the altar of childhood innocence, Carroll gets tremendous comic mileage here out of the discrepancy between real and ideal young people. Similarly, his photographs frequently undermine standard sentiments about the purity and simplicity of children. For instance, just as he caricatured *The Age of Innocence*, he also produced a subversive revision of Reynolds's *Penelope Boothby* (figure 3.3), another iconic figuration of the Romantic child. Reynolds employs many of the same markers of purity here: once again, he focuses on an angelic child attired in spotless white, whose modestly averted eyes and clasped hands attest to her inwardness and inaccessibility. As Anne Higonnet observes, "the image of the Romantic child is an unconscious one, one that does not connect with adults, one that seems unaware of adults. The child in *Penelope Boothby* is presented for us to look at, and to enjoy looking at, but not for us to make any psychological connection with" (28). As adults, we have already been expelled from the Edenic garden of childhood innocence that Reynolds's girls inhabit. Their detachment enables them to maintain their difference—that otherworldly purity that made them attractive subjects for study in the first place. Critics such as Laura Mulvey who theorize "the gaze" would note that even as Reynolds exalts his child sitter, he also objectifies her by refusing to grant her the power of looking back.

FIGURE 3.3 "Portrait of Penelope Boothby" (1788) by Sir Joshua Reynolds. On loan to the Ashmolean Museum, University of Oxford, from a private collection.

While Carroll's photographs of sleeping girls seem perfectly in line with this ethos of gloating over the child's unconscious innocence, such shots are the exception rather than the rule in his oeuvre. To be sure, his adult sitters often look off to one side, seemingly unaware of the photographer's presence. But his child sitters frequently return the gaze focused on them, as Alexandra (Xie) Kitchin does in Carroll's markedly resistant reenactment of Reynolds's work (see figure 3.4). Far from emphasizing the separateness of adult and child, Carroll downplays or eliminates every aspect of *Penelope Boothby* that attests to the child's otherness. Xie's level stare instantly reveals that she inhabits precisely the same world as those who observe her, not some exotic wilderness. To reinforce this point, Carroll dispenses with the natural background, substituting a pointedly artificial one that locates Xie firmly within the social setting of an artist's studio. And rather than swath his young sitter in pure white, Carroll gives Xie only a crisscross of light material to place over her shoulders, even though other photographs of her from this period reveal that he had plenty of all-white garments at his disposal. Moreover, whereas the original Penelope's oversized costume highlights her dissimilarity from adult women, Xie's does not: Reynolds's girl is adorably miniaturized by her huge mobcap, whereas Xie's hat fits fine.

FIGURE 3.4 Alexandra (Xie) Kitchin as Penelope Boothby (1876) by Lewis Carroll. Gernsheim Collection, Harry Ransom Humanities Research Center, University of Texas at Austin.

As a result, Xie seems less like a Child of Nature, spontaneous and unconstrained, and more like a scripted performer who collaborates with the photographer-director in the production of an artistic scene. Indeed, far from trying to freeze his favorite child sitter in place as an icon of innocence, Carroll invited Xie to inhabit a tremendous range of roles, many of which seem to fit her better than Penelope: Shakespeare's Viola; Kingsley's "The Lost Doll"; a Chinese tea merchant; "Penitence"; a "Captive Princess"; a Greek maiden; a violinist; an Indian woman; a Danish girl, and so on. His habit of asking child friends to dress up in elaborate costumes and play various roles complicates Lindsay Smith's contention—in an otherwise compelling analysis of Carroll's photographic practices—that his shots of young people fetishize "the 'natural' child (as encoded in tousled hair and bare feet, for example), itself a fantasy of the child as exempt from the civilising and regular sartorial characteristics of Victorian culture" (102).

Trying to make sense of Carroll's obvious penchant for involving children in artifice, Smith asserts that his elaborately costumed and posed child sitters are "always enacting a fantasy of cultural and / or ethnic difference" (103). But this description does not acknowledge the range of Carroll's references. To be sure, his child sitters do don Turkish, Chinese, and Indian garb, but they also impersonate English children pictured in famous paintings such as *Penelope Boothby* and William Mulready's *Open Your Mouth and Shut Your Eyes* (1838), as well as girl characters from English poems such as Tennyson's "The Beggar-Maid" and "The May Queen." Sometimes they purport to be classical statues by putting on flowing white robes; other times they pretend to be fairy tale heroines such as "Little Red Riding Hood" and "Cinderella" or famous figures from English history such as Eleanor of Aquitaine, Shakespeare, and Saint George.

Rather than enacting an escape from contemporary civilization, these child sitters function as partners in a type of trendy theatrical play based on a wide-ranging knowledge of cultural artifacts: the popular parlor game of producing *tableaux vivants*. Entire families would participate in these amateur performances, which involved adopting the dress and posture of familiar ethnic "types," abstract qualities (like Faith, Hope, and Charity), famous historical or mythological scenes, and especially figures from well-known paintings, sculptures, or literary works. The fun depended on knowing the source material, so as to embody it (as an actor) or to guess what it was (as an audience member). Thus, as Mary Chapman notes, "Parlor performances of *tableaux vivants* allowed middle-class families to display . . . a shared knowledge of literature and the fine arts" (29). In December 1860, the Liddell family hosted such an event, which Carroll described in glowing terms:

> The *tableaux vivants* were *very* successful. . . . Lady Williamson was there, and supplied the costumes, and herself appeared in one scene. One of the prettiest was Tennyson's *The Sleeping Princess*, acted entirely by children.

> The grouping was capital, I believe by Lady W. . . . I shall try to get them to go through it by daylight in the summer. It would make a beautiful photograph. (quoted in Foulkes 38)

Carroll's focus here on the skill of the adult director as well as the child performers is a characteristic feature of discourse on *tableaux vivants*, which were also known as "living pictures," "living statuary," or *poses plastiques*: stage managers were routinely credited with playing a crucial role in their construction.[3] This point is important to stress because some critics suggest that Carroll's costume shots showcase the natural playfulness of children indulging in an impromptu game of dress-up.[4] On the contrary, these photos immortalize carefully scripted events that attested to—and continued the process of—the child's "cultivation," to quote an 1882 instruction manual for producing amateur *tableaux vivants* (Harrison 113). Living pictures were considered an excellent amusement for young people because they were said to "arouse a taste for history and biography, and turn wavering thoughts toward the great world of literature, painting, sculpture and archeology" (*Tableaux* 11). Indeed, the French aristocrat Madame de Genlis, who helped originate the practice of producing private *tableaux vivants*, conceived of them as an educational tool. Under her coaching, groups of children would enact a series of historical or mythological scenes, while others in the audience guessed what they were.[5]

In choosing to model his pictures around this communal activity, Carroll implicitly characterizes the child as a sociable and socialized being, involved with adults and enmeshed in their culture. Indeed, his albums are full of photographs of the cultivated child: of young people playing musical instruments (guitars, pianos, violins), reading books, looking at sculptures, studying mathematics, attending school, playing chess and whist, brushing their hair, and so on. His photographs of children playing various roles should be added to this list. Even when his child sitters perform the part of uncivilized Other, they remain firmly embedded within the confines of "civilized" English life, as Carroll's (in)famous shot of Irene MacDonald swathed in oriental drapery demonstrates (see figure 3.5). Unlike the barefoot child in *The Age of Innocence*, Irene is properly shod. Her white socks and patent-leather shoes, coupled with the presence of an end table with a house-plant on it, reveal that her natural habitat is not the untamed wilderness. Posed like an odalisque, and clearly aware that she is being observed, she is a conscious collaborator rather than an artless naïf. Thus, when Carroll placed this picture in an album, he invited Irene to sign her name underneath it, in a manner "reminiscent of an artist's own signature at the bottom of a painting" (Mavor 29). But he also drew attention to his own role as the stage manager of this scene by cropping the photograph into an oval shape, thereby dramatizing the presence of his own eye, focused on the child.

FIGURE 3.5 Irene MacDonald (1863) by Lewis Carroll. Gernsheim Collection, Harry Ransom Humanities Research Center, University of Texas at Austin.

Noting that many other Victorian artists composed equally provocative images of children, Karoline Leach argues that if photographs like this "are taken to illustrate some kind of perversion, then it is the mass perversion of a mass culture" (68). And it is true that the eroticism and exoticism that pervade this picture seem to have been an accepted part of the *tableaux vivants* tradition. London theatres and music halls routinely exploited audience fascination with the Orient by composing titillating living pictures with titles like "The Daughter of the Sheik" and "The Moorish Bath." In *The Shows of London* (1978), Richard D. Altick marvels at how little protest these glorified strip-shows engendered; lofty claims that *tableaux vivants* assisted in the transmission of cultural knowledge seem to have trumped concerns about the public display of the female body. Thus, although a character in an 1846 pantomime joked that each new tableau tries "to *outstrip* the others," no real objection was raised against this form of entertainment until the Social Purity campaign of the 1890s (Altick 347).

Impersonating foreign or lower-class characters likewise allowed performers in private homes to show more skin than usual. *Tableaux, Charades and Conundrums* (1893) proposes that young people pose as vagabond or gypsy children in rags, as well as alluringly costumed Dutch and Japanese characters: "*The Industrious*

Fraulein is a dear little Dutch maiden in typical dress . . . industriously knitting . . . The arms may be bare, and should be round and plump" (14). Similarly, *Maud Müller* displays a "pretty girl in Dutch peasant costume, raking hay; portly squire in riding costume looking at her with admiration" (6).

It is no coincidence that in both of these *tableaux*, the girl is depicted as absorbed in an innocent activity, unaware of the eyes fixed on her. As Chapman and other critics have pointed out, Victorian "living pictures"—like many of the artworks they were based on—tend to transfix the female as the passive object of the controlling male gaze.[6] Instruction manuals like this one called on girls and women to embody icons of "piety, purity, submissiveness, and domesticity" (Chapman 32). Or they selected rebellious characters like Bluebeard's wife or Beatrice Cenci but defused their power by selecting for representation moments when these figures are being punished for challenging masculine authority. (Models of feminine action, Chapman explains, are thus transformed into mere objects of male desire.) Either way, female performers "have no gaze themselves. Their eyes are perpetually 'modestly cast down,' and 'face[s] . . . bent downward as if blushing' to signify their chastity. The female gaze is taboo" (Chapman 31).

In this context, the bold outward stares of Carroll's female sitters seem even more remarkable. Though he has been widely attacked for his voyeurism, Carroll declines to objectify these girls, preferring to evoke a sense of charged complicity between viewer and viewed. Indeed, even when his source material explicitly calls for the child performer to function as a passive object of desire, Carroll refuses to comply, as his photograph of Alice Liddell as "The Beggar-Maid" illustrates (see figure 3.6). Rather than selecting a strong character and enfeebling her, Carroll chooses a weak one and endows her with newfound power and agency, since the heroine of Tennyson's 1842 poem exists only to be observed and idolized. Her one action, on arriving at the court of King Cophetua, is to lay "her arms across her breast," presumably to shield herself from the piercing gaze of the king and his lords:

> She in her poor attire was seen:
> One praised her ancles, one her eyes,
> One her dark hair and lovesome mien.
> So sweet a face, such angel grace,
> In all that land had never been:
> Cophetua sware a royal oath:
> "This beggar maid shall be my queen!" (Tennyson 552)

Whereas Tennyson focuses solely on the excitement of the male voyeur(s), Carroll's photograph of Alice Liddell in this role invites viewers to wonder what the beggar-maid wants. Alice's posture does not suggest embarrassment; not only does she boldly return the gaze focused on her, she also cups her hand in

FIGURE 3.6 Alice Liddell as "The Beggar Maid" (1858) by Lewis Carroll. Morris L. Parrish Collection, Department of Rare Books and Special Collections, Princeton University Library.

a gesture that suggests that she is asking for something or beckoning the viewer to come closer. In doing so, she flouts one of the key rules the Victorians used to distinguish good girls from bad ones, respectable women from prostitutes; as both Tracy C. Davis and Judith Walkowitz point out, the act of meeting the male gaze in a public place signaled erotic availability or sexual complicity.[7] Whereas Tennyson adheres to this binary, representing his sweet heroine as a mere object of desire, Carroll entertains the idea that even an "angel" might be a sexual being with desires of her own. As Auerbach notes, this subversive notion also informs a shot Carroll titled "The Elopement" (figure 3.7), in which eleven-year-old Alice Jane Donkin takes her sexual fate into her own hands. Climbing out of her bedroom window using a rope ladder, this adventurous Alice is not just an erotic object but an active agent in her own "fall."

Similarly, as I have already noted, Xie Kitchin's indomitable gaze as Penelope Boothby bespeaks an immodest assertiveness wholly absent from Reynolds's

FIGURE 3.7 Alice Jane Donkin in "The Elopement" (1862) by Lewis Carroll. Gernsheim Collection, Harry Ransom Humanities Research Center, University of Texas at Austin.

painting; she is not merely an object for contemplation but an unabashed voyeur in her own right. Her posture is more aggressive, too; although one arm remains on her lap, the other is raised into a loose fist, a pose that seems defiant, even threatening. Carroll was not afraid to acknowledge the violent tendencies of children, as the vicious behavior of the children in "A Photographer's Day Out" indicates. Whereas traditional framers of "living pictures" pressured female performers to adopt "passive, unaware, and sexually vulnerable" poses (Davis, *Actresses* 125), Carroll often portrays girls as active, conscious, aggressive beings. His photo of Evelyn Dubourg as Joan of Arc (1875) exemplifies this tendency. *Tableaux, Charades and Conundrums* (1893) suggests that this "favorite" figure should appear in "simple peasant dress. . . . Represent her as in Kaulbach's picture, kneeling and looking upward as though rapt in some heavenly vision" (15). In contrast, Carroll dresses his Joan in chain mail, arms her with a sword, invites her to gaze directly forward, and inscribes under the photo "Dulce et decorum est pro patria mori."

Moreover, in "Hiawatha's Photographing" (1857), a poem whose plot closely follows that of "A Photographer's Day Out," Carroll makes merciless fun of the daughter who insists on assuming a "look of 'passive beauty'" for the camera (770). Indeed, one glance at Agnes Weld as "Little Red Riding Hood" (figure 3.8) reveals his willingness to jettison sentimental notions about the sweet gentleness of children. Agnes scowls darkly at the camera, leading Carol

FIGURE 3.8 Agnes Weld as "Little Red Riding Hood" (1857) by Lewis Carroll. Morris L. Parrish Collection, Department of Rare Books and Special Collections, Princeton University Library.

Mavor to read her expression as one of voracious hostility toward the viewer: "Hers are the eyes of the wolf that has presumably just eaten her grandmother; we wonder whether she has eaten the wolf, and whether she is about ready to eat us up" (29).

Once again, a comparison to the specific source material demonstrates that Carroll often declines to freeze the child in place as an icon of purity. This shot is based on a two-verse poetic retelling of the fairy tale, which Carroll inscribed in the album next to the photograph. Although the poem includes a stanza that portrays Little Red as a standard-issue Romantic child, skipping though the woods in solitary delight, Carroll chooses not to build his tableau around this moment. Instead, he asks Agnes to act out the second stanza, which chronicles the moment when the child refuses to be arrested by contact with an outside force:

> And now at last she threads the maze,
> And now she need not fear;
> Frowning, she meets the sudden blaze
> Of moonlight falling clear;
> Nor trembles she, nor turns, nor stays,
> Although the Wolf be near. (quoted in Taylor and Wakeling 140)

This photograph celebrates the steps taken by an ingenious, determined child who keeps moving forward despite the danger she faces in doing so. This threat, not coincidentally, is linked to a moment of suddenly enhanced visibility: the wolf's nearness coincides with the child's exposure to light. Thus, the photographer is associated with the unseen wolf; although he remains invisible, his threatening presence can be palpably sensed.

This is true of many of Carroll's shots of children; he insistently draws attention to his own presence, putting the focus on the intimate and sometimes fraught relationship between photographer and subject. His most famous portrait of the three Liddell sisters provides a perfect example of this tendency (see figure 3.9). Slumped together on a sofa as if unwilling to put their bodies on display, these glowering girls are sitters who refuse to sit nicely. As a photographer, Carroll knew that the demands he made on his subjects were discomfiting. Recognizing that the long minutes of stillness required by the collodion process were tedious, he often referred to his child sitters as "victims" of his passion for securing shots.[8] Held hostage by the unseen shutterbug, the Liddell girls respond to this imposition with some serious hostility of their own, in a photograph that encapsulates the phenomenon I am calling reciprocal aggression. As in the picture of "Little Red Riding Hood," here too the child fights back against an encroachment on her liberty.[9]

FIGURE 3.9 The Liddell sisters (1858) by Lewis Carroll. Gernsheim Collection, Harry Ransom Humanities Research Center, University of Texas at Austin.

Such shots belie Diane Waggoner's assertion that Carroll portrays children as "playful, relaxed, spontaneous, [and] uncontrolled" (159). On the contrary, his photographs are records of engagement and influence. His child sitters are scripted—and sometimes, it seems, *con*scripted—partners in the process of producing art; their individuality most often manifests itself through resistance to the unseen stage manager. Their outward gaze and often annoyed expression draws attention to the man behind the curtain, as does the obviously artificial environment Carroll prefers to use. As Waggoner herself acknowledges, Carroll's preference for imperfect backdrops and costumes "disrupt[s] the artistry of representation" and publicizes the fact that the shots were taken in a private rather than a professional setting (155). The decisions Carroll makes about how to display these photos likewise seem motivated by a desire to leave traces of his own presence, his own touch: they are carefully cropped, painted, pasted in albums, framed by his own handwriting.[10] His aim is to immortalize an intimate *relationship*: interaction, not objectification, is the governing dynamic that informs these images.

Describing Carroll's photographs of little girls, Vladimir Nabokov comments, "His were sad scrawny little nymphets, bedraggled and half-dressed, or rather semi-undraped, as if participating in some dusty and dreadful charade" (quoted in Nickel 11). While attentive to the theatricality of these shots, this description fails to do justice to the powerful presence of sitters like Xie and Alice Liddell, who seem neither pathetic nor submissive. Carroll resists patriarchal artistic conventions that enable undisputed male voyeurism. Yet these images are still upsetting. The sitters are not women, after all, but children, so the intimacy and intensity of their relationship with the adult photographer sometimes seems disturbing. However much we decry the tendency of nostalgic artists to fixate on the preservation of innocence, most of us support the idea of establishing a boundary between child and adult that precludes the formation of romantic, erotic, and even some kinds of artistic partnerships. Carroll's photos are disturbing not because they portray the child as an innocent, untouchable inhabitant of a separate sphere—that is, after all, the image of childhood that has gained widespread acceptance today—but because he *declines* to establish a firm line of division, representing child and adult as genuine collaborators. At the same time, he hints that the smaller party might not be an entirely willing partner—an idea he dwells on at length in the *Alice* books.

"WILL YOU, WO'N'T YOU, WILL YOU, WO'N'T YOU, WILL YOU JOIN THE DANCE?"

In creating the character of Alice, Carroll once again departs from the Romantic ideal of innocence on display in Reynolds's paintings. Far from inhabiting a childhood Eden, Alice is already excluded from the beautiful garden, which she struggles to regain access to during her first adventure in Wonderland. Moreover, like the heroine of "The Elopement," this Alice precipitates her own "fall"; "burning with curiosity," she leaps down the rabbit hole and, once underground, continues to insert herself into a variety of social situations, including parties, games, and conversations (16). Once again, Carroll focuses his attention not on the Child of Nature but on the drawing-room child, who has read and been taught "all sorts of things" (25). Alice knows the rules of games like croquet and chess; she knows how to curtsey and make polite conversation; she knows that her own comfortable home is preferable to that of poor Mabel, who lives in a "poky little house" and has "next to no toys to play with" (26). Her adventures may take place "in a realm beyond the confines of nurseries and schoolrooms," but Alice herself is and remains firmly enmeshed in that milieu (Taylor and Wakeling 53).

Thus, even as Carroll characterizes his heroine as a dreamer and a storyteller in her own right, he also acknowledges that she is always already the subject of other people's stories, other people's dreams. "'There ought to be a book written about me, that there ought!'" Alice exclaims early on in her first Wonderland adventure, "'And when I grow up, I'll write one'" (40). But clearly, her story has already been written for her. A scripted being rather than a blank slate, Alice must wrest away a writing utensil from a male figure—as she does twice during the course of her adventures—if she hopes to usurp some control over her own self-fashioning.

Moreover, Carroll's target audience clearly consists of similarly socialized children. The humor of the opening scenes, in which Alice misremembers what she has been taught, depends on child readers knowing the right answers.

Educated audience members are expected to giggle at her assertion that "four times five is twelve" and "London is the capital of Paris," not to mention her mangling of Isaac Watts's popular children's poem "How Doth the Little Busy Bee" (25). This focus on the knowing, literate child conflicts with the Child of Nature paradigm, as John Ruskin seems to have recognized. In his essay "Fairy Stories," which was published three years after *Alice's Adventures in Wonderland*, Ruskin criticizes children's authors who conceive of their audience as civilized beings: "In the best stories recently written for the young, there is a taint which it is not easy to define, but which inevitably follows on the author's addressing himself to children bred in school-rooms and drawing-rooms, instead of fields and woods—children whose favourite amusements are premature imitations of the vanities of elder people" (127). Lamenting a lost "simplicity" (128), Ruskin particularly objects to the "fine satire . . . gleaming through every playful word" of recent fairy stories (127). "Children should laugh but not mock," he cautions, "and when they laugh, it should not be at the weaknesses and the faults of others" (128).

Just as Ruskin's own child-related prose (and practices) did not always align with this Romantic rhetoric, so too Carroll oscillates between celebrating children's sweet naïveté and conceiving of them as knowing, judgmental, and capable of appreciating satire. Besides encouraging child readers to laugh at Alice's errors, he allows Alice herself to deem various Wonderland creatures "absurd" (34), "perfectly idiotic" (59), and "stupid" (105), and to emit "a little scream of laughter" when she hears that the Duchess has boxed the ears of the Queen of Hearts (81). Auerbach brilliantly demonstrates how Carroll's belated efforts to characterize his heroine as "loving and gentle" are belied by her actual behavior in Wonderland (quoted in Auerbach 131); Alice functions less as an icon of purity and simplicity than as a creature of appetite and aggression. Yet her often menacing manner does not differentiate her from the inhabitants of Wonderland, since they, too, often lose their tempers and act in autocratic, insensitive, or insulting ways. Indeed, Alice and the creatures take turns intimidating each other. Addressed by an enormous Alice, for instance, the terrified White Rabbit "started violently . . . and scurried away into the darkness as hard as he could go" (24), but a few scenes later, the situation is reversed: the Rabbit abruptly issues orders at Alice, who "was so much frightened that she ran off at once in the direction it pointed to" (38). Similarly, Alice petrifies small animals by threatening to set her cat Dinah on them, but immediately afterwards finds herself "terribly frightened" by a giant puppy who "might be hungry, in which case it would be very likely to eat her up" (46).

Rather than demonize either Alice or the creatures, Carroll dwells on difficulties that ensue when big and little creatures interact. The sociable Alice *wants* to play with the puppy, but she cannot enjoy their game because she is not "the right size," and therefore "it was very like having a game of play with a cart-horse, and expecting every moment to be trampled under its feet" (46). In a cat and mouse game like this one, as Kathleen Blake notes, the power imbalance between the two parties precludes mutual pleasure. Indeed, Blake contends that such unbalanced contests do not even deserve to be called games, since no real reciprocity is possible when "the power and the will to play are all on one side" (114–15). The Queen of Hearts's croquet game is the paradigmatic example of a "pseudogame" of this sort (213), but Blake argues that "play" in the *Alice* books always involves a degree of imposition. In doing so, she persuasively counters the claim—forwarded by Roger Henkle, Kincaid, and others—that Carroll sets up a neat dichotomy between play and power. Pointing to the caucus-race, these critics contend that the Wonderland creatures engage in joyous, anarchic "free play," which the power-hungry Alice resists because of her obsession with rules and mastery. But Blake points out that this event "is after all a contest, marked out and directed, solo, by the Dodo," who pressures an uninterested Alice into participating and unilaterally determines who wins (117).

Indeed, the problem of unequal engagement is even more central to the *Alice* books than Blake suggests. It shows up not only in incidents involving Alice but also in the songs the creatures sing. Both "The Walrus and The Carpenter" and the Mock Turtle's ditty about the whiting and the snail elaborate on the theme of how dangerous it is to collaborate with individuals who are more powerful than you are. Invited to share "a pleasant walk, a pleasant talk" with the Walrus and the Carpenter, the young oysters suffer the usual fate of mice engaged by cats: they are consumed (169). Similarly, in the Mock Turtle's song, a large sea creature invites a small one to join in a communal dance. The whiting exclaims,

> "You can really have no notion how delightful it will be
> When they take us up and throw us, with the lobsters, out to sea!"
> But the snail replied "Too far, too far!" and gave a look askance—
> Said he thanked the whiting kindly, but he would not join the dance. (98)

Refusing to take no for an answer, the pushy whiting tries to sweet-talk the snail into participating—"turn not pale, beloved snail, but come and join the dance"—and then continues to beleaguer him: "Will you, wo'n't you, will you, wo'n't you, will you join the dance? / Will you, wo'n't you, will you, wo'n't you, wo'n't you join the dance?" (98). Since the song ends with this question still hanging in the air, we do not know whether the snail ultimately succumbs, as the poor little oysters do, to the solicitations of the larger animal. But we can guess that no good will come of it if he does.

Critics often speak of Carroll's "compulsive interest in smallness," assuming that he embraces an "erotics of tininess" (L. Smith 101; Mavor 22). But as the foregoing examples indicate, he often associates littleness with dire vulnerability. As Alice observes, "three inches is such a wretched height to be" (53). Had

Carroll truly been obsessed with freezing Alice in place as an eternal child, one might expect that her many size changes would demonstrate the advantages of being small. And indeed, when she shrinks for the first time, Alice is delighted to discover that "she was now the right size for going through the little door into that lovely garden" (21). But being little does not earn Alice entry into the Edenic garden. Indeed, shrinking proves as dangerous as growing: just as her rapid expansion in the rabbit's house almost breaks her neck, her unexpectedly speedy diminution puts her at risk of drowning in her own (previously shed) tears and "going out altogether, like a candle" (21).

Rather than suggesting that either state is preferable, Carroll uses the occasion of Alice's size changes to dwell on the difficulties small creatures face when interacting with large ones. At first, Alice cannot comprehend why little mice and birds might not enjoy playing with her cat Dinah. But after her encounter with the huge puppy, she understands their position, as indicated by her conscious decision to minimize the disparity between herself and others in order to grease the wheels of interaction. Spotting the Duchess's tiny house, she exclaims, "'Whoever lives there . . . it'll never do to come upon them *this* size: why, I should frighten them out of their wits!' So she began nibbling at the right-hand bit [of the mushroom] again, and did not venture to go near the house till she had brought herself down to nine inches high" (57). Similarly, when she arrives at the March Hare's house, which is larger, Alice snacks on the other side of the mushroom to make herself bigger. Endowed with the ability to manipulate her size to suit her surroundings, she finally manages to get into the beautiful garden.

In other words, rather than fetishizing smallness or imagining a world in which growth is arrested, Carroll constructs a fantasy about being able to control one's own size so one can match up evenly with anyone one happens to meet. For an adult who loves to interact with children, this is a natural reverie to indulge in; anxious that the disparity between big and little creature means that collaboration endangers the smaller party, Carroll dreams up a magical mushroom that enables any two creatures to engage as equals. But Carroll's attentiveness to the issue of asymmetrical engagements does not simply stem from a generic anxiety about adult–child relationships. It also reflects his more particular concern about the potentially coercive nature of the adult author–child reader relationship. The opening chapters of the first *Alice* book reveal Carroll's intense self-consciousness about working in a genre that had habitually tried to bully young people into submissive compliance.[11] He quickly tries to distance himself from this didactic tradition by parodying the pious poetry of Watts and underscoring the sadism of cautionary tales, those "nice little stories" in which children get "burnt, and eaten up by wild beasts, and other unpleasant things, all because they *would* not remember the simple rules their friends had taught them" (19–20).

Carroll here objects to the tendency of children's authors to pass themselves off as the kindly "friends" of young people, even as they dream up terrible tortures for child characters in an effort to frighten child readers into submission. In her autobiography *A London Child of the 1870s* (1934), M. V. Hughes recalls two such books, both of which promoted "only one virtue, obedience to parents and kind teachers" (52–53). One was entitled *The Safe Compass*, yet in it "the disobedient were gored by bulls, those who laughed at the infirm fell down wells and were crippled for life, busy mockers died in want" and so on (52). Alice has thoroughly absorbed the cruel logic of such stories; when she falls into the pool of salt-water, she exclaims, "'I shall be punished for [crying so much] now, I suppose, by being drowned in my own tears!'" (28).

Hughes also reports that "many people of my age must have imbibed their early religious notions from the same book I did": *The Peep of Day* (1833), by Favell Lee Mortimer. Indeed, this macabre text reportedly sold over a million copies. It featured such tidbits as:

> God has covered your bones with flesh. . . . Will your bones break?—Yes, they would, if you were to fall down from a high place, or if a cart were to go over them . . . How easy it would be to hurt your poor little body! If it were to fall into the fire, it would be burned up. If hot water fell upon it, it would be scalded. If it were to fall into deep water, and not taken out very soon, you would be drowned. If a great knife were run through your body, the blood would come out. If a great box were to fall on your head, your head would be crushed. (5)

And so on. Just as the Duchess digs her "uncomfortably sharp" chin into Alice's shoulder to drive home her morals (88), Mortimer (and others) used the threat of violence to pressure children into passive compliance with their didactic agenda: "God only can keep your body from all harm. . . . Kneel down and say to God, 'Pray, keep my poor little body from getting hurt'" (Mortimer 6).

Carroll indicates his determination to forge a different path right from the start of the first *Alice* story: though she falls from a great height, "Alice was not a bit hurt" (18). Moreover, her adventures begin when she rejects the tedious book her sister is reading. Besides signaling Carroll's desire to depart from what he viewed as an uninspiring literary tradition, this moment also attests to his commitment to encouraging child readers to take an irreverent attitude toward texts. Despite her bold opening act, Alice at first exhibits an unfortunate tendency to parrot back bits of information gleaned from books, but Carroll quickly attempts to persuade readers that adopting this slavish stance is silly; it is much more fun to spoof, transform, or creatively (mis)interpret texts, as Alice does unwittingly with the Watts and Southey poems and then purposefully with "Jabberwocky." Indeed, an extremely large proportion of Wonderland conversations center around texts: besides reciting poems herself, Alice listens, interrupts, and analyzes the songs, stories, and verses performed by the irrepressible creatures. Literature, Carroll thus suggests, should be actively *engaged* with, not merely echoed back and obeyed.

Carroll further encourages child readers to talk back to texts by employing a chatty narrator who addresses his young audience directly, often in a way that requires response. For example, during Alice's journey down the rabbit hole, the narrator parenthetically remarks, "fancy, *curtseying* as you're falling through the air! Do you think you could manage it?" (17). Similarly, the last line of *Through the Looking-Glass* telegraphs his desire to draw child readers into a dialogue; after describing how Alice ponders the question of whether she or the Red King dreamed up the story, the narrator concludes by inquiring "Which do *you* think it was?" (249). As his decision to end with a question indicates, Carroll wants children to conceptualize texts not as the last word on any given subject but as a starting point that enables their own creative responses. Unlike Mortimer, whose catechistic questions offer no opportunity for original input ("Will your bones break?—Yes"), Carroll asks open-ended questions that do not have a single right answer. As Barbara Wall observes, he seems eager to establish a "close and comfortable . . . partnership" between the adult narrator and child readers (100, 102).

To that end, he undermines the omniscience of his omniscient narrator, refusing to present him as an all-knowing authority figure. For instance, after describing how the creatures accompanying Alice in the train carriage respond to her by thinking in chorus, the narrator adds, "(I hope you understand what *thinking in chorus* means—for I must confess that *I* don't)" (155). Similarly, when Humpty Dumpty mysteriously remarks that he pays words when he asks them to do extra work, the narrator explains that "(Alice didn't venture to ask what he paid them with; and so you see I ca'n't tell *you*)" (197). Here Carroll attempts to lessen the disparity between adult storyteller and child reader by suggesting that the narrator's knowledge is limited (just like Alice's). Rather than attempting to effect a strict separation between adult and child, he aims to inspire intimate interaction. As should be evident by now, parentheses function as his preferred tool for establishing a congenial rapport with children; he uses them not just to address the child reader but also to confirm his closeness with Alice. When she mentions Dinah, for instance, his interpolated explanation "(Dinah was the cat.)" demonstrates his familiarity with her household and represents an effort to endear himself to child readers by acting as a helpful informant (17).

Other parenthetical comments attest to the narrator's intimate knowledge of the way Alice's mind works. During her fall down the rabbit hole, for example, he uncovers her private motivation right in the middle of one of her speeches:

> "I must be getting somewhere near the centre of the earth. Let me see: that would be four thousand miles down, I think—" (for, you see, Alice had learnt several things of this sort in her lessons in the school-room, and though this was not a *very* good opportunity for showing off her knowledge, as there was no one to listen to her, still it was good practice to say it over) "—yes, that's about the right distance." (17)

Carroll's desire to achieve intimate intercourse with children manifests itself strongly in this passage. He attempts to form a chummy relationship with child readers by using the casual phrase "you see" and poking fun at Alice for their amusement (two tactics he employs repeatedly in the opening chapters). At the same time, though, he implies that he and his heroine share an extremely close connection. By insinuating his remark within hers, he visually signals his ability to penetrate her thoughts. It is as if they are engaged in a kind of conversation, an impression that is confirmed a few pages later when Alice overhears his thoughts just as he does hers. As a number of critics have pointed out, she responds to his observation that she enjoys "pretending to be two people" by exclaiming, "But it's no use now . . . to pretend to be two people!" (21). Similarly, when he confidently declares that "wise little Alice" would never drink from an unidentified bottle, she agrees, "No, I'll look first . . . and see whether it's marked '*poison*'" (19).

As the presence of so many parenthetical intrusions indicates, Carroll strives to create a kind of children's literature characterized by dialogic exchange rather than unidirectional indoctrination. In other words, he wants to produce texts that encourage audience intervention rather than enforcing the author's intention. "Jabberwocky" stands as a shining example of this sort of writing; incomprehensible at first, it can only be understood after the reader engages in good deal of creative work. During their long conversation about the meaning of various words in this poem, Alice and Humpty Dumpty show readers how this process works. Puzzled at first, Alice quickly catches on when Humpty Dumpty makes up his own meanings for words like "gyre" and "gimble." Entering into the spirit of this new game, she ingeniously proposes that "'the wabe" is "the grass-plot round a sun-dial" (199). But the two intrepid interpreters only explicate the very first verse, leaving five more stanzas full of mysterious words and phrases—such as "frumious Bandersnatch"—for child readers to define for themselves. A text, Carroll suggests, should function like a riddle that has no definite answer (the Mad Hatter's favorite party trick). Thus, during Alice's final moments in Wonderland, the White Queen recites to her a poem that is also a riddle, and invites her to respond: "'Take a minute to think about it,'" she says, "'and then guess'" (202).

Other similarly provoking texts dot the pages of the two *Alice* books, including Humpty Dumpty's own poem, which concludes with the spectacularly inconclusive line "I tried to turn the handle, but—" (202). Like the final line of *Through the Looking-Glass* itself, this ending makes room for audience participation; any reader hoping to make sense of this poem, which features multiple dashes of this sort, would have to fill in the blanks for himself. The flocks of asterisks Carroll incorporates into both *Alice* stories perform a similar function, breaking up the flow of the narrative at unpredictable moments. Indeed, all of these orthographic devices—asterisks, dashes, parentheses—combine to create an atmosphere that actively encourages interruption. John Tenniel's brilliant illustrations pick up on and exacerbate this rowdy ambiance; they too appear erratically, pushing the text around the page in odd and unexpected ways, breaking up sentences, paragraphs, poems, chapters, even individual words. At the same time, the episodic structure of both narratives might be said to invite additions; since they essentially consist of a series of unconnected encounters, it would be easy to alter them, to insert a new incident into either one.

Arguing that readers derive pleasure from places where the text can be perforated—"the seam, the cut, the deflation, the *dissolve*"—Roland Barthes claims that we are drawn to texts that we can imagine ourselves rewriting, that prompt us to become producers as well as consumers of meaning (*Pleasures* 7). Barthes dubs such stories "writerly" texts (*S/Z* 4). Clearly, Carroll's stories fit into this category, as indicated by the fact that both *Alice* books include a scene in which the heroine wrests away a pencil from a male figure. During her first adventure, Alice steals the squeaky pencil of one of the jurors in the trial scene. Then, near the start of *Through the Looking-Glass*, she interferes when the White King attempts to write a note in his memorandum-book: Alice "took hold of the end of the pencil . . . and began writing for him. The poor King looked puzzled and unhappy, and struggled with the pencil for some time without saying anything; but Alice was too strong for him" (139–40).

Ultimately, though, Carroll is too aware of the fact that the *Alice* stories are—to quote the White Knight—"my own invention" to allow himself to indulge in the fantasy that the child functions as an equal partner in the production of narrative (217). His prefatory poem, as I have suggested, simultaneously floats and retracts this idea; immediately after celebrating Tertia's constant interruptions, Carroll admits that when he begins to tell the story, the children actually lapse into "silence" (11). Such vacillation continues in the body of the books. During his description of Alice's encounter with the Tweedle brothers, for example, Carroll characterizes his heroine as a storyteller in her own right: "'But it certainly was funny,' (Alice said afterwards, when she was telling her sister the history of all this), 'to find myself singing *Here we go round the mulberry bush*'" (167). Soon afterward, however, the brothers show her the sleeping Red King and inform her that she is merely a made-up character: "'you're only a sort of thing in his dream,'" they jeer, causing Alice to break down in tears (174). Here Carroll hints that his "dream-child" functions not as the source of the fantasy but as the object of it (11).

Moreover, Carroll suggests that the fantasy he weaves around his heroine is not necessarily one she would have chosen for herself; he actively entertains the idea that his own brand of nonsense, which he finds so entertaining, is not something children will necessarily enjoy. Thus, Alice derives no pleasure from her inadvertent parody of Isaac Watts's poem; on the contrary, she bursts into tears when she finds that she cannot recite the poem correctly. Later, the Gnat tries to tease Alice into making puns, rhymes, and other jokes based on wordplay, but she remains completely uninterested in this form of fun. More than that, her decidedly unpleasant experience at the Mad Tea Party attests to Carroll's recognition that nonsense can easily make children feel frustrated, shut out, and stupid. Echoing their quirky creator, the creatures attending this party produce statements that are just as inscrutable as "Jabberwocky": "The Hatter's remark seemed to [Alice] to have no sort of meaning in it, and yet it was certainly English" (70). But rather than enabling Alice to engage in creative play, such impenetrable declarations make her feel "dreadfully puzzled" and incapable of maintaining a conversation (70); when the Dormouse makes another baffling comment, Alice is "so confused" that she falls silent (75), a state the creatures themselves seem to encourage, by shushing her, calling her "stupid" (75), and telling her that she "shouldn't talk" (76).

Indeed, although the two *Alice* books are filled with nonsensical moments that seem aimed at opening up a dialogue with readers, the word itself is invariably used as a negative term to shut people up. To choose just one of many examples: when the Queen of Hearts begins screaming, " 'Off with her head!' " Alice barks out " 'Nonsense!' " in order to silence her (80).[12] "Jabberwocky"-type writing may grant readers lots of room to exercise their creativity, but Carroll realizes that the act of withholding meaning can easily be experienced as a form of deprivation, punishment, or exclusion. Thus, although there is plenty of space at the Mad Hatter's tea table, the creatures greet Alice with the rude cry " 'No room! No room!' " (68). And the revelation that the Hatter's riddle has no right answer makes Alice feel disappointed and stumped, not liberated and inspired to come up with her own solution. Rather than scorning his heroine for her lack of creativity, Carroll hints that there *is* something punitive about the act of producing open-ended texts, since the Hatter poses his riddle right after Alice chastises him "with some severity" for being rude: "The Hatter opened his eyes very wide on hearing this; but all he *said* was 'Why is a raven like a writing desk?' " (68). Textual incompleteness emerges here as a retaliatory act, an idea that recurs later in the scene when the Dormouse threatens to deprive Alice of the rest of his story because she offends him: " 'If you ca'n't be civil, you'd better finish the story for yourself' " (74).

Such moments indicate Carroll's recognition of the fact that the kind of literature he prefers demands a great deal of imaginative exertion from child readers; it prods them into participating at a higher level of engagement. Taking someone who is used to being passive and forcing them to be creative is an aggressive act, as the Dormouse's own experience at the party demonstrates. This dozy creature would prefer to remain dormant, but the March Hare and Mad Hatter pour hot tea on its nose to make it wake up and join in the conversation, then pinch it "on both sides at once" to pressure it into telling them a story (73). Even as Carroll tries to differentiate himself from overtly didactic authors like Watts and Mortimer, he realizes that his effort to promote creativity and linguistic playfulness constitutes a pedagogic agenda in its own right. Thus, Alice is *educated* into liking nonsense; under Humpty Dumpty's tutelage, she learns to appreciate rather than dread the opportunity to make her own meaning. Readers also watch her develop a willingness to take on the work of authorship. When the March Hare asks her to tell a story, an "alarmed" Alice begs off with the excuse " 'I'm afraid I don't know one' " (73). But a few scenes later, she "timidly" agrees to recount some of her adventures for the Mock Turtle and Gryphon, and by the time she leaps through the looking-glass, as I have shown, she comfortably inhabits the role of storyteller (100).

Alice herself recognizes that her fall down the rabbit hole does not free her from didacticism: " 'How the creatures order one about, and make one repeat lessons! . . . I might just as well be at school at once' " (101). The realm of fantasy offers children no reprieve from the overtures of pushy adults. Thus, even after Alice achieves her dream of becoming a queen, she cannot escape other people's efforts to direct, control, and contain her; two other queens immediately turn up and begin barking out orders, criticizing her behavior, and subjecting her to an extended examination on arithmetic and other unpleasant topics (230). Like many other fantasy lands created by Golden Age children's authors, including Neverland and Oz, Wonderland does not offer its child protagonist an idyllic safe haven from adult power and social demands.[13] Indeed, Alice resembles the poor Dormouse, in that she encounters pressure from every direction; Tenniel's famous picture of her squished between the two queens was inspired by more than one passage that describes how they "pushed her so, one on each side" (244).

As Judith Plotz persuasively demonstrates in *Romanticism and the Vocation of Childhood* (2001), writers who embraced the Child of Nature paradigm characterized childhood as a time of blissful freedom from societal constraints; their urge to arrest the child in place arose out of a belief that the young enjoyed an autonomy unavailable to adults. In contrast, Carroll recognizes childhood as *the* period during which socialization takes place. Thus, when Alice contemplates what it would mean to remain a child forever, she concludes that it would not be nice: " 'always to have lessons to learn! Oh, I shouldn't like *that!*' " (40). Carroll's point in this lighthearted passage is not to bemoan the evils of adult influence; he cheerfully accepts education as an unavoidable fact of child life. More than that, he portrays adult–child interaction as a major source of pleasure for both parties and a crucial enabler of identity formation (rather than the death knell of autonomy). Alice's disorientation after her fall down the rabbit hole ("Who in the world am I?") stems from the fact that she is so used to being enmeshed in a network of relationships—with family members, nurses, governesses, other children, pets and so on—that she does not know how to define herself in their absence (24). Her worst moments in Wonderland come not when creatures order her around but when no one pays any attention to her at all, making her feel miserably lonely.

Since contact with other people is both inevitable and desirable, the question is how to protect yourself from being overwhelmed by outside influences. Faced with a variety of creatures who aggressively order her around, Alice repeatedly exercises the power of saying no: she objects to the idea of belonging to the Red King's dream; she declines to become the White Knight's prisoner; she physically turns on the Red Queen; and twice she rejects Wonderland entirely, ultimately declaring " 'I ca'n't stand this any longer!' " (244). Since young people are always already subject to external pressure from adults, the power of negation functions not as a naughty luxury (as Kincaid suggests) but as the essential tool for shaping a sense of self.[14] Carroll's habit of conceiving of identity formation in terms of denial reveals itself near the start of *Alice's Adventures in Wonderland*, when Alice worries that if she returns home, she will discover that she is her slow-witted friend Mabel. To avoid this uncomfortable fate, she decides that she will stick her head out of the rabbit hole and demand " 'Who am I then? Tell me that first, and then, if I like being that person, I'll come up: if not, I'll stay down here till I'm somebody else' " (26).

Formless at first ("Who am I?"), the child's identity develops not in isolation but in response to the demands placed on it by others. This is a kind of agency—limited, reactive—that does not pretend to autonomy, and it stands in direct contrast to the Child of Nature paradigm, which posits an authentic core of selfhood that emanates from within and can only be destroyed by contact with the outside world. Carroll once again endorses the rubric of reciprocal aggression: acknowledging that adults (including himself) inflict their ideas about childhood on the child, he suggests that the sanity of young people depends on rudely rejecting the most unwelcome overtures.

Crucially, one of the adult ideas Alice resists most vehemently during her adventures is the message that she should remain a child forever. "Now if you'd asked *my* advice," Humpty Dumpty pompously observes, "I'd have said 'Leave off at seven' " (194). Unmoved by this absurd proposal, Alice indignantly informs him that "I never ask advice about growing" and—when he continues to press her—she firmly changes the subject: "They had had quite enough about the subject of age, she thought" (194–95). Similarly, when the officious railway guard tells her, "You're traveling the wrong way," Alice completely ignores this complaint, even when another gentleman on the train seconds it by suggesting that she take a return ticket. "Indeed I sha'n't!" Alice retorts (157), and a few pages later she reaffirms her commitment to moving forward: "for I certainly won't go *back*" (162).

Rather than interpreting such moments as unproblematic evidence for Carroll's own desire to arrest the girlchild in place, we should instead recognize that they represent his willingness to grapple, quite self-consciously, with the question of how damaging this particular adult yearning is, and how young people should respond to it. In other words, Carroll acknowledges this arresting impulse as one of the impositions that pushy adults place on children. What should children do when confronted with such nudging? If we assume that Alice is intended to function as a positive role model, the foregoing incidents send the message that young people should refuse to listen to such nonsense and get away from the adult in question as fast as possible. Alice's encounter with the White Knight toward the end of *Through the Looking-Glass* likewise promotes this idea. Many critics maintain that the White Knight functions as a stand-in for Carroll, interpreting his determination to hold Alice prisoner as an admission of the author's own longing to freeze the child in place.[15] Indeed, this scene does stage a skirmish between an adult who wants to capture and slow down a child and the child herself, who is determined to move forward and graduate to more grown-up status: "'I don't want to be anybody's prisoner,'" Alice announces, "I want be a Queen" (216).

What critical accounts of this scene rarely acknowledge is that this conflict is *instantly* resolved in favor of Alice; in response to her declaration, the Knight promptly gives up his claim on her and agrees to help her move forward: "'So you will, when you've crossed the next brook. . . . I'll see you safe to the end of the wood—and then I must go back'" (216-17). Like many other scenes in the *Alice* books, then, this one invites children to regard adult desires as something they can say no to: it is less about arrest than about *resisting* arrest, something Alice does over and over again during the course of her adventures. Constantly disengaging herself from a variety of unpleasant interactions, Alice operates as an escape artist from the very first scene—in which she flees the prosaic company of her sister—to the final moments of both adventures, when she busts out of the chaotic fantasyland created by Carroll.

Moreover, Carroll strongly implies that Alice is right to resist the pressure to remain childlike by introducing readers to a number of characters who are absurd and unattractive precisely because they are cases of arrested development. Although they are clearly identified as "men," for example, the Tweedle brothers look "like a couple of great school-boys" and behave like infants (166); besides their fussing and fighting over a rattle, their extreme egotism leads Alice to denounce them as "Selfish things!" (174). They and the equally querulous Humpy Dumpty are literally arrested; when Alice first sees the Tweedles, they stand so still that she forgets they are alive and gazes at them as if they are "wax-works"

(165). Here Carroll links being frozen in place with being objectified; elsewhere he goes so far as to link this state with death. When Alice spots Humpty Dumpty, his expression is so "fixed" that she assumes "he must be a stuffed figure" (191). Although this embryonic character tries to persuade Alice of the benefits of remaining frozen at an early age, his own dire fate demonstrates the nonviability of that kind of life. By emphasizing the self-centeredness of these childlike figures, Carroll anticipates Barrie's un-Romantic habit of associating eternal innocence with "heartless" egocentrism (*Peter and Wendy* 166).

Despite these indications that Carroll intends to deride the adult yearning for eternal youth, the characterization of the White Knight shows how conflicted he remains in regard to this issue. A decidedly childish figure himself, the Knight seems designed to elicit amused sympathy rather than harsh ridicule. Although he clearly desires to detain Alice and delay her development, this "gentle," "mild," "kindly" figure is hardly portrayed as a villain (224). Indeed, the narrator informs us that in later years, Alice recalls the occasion of listening to his song very fondly. Moreover, however problematic the Knight's desire to control and arrest Alice may be, this "foolish" character is so ineffectual, so easy to resist, that such solicitations wind up seeming fairly harmless (224). Yet at the same time, as U. C. Knoepflmacher has noted, this scene rather ruthlessly exposes and mocks the tendency of narcissistic adults to assume ownership over and project their own feelings onto children. Wandering through the world "with his eyes shut, muttering to himself" (220), the Knight ignores and misreads Alice, making this one of many scenes in the second *Alice* book that explore the "subjective distortions by which we remake others into imaginary self-reflections" (Knoepflmacher, *Ventures* 222).

Moreover, by having the White Knight spout a parody of Wordsworth, Carroll associates such self-involved fantasizing specifically with Romantic discourse. Like so many other interpolated texts in the *Alice* books, the Knight's song dwells on the perils of entering into a relationship characterized by fake or failed mutuality. In it, Carroll sends up the self-absorption of the poet-narrator of "Resolution and Independence" (1807), suggesting that his efforts to draw the old leech-gatherer into conversation do not attest to any desire for genuine communication or reciprocity. Thus, in Carroll's version, the Wordsworthian narrator ignores everything the "aged aged man" says in response to his questions. His extreme egotism is hilarious, but the parody conveys a real concern that artists, in their narcissism, can actually harm the hapless objects of their attention. Thus, Carroll's poet-narrator physically abuses the subject of his tale, shaking the old man "from side to side, / Until his face was blue" and accompanying his often-reiterated question with violence: "I cried, 'Come, tell me how you live!' / And thumped him on the head" (224–25).

As Ruth Berman notes, Carroll's phrasing here recalls another Wordsworth poem in which the object under interrogation is a child; in "Anecdote for

Fathers" (1798), the speaker repeatedly demands that his child explain himself ("Why? Edward, tell me why?") while physically accosting him ("I said and took him by the arm") [lines 48, 26]. Rather unfairly, Carroll suggests that the Wordsworthian narrator is himself unaware of how his desires constrain the liberty, self-expression, and well-being of his child addressee.[16] Keen to avoid what he views as a highly unself-conscious and aggressive authorial stance, Carroll repeatedly emphasizes his own recognition that being figured as the subject of other people's imaginings can constitute a painful form of subjection for the child.

Indeed, Alice so dislikes the idea of belonging to another person's dream that a few scenes after she tearfully dismisses this possibility as "nonsense" (174), she contemplates going back to rouse the Red Knight in order to reassure herself that her Wonderland adventure really is "*my* dream" (214)—and this despite the fact that the Tweedles have warned her that waking him up might make her vanish like a blown-out candle. Just as Carroll's photographs often alert viewers to his own invisible presence, the many moments in the *Alice* books that raise the possibility that Alice is "fabulous" rather than "real" draw our attention to the author hovering behind the scenes (210, 174). Indeed, the very last line of *Through the Looking-Glass* invites such exposure; although it asks child readers to decide whether the Red King or Alice dreamed up the preceding story, an astute audience member might well propose another answer entirely.

At the same time, by creating a child protagonist who constantly finds herself having poems, stories, and songs inflicted on her by nonsensical men, Carroll dramatizes the plight of the child bombarded by other people's discourse, which of course includes Alice Liddell and other young readers of his books. In the process, he manages to undercut the cheery notion that children's literature exists merely to entertain children—an idea the *Alice* books are often credited with popularizing. After hearing that the Tweedle brothers regaled Alice with verse, Humpty brags, " '*I* can repeat poetry as well as other folk, if it comes to that' " (199). "Hoping to keep him from beginning," Alice hastily exclaims " 'Oh, it needn't come to that!' " (199). But of course it does:

> "The piece I'm going to repeat," he went on without noticing her remark, "was written entirely for your amusement."
>
> Alice felt that in that case she really *ought* to listen to it; so she sat down, and said "Thank you" rather sadly. (200)

Carroll here sends up the whole idea of writing "for" children. Humpty Dumpty professes to have composed children's literature: a poem created solely to entertain a particular child. Yet this claim is obviously specious, since he has just met Alice (and in any case seems far less interested in her than in himself and his own pronouncements). Worse that that, Carroll suggests, the mere act of designating the child as the intended addressee can exert a coercive, silencing effect; the child is essentially being asked to sit down and shut up, a point made explicit during Humpty's rendition of the poem, when he "severely" informs Alice that she should stop inserting her own commentary in between his lines (200): "'You needn't go on making remarks like that,' Humpty Dumpty said: 'they're not sensible, and they put me out'" (200).

Carroll's decision to represent Alice as immersed in discourse not of her own making and his habit of dwelling on his heroine's artificiality—her status as a figment of someone else's imagination—are closely related. If we acknowledge that outside influences strongly shape selfhood, we must face the possibility that even our dreams are not our own—an idea that might make anyone weep. Alice's tears attest to how painful it is to conceive of oneself as a scripted being rather than an autonomous, totally authentic agent. Yet rather than regard this problem as unique to childhood, Carroll conceives of such belatedness as another point of connection between young and old. For the White Knight scene vividly illustrates that children are not the only ones imbued with ideologies not of their own making; adults, too, must cope with their profound unoriginality. Although the Knight prides himself on his power of invention, his ideas are either absurd or—in the case of his song—derivative. Not only does the plot of his poem come from Wordsworth, "the tune *isn't* his own invention"; according to the highly acculturated Alice, "it's '*I give thee all, I can no more*'" (225). Adults, Carroll suggests, absorb, conform to, and improvise on various cultural influences, too, including and especially the kind of Romantic discourse about childhood that he himself frequently reiterates, reanimates, and caricatures.

Such keen recognition about the difficulty of being genuinely inventive and innovative might help explain why Carroll never allows his heroine to evolve into a full-fledged creative agent. Despite her willingness to say no, Alice ultimately remains a relatively unresistant reader: just as she wants to echo Watts when she first arrives in Wonderland, so too she promises after her final departure to "repeat 'The Walrus and the Carpenter'" to Dinah the next morning (248). And although Carroll flirts with the idea that children can wrest away the pen, he does not really take it seriously as a genuine possibility. It is grown-ups who control the world of children's fiction, as Alice herself recognizes. As I will demonstrate in the next chapter, E. Nesbit concedes this point yet insists that being saturated in other people's stories is precisely what enables creativity. She emphasizes the sheer variety of discourses children are exposed to, suggesting that young people can pick and choose, fusing different strands of preexisting rhetoric together in new and unexpected ways. Mutual aggression thus gives way to a more optimistic vision of reciprocal exploitation.

4

PARTNERS IN CRIME

E. Nesbit and the Art of Thieving

"Suppose," Matthew Sweet has recently enjoined us, "that everything we think we know about the Victorians is wrong" (ix). In his compelling book *Inventing the Victorians* (2001), Sweet inveighs against the time-honored tradition—inaugurated by Lytton Strachey's *Eminent Victorians* (1918)—of condescending to the Victorians, characterizing them as sentimental, prudish, hypocritical, and generally unsophisticated "in order to satisfy our sense of ourselves as liberated Moderns" (ix).[1] With a showman's flourish, Sweet reveals that many of the anecdotes critics use to encapsulate the spirit of the age are specious: the often-repeated notion that the Victorians were so modest that they felt compelled to cover up their piano legs was fabricated by a radio commentator in 1947, while the first documented appearance of the motherly recommendation "Lie back and think of England"—often attributed to Queen Victoria—is in a private diary from 1912 (xii–xv).

The idea that Golden Age children's authors such as Carroll, Stevenson, and Barrie were frozen in eternal childhood is an equally condescending canard. Indeed, we inherit this line of thinking from Strachey's contemporaries: Max Beerbohm's first review of *Peter Pan* was entitled "The Child Barrie" (1905); G. K. Chesterton declared in 1928 that Stevenson had "barricaded himself in the nursery and almost tried to creep into the dolls'-house" (159); and Virginia Woolf characterized Carroll as having an "impediment in the centre of his being . . . [a] hard block of pure childhood [that] starved the mature man of nourishment" (82). This habit of infantilizing authors who wrote for an audience that included children also manifested itself on the other side of the Atlantic. As Beverly Lyon Clark has noted, Van Wyck Brooks made "constant derogatory use of metaphors of juvenility" in his 1920 study of Mark Twain (91), while Odell Shepard claimed in 1938 that Louisa May Alcott "never emerged from adolescence"—"she never grew up" (quoted in Clark 119). Both Clark and Felicity A. Hughes have shown that the tendency to denigrate children's texts and their authors was part of a broader campaign waged by turn-of-the-century writers and intellectuals (including and especially Henry James) to differentiate serious "adult" literature from popular works aimed at mixed audiences—to effect a strict bifurcation between child and adult audiences, children's books and books for grown-ups.

Unfortunately, this impulse to belittle children's authors has proven astonishingly persistent. Following in the footsteps of Peter Coveney, who diagnosed Carroll and Barrie as "neurotic" cases of arrested development (249), Humphrey Carpenter contends in *Secret Gardens: The Golden Age of Children's Literature* (1985) that Nesbit "was a child in adult clothes" (129). Similarly, Jackie Wullschläger bases her study *Inventing Wonderland* (1995) on the premise that Carroll, Barrie, Edward Lear, and Kenneth Grahame were "writers who could not grow up" (3). Infantilizing and pathologizing the author often corresponds with a tendency to devalue the work, as when Coveney calls Barrie an "artistic failure" whose writing reflected "a generally sick sensibility" (249, 242) or Carpenter dismisses Nesbit as "an energetic hack" (126).

Adopting such a disdainful stance prevents us from noticing that these authors grappled in a sustained and sophisticated way with the very issues that concern contemporary critics who focus on Victorian child-loving. Keenly aware that their age was witnessing a major shift in the value accorded to children and childhood, these writers used their fiction as a forum to explore the question of what effect this newly intense investment in the young might have on both adult and child. For example, Carroll and Barrie wrote long, complex novels about the act of romancing the child; *Sylvie and Bruno* (1889) and *The Little White Bird* (1902) both feature aging male narrators who chase obsessively after children. As I have argued elsewhere, *Sylvie and Bruno* portrays such child-loving as destructive to the well-being of both adult and child,[2] while *The Little White Bird* characterizes the act of telling stories to children as a means of seduction (thereby anticipating a central tenet of the colonization paradigm). In it, a Barrie-esque narrator relates fantastic tales about Peter Pan and the fairies to a beloved child-friend as part of his campaign to "take him utterly from [his mother] and make him mine" (99). Children's stories penned by these authors have a similarly metafictional bent.

Indeed, my argument in this book has been that many celebrated Golden Age children's authors were extremely self-reflective about their own genre, producing children's books that attend to the issue of the complications that ensue when adults write books for children. Famous texts like the *Alice* books and *Treasure Island* reflect a deep anxiety about the power imbalance that complicates the adult author–child reader relationship: Carroll frets over the possibility that even nonsense literature can function as a form of coercion, while Stevenson worries that authors of adventure stories aim to indoctrinate and exploit youngsters like his impressionable boy hero. Female authors such as Craik, Ewing, and Molesworth also dwell on the issue of influence, although they seem more optimistic about the child's chances of coping in a creative way with the pressure exerted on them by adults and adult-produced texts. Their decision to employ child narrators attests not just to a desire to speak for and thereby shape juvenile readers but also to an interest in helping the young find their own voices despite the existence of preexisting stories about who they are and how they should behave. (Perhaps women writers tended to be more hopeful than their male colleagues because their own experience as women in a patriarchal culture had convinced them of the possibility of writing and acting from a subordinate position—or because they often had the chance to observe children's development at closer range than their male colleagues.)

The most obvious objection to such readings would be that I am overreacting to accounts of Victorian cluelessness by attributing an improbably high level of reflective self-awareness to these authors. Is it really credible to contend that they worried so much about the potentially prescriptive effects of their own genre? In a word, yes. Children's literature had been highly metafictional from very early on; Sarah Fielding's *The Governess* (1749)—often described as the first children's novel—is, more than anything else, a book about reading. Fielding intersperses interpolated stories in her narrative precisely in order to explore the issue of how children should react to texts. Being able to extract and act on the morals of stories is a key lesson, as is the importance of paying "the most exact Obedience" to benevolent adult authority figures such as herself (176). Similarly, in her immensely popular book *The History of the Fairchild Family* (1818), Mary Martha Sherwood shows the Fairchild children reading aloud—and being improved by—a trio of tracts. Like the overarching story in which they appear, these interpolated tales present themselves as "The History of" a particular sinner or group of godly people, and each one ends with a prayer that child readers are encouraged to use on their own behalf, just as all of Sherwood's chapters do. This metafictional focus on the scene of storytelling is aimed at teaching young readers to swallow didactic narratives whole, to internalize without question the "beautiful books" given to them by adults (Sherwood 159).[3]

Right from the start, in other words, children's books addressed the issue of how children should read. Moreover, as Burnett's autobiography and Carroll's *Alice* books indicate, Victorian children's writers knew that some of their predecessors and peers aimed to encourage strict obedience and passive literacy, so it is not odd that they should map out other ways of responding to literature in their own books. Then, too, Golden Age authors were undoubtedly aware of the critical discussions of their genre that regularly appeared in a wide variety of periodicals. Indeed, Charlotte Yonge, George MacDonald, Mary Louisa Molesworth, William Brighty Rands, and other children's writers contributed to this lively discourse about the origins and aims of children's literature.[4] Self-identified members of "an age much occupied in self-analysis and in criticism" ("Children's Literature" 299), nineteenth-century essayists recognized that the explosion of fiction aimed specially at children was a relatively recent phenomenon, and some of them regarded the whole genre with suspicion, precisely because of the "excessive ardour for *teaching*" evident in so many children's books (Rigby, "Children's Books" 2).

Indeed, the question "Should Children Have a Special Literature?" (1890)—to quote the title of one late Victorian article—remained pressing even in the final decade of the century (Salmon 332). Not everyone agreed that it was a good idea to cater books specifically to the young. For instance, the anonymous author of "Writers for the Young" (1898) reports that noted novelist and travel writer Matilda Betham-Edwards

> tells us she got her education from a leather-bound copy of *Shakespeare*; she disapproves of purely children's books. "I had few in my own childhood, and read only the English classics, and found them entertaining enough. The present fashion of writing story-books especially for children is, I think, a mistake. It tends to weaken their taste for literature, and when they grow older they are not able to appreciate the best forms of literary style." (717)

Also in 1898, investigating the question of "What Children Like to Read," a reporter for the *Pall Mall Gazette* asserted that "it is by no means certain that even under ten years of age children are so easily persuaded to attend precisely to what is addressed to them, and do not rather love to overhear, to listen by permission, and to have a share in" books aimed at their elders (1).

In my next chapter, I concur with those who contend that the nineteenth century was *not* a time when a sharp division between adult and child was automatically assumed and strictly enforced but an era when some people campaigned for this to happen while many others resisted. The realm of literature provides one example of this struggle. Various authors and critics did indeed conceive of children as innocent, incompetent readers who needed to have their own specially simplified stories. But others strongly objected to "the parade of protection" that aimed to deprive children of access to the work of writers like Shakespeare and Scott and substitute instead "simple little books which any little simpleton can understand" (Rigby 8, 25–6). This scathing indictment of the genre comes from Elizabeth Rigby's essay "Children's Books" (1844); Yonge likewise endorsed a kind of "wholesome . . . neglect" whereby children should be allowed to read whatever adults did (230). In her lengthy account of "Children's Literature of the Last Century" (1869), she observes that "infantine literature . . . is a recent production," speaking wistfully of the time when "elders [did not] trouble themselves with scruples" about whether children would be "corrupted" by reading grown-ups' books (229).

Writing some twenty years earlier, Rigby can still celebrate such liberty as a positive feature of the literary scene. Indeed, she coins the marvelous phrase "promiscuous reading" to explain why members of "the rising generation" have such lively, well-cultivated minds (16, 2). Such sophistication, she insists, is the result not of "any efforts which have been made of late in their own department" but of "the liberty now allowed them in promiscuous reading" (16). To be sure, Rigby had absorbed enough of the emerging ideology of innocence to make her uncomfortable with the salacious implications of this phrase, so she switches metaphors in midstream—from sex to farming! The sentence that begins by lauding literary profligacy as the key to the modern child's cultivation ends by recasting this freedom as rural rather than erotic: the cultivation of modern children comes from having been granted "the power of ranging free over field and pasture" rather than being force-fed "all the little racks of ready-cut hay that have been so officiously supplied them" (16).

The hyperliterate heroes and heroines of E. Nesbit's children's stories are promiscuous readers par excellence, having read everything from didactic tracts to adventure stories, from novels by Dickens and Thackeray to children's books by Kipling and Grahame. Nesbit was even relaxed enough to allow them access to the penny dreadfuls and yellow-covered novels that so many of her peers denounced as devastatingly destructive to youthful purity. Nevertheless, she (too) has recently been accused of depicting the child as an innocent Other so as to persuade child readers to identify with—and mold themselves to match—this static image. In this chapter, I contend that such attacks are off the mark; far from representing children as a race apart, Nesbit follows in the footsteps of the female authors discussed in chapter 1 by portraying young people as deeply enmeshed in a social, cultural, and literary scene that influences but does not entirely constrain them. Commenting on his own development as a writer, Nesbit's famous child narrator Oswald Bastable observes, "Albert's uncle says your style is always altered a bit by what you read" (*Wouldbegoods* 109). This line encapsulates Nesbit's habit of representing the child as marked but not disabled by the influence of adults and their texts.

Like Rigby, Nesbit experiments with multiple metaphors in her quest to celebrate this productive permeability. For instance, she suggests that in order to participate actively in the shaping of their own lives and life stories, children should function like the discriminating editors who often turn up as characters in her books: rather than simply accepting everything they receive from the culture at large, they should criticize, edit, rewrite, even reject the endless submissions pouring in from all quarters. Still more often, as I will show, Nesbit employs the metaphor of theft, depicting children as avid appropriators who steal a little bit from a variety of sources. Because her child protagonists manage to enrich themselves by exploiting the resources of adults and their culture, they provide the most perfect example of how children's authors from this period portray the child as a genuinely artful dodger, capable of eluding the most paralyzing forms of social and literary pressure.

Yet Nesbit combines this sanguinity about children's resourcefulness with a down-to-earth recognition of the limited nature of their power over other people, the circumstances of their daily lives, and even their own actions and voices. As Erika Rothwell notes, her child protagonists often fail in their efforts to "exercise any real or lasting influence over the outcome of events in the adult world" and in their aspiration to produce original creative work—to find their own artistic voices (65). Just as Stevenson and Carroll worry about children acting as parrots, Nesbit dwells on the problem of the child plagiarist, repeatedly stressing that young people should not simply absorb and echo back material appropriated from adult culture. Instead, she intimates, child readers should follow her lead in becoming more daring and ingenious thieves. For Nesbit repeatedly acknowledges her own indebtedness to outside sources in her children's novels, often mentioning by name the well-known authors whose work she improvises on. In doing so, she invites children to view their own belatedness as a benefit rather than a source of inevitable oppression; far from being forced to conform to the narratives about childhood already in existence, she suggests, children can treat such stories as raw material to exploit, contradict, or retool. By vouching for the child's resilience and resourcefulness while simultaneously acknowledging the adult's primacy, power, and influence, Nesbit provides us with a far more nuanced picture of the adult author–child reader relationship than the draconian colonization paradigm, which inserts adult and child into the unpleasant roles of perpetrator and victim rather than entertaining the possibility that they can operate as partners in crime.

It is not surprising that Nesbit manages to maintain this delicate balance, since she straddles many different fences as a children's author. Writing at the turn of the century, she seems both quintessentially Victorian and amazingly modern; her tales of large families coping with the ups and downs of nineteenth-century life are chronicled in "miraculously colloquial, flexible and revealing prose" that anticipates (and influences) the voices of many twentieth-century children's authors (Crouch 16).[5] Her habit of producing stories that blur the line between realism and fantasy has also been much imitated; although Nesbit did not invent the practice of suddenly introducing magic into the lives of everyday children, she did it with such panache that her novels are the ones writers like Edward Eager (1911–1964) and J. K. Rowling (1965–) allude to as important influences.[6] Then, too, Nesbit's biographers and critics have had no end of fun exploring how she teetered back and forth between conventional and radical stances: she was an early feminist who opposed female suffrage, a Fabian socialist whose work "frequently revealed a conservative's nostalgia for idealized versions of the past" (R. Jones ix). In keeping with this habit of having a foot in two camps, Nesbit embraces the optimism about the child's creativity and agency that suffuses stories by female authors like Craik and Ewing but seasons it with a dash of the pessimism present in the work of their male colleagues.

RECIPROCAL ROBBERY

Catching a burglar in the act of creeping into her family's nursery, the youngest heroine of Nesbit's novel *The Phoenix and the Carpet* (1904) knows better than to succumb to fear. For Jane, despite her youth, "had read a great many nice stories about burglars, as well as some affecting pieces of poetry, and she knew that no burglar will ever hurt a little girl if he meets her when burgling" (192). Elaborating on the conventions of this Victorian mini-genre, Nesbit explains that

> in all the cases Jane had read of, [the thief's] burglarishness was almost at once forgotten in the interest he felt in the little girl's artless prattle. . . . [But Jane] could not at once think of any remark sufficiently prattling and artless to make a beginning with. In the stories and the affecting poetry the child could never speak plainly, though it always looked old enough to in the pictures. And Jane could not make up her mind to lisp and "talk baby," even to a burglar. And while she hesitated he softly opened the nursery door and went in. (192–93)

Even as Nesbit parodies the tendency of other authors to domesticate the figure of the burglar, she enthusiastically purloins and reproduces this scenario, both here and in her other works. Just as the burglar Jane discovers gets converted into a family friend (later referred to as "that nice chap—our own burglar"), the thief caught by the child protagonists in *The Story of the Treasure Seekers* (1899) is quickly adopted and transformed into "our own dear robber" (*Phoenix* 210; *Story* 201).[7] Such encounters testify to Nesbit's self-conscious sense of herself as an author who plunders or colonizes the realm of childhood, as well as the work of other authors of children's literature. Yet Nesbit optimistically insists that children, too, can fruitfully practice the art of thieving, as indicated by the fact that these burglars are themselves seized and exploited by the very youngsters they hope to rob.

Far from being artless prattlers, Nesbit's child heroes are artful dodgers, adept at appropriating and recycling the work of adult authors. But as Julia Briggs, Erika Rothwell, and Mavis Reimer all point out, Nesbit's young protagonists frequently misinterpret or misapply the material they steal, experiencing a great deal of trouble as a result of their naïveté. These difficulties, however, do not indicate that Nesbit believes children should cease such stealthy operations entirely. Rather, they convey her conviction that young people must learn to pull off more savvy and sophisticated heists, ones that more closely resemble Nesbit's own appropriations. By simultaneously lampooning and propagating literary conventions—such as the burglar motif in the passage just quoted—Nesbit models for her readers the kind of balancing act she wants them to master; even as she encourages children to take pleasure from and make use of texts, she coaxes them to become more critical readers. Keenly aware of the power that adults and their narratives wield over children, Nesbit incites young people to commandeer more completely the scripts they are given, to revise rather than simply reenact them.

A number of critics have noted the extraordinary extent to which Nesbit's child characters are saturated in and fascinated by all kinds of literature.[8] In book after book, Nesbit portrays young people as irrepressible mimics who shape their games, ideals, behavior, and even speech around texts created by adults. In *The Story of the Treasure Seekers*, for example, the Bastable children swipe scenarios for their activities from Kipling, Conan Doyle, Marryat, Edgeworth, de la Motte Fouqué, Pope, and the *Arabian Nights*, as well as assorted picture books, newspaper stories, and advertisements. At the same time, Nesbit herself reworks the material of Dickens, Ewing, Burnett, and Grahame. In her numerous studies of Nesbit, Briggs meticulously details both sets of borrowings, but she never quite makes explicit their ultimate effect, which is to break down the divide between adult writer and child reader by suggesting that both parties can improvise on other people's stories to produce their own narratives. While this strong sense of equivalence may be a fantasy on Nesbit's part, it is nevertheless a fantasy about equality, about sharing a propensity for the same game; and it therefore conflicts with the claim, advanced by both Reimer and Rothwell, that Nesbit constructs the child as "irremediably Other," an innocent, vulnerable victim unable to comprehend adult language or cope with the adult world (Reimer 54).

Rather than setting up the child as an innocent Other, Nesbit confounds the very categories of child and adult, reader and writer, by presenting highly literate young protagonists who inhabit the same position as herself; like their creator, the Bastables and their counterparts appropriate and adapt texts to suit their own purposes. This constant trolling for material finds a metaphorical equivalent in the activity of treasure seeking, a close cousin to burglary in Nesbit's fiction. *The Story of the Treasure Seekers* and *The New Treasure Seekers* (1904) chronicle the efforts of six siblings—Oswald, Dora, Dicky, Alice, Noël, and Horace Octavious (nicknamed H.O.)—to "restore the fallen fortunes of [our] House" in the wake of their father's business troubles and their mother's death (*Story* 11). The Bastables' many efforts to garner funds derive from ideas they have stolen from various texts; for example, they decide to try "Being Detectives" after reading "Mr. Sherlock Holmes, as well as the yellow-covered books . . . [by] Gaboriau" (*Story* 32). Stressing the "burglarishness" of such borrowings, Nesbit frequently connects literary theft with literal larceny. For example, feeling "quite certain that the books were right, and that the best way to restore fallen fortunes was to rescue an old gentleman in distress," Oswald picks up a coin dropped by an elderly man "and was just thinking what he should say when he returned it, [when] the old gentleman caught him by the collar and called him a young thief" (*Story* 127–28).

As the narrator of the Bastable books, Oswald constantly capitalizes on other authors' material, displaying a penchant for creative recycling that matches Nesbit's own. Needless to say, the very act of delegating the power of narration to a child surrogate reveals Nesbit's interest in dissolving any strict division between author and audience. Furthermore, from the first page of his narrative, it is clear that Oswald's writing style will be heavily influenced by his experience as a reader. He immediately announces,

> There are some things I must tell before I begin to tell about the treasure-seeking, because I have read books myself, and I know how beastly it is when a story begins, "Alas!" said Hildegarde with a deep sigh, "we must look our last on this ancestral home"—and then some one else says something—and you don't know for pages and pages where the home is, or who Hildegarde is, or anything about it. (*Story* 10)

Here Oswald models the kind of thieving Nesbit advocates; simultaneously exposing and exploiting literary conventions, he allows himself the pleasure of performing exactly the routines he swears never to revisit. Thus, in the midst of another commentary on authorial techniques, he vows "You will not catch me saying, 'thus the sad days passed slowly by'—or 'the years rolled on their weary course'—or 'time went on'—because it is silly; of course time goes on—whether you say so or not" (*Story* 21). Rather than choosing whether to "say so or not," Oswald both deploys and denigrates these phrases, just as his creator simultaneously uses and abuses literary conventions like the good-hearted burglar and the wealthy "old gentleman" who saves the day.[9] Both Nesbit and Oswald excel at revising other people's plots; she recycles Burnett's *Editha's Burglar* in the chapter entitled "The Robber and the Burglar," while he promises at the start of his story to improve on the work of previous authors of children's literature, asserting "I have often thought that if the people who write books for children knew a little more it would be better. I shall not tell you anything about us except what I should like to know about if I was reading the story and you were writing it" (*Story* 21–22).

Of course, Nesbit's habit of conceptualizing the reader–writer dyad as reversible may be mere wishful thinking, particularly since she mainly produced children's fiction, a genre that, as Rose notes, "rests so openly on an acknowledged difference, a rupture almost, between writer and addressee" (2). Yet imagining this binary as violable is precisely what enables Nesbit to jettison the ideal of the innocent child that Rose identifies as a defining characteristic of children's literature. In *The Case of Peter Pan*, Rose contends that children's fiction "fixes the child and then holds it in place" as sexually and textually innocent (4), an enticingly blank and remote point of origin. Nesbit's work challenges this paradigm, not only by embracing the archetype of the literate, critical child but also by championing trespassing as a productive mode that enables self-expression. Rather than keeping the categories of adult and child "safely" quarantined on the page (Rose 69), Nesbit demonstrates how saturation in the work of adult authors—coupled with the power of discrimination—enables her child protagonists to usurp the role of author for themselves.

For example, the fact that Oswald opens his first three chapters with sharp-eyed critiques of various kinds of literature suggests that reading enables writing—or rather that *critical* reading releases or empowers one's own creative efforts. Wide-ranging knowledge of texts must be coupled with the ability to edit and editorialize. Thus, the Bastables' whiny next-door neighbor Albert "cannot play properly at all . . . [because he] doesn't care for reading, and he has not read nearly so many books as we have" (*Story* 23). But Dora lacks the ability to dream up or participate in entertaining amusements as well, because she behaves too much "like the good elder sister in books" (*Story* 17). Having uncritically absorbed the material she has read, Dora has failed to master the skill of selection; she swallows preachy texts like *Ministering Children* (1854) and *What Katy Did* (1872) whole rather than extracting, revising, and (mis)applying particular lines or scenes in order to manufacture adventures. Underscoring the productive possibilities of discrimination of this sort, Nesbit notes that useful ideas can be gleaned from even the trashiest sources; Oswald prefaces his narration of one of their adventures with the explanation that "we had just been reading a book by Dick Diddlington—that's not his right name, but I know all about libel actions, so I shall not say what his name is really, because his books are rot. Only they put it into our heads to do what I am going to narrate" (*Story* 32).

Like Jane's resistance to the paradigm of the artless child, Oswald's selectivity illustrates Nesbit's interest in conceptualizing children as active receivers of texts, capable of improvising on—not just slavishly adhering to—other people's stories. The transformative power of revision of this sort emerges not only in the Bastable books but also in Nesbit's popular *Five Children and It* (1902) series; the second book in this sequence, *The Phoenix and the Carpet*, repeatedly dramatizes the process by which old stories inspire new ones, highlighting the connection between the consumption and the production of texts. The adventures of Cyril, Robert, Anthea, and Jane, like those of the Bastables, commence as a result of their familiarity with fiction; while acting out scenes from the *Ingoldsby Legends*, the children accidentally knock into the fire a mysterious egg they have discovered wrapped up in their new nursery carpet. When a magical phoenix rises out of the ashes and informs them that their new rug will obey their every wish, the resurrection of this fabulous beast mirrors the process by which *The Phoenix and the Carpet* itself rises out of the ashes of other texts, including and especially the *Arabian Nights*. Not only does Nesbit nab the magic carpet motif and other scenarios from this source, the very idea of using *Arabian Nights* in this way is borrowed from F. Anstey's novel *The Brass Bottle* (1900). Nor does Nesbit hide her debts; she makes frequent references to texts that have inspired her own, as when she describes a desert island visited by the children as covered with "all the tropical flowers and fruits that you read of in *Westward Ho!* and *Fair Play*" or compares a conflagration to "the rose of fire in Mr. Rider Haggard's exciting story about Allan Quatermain" (*Phoenix* 67, 5).

"A bird of its word" who can "speak and understand *all* languages," the Phoenix's first act reveals how closely his regenerative ability is associated with the art of literary reinvention (60, 75). As Robert reads him an encyclopedia account of the habits and physical features of "the Phoenix," the bird maintains a running commentary, finally declaring, "'That book ought to be destroyed. It's most inaccurate'" (21). As in the Bastable books, criticizing other texts emerges as a crucial prelude to the act of storytelling; eager to correct the faulty account, the Phoenix promises the children, "'I will tell you my story'" (22). Under his influence, the children master the art of effectively altering texts as well; in order to summon the Phoenix quickly, Robert condenses "the whole of the Greek invocation song of seven thousand lines . . . into one English hexameter" (111), while Anthea learns to revise "Rain, rain go away" into a more effective spell so that the family can show the Phoenix around London without getting wet (113). In particular, Cyril's triumphant turn as "a heaven-born teller of tales" attests to Nesbit's determination to portray the process of revising preexisting stories as a creative act (93). Transported to an Indian palace by the magic carpet, Cyril enchants the royal court by retelling some of the adventures chronicled in the first half of the narrative; he relates the story of "the Phoenix and the Carpet, and the Lone Tower, and the Queen-Cook, in language that grew insensibly more and more Arabian Nightsy" (93).

As this final bit of description indicates, however, the line separating retelling or rewriting stories and plagiarism is an extremely fine one. Keenly aware of the criminal aspects of scavenging material from other authors, Nesbit associates the actions of both the children and the Phoenix with theft.[10] The children are mistaken for "members of a desperate burgling gang" in one adventure and dealers in stolen goods in another, while the Phoenix defends his own scavenging ways by saying, "'Birds always take what they want. It is not regarded as stealing, except in the case of magpies'" (241, 44). Himself stolen by two pickpockets who mistake him for a parrot, the Phoenix "scornfully" denies this charge (126); but numerous other characters—and even the narrator—associate him with this avian mimic, signaling Nesbit's anxiety about the close correlation between revision and repetition. Further proof of this concern comes when the children, the narrator, and even an actual burglar follow the Phoenix's footsteps and attempt to absolve themselves of the crime of stealing; bent on distinguishing Phoenix-like regeneration from parrot-like plagiarism, the narrative offers a number of different answers to Anthea's unfinished remark "'It can't be stealing if—'" (144).

For example, trying to convince his siblings that taking an abandoned pile of treasure does not qualify as theft, Cyril argues that "stealing is taking things that belong to someone else, and there's no one else'" (144). Drawing an even finer distinction, the narrator defends the fact that the children entertain themselves with "chalk that Robert had nicked" from school by explaining, "You know, of course, that it is stealing to take a new stick of chalk, but it is not wrong to take a broken piece, so long as you only take one" (15). Caught in the act of breaking into the children's nursery, the burglar Jane surprises exculpates himself by declaring, "'I was druv to it by dishonest blokes'" (219). And when the magic carpet accidentally gets sold at a bazaar, Cyril defends the idea of breaking into the new owner's home and taking it with yet another excuse: "'It's our own carpet. It wouldn't be burglary'" (104). By far the most compelling and frequently employed rationalization of theft centers around the idea that exploitation can be mutual, a view Noël Bastable sums up when he insists that "'there are ways of being robbers that are not wrong. . . . If you can rob a robber it is a right act'" (*Story* 180). Throughout her fiction for children, Nesbit characterizes burglary as a comic mode of reciprocal exploitation; by portraying both children and adults as thieves and by devising scenes in which they take advantage of each other, she continues her campaign to conceptualize the reader–writer divide as traversable. For these encounters emphatically attest to the possibility of cross-colonization; and since thieving is specifically linked to approaching (and producing) literature, these moments imply that both children and adults can annex and improvise on texts.

The Phoenix and the Carpet chapter entitled "The Cats, The Cow, and the Burglar" provides a perfect example of this phenomenon. When a burglar breaks into their home hoping to rob them, Cyril, Robert, Anthea, and Jane ingeniously manage to take advantage of him, even as he profits from their interference. Desperate to feed and dispose of 199 starving Persian cats that the magic carpet has deposited in their nursery, the children convince the burglar—whom Jane has cornered—to help them out: first, Jane persuades him to milk the cow brought by the carpet to provide food for the cats, and then Cyril talks him into getting rid of the cats for them by explaining that he can sell them and keep the profits. What could have been a scene about the adult's power to exploit the child turns into a dramatization of the way children and adults can use each other in a way that works to their mutual advantage. Furthermore, since this scene explicitly parodies other stories for children, the siblings' creative reception of the intruder takes on a specifically literary application: their refusal to fall victim to the plot of a scheming adult—the burglar—parallels their ability to resist the limiting and condescending picture of themselves presented to them by texts.

For just as the Phoenix repudiates the picture of himself contained in the encyclopedia, Jane rejects the paradigm of childhood offered to her by books; although she knows from her reading how little girls ought to behave in her situation, she simply cannot "bring herself to say, 'What's 'oo doing here, Mithter Wobber?' " (193). At the same time, even as she resists being typecast as an adorable innocent, she infantilizes the burglar, dubbing him "my own dear pet burglar" (213). Thus, Nesbit confounds the categories of (adult) perpetrator and (child) victim, representing relations between the two parties as an endless cycle of exploitation.[11] In order for children to avoid being victimized by adult plotters, Nesbit suggests, they must learn not to identify blindly with their literary counterparts. Thus, the climax of *The Phoenix and the Carpet* finds the children trapped in a burning theatre; Anthea quavers, " 'Father said [to] stay here' " and Robert replies, " 'He didn't mean stay and be roasted. . . . No boys on burning decks for me, thank you' " (261). His refusal to mimic the obedient boy hero of Felicia Hemans's poem "Casabianca" (1826)—who declines to leave a burning ship "Without his father's word"—demonstrates the critical importance of resistant reading (line 10). Like Oswald's scornful treatment of various literary conventions, Robert's stubbornness reminds us that one way children can capitalize on texts is by using them as examples of what *not* to do. Indeed, Nesbit's notion of reciprocal robbery depends on the idea that adult narratives do not exercise prescriptive power over children; optimistically, she suggests that readers of all ages can plunder texts selectively, heisting only what appeals to them and rejecting—or revising—the rest.

The Bastable books likewise portray burglary as a mutually enriching activity; in keeping with Nesbit's notion that thieving can go both ways, both children and adults are repeatedly associated with robbers throughout the series. Such parallels are particularly pronounced in *The Story of the Treasure Seekers*. In "Being Detectives," for example, the Bastables suspect that burglars have broken in to their neighbors' house; snooping around in an effort to find out, they themselves are suspected of being burglars. In "The Robber and the Burglar," the Bastables, as they "play at burglars," surprise a man whom they assume is an actual burglar; actually, he is a friend of their father, but he (too) pretends to be a thief, so as not to disappoint them (*Story* 184). As this "robber" recounts to his ecstatic captors fabulous stories about his past misdeeds, a real thief breaks into the house. Commenting on the capture of this genuine bandit, Oswald makes explicit the link Nesbit forges between child and adult adventurers; he remarks, "It was the most wonderful adventure we ever had, though it wasn't treasure-seeking—at least not ours" (*Story* 197).

Nesbit's decision to portray both children and adults as treasure seekers reflects her belief that literary exploitation goes both ways; children use texts penned by adults to entertain themselves, while adults use children as material for their literary efforts. In particular, "The Poet and the Editor" dramatizes the possibility of productive cross-colonization of this kind. In this story, Oswald and his brother Noël take a collection of the Noël's poems to the editor of a London newspaper, in the hope that he will purchase and publish them. The Editor accepts the poetry and thrills Noël by paying him a guinea; but Oswald concludes his story by noting that

> [the Editor] never put Noël's poetry in the *Daily Recorder*. It was quite a long time afterwards we saw a sort of story thing in a magazine, on the station bookstall, and that kind, sleepy-looking Editor had written it, I suppose. It was not at all amusing. It said a lot about Noël and me, describing us all wrong, and saying how we had tea with the Editor; and all Noël's poems were in the story thing. I think myself the Editor seemed to make game of them, but Noël was quite pleased to see them printed—so that's all right. (*Story* 68)

Here Nesbit not only acknowledges the way adults capitalize on the naïveté of children, she also implicates herself as a participant in this dubious "game," since her own fiction—including *The Story of the Treasure Seekers*—appeared in magazines such as the *Strand*, which were read by adults as well as children. Furthermore, like the Editor, Nesbit frequently pokes fun at her child characters for the benefit of the adults in her audience. For example, when the Editor turns his back to the boys after reading one of the poems, adult readers are expected to guess that he is laughing, despite Oswald's comment that "Noël thinks he did it 'to conceal his emotion,' as they do in books" (*Story* 62).

Of course, child readers might pick up this joke, too, particularly after learning how the Editor treats Noël's poetry; ultimately, this encounter warns children that adults who appear to be taking them seriously may in fact be making fun of them, even cashing in on their foibles. Yet *The Story of the Treasure Seekers* posits the hopeful notion that exploitation of this kind can be playful, productive, and reciprocal. For this reason, both the Editor and Noël profit from this shared experience; Noël gets a guinea and his poems printed—no mean feat, despite the context—while the Editor obtains priceless material. At the same time, however, Noël and his siblings turn the Editor into grist for *their* imaginative mill; the Editor may "make game" of Noël's poems, but in a later story, entitled "Being Editors," the Bastables fashion their play around their new friend's professional identity. Furthermore, by the time the Editor uses Noël as material for his writing, Noël has already used him. In a moment that crystallizes the way this exchange works to their mutual advantage, Noël—thrilled by the success of this particular treasure hunt—composes a poem to his new friend on the spot, entitled "Lines to a Noble Editor," causing the object of his appreciation to comment, " 'I shall treasure it' " (*Story* 68).

Critics who claim that Nesbit "constructs childhood as a period of helplessness, ignorance, and incompetence" might argue that the reciprocity of such encounters is undermined by the various mistakes and malapropisms the children unknowingly commit (Stephens 130). When Oswald describes the family's attempts to offer aid to "the poor and indignant" or to prove themselves innocent of a crime even though "the evidence [was] convulsive" (*Wouldbegoods* 127, 183), many commentators maintain that such jokes not only are aimed at adult readers but also come "at the expense of children—because the joke is often between the adult reader and the author at Oswald's expense" (Rothwell 62). But to presume that young people will not appreciate these moments is to promote a vision of the child that is far more "dominated by limitation and condescension" than Nesbit's own (Rothwell 69). As Barbara Wall points out, Nesbit "never pays her young readers [a] greater compliment than in her readiness to trust them to cope" with irony, parody, and other linguistic challenges; by believing that her audience is "capable of sharing a joke," she consistently gives children "the opportunity to extend their range" (153, 156–57). Eager for *all* of her readers to get in on the fun, Nesbit broadcasts the fact that knowing exactly what a word means can provide extra enjoyment and even indicates how such information may be obtained: when an adult friend of the family makes a joke based on a difficult word, Oswald explains, "We laughed—because we knew what an amphorae is. If you don't you might look it up in the dicker" (*Wouldbegoods* 189).[12]

Moreover, although the Bastables frequently misread texts and situations, and rarely manage to affect the adult world as they hope to do, the idea that such disappointments are disempowering to child readers assumes that young audience members have no choice but to identify with the misguided, often demoralized child characters. Such a stance is in keeping with Rose's characterization of children's fiction as a form of colonization in which adult authors construct an image of the child as an innocent Other and then coerce young readers into identifying with that limited (and self-serving) representation. This dark vision of children's literature as oppressive and deeply manipulative takes little account of the possibility that responses other than identification are possible, and sometimes encouraged. From the very start of Oswald's narrative, Nesbit invites audience members to feel superior to (and amused by) her self-important storyteller. For although Oswald announces his intention to keep it a secret which Bastable is telling the story, he immediately gives himself away, inadvertently broadcasting the truth when he tells his readers, "While the story is going on you may be trying to guess [who is narrating it], only I bet you don't. *It was Oswald* who first thought of looking for treasure" (*Story* 11, my emphasis). Any remaining doubt about the identity of the narrator swiftly dissipates as Oswald proceeds to heap praise on himself and criticize his siblings. As Briggs and Moss have pointed out, Nesbit particularly foregrounds Oswald's condescending attitude toward girls and women, prodding her readers to recognize the limitations of his self-satisfied, sexist point of view.[13] In a final effort to impede the process of identification, Nesbit sets up a neat double bind: even if child readers *do* identify with Oswald, they are identifying with a child who refuses to identify with fictional child characters. In other words, since Oswald himself smugly looks down on most "boys in books," child readers wishing to emulate him should by rights make sport of *his* mistakes and idiosyncrasies (*Wouldbegoods* 28).

Nesbit's interest in fostering such detachment emerges not only in the Bastable books but also early on in *Five Children and It*, the first adventure featuring Robert, Cyril, Anthea, and Jane. When the children discover a sand-fairy who agrees to grant them wishes, the narrator remarks to her audience, "I daresay you have often thought what you would do if you had three wishes given you, and have despised the old man and his wife in the black-pudding story, and felt certain that if you had the chance you could think of three really useful wishes without a moment's hesitation" (17). This passage exemplifies how Nesbit's texts both presuppose and create skeptical, educated, active readers. To begin with, if readers are not familiar with "the black-pudding story," it is up to them to find out about it, or to imagine what it might be about. Then, too, this comment reminds audience members that they can practice differentiation rather than identification as the rest of narrative unfolds. That is to say, rather than feeling personally implicated when child characters make one careless, disastrous wish after another, readers have the option of feeling exasperated with and wiser than their textual counterparts.

The nature of the mistakes Nesbit's child protagonists make also serves to discourage young readers from aligning themselves too closely with their literary counterparts, since the worst trouble the Bastables and company get into comes when they adhere too closely to treasured texts. For example, the most upsetting incident in *The Story of the Treasure Seekers* occurs when the Bastables, bent on imitating the fictional children who make their fortune by intervening "to rescue an old gentleman in distress," manufacture such a situation by setting their dog on an elderly man (127). After the furious victim of this fiasco reduces the children to tears by threatening to have them arrested and telling them that he might have died as a result of their dishonest action, Alice miserably explains that "'we wanted to be like the children in books—only we never have the chances they have. Everything they do turns out all right'" (*Story* 136). Efforts to emulate the virtuous child heroes of texts like *Ministering Children* prove equally disastrous; in stories like "The Benevolent Bar" and "The Conscience-Pudding," poor people *do* become "indignant" and even verbally and physically abusive when the children attempt to help them (*Wouldbegoods* 127). Even favored fiction like Kipling's *Jungle Books* causes problems when the children try to reproduce it too exactly: the Bastables' extended reenactment of Mowgli's experiences in the jungle leads them to be beaten and banished to the country at the beginning of *The Wouldbegoods*. When Oswald admits that their most egregious offense that day consisted of taking their uncle's tiger skins and dead "stuffed animals" without permission, propping them up, and playing with them, it becomes clear that this incident illustrates the dangers of borrowing and attempting to reanimate someone else's stuff (17).

In matters of style as well as substance, Nesbit encourages young people to practice fickleness rather than fidelity to texts, to revise rather than plagiarize the discourse of other authors. At the beginning of *The Enchanted Castle* (1906), for example, young Gerald bores and annoys his siblings by narrating his life in the fashion of his favorite novels; exploring a cave with his brother and sister, he intones, "'But their dauntless leader, whose eyes had grown used to the dark while the clumsy forms of the others were bunging up the entrance, had made a discovery'" (11). As Nesbit's narrative unfolds, however, Gerald gradually finds his own storytelling style and stops parroting other authors. Similarly, Noël Bastable learns to deviate from rather than simply ventriloquize the voices that influence his own work. Describing the genesis of the poem Noël writes after the Bastables' housekeeper, Eliza, takes them to see a "Reviving Preacher," Oswald relates:

> everybody cried, and Father said it must have been the Preacher's Eloquence. So Noël wrote:
>
> O Eloquence and what art thou?
> Ay what art thou? because we cried
> And everybody cried inside
> When they came out their eyes were red—
> And it was your doing Father said. (*Story* 51)

The fact that Noël constructs this entire poem around a word he does not understand brings home the point that he does not fully absorb the material he usurps; his use of archaic poetic language and his reference to his father suggest that he has not yet found his own poetic voice. Similar symptoms manifest themselves in Noël's "Lines on a Dead Black Beetle that was poisoned," which begins "Beetle how I weep to see / Thee lying on thy poor back!" and concludes "I wish you were alive again / But Eliza says wishing it is nonsense and a shame" (*Story* 51). Like the paean to the preacher, this poem testifies to other people's eloquence rather than Noël's own; in both cases, he begins by mimicking the high-flown language of other poets and concludes by incorporating unreconstructed comments made by other people.

Here and elsewhere, Nesbit shows children struggling with the same problem all artists grapple with: inundated by other people's narratives, one must strive to prevent these stories from exerting undue influence on oneself. Nesbit dramatizes the difficulties (and rewards) of this quest for originality in her two Arden books, *The House of Arden* (1908) and *Harding's Luck* (1909). To induce the magical Mouldiwarp to appear and work his spells, Elfrida and Edred Arden must produce and recite original poetry. Edred cannot manage this feat at all, and even Elfrida's efforts sometimes fail; on one such occasion, she recognizes that her derivative verses are of "no use," prompting her brother to declare, "'I should think not. . . . Why, it isn't your own poetry at all. It's Felicia M. Hemans'" (*Harding's* 184–85). As a poet, Nesbit herself struggled with this very problem; Briggs notes that "she secretly dreamed of becoming a great poet . . . but in order to write verse at all, she had to imitate, and both the sentiments and techniques she used were usually rather secondhand" (*Woman of Passion* 36). Although Nesbit's work for children allowed her to celebrate rather than hide her debts to other texts, anxiety about recycling the work of others does surface, particularly in *The House of Arden*; given that Nesbit's childhood nickname was Daisy, it is telling that the Mouldiwarp explains one of his magical acts with the words "'The daisies did it. Poor little things! They can't invent at all. But they do carry out other people's ideas quite nicely'" (*House* 79).

However, self-deprecation of this sort should not lead us to dismiss Nesbit as "an energetic hack," as Carpenter does in *Secret Gardens* (126). Objecting strenuously to the inclusion of Nesbit in the canon of great writers for children, he disparages even her "best achievement[s]," remarking that "she knew how to borrow, and the degree of originality in [these stories] is comparatively small" (136). What this reading fails to recognize is that Nesbit's extreme allusiveness itself constitutes an innovative technique, one that her child characters practice constantly and to great effect. At once inimitable and imitative, Oswald's instantly recognizable style suggests that authors can in fact find their own unique voices by mimicking, revising, or elaborating on other writers' work. "Trespassers of the very deepest dye," Nesbit's child protagonists must follow Oswald's lead and become more savvy thieves (*Oswald* 114); the innumerable encounters with real and imaginary "smugglers, and bandits, and highwaymen, and burglars, and coiners" that Nesbit sets up represent efforts to train these children to become better borrowers (*New Treasure* 192). In *The Enchanted Castle*, for example, observing and empathizing with a gang of burglars transforms Gerald from a tedious parrot into a mesmerizing storyteller. After helping some thieves escape with their loot, Gerald recounts his adventures to his siblings, and Nesbit notes:

> As he told [his story] some of the white mystery and magic of the moonlit gardens got into his voice and his words, so that when he told of the statues that came alive, and the great beast that was alive through all its stone, Kathleen thrilled responsive, clutching his arm, and even Jimmy ceased to kick the wall with his boot heels, and listened open-mouthed. (*Enchanted* 96)

Yet even as Nesbit sets up the child as a creative agent in his or her own right, even as she fantasizes about the possibility of mutually productive exploitation, she never fails to acknowledge the tremendous power adults have over children. The complexity of this position is fully embodied in her presentation of a child narrator. Complimenting Nesbit on her seamless channeling of a child's voice, W. W. Robson claims that "in the Bastable books there seems to be no storyteller behind Oswald" (257). In fact, it would be hard to imagine a character more obviously affected and shaped by adult scripts, not only because he ventriloquizes the words of so many different authors but also because Nesbit inserts into his narrative a parade of adult characters who are themselves writers. Besides introducing the kindly, creative Editor, she brings the Bastables into contact with Mrs. Leslie, a professional poet and short story writer, and "Albert-next-door's uncle," a novelist who tells the children "first-rate" stories and advises Oswald on writing matters (*Story* 92). The presence of this charming, avuncular character reminds readers that adults tend not only to be the authors of books but the purchasers as well; praising his favorite neighbor, Oswald says "He gave us our Jungle books" (*Story* 211).

These figures alert us to Nesbit's own presence as a behind-the-scenes storyteller; indeed, at least one of them—Mrs. Leslie—is an explicit self-portrait. Travelling by train to meet the Editor, Oswald and Noël befriend an "awfully jolly" woman writer who turns out to be a famous poet—a glorification of Nesbit's own prolific but never entirely successful career as an author of verse (*Story* 54). Like her creator, Mrs. Leslie writes humorous poems for children; and she gives the boys a sample of her efforts, saying, "'I think you will like [it] because it's about a boy'" (55). Fittingly, this poem is not only about a boy, it is narrated by a boy; and it therefore operates as a microcosm of *The Story of the Treasure Seekers* itself. By providing a detailed demonstration of the way children can be tricked into identifying with an adult-produced image of childhood, this scene challenges Rose's claim that narratives aimed at children seduce their subjects "without the child being given the chance to notice, let alone question, the smoothness and ease of that process" (63).

After describing the pleasures of play and the limited understanding of grown-ups, Mrs. Leslie's young narrator gripes:

> I often wonder whether they
> Ever made up our kinds of play—
> If they were always good as gold
> And only did what they were told. (*Story* 56)

As these lines indicate, the poem draws a clear distinction between "us" and "them"—children and adults—and insists that the narrator is on the side of the child. Yet the scene as a whole unmasks the child narrator as an adult construction; Mrs. Leslie's ability to speak *as* a child, for the express amusement of children, invites readers to recognize the artificiality of Oswald himself. Indeed, Oswald's observation that Mrs. Leslie "didn't talk a bit like a real lady, but more like a jolly sort of grown-up boy in a dress and hat" effectively outs Nesbit as an adult who talks like a boy (57). Before sharing the full text of Mrs. Leslie's poem with his readers, Oswald explains that "she gave it to us . . . so I can copy it down" (55), an act that likewise signals his status as a conduit for someone else's voice.

Prodding children to recognize that adults have indeed "made up our kinds of play," Nesbit here acknowledges the existence of the reader–writer divide, the imaginary nature of the reciprocity she envisions. Thus, although the encounter between Mrs. Leslie and the children begins with a show of mutuality—" 'if you show me [your poems,] I'll show you some of mine,' " Mrs. Leslie tells Noël—there is no question as to who emerges as the real talent; referring to Mrs. Leslie's piece, Oswald admits, "I like it better than Noël's poetry, though I told him I did not, because he looked as if he was going to cry" (55–56). Ultimately, this scene broadcasts the upsetting news that adults can speak for children better than children can speak for themselves; grown-ups, Nesbit suggests, make more convincing children than children do.

The climactic resolution of *The Story of the Treasure Seekers* provides another example of a seemingly mutual moment that actually broadcasts the pervasiveness of adult power. As the narrative draws to a close, the Bastables are reunited with their long-lost "Indian Uncle," whom they assume is "the Red kind" but who ultimately turns out to be a British colonist who has been living in India (231). Noting that the children mistake their uncle for "an imperial subject rather than an imperial functionary" and observing the colonialist nature of the games the children play with their newfound relative, Reimer argues that these final chapters ignore or minimize the exploitative nature of the imperialist project (52). Certainly, the remarkable symmetry of the Bastables' encounter with the Indian Uncle seems to support her claim; just as Nesbit insists on blurring the line between adult and child, writer and reader, she also appears to downplay the division between colonizer and colonized, by setting up a finale that depends on and celebrates the idea of perfect reciprocity.

Pitying their uncle for his poverty, the Bastables invite him to share a special dinner with them, and urge him to take the little money they have. During this meal, the Indian Uncle discovers *their* poverty, whereupon he repents of his refusal to invest in their father's ailing business, secretly showers the family with money and gifts, and finally reveals himself as their benefactor at a dinner party explicitly linked to their own; he invites them to this event by saying, " 'You remember when I dined with you, some time ago, you promised to dine with me some day' " (233). Because this denouement revolves around a fantasy of mutuality, child and adult alike are associated with treasure. Noël writes a poem about the Indian Uncle that concludes "We looked for treasure, but we find / The best treasure of all is the Uncle good and kind" (241). In response, the Indian Uncle "kissed Alice and he smacked Noël on the back, and he said, 'I don't think *I've* done so badly either, if you come to that, though I was never a regular professional treasure seeker' " (242).

But the logic of Nesbit's narrative contradicts the Indian Uncle's claim, thereby revealing her recognition that imperialist projects rarely constitute cases of reciprocal exploitation. For the fact that the Indian Uncle's immense wealth is signified by and associated with the booty he brings back from abroad implies that to be a colonist *is* to be a "professional treasure seeker." Describing the profusion of presents proffered by his newfound relative, Oswald lists

> Japanese china tea-sets for the girls, red and white and gold . . . and long yards and yards of soft silk from India, to make frocks for the girls—and a real Indian sword for Oswald and a book of Japanese pictures for Noël, and some ivory chess men for Dicky. . . . There were carved fans and silver bangles and strings of amber beads, and necklaces of uncut gems . . . and shawls and scarves of silk, and cabinets of brown and gold, and ivory boxes and silver trays, and brass things. (231–32)

Not only does this description connect the act of colonizing to the enterprise of treasure seeking, it also links the Indian Uncle to another purveyor of purloined goods, an avaricious Jewish moneylender whom the Bastables mistake for "a Generous Benefactor, like in Miss Edgeworth" (114). Z. Rosenbaum's luxurious office prefigures the scene of excess just described; Oswald compares the moneylender's room to "a king's palace . . . full of the most splendid things" (121, 118), including "black and gold cabinets, and china, and statues, and pictures . . . and gilt looking-glasses, and boxes of cigars and scent and things littered all over the chairs and tables" (118). Like his Jewish counterpart, the Indian Uncle enters the text in the role of moneylender; during the Bastables' first encounter with their newfound relative, Oswald overhears his father unsuccessfully entreating his wife's brother to loan him "a little capital" to help save his sinking business (215). As the narrative continues, the parallel grows even more pronounced; both Z. Rosenbaum and the Indian Uncle at first refuse to extend financial aid to Mr. Bastable, then relent as a result of meeting the children.

Entitled "The G. B." (the Bastables' shorthand for "Generous Benefactor"), the chapter that chronicles the family's dealings with the Jewish moneylender unsettles the whole idea of benevolent adult intervention. For the character the Bastables read as an openhearted philanthropist turns out to be self-interested, stingy, and unreliable. Moved by the children's poverty, Rosenbaum at first promises to give them a sovereign, but after "stroking the sovereign and looking at it as if he thought it very beautiful," he suddenly puts it back in his pocket and says, "'I'll give you fifteen shillings, and this nice bottle of scent. It's worth far more than the five shillings I'm charging you for it. And, when you can, you shall pay me back the pound, and sixty per cent interest'" (123). Although this encounter convinces Rosenbaum to extend Mr. Bastable's loan, his slimy turnaround after being "touched" by the children encourages readers to question the motives, merit, and dependability of the Indian Uncle, another "kind gentleman who has a lot of money" and who seems to desire, out of the goodness of his heart, to give it to the poor (114).[14]

By linking the Indian Uncle to this unsavory character, Nesbit acknowledges the dark side of appropriation, a process she so often presents as enabling and inspiring. Even as she champions reciprocal exploitation as a viable and valuable mode, she recognizes that colonization generally involves one party exercising power over the other.[15] In particular, as Briggs points out, Nesbit "never forgot . . . that all children, for better or worse, are ultimately at the mercy of all adults" (*A Woman of Passion* xx). While both children and adults seek for treasure in her books, it is invariably adults who possess, disburse, and control assets of all kinds. Indeed, Nesbit repeatedly portrays children as beggars as well as burglars. By presenting the majority of her child characters as impoverished, she demonstrates her keen sense of the limited power and resources of children, their deep dependence on outside sources for inspiration and support. In the Bastables' case, the paucity of their stock renders them poor targets for thieves; thus, the real thief in "The Robber and the Burglar" cheerfully promises never to return to their house, having noticed that they possess nothing worth stealing.

Like *The Treasure Seekers* series, *The Railway Children* (1906) often casts its child characters in the role of beggars. Even after their mother chides them, saying, "you must never, never, never ask strangers to give you things" (63), Roberta, Peter, and Phyllis entreat all kinds of favors from adults outside of their own family. When their mother falls ill, for example, they request an elderly gentleman whom they have never before met to purchase food for her, and Roberta asks the doctor not to charge them the regular rate because of their poverty.[16] Even their thieving savors of begging; acting as "an engine-burglar," Roberta sneaks onto a train and implores the engineer to fix Peter's broken toy engine (78), while Peter gets caught illegally "mining" for coal after his mother tells him that they are "too poor to have a fire" (40). Sympathetic to the family's plight, the Station Master who collars Peter lets him off with the warning "'remember, young gentleman, stealing is stealing, and what's mine isn't yours, whether you call it mining or whether you don't'" (40).

Not only does Nesbit repeatedly characterize children as beggars, she also depicts them as reduced to the condition of breaking into their own home. In *The House of Arden*, poverty-stricken siblings Edred and Elfrida worry about the "burglarish" aspects of sneaking into their former family estate without permission (18). Similarly, before discovering his true identity as the next Lord of Arden, the destitute, homeless Dickie Harding burgles the home of his own wealthy relatives in *Harding's Luck*. The rich image of the child forced to break into his or her own home illustrates Nesbit's shrewd awareness of the way "children's fiction sets up the child as an outsider to its own process" (Rose 2). Presenting youngsters as trespassers in their own domain, Nesbit suggests that adults have colonized childhood so completely that children must struggle to obtain control over their own identities, to steal back their own selfhood. Refusing to portray children as natural phenomena, innocent of influence, Nesbit exposes the extent to which adults—and their texts—teach children how to be children. Indeed, in *Harding's Luck* she dramatizes this process explicitly by documenting Dickie Harding's indoctrination into his own identity as Lord Arden:

> very gradually, yet very quickly, Dickie learned about this new boy who was, and wasn't, himself. [His nurse] would sit by his side by the hour and tell him of things that had happened in the short life of the boy whose place he filled. . . . And as soon as she had told him a thing he found he remembered it—not as one remembers a tale that is told, but as one remembers a real thing that has happened. (69)

Earlier in the narrative, Dickie experiences the same strange feeling when he breaks into the house that contains the secret documents that reveal his true heritage; as he navigates this unfamiliar space, the narrator notes that "he did not need to remember what he had been told. For quite certainly, and most oddly, he *knew* exactly where the door was . . . which way to turn and what passages to go along" (38). For those who have read Dickens, reading about this uncanny experience is an uncanny experience in itself, since (as Briggs points out) the image of the child breaking into a home that will later offer him shelter is stolen from *Oliver Twist*.

Similarly, it could be argued that Nesbit lifted the whole idea of representing young people as thieves from Grahame's *The Golden Age*. In chapters such as

"The Burglars," Grahame emphasizes the "fertility of resource and powers of imagination" of his child characters while simultaneously stressing that they do not fully understand everything they read and hear (114). In keeping with her habit of openly acknowledging her literary debts, Nesbit has Oswald declare that "*The Golden Age* . . . is A1 except where it gets mixed with grown-up nonsense" (*Wouldbegoods* 83). Yet however negatively Oswald may regard Grahame's strategy of blurring the line between innocence and experience, Nesbit herself follows firmly in Grahame's footsteps by suggesting that young people can never escape being mixed up with and shaped by adults and their texts. For this reason, their attempt to find their own voices depends on their willingness to choose which elements they want to reject and which they want to absorb and improvise on and they navigate through a sea of competing discourses.

The colonization paradigm that has proven so popular and influential with theorists of childhood and children's literature assumes that all acts of influence are oppressive, one-way transactions in which adults exploit and manipulate the child for "often perverse and mostly dishonest . . . purposes" (Rose 10). But Nesbit offers a more nuanced vision of this problematic—but not impossible—relationship. Acknowledging the extent to which adults and their texts form and influence children, she nevertheless insists that such power does not preclude the possibility that children can tweak, transform, and renew the scripts they are given. Her narratives dramatize the dangers of buying into a fictional image of oneself, but they also highlight the crucial link between the consumption and the production of texts, reminding us that reading can enable as well as inhibit creativity. The manufacturing of childhood can be a mutual process, Nesbit suggests, if children learn to function as selective, resistant readers. In other words, Nesbit posits the hopeful notion that cross-colonization can occur—that the child, as well as the adult, can appropriate and exploit texts for her own purposes. At the same time, though, she acknowledges that the stubborn power structure that divides reader from writer, child from adult, and colonizer from colonized can never be completely dissolved. Since the categories of perpetrator and victim are perhaps the least interchangeable of all dyads, crime provides Nesbit with an appropriately ambivalent metaphor; the motif of the burglar allows her to simultaneously entertain and disclaim the possibility of reciprocal exploitation.

5

THE CULT OF THE CHILD AND THE CONTROVERSY OVER CHILD ACTORS

Just how different did the Victorians think children were (or should be) from adults? Recent commentators have suggested that "in this period, ideal childhood is generally imagined as a wholly separate estate from adulthood," an Edenic realm that offers a means of detachment and retreat from the painful complexities of adult life (C. Robson 136). In keeping with George Boas's argument in *The Cult of Childhood*, child-loving authors such as Ruskin, Carroll, and Barrie are held especially culpable for erecting "a barrier of nostalgia and regret" between childhood and adulthood by associating youth with an innocence and spontaneity that adults have lost as a result of their worldly experience (Coveney 240). In other words, the cult and the children's literature penned by some of its members are viewed as the most pronounced manifestation of a widespread tendency to regard the child as a primitive Other and childhood as an idyllic separate sphere, a sort of escape hatch from the artificiality of contemporary culture and the complications of engaging in intimate relationships with other adults.

There are a number of serious problems with this account. To begin with, very few Golden Age children's classics wholeheartedly embrace the Child of Nature paradigm, as even Humphrey Carpenter—a key advocate of this critical story—is forced to admit.[1] For this reason, as I showed in my introduction, nineteenth-century proponents of primitivism objected to the work of many prominent children's authors on the grounds that they had failed to differentiate clearly between innocence and experience. Moreover, the same sort of criticism was leveled at the cult of the child, which the Victorians recognized was partly responsible for the "excessive elaboration of . . . toys, books, pictures, and literature" aimed at children ("Worship" 1298).

Writing for the *Spectator* in 1869, the anonymous author of "The Worship of Children" noted the emergence of a new and "fanatical cultus of children" (1299), characterizing the explosion of sophisticated children's stories by such authors as Ruskin, Kingsley, Margaret Gatty, and George MacDonald as an outgrowth of this movement. In no uncertain terms, this commentator complains that the cult constitutes an affront to his own more Romantic conception of the child, since child-lovers such as Ruskin foolishly assume that youngsters are capable of appreciating "high art" (1300), serving up "luxurious, elaborate, and refined" fare rather than recognizing that "a bare, rugged, and almost grotesque simplicity of material is . . . the best possible food" for primitive young minds (1299). Children, he insists, cannot understand allegory, parody, or any technique that evokes the "complexity of real life" (1299); their literary diet should be limited to ancient fairy tales and nursery rhymes, and didactic stories in which moral messages are presented in stark black-and-white terms.

Contrast this condescending attitude with that of one of the Golden Age authors this critic attacks: William Brighty Rands, author of the popular—though now sadly neglected—*Lilliput Levee* (1864), a collection of children's poems. Not only did Rands produce both reverent and irreverent work that contemporary critics deemed "far beyond" the comprehension of children ("Worship" 1299), he also penned a passionate essay, "Children and Children's Books" (1866), in which he argued that adults should respect the abilities of children enough to give them access to "adult" poetry, as Lucy Aiken did when she published excerpts from Alexander Pope, John Dryden, and Walter Scott in *Poetry for Children* (1802), a book Rands adored as a child. Rands's rallying cry is not simplicity but "sympathy" ("Children" 464); he argues that children should be treated not "as if they were crude, shapeless lumps, that had to be 'turned' into figures on the . . . potter's wheel" but "as we do our equals in a noble friendship" (465).

As his careful phrasing here suggests, Rands recognized that children did not in fact enjoy perfect equality with adults. Anticipating the basic plot of Dickens's *Holiday Romance*, the poem "Lilliput Levee" chronicles what happens once "the Children, clever bold folks,/Have turned the tables upon the Old Folks!" (1), a setup that takes for granted the existence of the adult–child hierarchy. Having wrested away the role of top dog, the children inflict lessons and "catechisings" on the adults (4), down sherry and negus, and compose an alternative value system for themselves:

They offered a prize for the laziest boy,
And one for the most Magnificent toy,
They split or burnt the canes off-hand,
They made new laws in Lilliput-land. (3)

The best twist comes at the very end of the poem, when the previously inconspicuous narrator suddenly announces:

> I noticed, being a man of rhymes,
> An advertisement in the *Lilliput Times*:—
> "PINAFORE PALACE. This is to state
> That the court is in want of a Laureate. . . .
>
> Said I to myself, here's a chance for me,
> The Lilliput Laureate for to be!
> And these are the Specimens I sent in
> To Pinafore Palace. Shall I win? (7)

In a move that neatly parallels the plot of the poem, the adult author—previously a distant, omniscient figure—is here abruptly reduced to the rank of a nervous "candidate" whose fate hangs on the judgment of children (8). This moment alerts young readers to their own power of discrimination, of weighing rather than simply absorbing the literary offerings of adults. Since this poem prefaces the rest of the collection, it invites child readers to view the rest of Rands's work with an evaluative eye. Just as the children in the poem function as artful dodgers who creatively rewrite the rules of their society, Rands assumes that his child readers are intelligent enough to cope with puns, topical references, and other material that commentators like the critic quoted earlier deemed both impure and impossible for children to comprehend.

Far from promoting primitivism, then, Rands and many other Golden Age authors resisted "the cry for extreme simplicity—almost inanity" made by cultural commentators who urged children's writers to regard the child as a less evolved breed of being ("Writers" 717). Similarly, this chapter argues that in general, members of the cult of the child were at best ambivalent and often hostile to efforts to conceive of the child as an innocent Other. Far from being wedded to the notion that a firm barrier separated child from adult, they enjoyed engaging in intimate intercourse with clever, artful children whose precocious abilities enabled them to blur the line between innocence and experience.

Before I launch into that argument, it is necessary to note that the critical story just outlined rests on another, larger error: our habit of overestimating the general extent of the Victorians' investment in innocence. As Kincaid observes, it is simply a mistake to assert, as Jeffrey Weeks does, that "the separateness of childhood was axiomatic in Victorian ideology" (Weeks 48). To be sure, over the course of the nineteenth century, artists, journalists, and activists unleashed a host of new efforts to establish a strict dividing line between childhood and adulthood, innocence and experience. But the very vehemence with which they had to make their case—coupled with the glacial pace of reform relating to child labor,[2] education,[3] and the age of consent[4]—indicates that many Victorians remained unconvinced of the separateness and sanctity of childhood.

As both Deborah Gorham and Matthew Sweet point out, nineteenth-century England was not a nation that had wholeheartedly embraced the equation of youth with purity but rather one "in which the concept of childhood was being actively developed and redrafted" (Sweet 171). Throughout this period, all kinds of debates were taking place about the definition of childhood and the child's proper role within the family and society at large. Were children full of original sin or original innocence? How young was too young for sexual intercourse? When did childhood end and adulthood begin—or was there a state in between that needed to be identified and studied? (According to Gorham and John R. Gillis, it was not until the end of the century that the concept of adolescence emerged as a meaningful category.) Did children have any legal rights at all, or were they simply the property of their fathers? Should poor children be inured to labor as soon as they were old enough to work, or should the state intervene to ensure that they received some sort of education? What sort of education should they get? Far from being settled, these were live questions right up until (and past) the end of the nineteenth century, as Hugh Cunningham and Viviana Zelizer have noted.[5]

In other words, the "otherness" of children was not a settled fact during the nineteenth century but the subject of a long, drawn-out fight. Trying desperately to persuade the general public to share their dismay at the plight of the uneducated, unprotected child, nineteenth-century activists employed two quite different strategies. The first was to emphasize the incompetence of children: their pathetic unfitness for the demands being made on them, their inability to survive in an uncaring, materialistic world. Dickens uses this tactic repeatedly, confronting his audience with a host of sad cases, including poor Jo, the crossing sweeper in *Bleak House* (1853), who "never know'd nothink" and can only parrot back the Lord's Prayer as he dies, with no understanding of its meaning (571). Social reformers like Josephine Butler, William Allen, Mary Carpenter, and W. T. Stead shared this habit of characterizing quite old children as pathetic lost lambs, unable to speak, think, or act on their own behalf.[6] Indeed, as Cunningham notes, child-savers routinely applied the word "infant" to poor children of all ages in order to characterize them as fragile, helpless beings (*Children of the Poor* 88). In other words, efforts to champion the rights of working-class youth often entailed their dehumanization and objectification.

The other strategy that activists favored involved acknowledging the impressive skills acquired by young people but characterizing such competence as horrifying—a dreadful precocity. The most obvious example from Dickens's oeuvre is "sharp" little Jenny Wren, who has been prematurely burdened with (and deformed by) "sordid shames and cares," such as the need to support her drunken father by toiling away as a dolls' dressmaker (*Our Mutual Friend* 402, 294). Campaigning in 1851 for state-funded education, one activist characterized the London street child as a "hideous antithesis, an infant in age, a man in shrewdness and vice" (quoted in May 21), a description reminiscent of the Artful Dodger and his mates, who intersperse their thieving with periods of leisure in which they enjoy "smoking long clay pipes, and drinking spirits with the air of middle-aged men" (*Oliver Twist* 105). In his famous series of articles on *London Labour and the London Poor* (1861–62), journalist Henry Mayhew likewise focused on quick-witted children like the little watercress seller who, "although only eight years of age, had entirely lost all childish ways, and was, indeed, in thoughts and manner, a woman" (64). Clearly disturbed by the girl's precocious competence, Mayhew observes: "there was something cruelly pathetic in hearing this infant" describe her proficiency at conducting business and coping with "the bitterest struggles of life," while evincing no familiarity with the definition of a park or the fun of playing with other children (64).

We tend to assume that participants in the cult of the child shared a similar investment in the idea of the child's otherness—that they had thoroughly rejected the old view of children as miniature adults, capable of working and playing alongside grown-ups. But in fact, the cultists often opposed reformers' efforts to erect a strict line of division between youth and age, even as they voiced allegiance to the ideal of innocent simplicity. Take for example the case of Ernest Dowson, author of "The Cult of the Child" (1889), who repeatedly celebrated the child's stainless purity in both that essay and his poetry. Yet the actual content of the essay and Dowson's behavior toward real children vividly attest to his fascination with precocious competence. Although "The Cult of the Child" is full of Romantic effusions about the child's natural artlessness, it is nevertheless a spirited defense of the right of very young children to work as professional stage performers—a salvo *against* the campaign being waged by Dickens, Lord Shaftesbury, and others who opposed child labor.

Moreover, Dowson also resisted the new social and legal conventions that put girls off limits as erotic partners, such as the Criminal Law Amendment Act (1885), which raised the age of consent to sixteen. By actively wooing a series of precocious young girls—including Adelaide Foltinowicz, who was only eleven when he fell in love with her—Dowson indicated his opposition to what he viewed as an absurd "English tradition which assumes Heaven knows why? that a girl is not Amabilis when she is at her most amiable age" (*Letters* 221). And his desire for young girls was not merely chaste and sentimental; despite his poetic declarations about their redemptive purity, in 1889 he confided to his friend Arthur Moore that he had contemplated having sex with a fifteen-year-old "tart" named Bertha Van Raalte but decided that "in view of the new Act le jeu ne valait" (the game wasn't worth it) (*Letters* 116, 118).

How can we account for such contradictory behavior? One time-honored response is to suggest that the cultists were hypocrites who paid lip service to innocence as a sly cover for their fascination with the sexuality of young people. But this interpretation demands that we attribute a level of calculated malice to men like Dowson, Carroll, and Ruskin that ultimately seems untenable. As their diaries and letters reveal, these were thoughtful, morally sensitive, and highly self-critical men. Even Dowson, who at times seems so shameless in his pursuit of prepubescent paramours, engaged in tortured soul-searching about his own motives. For example, as Jad Adams observes, Dowson reacted with "morbid sensitivity" to the public scandal surrounding the arrest of Edward Newton (58), a thirty-nine-year-old journalist who had fallen in love with an eleven-year-old girl, just as Dowson himself had done. When this scandal broke, Dowson was avidly courting Adelaide. In an agonized letter to Moore, he declared that reading this "most disgusting story of a most disgusting person" in the newspaper has given him "a moral shock . . . which has racked me ever since with an infinite horror":

> The worst of it was, that it read like a sort of foul and abominable travesty of—pah, what is the good of hunting for phrases. You must know what I mean, and how I am writhing. . . . I can't help feeling that even her people—and mine, as far as that goes—might take alarm and suspect my motives. And yet I swear there never was a man more fanatically opposed to the corruption of innocence . . . than I am. (*Letters* 213)

At some level, Dowson was aware that his own behavior was not in keeping with this avowed allegiance to innocence, as indicated by the fact that he concludes his letter to Moore hopelessly: "I don't expect consolations from you: I don't see that there are any" (213). Charging him with hypocrisy does not help us to understand his predicament.

The second and more popular way of accounting for the often contradictory behavior of the cultists is to maintain that they were so convinced of the unclouded innocence of young people that they felt no need to shield them from sexual matters. For example, faced with the undeniably erotic photographs of naked or semi-undraped children taken by Carroll and Julia Margaret Cameron, commentators such as Morton N. Cohen, Karoline Leach, and Douglas R. Nickel contend that the Victorians could feel comfortable placing (and viewing) children in these quasi-pornographic poses because they "believed so emphatically in their total insulation from the implications of such postures" (Nickel 66).

The problem with this line of argument is that it assumes that the ideal of innocence was completely entrenched by midcentury, so much so that middle-class artists and their audiences could not possibly have entertained the idea that the child might function as a sexual being. But in a culture in which innumerable prepubescent Londoners "[went] about openly soliciting prostitution"—according to the policemen who testified before an 1881 House of Lords committee—such naïveté seems incredible (quoted in Linnane 184). Throughout the final decades of the century, the popular press publicized multiple instances of adults dallying with minors, including the (fake) rape of a thirteen-year-old chronicled in "The Maiden Tribute of Modern Babylon" (1885) by W. T. Stead, a series of articles we know Carroll saw. According to a correspondent for *Figaro in London*, "every evening towards midnight more than five hundred girls in ages between twelve and fifteen parade between Piccadilly Circus and Waterloo Place," while the Cleveland Street scandal and the Wilde trial drew attention to the presence of boy prostitutes on the city streets (quoted in Pearsall 350). According to Ronald Pearsall, there were frequent references in pornographic periodicals to men with a taste for "unripe fruit" (316), and brothels specializing in children existed "in all parts of London, and particularly in the East End" (350).

Moreover, it was not just poor children who were routinely regarded as potential erotic partners. The battle over the question of when girls in particular became fair game for suitors was fought at all levels of society. Throughout the nineteenth century, twelve remained the legal age at which females could get married, and many prominent men—including Ruskin, Frederic Harrison, Edward White Benson, and Philip Wilson Steer—courted and even proposed to well-bred prepubescent girls. We tend to assume that middle- and upper-class Victorians youngsters were sequestered away in nurseries, but biographies and autobiographies of writers, artists, academics, and religious leaders from this era suggest that after infancy, frequent and intimate contact with adult society was fairly routine. For example, artist Henrietta Ward (1832–1924) went to her first ball at eleven; around the same time, she fell in love with her future husband, who had been hired as her drawing tutor. They got engaged when she was just fourteen.[7] A few decades later, Carroll's own brother Wilfred fell in love with a fourteen-year-old, Alice Donkin, though he was persuaded to wait six years before marrying her. Given this state of affairs, it seems highly unlikely that when Carroll photographed young Miss Donkin in the act of pretending to elope, he believed her to be completely cut off from such an "adult" activity!

Rather than assuming that members of the cult were calculating hypocrites or clueless naïfs, a better way to make sense of their inconsistent behavior is to view this movement as a cultural phenomenon that reflected competing—and incompatible—conceptions of childhood. More specifically, it is the site where the relatively new concept of the child as an innocent, helpless Other clashed most dramatically with an older vision of the child as an adult in the making. Take for example the case of Edward White Benson, who became archbishop of Canterbury in 1882. When speaking in the abstract about children, Benson—like Dowson and Carroll—was prone to rhapsodize about their "playfulness" and "purity" (quoted in Millais 378). Yet when he fell in love with eleven-year-old Mary ("Minnie") Sidgwick, his behavior toward her prompted one of his biographers to observe that "the Victorian child was very much thought of as the Victorian grown-up only not yet quite so large" (Williams 13). Describing the night he proposed, for example, Benson records approvingly that the twelve-year-old Minnie "said nothing silly or childish" (56). Indeed, his diary entries are filled with tributes to his future bride's emotional and intellectual precocity: her love for poetry; the "keenness and depth of her thought"; the "great parts and peculiarly strong affection [that] have been discernible in her . . . [since she was] a very young child" (quoted in Benson 55, 52).

Benson's stance toward children thus reflects both a sentimental preoccupation with innocence *and* a lingering commitment to an older conception of childhood that held that young people could function as knowing, competent, and romantically available beings. Indeed, reading his and other cultists' statements about children, one gets the sense that this radical uncertainty about the child's status was itself erotically exciting. Pondering Rose La Touche's mixture of childish and coquettish qualities, for example, Ruskin noted, "I don't quite know what to make of her. . . . She wears her round hat in the sauciest way possible—and is a firm—fiery little thing" (*Winnington Letters* 121). Similarly, recounting his delicious uncertainty in regard to the Jamesean question of just how much an attractive young girl named Lena knew, Dowson observed, "I am in the condition of the perplexed lover in 'Daisy Miller.' Is she amazingly innocent or impudence personified?" (*Letters* 62). In just the same way, Benson wondered in his diary whether little Minnie's seemingly "guileless" manner masked a secret knowledge of—and determination to encourage—his romantic intentions toward her (54). Fittingly, it was he who, years later, told Henry James an anecdote about corrupt innocents that served as the germ for *The Turn of the Screw* (1898).

Of all the cultural sites where the cult manifested itself, the theatre provides the best arena in which to trace how strongly Victorian and Edwardian child-lovers were drawn to precocious youngsters who blurred the line between innocence and experience. Carroll, Dowson, Barrie, and many other members of the cult adored the stage, often taking their child-friends with them to watch the work of professional child actors. This act in itself suggests they were not fully committed to establishing and preserving the innocent otherness of children, since reformers determined to erect a binary opposition between adult and child strongly opposed such activities, as I will show. In my introduction, I traced how nineteenth-century commentators who embraced Romantic primitivism often complained that the work of Golden Age fantasy authors was not sufficiently respectful of the child's difference because it included "adult" content, addressed a mixed audience, and presupposed the presence of worldly or "blasé" child audience members. The very same criticisms were leveled at the theatrical events beloved by Carroll and his fellow cultists, which included pantomimes, stand-alone performances by child prodigies, and other kinds of shows in which child performers played featured roles.

Yet even as members of the cult defied "Mrs. Grundy" by indulging a fascination for precocious competence that many of their peers found revolting, they were not deaf to calls of impropriety. Sometimes, their response was to make distinctions so fine that they now seem absurd. For example, Carroll protested vigorously when he witnessed "a bevy of sweet innocent-looking little girls sing . . . the chorus 'He said 'Damn me!' He said 'Damn me!''" in *The Children's Pinafore* (Opera Comique 1879), an all-child production of the Gilbert and Sullivan operetta ("Stage and the Spirit" 221). Yet he went six times to another all-child production, taking "at least three child friends to each performance" (Foulkes 110), even though it featured child actors impersonating adult lovers and rolling around the stage as if "in a drunken and incapable state" (review of *Robin Hood, Times*). Similarly, as an avid fan of pantomime, Ruskin regularly enjoyed watching cross-dressed actresses cavort about the stage, but when a chorus of girls dressed as boys pulled out cigars and begin to smoke them during a performance of *Ali Baba and the Forty Thieves* (Covent Garden 1866), he suddenly pronounced himself horrified at the evident amusement of his fellow audience members.[8]

In a similarly inconsistent move, after critics of the craze for child actors finally succeeded in their attempts to associate precocity with exploitation and abuse, cultists and other fans of this phenomenon simply carried on celebrating the prematurely developed skills of professional child actors while simultaneously denying that the term "precocious" applied to them, as I will show. Such commitment to a trend that was so widely denounced as destructive of youthful purity should prompt us not only to reconsider our definition of the cult of the child but also to speculate on the question of why so many Victorian playgoers continued to flock to see precocious child performers. For as Hugues Lebailly and Richard Foulkes have emphasized, literally "thousands of enthusiasts" embraced this trend (Lebailly 27); fans included not just child-loving men such as Carroll and Ruskin but women and children as well. During her first trip to the playhouse as a little girl, for instance, Kate Terry Gielgud was impressed by seeing "*H.M.S. Pinafore* acted by children—professional children [who had] already played . . . innumerable" roles despite their youth (53). Similarly, drama critic Henry A. Clapp recalled his glee at seeing a company of Viennese child performers when he was eight years old (7).[9]

Because of the ephemeral nature of such performances, we cannot pretend to know for certain why featured child performers—that is to say, children who did more than mere chorus work, who had solo speeches, songs, and dances to perform—were so popular. However, since both fans and critics of this vogue often emphasized the prematurely developed proficiency and professionalism of child actors and noted their ability to skillfully inhabit adult roles, it seems worthwhile to speculate about why nineteenth-century audiences so enjoyed seeing children act like grown-ups. Perhaps we can read this fascination with precocity as a form of resistance to the growing pressure to conceive of the child as incompetent, weak, and artless, a separate order of being who could not work alongside or enter into intimate relationships with adults. Then again, since many child performers were working class, perhaps their competence appealed to people because it seemed to justify a socioeconomic system in which childhood in the idealized state was not very widely available. In other words, if the professionalism of child actors "proved" that lower-class children were not that different from adults, then people might feel reassured that such children did not really *need* to enjoy an extended period of protection, dependence, and development.

For whatever reason, though, the public "frenzy" over child stars was not a short-lived fad that died out in the 1820s, as Allardyce Nicoll asserts in his magisterial *History of English Drama* (21).[10] On the contrary, featured child performers remained so visible that an 1878 issue of the *Theatre* included a lengthy editorial calling for their banishment from the stage.[11] A decade later, responding to the popularity of *Little Lord Fauntleroy* and other plays centered around child characters, the leading theatrical trade paper the *Era* declared: "This is an age of juvenile prodigies. We have juvenile musicians, juvenile acrobats, juvenile reciters, and juvenile actors and actresses" ("Child Drama"). Advertisements for and reviews of late Victorian child stars such as Baby Benson, Lydia Howard, Harry Grattan, and Vera Beringer provide support for this claim. Indeed, as late as 1899, a critic evaluating the new crop of "Leading Little Actors and Actresses of the Day" for the *English Illustrated Magazine* felt he could declare that "as regards to the youthful Roscius, things seem pretty much as they were" (Dolman 177).[12]

The craze for child performers who combined "the artlessness of the nursery with the skill of the Conservatoire"—praise earned by Beringer in the role of Little Lord Fauntleroy[13]—was therefore not just coincident with the Golden Age of children's literature but intertwined with it. Authors such as Burnett, Carroll, Twain, and Barrie provided golden opportunities for child performers, and their interest in the phenomenon of the theatrical child suggests yet another possible explanation for the appeal of such performers. One of my contentions here has been that Golden Age children's authors used the trope of collaboration to grapple with the issue of how much agency one can have as an acculturated subject. It therefore makes sense that these writers were fascinated by child actors. Involved in an inherently collaborative art form, successful child performers were perceived as being both artful and natural, both inscribed and original. In other words, they modeled a form of nonautonomous agency in which being scripted by adults did not necessarily preclude them from functioning as intelligent, creative individuals.

PHENOMENAL INFANTS

It is no secret that many members of the cult of the child were fans of child actors.[14] But because so little work has been done on the reception of shows that prominently featured children, the full import of this predilection has gone unnoticed: in enjoying and endorsing such performances, the cultists were positioning themselves in opposition to a long, loud tradition of commentators who vociferously attacked the vogue for child performers, viewing it as a threat not only to the purity of the young but to the maturity of the old as well.

Concerted opposition to this fad began during the first decade of the nineteenth century, after the tremendous success of William Henry West Betty—also known as the Infant Roscius—triggered a craze for child prodigies who performed adult parts such as Shylock, Richard III, Lady Teazle, and Widow Cheerly. During his tenure as a drama critic for the *News* from 1805 to 1807, the Romantic poet and essayist Leigh Hunt launched a furious (and extremely entertaining) series of attacks on "this inundation of infants . . . who are so hastily forsaking their bibs and tuckers for the sock and buskin" ("Theatricals," 11 Aug. 1805). Besides panning the work of all-child acting companies such as the Academic Theatre and individual child prodigies such as Master Betty, Miss Fisher, and Miss Mudie, Hunt also suggested that the public's avid admiration for such performances revealed a deplorable deficiency in "the national taste" ("Theatricals," 11 Aug. 1805).

In his pungent diatribes against this fad, most of which have never been reprinted, Hunt employed the binary strategy I just outlined, helping to set the pattern for the many critiques of child performers that followed.[15] On the one hand, he repeatedly characterized child actors as incompetent naïfs shoved into the limelight by greedy parents and managers. Their appeal, he insisted, was based on novelty rather than talent, making audiences who admired them as "deluded" as those credulous souls who gape when showmen trot out learned pigs and five-legged rams (review of *The Country Girl*). Indeed, he declared that young actors could never achieve excellence as artists: since their immature minds can form no conception of "manly or womanly character," juvenile performers are mere puppets who mechanically parrot back material they cannot comprehend ("Abstract"). After all, Hunt explained, children have not experienced the emotions they are called on to convey, and "no one can be expected to represent what he cannot feel" ("Some Remarks"). Moreover, the young lack "a sufficient acquaintance with that world which it is the business of the stage to imitate, and with which a child [has so] little mingled" ("Abstract").

On the other hand, to the extent that acclaimed child prodigies such as Master Betty and Miss Mudie *did* seem capable of understanding and conveying "adult" emotions, complex ideas, and worldly humor, such "prematurity of knowledge" rendered them "disgusting" to Hunt ("Abstract"). He thus disparaged the "confident vulgarity" of a thirteen-year-old child comedian ("Accurate List") and questioned whether "a delicate little female seven years of age is the proper representative of a royal tyrant or a vulgar masculine scold" ("Theatricals," 11 Aug. 1805). Hunt reserved his most withering scorn for all-child performances of bawdy plays such as William Wycherly's *The Country Wife*.[16] In a passage that drips with irony, he observed that the opportunity to perform in this type of show gives a baby actress

> such new ideas and induces her to get rid of that foolish innocent behaviour which makes the other sex so distant and so cold: the little boys too in the performance of such a comedy gain much improvement of this kind, they become what is called *knowing fellows*, and can stare a female audience in the face with as much unconcern as they would contemplate a piece of gingerbread: this shews that they have no ridiculous bashfulness, which might be detrimental to their advancement in knowledge. ("Academic Theatre")

Before long, Hunt cheerfully assures his audience, "these sprightly children, totally exempt from the uncomfortable restrictions of childhood, such as regular hours, simplicity of manners, and innocence of mind . . . will present a delightful spectacle to the whole town" by becoming playboys and prostitutes ("Academic Theatre").[17]

Though Hunt himself was later caricatured by Dickens as a boy who refused to grow up, as a drama critic he vehemently insisted that a strict line should be drawn between age and youth.[18] Over and over again, he complained that the adoring crowds who enjoyed watching children act like adults were insufficiently attuned to and protective of the innocent otherness of children. Rather than allowing children to stay up late and accustom themselves to the glare of the public spotlight, adults should sequester them in the nursery where they belonged. Otherwise, he warned, children would become repulsively precocious, even as their adult fans would be infantilized by indulging their taste for such puerile entertainment. "Let us admire children as children," he exhorted his readers in another impassioned attack on what he dubbed "Rosciuscism": "to admire them as men is to become children ourselves" ("Abstract"). If they must take to the stage, he declared, children should be confined to playing child roles, since pretending to be adults "destroys that innocent simplicity of thought and behaviour which is the beauty and the happiness of childhood" ("Academical Theatre").[19]

All of the points Hunt made in regard to featured child performers recur in the attacks on this craze that continued to appear throughout the nineteenth century. Reviewers on both sides of Atlantic echoed Hunt's insistence that infant wonders were incompetent novelty items rather than skilled artists.[20] Those opposed to child labor in all its forms were especially prone to characterizing stage children as utterly inept victims, as indicated by the example of Dickens's infamous "infant phenomenon" in *Nicholas Nickleby* (1839). Dosed with gin by her parents "to prevent her growing tall" (365), little Miss Crummles cannot even manage to embody girlish purity in a convincing manner, stumbling though an absurd "little ballet interlude" in which she wordlessly attempts to mime maidenhood (364). Just as Hunt complained that the popularity of stage children came at the expense of more mature, talented actors, Dickens allows an older member of the Crummles's company to object that this bungling "little sprawler" is "forced down the people's throats, while other people are passed over" (366). Dickens also follows Hunt's lead by associating child performers with trained animals. Just after Mr. Crummles announces to Nicholas that his children are in the theatrical profession, he adds that he also likes to trot out his dog and pony, since he is always looking to add more "novelty" to his shows (359).

This profoundly negative image of the stage child proved so influential that decades later, critics who wanted to praise child prodigies still felt compelled refer to it, as when a reviewer evaluating Master Bertie Coote's performance in an 1876 pantomime assured his readers, "Here we have no trace of the 'infant phenomenon' so ridiculed by Dickens."[21] Yet, as I have argued elsewhere, Dickens warped his source material significantly in his drive to portray child performers as incompetent, voiceless victims.[22] Whereas Miss Crummles exhibits no dramatic range or skill of any kind, her real-life counterparts were called on to display "amazing versatility" by inhabiting a dizzying variety of roles—tragic and comic, male and female, old and young, English and foreign—often in the course of single evening (Waters 86). Indeed, many child prodigies, including Jean Davenport (who has been identified by Malcolm Morley as a probable model for Miss Crummles)[23] performed in vehicles specially designed to showcase their protean powers: virtuoso showpieces such as *The Manager's Daughter*, *An Actress of All Work*, *The March of Intellect*, and *Whirligig Hall* offered child prodigies the opportunity to play five or six radically different roles and sometimes to sing, dance, and play instruments as well.

Featured children in plays, pantomimes, and all-child productions likewise took on extremely demanding roles. Before reaching the age of fifteen, for instance, Kate Terry had played a leading part in several Christmas pantomimes at the Princess's Theatre, as well as Ariel in *The Tempest* (1857) and Cordelia in

King Lear (1858). Kate's more famous sister Ellen made her official debut at age nine as Mamillius in *The Winter's Tale* (Princess's 1856); a year later, she performed the role of Puck in *A Midsummer Night's Dream* and the Fairy Goldenstar in *Harlequin and the White Cat.* Nor were the Terry sisters alone in playing featured roles at a young age. The Victorian stage was crowded with families of young siblings with similar résumés, including the Batemans, the Grattans, the Lloyds, the Vokeses, the Cootes, the Bowmans, the Adesons, the Weblings, the Vaynes, and the Harrises.[24]

Many of these children began their careers as infant phenomena before making their official debuts in plays and pantomimes. For example, Harry Grattan (1867–1951) joined his brothers and sisters in an act called "The Little Grattans" before playing featured roles in *Uncle Tom's Cabin* (Surrey 1871), *Rip Van Winkle* (Princess's 1875), and *Richard III* (Drury Lane 1876). He then tackled starring roles in all-child productions of *Little Goody Two-Shoes* (Adelphi 1876), *Robin Hood* (Adelphi 1877), and *H.M.S. Pinafore* (Opera Comique 1879). He and other youngsters who participated in all-child productions of burlesques, operettas, and pantomimes had to memorize and execute long passages of difficult music, as well as complicated choreography, stage business, and dialogue.

Of course, the fact that these children took on challenging roles does not mean that they played them well. Working on the assumption that nineteenth-century children were prized for their innocent otherness, Carolyn Steedman suggests in her otherwise compelling study *Strange Dislocations* (1994) that featured child performers were valued for their adorable incompetence: "What is 'priceless' in the child's performance is its attempt to be part of the adult world, and the very uselessness of that attempt" (144).[25] But a broad survey of contemporary responses to child stars and all-child productions reveals that when nineteenth-century children tackled featured roles, they were valued not for their comic ineptitude but for their "extraordinary precosity of talent" (review of *Hamlet*).[26] Over and over, commentators marvel not at the comic incongruity of young people pretending to be adults but at "the marvellous manner in which the children fitted their parts, and their characters fitted them. . . . All were competent, and more than competent indeed, for sometimes they displayed absolute genius" (review of *Children's Pinafore*, *Era*).

Indeed, it was seen as a benefit of all-child productions that they did not lessen the audience's appreciation for the skill of child actors by placing them alongside adult performers, whose greater experience and ability would naturally have made the young people seem less outstanding. The case of Miss Mudie—a child prodigy who was actually billed as "the Infant Phenomenon"—provides an early illustration of this point.[27] In 1805, this seven-year-old was hissed and hounded off the stage when she performed alongside adult actors who made her appearance in a grown-up role seem incongruous.[28] Yet when she performed another adult role in an all-child production a year later, even Hunt admitted that she had a decided and well-deserved success, though he could not resist prefacing his (quite fulsome) praise of her acting with rudeness about her previous performance: "Disgusting as this child appeared when contrasting the feebleness of infancy with the excellencies of matured age," he declared, her talents showed to better advantage "when opposed to that of her infant fraternity" (review of *Roxalana*). Decades later, reviewing the work of another all-child acting troupe known as the "Living Miniatures," the *Era* reiterated the notion that in general, child stars "are more advantageously seen together, or not at all" (review of Living Miniatures 11).[29]

What this and other similar reviews suggest is that midcentury child performers had to overcome a significant amount of prejudice in order to impress critics, thanks in large part to the efforts of Hunt and Dickens. Just as this review of the Living Miniatures announces that "very few persons are sanguine enough to expect [anything good] when they see the announcement of an infant or juvenile phenomenon in a playbill" (10–11), an 1876 review of the child prodigy Baby Benson states: "The announcement in a bill of an exhibition of juvenile precosity seldom awakens much expectation, and we are inclined to the opinion that even the 'infant phenomenon' which shed such remarkable celebrity on the family circle of Mr. Vincent Crummles would nowadays fail to excite a sensation. . . . As a rule, we like not children upon the stage" (review of Baby). Similarly, reviewing Vera Beringer's star turn in *Little Lord Fauntleroy*, Frederick Wedmore declared, "I generally detest child acting." Yet all three of these critics go on to acknowledge that despite their aversion to child performers, they were impressed by these phenomenally "clever and well-trained" child stars, who "seem to feel all they say, instead of following the general parrot-like rule" (review of Living Miniatures, *Era* 11).

These critics' shared insistence that child actors should fully understand their roles and exhibit "talent very far in advance of [their] years" is absolutely characteristic of responses to featured child performers throughout the nineteenth century (review of Baby). Rather than assuming that the innocence of young performers rendered them unfit to comprehend or inhabit their parts, commentators either marveled that the children's acting was "full of intelligence and meaning" and guided by a deep "sense of character" (review of *Children's Pinafore, Era*) or complained when they felt that "docility rather than appreciation of character . . . lies at the basis" of an impersonation (review of Living Miniatures, *Times*). Either way, they appreciated the difficulty "of procuring little folks competent to undertake characters hitherto associated with 'grown-ups,'"[30] a remark that reveals their shared assumption that the appeal of child performers depends on their precocious proficiency.

In other words, the appeal of such performers seems to have been based not on innocence per se but on the combination of youth (or at least the appearance of it)[31] with theatrical expertise "such as the 'oldest stager' might have envied" (review of *Children's Pinafore, Era*). Thus, the girl who played Little Buttercup in *The Children's Pinafore* garnered praise for combining "a woman's voice with a child's face" (review of *Children's Pinafore, Theatre* 39), while the boy impersonating Dick Deadeye was lauded for having "studied his comic business with the utmost attention and with the keenest ideas of humour. Never has 'an old head upon young shoulders' turned to more whimsical account" (review of *Children's Pinafore, Era*). Children performing in all-child productions of pantomimes earned similar praise: *Era* reviewers favorably compared Master Godfrey's song "I'm the Boy the Girls Run After" in *Dick Whittington* (Avenue 1882) to "the effort of a practised professional" (review of *Dick* 5) and marveled that the boy who played Pantaloon in *Little Goody Two Shoes* (Adelphi 1876) was "truly an old man in miniature" ("Children's Pantomime"). Whereas activist authors such as Dickens used descriptions just like these to characterize precocity as a cause for concern and even disgust, the theatre seems to have provided an arena for celebrating the prematurely developed talents of youngsters whose performances blurred the line between innocence and experience.

My contention that the appeal of featured child actors was based at least in part on their artistic abilities not only fits with a wide sampling of reviews by different critics but also helps make sense of the longevity of the fad for child performers, which persisted to the end of the nineteenth century (and beyond) despite all opposition. New infant wonders continued to emerge as the century wore on, appearing in music halls as well as in more respectable venues. Public enthusiasm for all-child shows heated up in the 1880s, even as more and more plays began to feature children in major roles.[32] As late as 1909, an anonymous *Times* reviewer summarizing the state of "Christmas Amusements" noted a recent flood of shows "in which the chief characters are children, and are often played by children," including *Pinkie and the Fairies* (His Majesty's Theatre 1908), *The Blue Bird* (Haymarket 1909), and *Where Children Rule* (Garrick 1909). The demand for companies of carefully trained child dancers likewise persisted past the century mark. Noel Streatfeild, who authored numerous children's novels about young performers beginning with *Ballet Shoes* (1936), was inspired by actual troupes such as Lila Field's Little Wonders and The Manchester Mighty Mites, which she saw in 1913 and 1925, respectively.

Some children's authors, most notably Mrs. O. F. Walton in *A Peep Behind the Scenes* (1877), followed in the footsteps of Dickens by representing juvenile performers as victims of adult oppression. But others resisted the tradition of characterizing such children as icons of artless vulnerability. Unlike the pathetic "infant phenomenon," for instance, Streatfeild's child prodigies—including Posy Fossil in *Ballet Shoes*—are portrayed as intelligent, self-determining agents who make use of their truly impressive talent and rigorous training to help support their families. Similarly, Louisa May Alcott's *Jimmy's Cruise on the "Pinafore"* (1879) chronicles the exploits of a twelve-year-old boy singer who finances his invalid sister's lifesaving trip to the country by getting himself cast in an all-child production of Gilbert and Sullivan's operetta. Like the equally gifted and generous Jo March, young Jimmy takes on the responsibility of acting as "the man of the family" (*Jimmy's Cruise* 7); clearly, the author of *Little Women* (1868–69) and *Little Men* (1871) was not invested in drawing a strict line of division between childhood and adulthood.

Jimmy's Cruise was inspired by a real show; in May 1879, the Boston Museum presented the Miniature Opera Company's production of *H. M. S. Pinafore*, anticipating the English all-child version by seven months. Yet the picture Alcott paints of what "jolly . . . fun" it is to be a professional child performer seems excessively rosy (10). This insistently optimistic stance was motivated by her amused exasperation with hyperbolic accounts of the fatal dangers faced by stage children that appeared in newspapers and in books like Ellen Barlee's *Pantomime Waifs: or, A Plea for Our City Children* (1884). Toward the end of her story, Alcott slyly notes that not one of the good ship *Pinafore*'s "gallant crew [was] killed or wounded . . . in spite of all the discussion in papers and parlours, no harm came to the young mariners, but much careful training of various sorts, and well-earned wages that went into pockets which sorely needed a silver lining" (22). Alcott was not alone in defending such work; besides Carroll and Dowson, whose statements on this subject I will discuss shortly, Lady Mary Jeune, John Coleman, and Lord Dunraven all maintained that critics of the craze exaggerated the dangers faced by child performers, while downplaying potential benefits to the children and their families.

Indeed, the continuing popularity of child performers reveals that many members of the public were ignoring the concerns expressed by commentators such as the anonymous author of "Children on the Stage" (1878), who followed in the footsteps of Hunt by arguing that playwrights and playgoers should avoid indulging their evident fondness for this phenomenon. "The text is an old one to preach from," this critic wearily observes, but child actors "grow old before they are young," having been subjected to a "premature apprenticeship" when "the proper place for [them] is the nursery" (186). Naturally, he cites Dickens's infamous infant as evidence for his claim and compares child actors to trained animals. Interestingly, although he clearly wishes he could echo Hunt in asserting that admirers of stage children are infantile themselves, he cannot help "admitting that with the more intelligent and better educated the child actor is really popular" (187). Rather than offering an explanation of why this might be so, he merely warns that "interest thus aroused cannot be healthy" (187).

As this commentator may have been hinting, the intimation of sexual as well as professional precocity was probably a key part of the appeal of child performers for some audience members. In a short story that appeared in the *Theatre* in 1878, Gerald Dixon introduces the enticing character of Minnie May, a young actress who has already played "quite a wide range of parts" since her debut at age twelve (128). Dixon quickly implies that Minnie's professional experience has accustomed her to intimate interaction with the opposite sex, since the action of the story begins when the bold fifteen-year-old accosts the older male narrator in a public stairway, inviting him to come see her perform. Observing her closely, the narrator notes: "There was a certain abandon in her movements which was at once attractive and strange. Her manner and utterance were easy, and her tone seemed to imply a thorough mastery of the situation, and a hint that, though she was young, she was experienced and was intimately acquainted 'with her way about'" (127–28). The precocious Minnie titillates the narrator by combining blushing youth and brash savoir faire; he finds her manner "both piquante and repelling" and admires the way "her slight girlish figure" gives "indications of future robustness" (129, 127).

Child labor activists likewise traced a connection between professional and sexual experience, but they characterized such premature development as horrifying rather than exciting. For instance, recounting her interviews with stage children in her book *Pantomime Waifs*, Barlee observes that even the littlest ones were "quick and sharp as needles" (14); despite her determination to represent them as "miserable little victims" (99), she is forced to admit that they exhibit "extraordinary prowess" and "independence of action," both onstage and off (10, 61). But she finds this premature professionalism deeply disturbing, particularly in the case of little girls: "The children soon learn to measure their own abilities and worth, and trade with their talents with the cupidity of grown women; whilst to hear them discuss amongst themselves their engagements, gains, and successes, one would imagine that, far from being in the realm of childhood, one was in the company of scheming adults" (55–56). Barlee contends that such "sad and evil precociousness" often spills over into the personal lives of child performers, often leading them to lose "their characters before they [are] fifteen years of age" (22).

Besides expressing concern about the moral and physical well-being of child performers who blurred the line between child and adult, later critics also echoed Hunt in worrying about the effect such shows would have on audiences. Pantomime in particular was attacked for not respecting and upholding the idea that children and adults were categorically different. One group of critics complained that its more "vulgar" elements—scantily dressed ballet girls, endless puns, topical jokes, and other music hall material—were "calculated to rob childhood of its innocence and purity!" (Barlee 30). Others were more upset that old people should enjoy such "childish" entertainment ("Christmas Amusements," 26 Dec. 1877). In a rant worthy of Hunt, Gilbert à Beckett declared:

> The twaddle about recurrence of youthful feelings is a very fine excuse for veteran idiots with vacant minds to grin over the silliness invented for the amusement of children. . . . One might as well suck lollipops at

> eighty, upon the strength of youthful reminiscences, as upon the same plan defend a relish for stupidity; and if we were to see an old man playing at the juvenile games of marbles, duck or leap-frog, we should not be more disgusted than we are to see some hoary father of a numerous family giggling with five year old *gusto* at the tricks of clown, or with eyes attentively fixed on the twaddle of Harlequin. ("Theatricals")

Either way, such commentary reflected a deep anxiety that popular entertainment was not drawing a strict enough line between child and adult. Many felt that pantomimes, with their mixed casts and mixed audiences, undermined the idea of childhood as a period of protected seclusion from the sordid adult world. Even Dickens—generally a staunch supporter of popular entertainment—attacked this theatrical genre for despoiling the innocence of fairy tales, "and having destroyed itself, its artists, and its audiences, in that perversion of its duty" ("Frauds" 111).

Adding his voice to this chorus, Max Beerbohm broached an even more upsetting possibility when he suggested that such shows did not defile childhood purity, they merely reflected the fact that contemporary children lacked this quality in the first place. In an 1898 review of two Christmas shows, Beerbohm declared that pantomimes had grown coarser over the past few decades "simply because children are different also" ("Two Pantomimes" 95). During his own youth, he observes, he and his equally "primitive" peers were enraptured by unembellished reenactments of "simple" fairy tales such as *Jack and the Beanstalk* (95). Now, however, children are too "sophisticated" to be "easily pleased by the things that ought to please them" (96). As an example, he cites the behavior of three little children whom he observed sitting near him during a performance of *Ali Baba* (Drury Lane 1898):

> The antics of the huge parrot and of the horse, which would have enchanted me at their age, did not raise a smile on their faces. On the other hand, they seemed to be interested in the dancing, and when a man came on, masked in the image of Captain Dreyfus, they applauded with such vigour. The references to Mr. Hooley and to the German Emperor made them laugh outright, but their attention wandered palpably whilst the story itself was proceeding. (96)

Beerbohm explicitly blames "the present cult for children" for engendering such worldliness (96). Echoing the authors of "Babyolatry" and "The Worship of Children," he complains that young people now "spend most of their time in the drawing-room or dining-room [or] wherever their elders may be"; adults treat them as "delightful companions" rather than confining them to the nursery and the company of other children and servants (95). Instead of viewing the cult as an expression of cultural primitivism, in other words, Beerbohm and other contemporary commentators objected that participants in this cultural trend failed to recognize and protect the otherness of children—a characterization in keeping with the actions of individual cultists such as Carroll, Dowson, and Burnett.

THE CULTISTS AND STAGE CHILDREN

Far from attempting to segregate children from the civilized world, many members of the cult—including Carroll, Barrie, and Dowson—took young people to see other young people onstage, enjoying the shows that critics complained so bitterly about: pantomimes, featured performances by child prodigies, and all-child productions. For example, Dowson took "2 demoiselles of tender years to the Surrey pantomime" *The Forty Thieves* (1888) (*Letters* 26), which featured "the topical songs and other contemporary 'gag[s]'" that many commentators considered unsuitable for children (review of *Forty* 4). Defying propriety still further, he took his young girlfriend Bertha to the music hall. His excited account of Bertha's physical precocity—"She hath the *torso* of seventeen, at least," he told Moore (*Letters* 116)—matches his thrilled description of a socially and theatrically experienced child prodigy whom he enjoyed watching and then meeting at the Bedford Music Hall in 1888: "an awfully clever little American child who sings and dances exquisitely. . . . I dare say you have seen her at the 'Pav'—'Little Flossie'—she figures in the bills. She was a most amusing little lady—aet 9—chattered like a jay—& I have promised to throw her chocolates at the 'Star' tomorrow" (*Letters* 18).[33] Dowson and Little Flossie corresponded a number of times after this meeting.

Although Carroll would never have gone to a music hall, he, too, routinely took child-friends to the theatre to see shows that featured professional child actors, and idolized, corresponded with, and sought out more intimate forms of interaction with stage children. Indeed, despite all the fuss that has been made about his fascination with Alice Liddell, Carroll's surviving letters and diaries contain far more proof of his obsession with "strangely clever" child actors (*Diaries* 2:318), including pantomime performers such as the Cootes and Vokes siblings, straight drama stars such as Ellen and Kate Terry, child prodigies such as Lydia Howard, and all-child acting troupes such as Warwick Gray's Children's Comic Opera Company.

Like many other fans of child performers from this era, Carroll seems less interested in sating a nostalgia for artless purity than in indulging a taste for "intelligent" children whose prematurely developed skills enable them to blur the line between child and adult (*Letters* 2:730).[34] Whereas activists such as Barlee decried the premature professionalism of stage children, Carroll expressed delight when ambitious youngsters proved themselves capable of performing their parts "in a manner quite worthy of an older actor" (*Diaries* 1:73). Describing the Living Miniatures, for example, he marveled at the "very remarkable" acting of a five-and-a-half-year-old boy and the naked ambition of his even younger sister, who, although she "is only four," pesters the management to let her take a larger role in the show (*Diaries* 1:251). Rather than embodying innocence, these children played distinctly "adult" parts, and this more demanding role was no exception; as Carroll noted, "the part of Mrs. Mite (taken by a very clever child) involves a good deal of talking, including a violent 'scene' with her sour-tempered little husband" (*Letters* 1:100). Unfazed by the idea of a four-year-old engaging in such nonangelic activities, Carroll deployed as terms of praise the same adjectives Barlee and company used to bemoan the child actor's precociousness: "certainly I *never* saw such clever little things—the sharpest of the sharp race of London children" (*Letters* 1:101).

Carroll was such a fan of seeing children act like adults that even the "pain" he felt at hearing children say "damme" in *The Children's Pinafore* was not strong enough to keep him away from the next production by the same company, which (like its predecessor) gave some of its child stars the opportunity to parody the performances of their adult counterparts. For example, according to the *Theatre*, the boy playing Frederick in the all-child version of *The Pirates of Penzance* (1884) was " 'made up' to resemble a popular English light tenor, of whom he is a curiously exact reproduction, supposing the latter to be contemplated through a pair of reversed opera-glasses. His àplomb and self-possession on the stage, the fervour of his love-making, and the smartness with which he fires off all his 'points,' are simply astounding" (Beatty-Kingston 82). Whereas Hunt was horrified to see children acting like adults, Carroll found this show "*very* charming" (*Diaries* 2:431). He was even more enthusiastic about the all-child pantomimes that E. L. Blanchard organized at the Adelphi Theatre, which assigned children to harlequinade roles previously associated with adults. Commenting on the first of these shows, Carroll singled out the performance of "Little Bertie Coote (about 10)," describing him as "a wonderfully clever little fellow" whose performance of Clown was "curiously" reminiscent of the grown-up Grimaldi (*Diaries* 2:359). He also expressed admiration for Bertie's younger sister Carrie "(about 8)" who played Columbine, the female lover figure. According to the *Era*, Carrie was "thoroughly efficient, whisking and flirting with all the airs and graces of a full-grown maiden" (review of *Little Goody*, 24 Dec. 1876, 13).

Not content merely to watch precocious child actors cavort on stage, Carroll wanted to meet and befriend them, as he did with the Cootes, Terrys, Bowmans, and Vanbrughs. Although he was much more fussy than Dowson about avoiding shows he deemed coarse, he was just as willing to thwart propriety in his drive to enjoy the company of young girls. His relationship with Isa Bowman—who played the title role in the 1888 revival of *Alice in Wonderland*—provides a case in point. Having spotted her in a small role in the original production of *Alice in Wonderland* (Prince of Wales's 1886), Carroll first arranged to meet her when she was thirteen years old, at which time he took her to an art exhibition and a comic opera before (successfully) petitioning her mother to let her join him for a visit to his holiday lodgings in Eastbourne. The following summer, she ended up staying "tête-à-tête" with him for five weeks; Carroll explained to a friend that he had been determined to "keep her over the normal *honey-moon* period" (*Letters* 2:730). Together they attended various social events, shows, and concerts, including a performance by the eleven-year-old piano prodigy Pauline Ellice, which Carroll described as "quite a treat. I have very seldom heard such playing in my life" (*Diaries* 2:464).

The cultists' obvious fascination with precocity and their desire to enjoy intimate interaction with young people hovering on the line between childhood and adulthood should prompt us to rethink our definition of the cult of the child. According to Peter Green, the "child-cult of the later nineteenth century" demanded that the young be arrested in place as an "ideal symbol of their elders' glutinous yearning for purity. There was no question of communication or understanding: the traffic of sentiment all went one way. Children were regarded as *objects*—dolls, pets, almost mythic symbols, which reflected nothing but the magnanimity and tenderness of their elders" (161). But such criticism is actually far more applicable to the child-savers than the child-lovers. Intent on convincing the public that young people should not be allowed to work and play with grown-ups, child labor activists portrayed young actors as helpless puppets or parrots whose survival depended entirely on the kindness of charitable adults (such as themselves) and who ideally should be removed not only from the workforce but from all of the worldly temptations associated with city life.[35]

In contrast, men like Dowson and Carroll maintained that even very young children had the ability and the right to earn their own living, and delighted in initiating their child-friends into a variety of urban pleasures, including theatregoing, an activity many of their peers considered a source of corruption. In doing so, they indicated their lingering allegiance to the old paradigm of the competent child, which held that the young did not necessarily need to be prevented from participating in adult occupations or pastimes. Carroll's commitment to this position emerges most vividly in an 1887 letter he wrote to the editor of the *St. James Gazette* specifically in order to protest the activists' habit of representing stage children as frail waifs in desperate need of adult protection. Pooh-poohing reformers' concerns that the "exceedingly heavy strain" on child actors will produce "fatal results," Carroll describes at length the "vigour of *life*" displayed by three strapping child actors who have been working for months in a provincial production of *Alice* (quoted in Lovett 214, 213). After freely acknowledging that their career is a demanding one, Carroll concludes with a defense of this activity that—as Catherine Robson notes—attests to his sense of these youngsters as powerful, "self-willed and self-determining beings" (186). He wrote: "I believe . . . that a taste for *acting* is one of the strongest passions of human nature, that stage children show it nearly from infancy, and that, instead of being miserable drudges who ought to be celebrated in a new 'Cry of the Children,' they simply *rejoice* in their work 'even as a giant rejoiceth to run his course' " (quoted in Robson 185). Clearly chafing against new efforts to erect a strict barrier between child and adult, Carroll rejects the notion that children can only be victimized by participation in the labor force, an idea epitomized for him by Elizabeth Barrett Browning's famous protest poem "The Cry of the Children" (1843), which decried the exploitation of hapless, doomed child workers.

As the simile of the giant suggests, Carroll and other members of the cult preferred to entertain the possibility that children could be both powerful and artful. This is not to say that scholars are wrong to find certain aspects of their stance on this subject disturbing, including the voyeuristic aspect of their fascination with child performers (Rose) and the self-justifying way they likened the work of stage children to play, downplaying its status as labor (Steedman). Nevertheless, it seems important to acknowledge that their position entailed a respect for the capacities of young people, in sharp contrast to those commentators who were so bent on protecting children from "commercial exploitation" that they characterized stage children as incompetent infants sleepwalking though roles that made no demands on their (nonexistent) talent (Shaw, "Van Amburgh" 456). The foil to Carroll's giant was Bernard Shaw's image of a pathetic "troop of infants" stumbling through a ballet "between eleven o'clock and midnight . . . in a sort of delirium induced by . . . intense sleepiness" (457–58). Shaw twice bemoaned the "epidemic of child exhibition" raging though the London theatre scene, adding his voice to the chorus of activists and critics calling for a "rigid rule" banning children under ten from the stage (457).

Like Dickens, Barlee, and other critics of the fad, Shaw drastically downplayed the opportunities child performers had to play featured roles, in order to make their situation seem more pitiable. Writing specifically to rebut such accounts, Dowson begins "The Cult of the Child" by carefully distinguishing between the case of ensemble children and that of " 'star' children" (433). He then goes on to dispute the idea that featured child performers are necessarily devoid of talent. On the contrary, he declares, they are "an enormous boon to the modern stage":

> There are cases within our recollection when a play, in itself foolish, or, at the very best, trivial, has been redeemed and made artistically possible by the marvelous acting of a tiny child. And there is no greater fallacy

> than the assumption which we have seen quite lately expressly stated in an article by one of our smartest dramatic critics, that a child's acting is necessarily inartistic. In our opinion it is generally the reverse. (433)[36]

Because critics of child performers had argued so vociferously that theatrical life was "sapping the root of all that should be pure and innocent . . . and producing a race of premature child-women" (Barlee 138), Dowson quickly insists that stage children are "not . . . precocious" but merely "spontaneously dramatic," as all "real" children are (433). Yet even as he celebrates the "playful instinct" of stage children, he simultaneously describes them as carefully "trained and cultivated" (434); even as he calls them "naïve" and natural, he admits that their innocence is an artful "counterfeit" (433, 435).

The same tension is evident in admiring reviews of child actors that appeared from the mid–nineteenth century onward: appreciative critics at once praised the "untutored spontaneity" of featured child performers and declared that "the little ones . . . are not above being taught, and . . . are all trained in a discipline that may conveniently affect their after life and future career" (review of *Robin Hood, Era*). There are a couple of explanations for this seemingly contradictory stance. First, as Lynn M. Voskuil observes in *Acting Naturally* (2004), the Victorians routinely lauded highly accomplished actors (of all ages) for their naturalness; where acting was concerned, they apparently did not conceive of the natural and the artificial as binary terms. For this reason, we cannot simply assume that critics who praised the naturalness of child performers fully embraced the Romantic ideal of the simple, spontaneous child; they may simply have been borrowing rhetoric commonly used to describe expert adult actors.

Second, because an admiration for precocity was becoming less socially acceptable, fans of child actors felt the need to disavow the term. They therefore lavished praise on the prematurely developed powers of stage children even as they insisted that such performers lacked even a "tinge of juvenile precocity" (review of *Children's Pinafore, Theatre* 38). Dickens and company had evidently succeeded in linking precocity with child abuse, as indicated by the fact that critical effusions on the naturalness of child actors were frequently triggered by the specter of the stage child as a browbeaten, broken-down animal.[37] For this reason, other cultists besides Dowson disavowed the term "precocity" despite their evident fascination with children who acted like adults. For example, as I have already noted, Ruskin gloried in Rose La Touche's artistic, intellectual, and emotional precocity while simultaneously denying that the word applied to her. Similarly, he justified his admiration for a featured child dancer in a pantomime by declaring that she "was not an infant prodigy":

> there was no evidence, in the finish or strength of her motion, that she had been put to continual torture through half her eight or nine years. She

> did nothing more than any child, well taught, but painlessly, might easily do. She caricatured no older person,—attempted no curious or fantastic skill. She was dressed decently,—she moved decently,—she looked and behaved innocently. (*Works* 17:337–38)

The pleasure Ruskin takes in the artistry of this young dancer is muted by his troubled sense that it is outré to admire precocity; purity and simplicity are the qualities he ought to be celebrating. Indeed, I believe that he and other cultists *did* admire these traits, having indisputably been affected by Romantic figurations of childhood innocence. But far from being the group who made the most frantic efforts to arrest the child in place as a primitive icon of purity, the cultists were ambivalent; even as they embraced the emergent ideology of innocence, they were also drawn to an older paradigm that assumed that the child could function as an active participant in "adult" activities such as the creation of art, courtship, and labor.

Understandably, this tension is especially evident in the cultists' attitude toward working-class children, since the ideology of innocence only slowly trickled down to affect how people perceived the juvenile poor.[38] The inconsistent stance that Carroll adopts in his essay "Stage Children" (1889) attests to this wider cultural trend. Focused on the case of working-class children employed mostly in chorus work, this piece is characterized by a kind of rhetorical confusion whereby the poor child is represented as both innocent and experienced, competent and incompetent. Carroll vigorously defends the right of children to help support their families by becoming wage-earners at an early age. Since underprivileged youth do not lead sheltered lives to begin with, he observes, it is absurd to argue that they must be protected from "late hours" and exposure to "impure air" and "the society of profligate men" (224–25). After all, their familiarity with "London alleys" and employment in bars and shops expose them to these hazards anyway (224).

Yet even as he represents poor children as self-supporting, experienced beings, Carroll simultaneously deploys the image of the clueless, innocent child; just a few paragraphs later, he contends that when stage children perform in "immoral" shows, they are protected from corruption by their "ignorance of the ways of the world, and of the meanings of most of the words they hear" (225). More strangely still, he insists that this naïveté furnishes stage children with a "powerful safeguard" against profligate men who hang around theatres (226), blithely disregarding the (much-discussed) possibility that such innocence might render children *more* vulnerable to entrapment into a life of sin.[39]

Rather than trying to resolve such contradictions and figure out what Carroll and the other cultists *really* thought about children, I believe we should view their inconsistencies as reflective of the divergent discourses circulating around the child throughout the nineteenth century. This after all was a society in which the Calvinist notion of original sin was still giving the Rousseauvian concept of original innocence a run for its money, even as constant reports about the sexual promiscuity of poor children shared cultural airspace with paeans to the purity of their more privileged peers. As Linda M. Austin notes, "the growing awareness of childhood through the nineteenth century did not bring a stable, shared definition of the phrase, only a sense that it differed somehow from adult life and lasted longer than it had centuries before" (79). Rather than supporting activists' efforts to define and defend the parameters of childhood, members of the cult often seemed to revel in uncertainty, as when Ruskin excitedly informed another young paramour, Kathleen Olander, that he was not clear "whether you are a child—an angel—a pretty girl—or a clever—woman!" (*Gulf* 63). He then invited Kathleen to join him in Paris and accompany him to the Comedie Française; "You can't think how naughty people are in Paris!" he exclaimed, entreating her to "be a *little* wicked, for once, and tell me" what sort of clothing she would wear on such an occasion (63).

Ruskin and the other cultists' fascination with child actors can also be interpreted as evidence of this interest in keeping age categories ambiguous. After all, the real age of child stars was often shrouded in mystery, and the well-known fact that quite old actors sometimes managed to pass themselves off as children meant that audiences could never be entirely sure whether a "child" star was in fact young in years. And even when child stars capitalized on their genuine youth by functioning onstage as icons of purity, their mere presence there—holding their own alongside adult actors, earning their own living, inhabiting a profession realm associated in the public mind with sexual corruption—undercut the notion that children were a race apart. The stage child could never simply be viewed as a Child of Nature; instead this figure blurred the line between nature and art, innocence and experience. Thus, praising Beringer's performance as Little Lord Fauntleroy, drama critic William Archer observed that she "really gives us a piece of pure nature, or, at least, of the art which conceals art" (quoted in V. Burnett 169). As I have shown, critics of the cult of the child used similar language to denounce its effect on children: "When artlessness gets to know its power, it is very near to art" ("Worship" 1299). The moment a child begins to *perform* purity, her status as a primitive, unselfconscious innocent comes into doubt.

The fact that the cult of the child was closely bound up with the craze for precocious child performers suggests that it was characterized not so much by an erotics of distancing and objectification (which involved fixing the child in place as an icon of otherness) as by an erotics of engagement and affiliation (which involved keeping the line between adult and child blurry). Acknowledging this tendency helps us to connect some of the cultists' seemingly disparate proclivities: their fascination with children who acted like adults; a parallel interest in adults who acted like children (such as seriocomics in music halls—grown women who pretended to be little girls, donning short white pinafores and clutching toys); a tendency to treat much younger people as romantic partners (whether in jest or not); a habit of conducting their own correspondence with loved ones in baby talk; and other actions that bespeak a desire to keep the boundary between childhood and adulthood indistinct and permeable.

This yearning also manifests itself strongly in child-centered plays written by Burnett and Barrie, two more members of the cult who produced iconic figurations of the adored child in their plays *Little Lord Fauntleroy* and *Peter Pan*. As my concluding chapter will show, these two writers at once participated in the creation of the emerging subgenre of children's theatre and resisted this movement, precisely because it was premised on the notion that children were a separate species, innocent beings who ought to consume their own specially sanitized shows. On the one hand, *Little Lord Fauntleroy* and *Peter Pan* drew large numbers of children into the playhouse, and turn-of-the-century commentators credited them with helping to establish the category of the children's play as a distinct dramatic subgenre. On the other hand, when we compare these two dramas to other productions that aimed to attract child theatregoers during this time, it becomes evident that Burnett and Barrie were resisting the increasing pressure to cater shows specifically and exclusively to the young. As I will show, besides including content some reviewers deemed too adult-oriented and aiming to attract a mixed audience, both of these plays thematize the issue of children acting like adults by featuring precocious child characters; Burnett's description of Little Lord Fauntleroy as "a mixture of maturity and childishness" applies equally well to Wendy.[40]

Burnett and Barrie's interest in the idea of keeping the line between childhood and adulthood blurry was also evident in their descriptions of the real children who helped inspire the creation of these dramas. The character of Little Lord Fauntleroy was closely modeled on Burnett's son Vivian, while the tale of Peter Pan grew out of storytelling, playacting, and photography sessions Barrie engaged in with George, Jack, Peter, Michael, and Nico Llewelyn Davies. (After befriending the eldest boys in Kensington Gardens, Barrie got to know the whole family and eventually adopted the brothers when their parents died.) Both authors penned accounts of the genesis of their most famous stories,[41] Burnett in a lengthy essay entitled "How Fauntleroy Occurred" (1894) and Barrie in the dedicatory preface "To the Five" (c. 1928) that he composed to accompany the published script of *Peter Pan*. Strikingly, in both of these essays the adult authors celebrate precocity, gleefully describing how they sometimes found themselves placed in an infantilized position because of their child-friends' preternatural maturity.

To begin with Burnett, she dwells at length on an incident in which little Vivian took care of her while she was ill in bed. Adopting a "protecting and comforting air" (193), she observes, he held her hand and tried to soothe her to sleep; then, believing he had succeeded, he slowly extricated his hand from hers and crept out of the room. Such behavior prompts Burnett to recall that "when he had been a baby I had sometimes laid him down to sleep with just such cautious movements" (194). So although "How Fauntleroy Occurred" contains plenty of sentimental effusions about Vivian's innocent simplicity and unconscious sweetness, it quickly becomes evident that—as in the case of child actors—it is actually the combination of youth and an unexpected maturity that makes this little boy so "seductive" (153). Thus, even as Burnett lauds Vivian's innocence she also characterizes him as an "artful" (147), "intelligent" (162), and "experienced" being (178).

Similarly, in "To the Five," Barrie delights in sharing stories in which the Llewlyn Davies boys have behaved maturely and he has behaved childishly. For instance, he exultantly recalls the time when Nico, though hardly out of childhood himself, was prone to "placing me against the wall of an underground station and saying, 'Now I am going to get the tickets; don't move till I come back for you or you'll lose yourself' " (85). He is also tickled by the fact that Michael, "while still a schoolboy" was nevertheless "the sternest of my literary critics":

> There was for instance an unfortunate little tragedy which I liked until I foolishly told [Michael] its subject, when he frowned and said he had better have a look at it. He read it, and then, patting me on the back . . . said, "You know you can't do this sort of thing." End of a tragedian. Sometimes, however, [he] liked my efforts, and I walked in the azure that day when he returned *Dear Brutus* to me with the comment "Not so bad." (85)

Interestingly, when the Llewelyn Davies boys and Vivian Burnett later offered their own accounts of these relationships, they, too, suggested that their adult companions were invested in keeping the categories of adult and child fluid and unfixed—in avoiding the sort of static, hierarchical relationship in which these two categories are perceived as completely separate states of being. Recalling their close connection, Nico observed that Barrie treated him "as a friend, not as a parent, even when I was very young (which, incidentally, is one reason why he got on so well with children—he always treated them as equals)" (quoted in Birkin 282). While he was at school, Nico added, he wrote to Barrie every day, "pouring out my thoughts and problems to him—not to a father, not to a brother, rather to a very intimate friend. I think Michael looked on him in much the same way" (282). Struggling to describe the "peculiar" form Barrie's affection for his brothers took, Peter Llewelyn Davies commented that it had "much . . . of the lover" in it, though he hastened to add that he did not think the relationship did George or Michael any harm (quoted in Birkin 235).

Similarly, Vivian suggests that his guardian preferred to be viewed as a partner rather than a parent. In his 1927 biography of his mother, which bears the subtitle *The Life Story of an Imagination*, the chapter that most closely chronicles his mother's relationship with him and his brother begins "The Imagination's sweetest and most complete romance was with her children" (129). His mother, he contends, wanted above all to function as a close "companion" to her boys (129), encouraging them to regard their bond with her as characterized by absolute intimacy and equality, an openness and mutuality that the adult Vivian recognizes was probably not as complete as it seemed. Describing how he and his brother related to his mother as children, he observes, "[We] never thought of keeping anything from her, and were sure that she never kept anything from [us]" (130). He also notes that when they were little, he and his brother regarded their mother as "a sort of little girl. She was little to look at and had curly hair like [our] own; and she used to sit on the nursery floor and build houses or play 'fish pond' with [us]" (131). In *Little Lord Fauntleroy*, which Vivian confirms was based closely on his relationship with his mother, all of these elements reappear; in the novel and in the play, mother and child often behave more like a romantic couple than a parent–child dyad, and both are represented as combining youthful sweetness with profound emotional maturity.

Acknowledging that both Burnett and Barrie were members of the cult of the child reminds us that we cannot simply characterize this phenomenon as one in which men romanced little girls. As Christine Roth notes, the few post-Boas scholars who have discussed the cult—such as Coveney and Wullschläger—contend that the Victorians confined their adoration to female children;[42] the advent of *Peter Pan*, they argue, then ushered in an opposing era of boy-worship. Though Roth questions whether this changeover was quite so abrupt, she agrees that such a shift occurred; during her discussion of what she calls "the Cult of the Little Girl," she maintains that boys were largely "excluded from Victorian images of childhood in Britain" (52, 51).

While I concur with Roth's point that many individual cultists shared a "fascination with the bounds of girlhood" (48), my sense is that the cult as a whole was never merely focused on one sex or the other. As I have shown, the Victorians' own discourse on this subject was general rather than gendered; they spoke of "Child-Worship" and "Babyolatry," of child-friends and dream-children. Moreover, artists and writers from this era created romanticized and eroticized images of boys as well as girls. John Everett Millais produced not just *Cherry Ripe* (1879) but also *Bubbles* (1865–66), while Henry Scott Tuke composed provocative paintings of naked boys, including *The Bathers* (1889) and *Ruby, Gold, and Malachite* (1902). Just as Dowson penned love sonnets to little girls, Swinburne and other poets composed passionate verses to and about adored boys. Even Carroll—who once claimed to be immune to the charms of male children—acknowledged their appeal; his *Sylvie and Bruno* books chronicle an adult man's obsession not merely with one but with both of these eponymous "Dream-Children" (Carroll, *Works* 473). By employing this phrase in *Sylvie and Bruno Concluded* (1893), Carroll indicates his indebtedness to Charles Lamb's "Dream-Children" (1822)—a foundational text for the cult—which features not merely the female dream-child Alice but also her brother John.

And then of course there is the example of Fauntleroy. Not only did this fictional boy inspire a widespread frenzy of admiration in the 1880s, Burnett's account of her relationship with his real-life counterpart exhibits what I view as the classic markers of cultural artifacts associated with the cult.[43] To begin with, "How Fauntleroy Occurred" sets up the child as the epitome of attractiveness and the primary focus of adult passion. Having usurped the central, most exalted position in the family, he is the ruling "conqueror" who exercises an "enslaving effect" on the adoring acolytes who orbit around him (157, 159). As often happens in texts associated with the cult, the child moves into the position vacated by an absent adult, acting more like a romantic partner to his remaining parent than an immature dependent. Indeed, Burnett omits virtually all mention of her husband and instead characterizes herself as the "victim" of her child's "seductive arts" (153): "Where did he learn—faithful and tender heart—to be such a lover as he was? Surely no woman ever had such a lover before! What taught him to pay such adorable childish court, and to bring the first-fruits of every delight to lay upon one shrine?" (185).

As this line suggests, even as Burnett sets up Vivian as the exalted object of her adoring gaze, she simultaneously portrays him as an attentive worshipper at *her* shrine. This, too, is characteristic of the cult; paradoxically, elevating the child for his or her appealing otherness often goes hand in hand with a tendency to confuse the adult–child binary, whether by fantasizing about the possibility of role reversal, celebrating precocity, or borrowing the language or imagery of mature romantic love to describe encounters with children. Indeed, as I have already noted, effusions about Vivian's innocent unconsciousness coexist with a tendency to characterize him as "coy" and "experienced" (157, 178).

Understanding the cult involves coming up with an explanation for such inconsistencies, which (as I have shown) crop up regularly in the art, utterances, and lives of many of its members. To say that the Victorians eroticized innocence, as Kincaid and others do, represents an effort to acknowledge the contradictoriness of the discourse surrounding children during this time. But in the context of the cult, it is not that purity per se gets eroticized; rather, the most titillating figures are those who vacillate between innocence and experience, blurring the line between child and adult and allowing those who interact with them to avoid being pinned down to one side of this binary as well.[44] "Alice Liddell as 'The Beggar-Maid'"; child performers such as Harry Grattan and Little Flossie; precocious characters such as Fauntleroy and Wendy; actual children such as Rose La Touche and the Llewelyn Davies boys—the appeal of all of these figures seems to have been based not on their alien otherness but rather on their ability to unsettle the whole idea of the child's absolute difference from adults.

As Leach observes, the cult was a "mass culture" phenomenon, not just a marginal trend involving a few peculiar men (Leach 68). Leach makes this point in the context of her discussion of visual arts such as photography and painting, but it also holds true for drama and children's literature. Just as both men and women flocked to see child actors, female children's authors such Burnett, Stella Austin, Martha Finley, and Annie Fellows Johnston were implicated in the cult of the child alongside their male counterparts. Leach and other scholars who emphasize how widespread and diverse the community of Golden Age child-worshippers was often use this fact to exonerate the cultists, contending that there was nothing "depraved" about the way they behaved toward and represented children, since everyone was doing it (Leach 67). This move makes me uneasy, for the obvious reason that the commonness of a behavior does not necessarily ensure its moral legitimacy. Moreover, it seems evident that the cult incorporated a spectrum of child-related activity, with some participants going further than others and actually making romantic or erotic advances on children in real life. Because I have been attempting to demonstrate that the cultists were not guilty of the precise brand of creepiness they have frequently been accused of—namely, objectifying and othering the child by erecting a strict barrier between age and youth—my own language may at times sound more positive than I intend. So let me close by emphasizing that my effort to reconceive the cult of the child stems neither from a desire to exculpate its members nor from a need to condemn them but merely from my conviction that its defining features were different from what we tend to think.

6

BURNETT, BARRIE, AND THE EMERGENCE OF CHILDREN'S THEATRE

The Victorians and Edwardians were intensely self-conscious about their own tendency to adore and interact intimately with young people. In his essay "Child-Worship" (1901), for instance, Augustin Filon worries that the new importance granted to children—who now function as "the undisputed masters of the house"—has made them aggressively self-confident and "conscious of their power" (41). Yet what truly upsets Filon is not so much a parent–child role reversal as a blurring of this binary: "We share our pleasures with them, unless we prefer to become children again, to join in theirs. Their interests are our interests, their talk is our talk. If you come as a guest to our houses, you will hear nothing but their tittle-tattle at the family dinner table" (43). Like the author of "Babyolatry," Filon complains that children are enmeshed in adult culture too soon: daughters trick themselves out in "complicated and expensive adornments" while sons "smoke cigarettes, write newspapers, plan agitations against their headmaster" (43). Moreover, "we take them to the play; we will have their company when travelling abroad. . . . We have created a literature for their amusement" (43).

The last point at first seems unconnected to the rest; it is not immediately obvious why the development of a special genre of literature aimed at children would promote the sort of intermingling that disturbs Filon. But my argument here has been that children's literature from this era did indeed participate in this trend: in keeping with the overarching tendency of the cult of the child to ignore, deny, or unsettle the adult–child binary that activists were struggling to establish, children's writers often seem intent on keeping the boundary between youth and age blurry. Thus, as contemporary critics of the cult noted, these authors insisted on providing children with literature of "the highest and subtlest refinement" ("Worship" 1299) rather than following the lead of those eighteenth-century children's authors who had begun to conceive of the young as primitive readers who needed to be addressed in radically simplified prose.[1] Instead of carefully calibrating their books to suit a very particular age group, authors such as Hood, Thackeray, Kingsley, Yonge, MacDonald, Rands, and Grahame persisted in addressing a mixed audience and, in the process, sometimes included content that reviewers declared was too sophisticated for children to appreciate.

In my readings of individual texts by Golden Age authors, I have tried to demonstrate that rather than producing an escapist literature that idealized the child as a wholly natural being, children's writers from this era frequently represented young people as complex, highly socialized individuals who (like adults) had to struggle with thorny issues of pressing contemporary relevance, including gender trouble, class division, ambivalence about imperial expansion, and the question of how much agency one can have as an acculturated subject. Instead of indulging in the fantasy that children can remain completely unaffected by the society they inhabit, these authors often acknowledged the powerful, inevitable influence of grown-ups and their social, cultural, and scholastic institutions. But rather than assuming that contact with the civilized world invariably oppresses and victimizes the young, they remained open to the possibility that children could cope with and even capitalize on the sometimes stifling—but also potentially inspiring—presence of adults and adult-produced texts.

In promoting this possibility, writers such as Ewing, Carroll, Stevenson, and Nesbit do not deny that children sometimes function as naïve or incompetent readers of the world around them. Rather, they dramatize the danger of ignorant or passive modes of engagement, suggesting that simply absorbing and accepting adult-produced scripts can be dull, damaging to the psyche, even deadly. When we recall Alice trying to echo back factoids and other peoples' poems, Jim Hawkins going along with dangerous plots he does not understand, and the felonious and infelicitous acts of plagiarism practiced by Nesbit's child protagonists, it becomes evident that the creators of these tales share a habit of emphasizing how easily one can fall into the trap of becoming a puppet, parrot, or pawn. Yet the very act of producing narratives that feature this message indicates that these authors hope and believe that young people *can* resist; they are not doomed to conform completely to the dictates of adult discourse, to identify with and emulate an adult-produced image of childhood in an uncritical, unreflective way.

Precisely because these writers were willing to entertain the idea that contact with adults and their culture does not necessarily oppress and smother the young, they chose not to portray precocity as a one-way ticket to the grave, as many of their peers did. Sometimes, as in the case of Burnett's Sara Crewe, they positively celebrated this quality. It therefore makes sense that many Golden Age children's authors were fascinated by—and provided golden opportunities for—child actors, who were both loved and hated for embodying precocity, as my previous chapter demonstrated. The job of such performers was to mouth adult discourse. Yet it was crucial to their success that there be "no parrot-like prating" in their delivery (review of *Children's Pinafore*, *Theatre* 39). Those who mechanically repeated back material they did not seem to understand were criticized; others who more artfully inhabited their roles were praised for having "nothing of the parrot" or the "drilled doll" about them (review of "Children's *Pirates*," *Era*). Thus, one possible source of the appeal of child actors to adults such as Carroll, Burnett, and Barrie was that they modeled a form of nonautonomous agency in which being scripted did not necessarily preclude being an intelligent, creative individual—an idea these authors also explored in their children's stories.

According to the Victorians, though, adults were not the only ones who loved to see child actors dominate the stage. "There is nothing that children like better than to see children act" one reviewer of *The Children's Pinafore* declared, and numerous other nineteenth-century commentators echoed this point (*Theatre* 38).[2] Because adults were so convinced of the truth of this claim, some of the first examples of the emerging genre of children's theatre featured all-child casts; reviewers commonly described them as being "by children for children."[3] Post-Rose, no scholar could simply accept this characterization as the whole truth, since adults evidently played a key role in the creation and consumption of such shows. Yet as I will show, viewing such productions *only* in terms of adult voyeurism is equally problematic, since considerable evidence does exist that large numbers of children attended and enjoyed them, including journalistic accounts that give detailed descriptions of their reactions, autobiographies that chronicle early theatregoing experiences, and fan letters from child audience members.

Previous studies of the Golden Age of children's literature generally assume that the greatness of this era is due almost entirely to fiction, particularly fantasy fiction. Yet I would argue that the rise of dramas aimed squarely (though not only) at a juvenile audience also played a role in making this a particularly rich, innovative, and productive period in the history of children's literature. The few theatre historians who have discussed the origins of Anglo-American children's theatre all concur with Mark Twain's characterization of it as "one of the very, very great inventions of the twentieth century" (quoted in McCaslin 5).[4] Similarly, *The Norton Anthology of Children's Literature* (2005) confidently asserts that "at the beginning of the twentieth century, no distinct theatre for children existed" (Zipes et al. 1294). While I agree that it was only with the creation of separate children's theatre companies in the early 1900s that children's theatre truly came of age, part of my purpose here is to show that the idea of creating professional dramas designed specifically to appeal to children—and some extremely popular examples of this subgenre—existed as early as the 1870s, making the rise of children's theatre fully coincident with the Golden Age.

By 1875, a journalist in the United States had already floated the idea that "a proper stage entertainment for young people could be made to bear the same relation to the average play that the juvenile story-book . . . does to the novel" ("Music and the Drama" 729). She (or he) noted that managers and dramatists in London had already begun to plot out shows "specially designed for children" (729), with one such "experiment" set to open soon (730). Indeed, besides producing numerous shows written for and marketed to the parent-and-child matinée crowd, late nineteenth-century dramatists even considered the possibility of forming children's theatre companies. While working on his dramatic adaptation of the *Alice* books in 1886, for example, playwright Henry Savile Clarke wrote to Carroll about his idea of creating a special theatre to produce plays intended for children, and Carroll wrote back proposing that it be named "St. Nicholas Hall" after "the patron saint of children" (quoted in Lovett 17). Clarke may well have been inspired by the all-child productions that became hugely popular in the 1870s, a decade before dramas based on children's books such as *Alice* began appearing. As I will demonstrate, many of these shows were premised on the notion that traditional theatrical fare consumed by mixed audiences—particularly pantomime—needed to be purified and simplified in order to suit children.

Had the Victorians been as deeply invested in innocence as we tend to think, the notion that child playgoers were a separate order of being who ought to be treated differently from adults would almost certainly have emerged even earlier or—at the very least—been embraced more quickly. Instead, this movement basically stalled: despite the critical and popular success of these early examples of children's theatre in the 1870s and 1880s, no immediate explosion of specially sanitized shows designed particularly for the young took place. Instead, what we see is the persistence of pantomime and plays such as Frances Hodgson Burnett's *The Real Little Lord Fauntleroy* (Terry's 1888) and J. M. Barrie's *Peter Pan* (Duke of York's 1904), which drew decidedly mixed audiences and included what some commentators complained was overly adult content: references to matters sexual, topical, political, financial, alcoholic, sentimental, and so on. As dramatists, Burnett and Barrie refused to limit themselves to an audience of children, construed as beings who needed to be shielded from such matters and addressed in very different terms from adults. Their plays thus provide a final piece of support for my argument that Golden Age authors often resisted the growing pressure to conceive of the young as a race apart.

CHILDREN IN THE PLAYHOUSE

Just as the question of whether or not children should have a literature of their own remained open to discussion into the 1890s, so did the issue of whether they should have a theatre of their own and (if so) what sort dramatic entertainment would suit them best. The evidence suggests that throughout the century, children continued to attend various kinds of theatrical entertainments that had *not* been written especially for them. Much to the dismay of Barlee, Mayhew, Gustave Doré, and Blanchard Jerrold, working-class children frequented rowdy penny gaffs and music halls, while more well-to-do youngsters were taken to see weightier straight dramas. At age seven, for example, Eleanor Farjeon saw Ellen Terry and Henry Irving in *The Dead Heart* (Lyceum 1889); she also attended *Charles I* (Lyceum 1891) and *Cymbeline* (Lyceum 1896). Popular plays such as *Rip Van Winkle, Hans the Boatman*, and *Uncle Tom's Cabin* were not written specifically for children, but they all featured child characters and seem to have attracted decidedly mixed audiences.[5]

Then, too, a broad range of children continued to consume pantomime, despite the genre's increasing appropriation of racy music hall content. In 1892, for instance, eight-year-old Compton Mackenzie's parents allowed him to attend the Drury Lane pantomime *Humpty Dumpty*, where he pronounced himself "not shocked" but "greatly surprised" by the sight of music hall star Marie Lloyd singing the hit song "Ta-ra-ra-boom-de-ay" and "showing her drawers!" (33–4). Ernest H. Shepard, illustrator of the *Winnie the Pooh* books, also saw this production when he was eight and found Marie "bewitchingly" attractive (186). The scantily clad Principal Boy inspired his ardent admiration as well, as he recalled in his autobiography:

> I did not think it possible that such feminine charms existed as were displayed by the Principle Boy. Ample-bosomed, small-waisted and with thighs—oh, such thighs!—thighs that shone and glittered in the different-coloured silk tights in which she continually appeared. How she strode about the stage, proud and dominant, smacking those rounded limbs with a riding crop! At every smack, a fresh dart was shot into the heart of at least one young adorer. (186)

Nevertheless, there were indications that some theatrical producers, playwrights, critics, and parents were beginning to regard the child as a separate order of being who ought to be treated differently from adults. One of the earliest signs of this shift came in 1853, when the first English matinée—billed as "a morning Juvenile Performance"—occurred at Drury Lane. It was a special showing of E. L. Blanchard's pantomime *Harlequin Hudibras*, coupled with "items rendered by the band of the Duke of York's School" (Armstrong 56).[6] The inclusion of these schoolboy musicians is interesting, because it reveals that from very early on in this process, producers assumed that young audience members would enjoy watching young performers, an attitude that remained in place throughout the Golden Age.

Escalating complaints that pantomime was too vulgar for children were another sign of the shift. In 1866, the *Era* cautiously suggested that since "a Pantomime is usually the first thing which attaches the recollections of a child to the Theatre," perhaps producers should consider eliminating "those elements of slang and courseness which are so often made the substitutes for wit and humour" ("Christmas Entertainments" 10). Two decades later, W. Davenport Adams expressed outrage that pantomime had not yet been "adapted" for the "special public" of children it attracts (86). And a decade after that, responding to the same production of *Humpty Dumpty* that Mackenzie and Shepard so enjoyed, the *London Entr'acte* objected that "the pantomime is designed rather with the intention of rejoicing adults than giving satisfaction to the young, many of the references requiring a mind educated in the most modern slang and scandals of the period to understand them" (quoted in Gillies 53–54).

As children's continued attendance at such shows suggests, the notion that they would be better off seeing specially sanitized shows designed particularly for them seems to have emerged quite late in the century—around the 1870s—and caught on fairly slowly. The same E. L. Blanchard who presided over the first matinée played a key role in popularizing this idea. After complaining in 1867 that contemporary pantomime was all "legs and limelight" (quoted in A. E. Wilson 169), Blanchard set about introducing an alternative. Hoping to attract crowds of children and their caretakers to the theatre, he composed the all-child pantomimes that so pleased Carroll. The first one, *Little Goody Two Shoes; or, Harlequin Little Boy Blue* (Adelphi 1876) was advertised as "a Children's Pantomime, performed entirely by Children. . . . At Morning Performances only . . . at Children's Prices" (see figure 6.1). Besides the reduced prices and the early start time—chosen "so the old objection to Pantomimes that they keep the children up late at night is at once disposed of"[7]—these shows also tended to be shorter than regular pantomimes and timed to coincide with school holidays. In terms of content, Blanchard aimed to cleanse the genre of the music hall vulgarity many people had begun to object to, and indeed

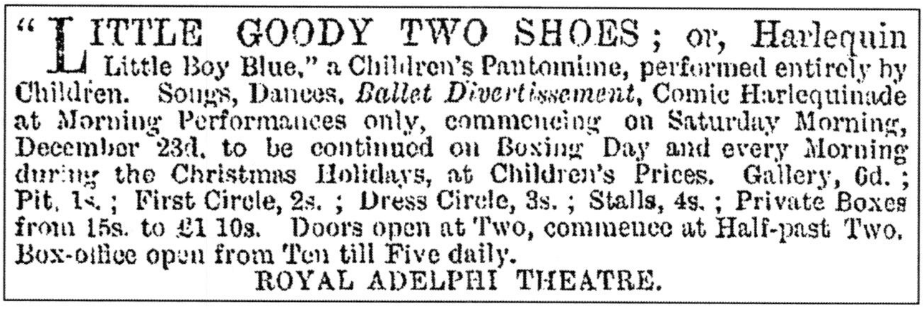

"LITTLE GOODY TWO SHOES; or, Harlequin Little Boy Blue," a Children's Pantomime, performed entirely by Children. Songs, Dances, *Ballet Divertissement*, Comic Harlequinade at Morning Performances only, commencing on Saturday Morning, December 23d, to be continued on Boxing Day and every Morning during the Christmas Holidays, at Children's Prices. Gallery, 6d.; Pit, 1s.; First Circle, 2s.; Dress Circle, 3s.; Stalls, 4s.; Private Boxes from 15s. to £1 10s. Doors open at Two, commence at Half-past Two. Box-office open from Ten till Five daily.

ROYAL ADELPHI THEATRE.

FIGURE 6.1 Advertisement for *Little Goody Two Shoes; or, Harlequin Little Boy Blue* (Adelphi 1876). *Era*, 17 Dec. 1876. British Library.

various reviewers praised him for avoiding topical jokes, political references, and other "adult" material.

Once we take into account Blanchard's all-child productions, F. J. Harvey Darton's claim that it was *Peter Pan* that inspired dramatists to begin producing shows "meant specially for children" becomes untenable (312). As Rose points out, Darton sets up children's drama in opposition to pantomime, suggesting that *Peter Pan* and its successors were "in no way like anything known before" (Darton 309). But as the example of *Little Goody Two Shoes* indicates, in trying to trace how children's theatre emerged as a distinct genre, we cannot sketch a simple progression from raucous pantomime (aimed at a mixed audience) to pure children's plays (designed only entertain youth). Rather, the existing evidence points to a messy situation in which both genres wavered back and forth: some pantomimes were geared more specifically than others to the perceived special needs and interests of children, and the same can be said of plays based on children's books, such as *Alice in Wonderland* (Prince of Wales's 1886) and *The Prince and the Pauper* (Gaiety 1890). For this reason, such dramas were condemned almost as often as pantomimes for including "distasteful, offensive, and [un]suitable" material (review of *Prince*). Moreover, as I will show, many of them were greatly influenced by the pantomime tradition.

Little Goody Two Shoes was a smash hit; it played for more than 150 performances and inspired Blanchard to produce two more all-child pantomimes at the Adelphi: *Little Red Riding Hood* (1877) and *Robin Hood and His Merry Little Men* (1877). These shows' popular success and the rave reviews they garnered prove that they pleased grown-ups, whether because they wanted to consume the child as spectacle, indulge a fascination with juvenile precocity, or find a less racy form of drama to attend with their children. At the same time, though, reviewers took seriously the proposition that if these shows aimed specifically to amuse young people, "*They* [should be] the real critics" (review of *Little Goody*, 24 Dec. 1876, 12). Numerous reviewers of Blanchard's shows therefore made a point of describing the composition and reactions of the audience, quoting specific remarks made by child audience members or recounting their general reactions at some length. For example, trying to capture what the atmosphere was like at a production of *Robin Hood*, the critic from the *Times* observed:

> It is eminently a children's pantomime, and on the first performance the theatre was taken by storm by children. Juries of at least 12, with a foreman and forewoman much larger and older than the rest, sat in several of the private boxes, and the gallery was full of persons of tender age who were always ready to assist Master Coote, the Clown, when he paused for a word in the time-honoured song of "Hot Codlings." A boy who would address a grown-up Clown as "Sir," pays, apparently, no respect to a Merryman of his own age; but the interrupters were vanquished by the satire

> of Master Coote, who begged to be excused for observing that "one fool is quite enough at a time." The audience of children vigorously applauded this and other sallies, and were evidently gratified by the compliment to themselves implied in intrusting all the parts to young actors. (review of *Robin Hood*)

To be sure, some of these accounts are colored by sentimental and sometimes downright voyeuristic delight in the wide-eyed adorableness of young audience members. In an article aimed at demonstrating that *Little Goody Two Shoes* was "a Children's Pantomime *par excellence*—a Pantomime written for children, enjoyed by children, and played by children," an *Era* critic declared that "little heads bent eagerly forward, little eyes sparkling with delight, little throats giving forth peal upon peal of laughter, little fingers pointing, and little hands clapping, afford in all parts of the house proofs inconvertible of the success of the Children's Pantomime at the Adelphi" ("Children's Pantomime"). Even as it strenuously attests to how child-oriented Blanchard's all-child productions were, this sort of report reminds us that the production of such shows was also driven by the adult desire to watch and listen to children (in the audience as well as on the stage). *Punch*'s review of *Little Red Riding Hood* provides another example of this phenomenon; in it, the critic quotes the naïve reaction of his child companion to the show, which had begun its run in the unseasonable month of August: " 'I suppose,' observed a small Boy who had been intensely delighted with the performance, 'I suppose they'll grow up by Christmas' " ("Our Representative" 83).

Clearly, the decision to cater to the young did not mean that producers could afford to ignore the tastes of adults (who, after all, were frequently the ones buying the tickets). In fact, most critics agreed that all-child productions like Blanchard's were "a thing for everybody to see, whether they are of tender years or are 'children of a larger growth' " (review of *Children's Pinafore*, *Era*). The frequent use of this expression—a predecessor to the phrase "children of all ages"—reveals that even those who admired such shows had internalized the idea that watching precocious children perform infantilized adult audience members. Gearing an all-child production specifically to children did not necessarily shield it from the familiar criticism that such shows actually had the effect of blurring the line between innocence and experience. For example, the author of "Children on the Stage" (1878) referred specifically to Blanchard's all-child pantomimes as evidence for his argument that modern dramatists were undermining the innocence of young people and encouraging an unhealthy preoccupation with precocity in their elders.

Indeed, even though Blanchard's goal was to produce more child-friendly shows, his adherence to the ideal of innocence was incomplete. His pantomimes featured child actors rolling around the stage impersonating drunkenness, as well as singing a song entitled "Capital Claret" and the aforementioned "Hot Codlings," a tune in which each rhymed verse ends with the performer falling silent and allowing the audience to shout out the missing word ("gin" and "drunk" are two of them). And Blanchard did not entirely avoid topical references; *Robin Hood*, his third such show, featured jokes about food adulteration, the price of American beef, and the training ship *Arethusa*, as well as a parody of the popular ballad "Nancy Lee." He and those who admired his productions also seemed comfortable with the idea that very young children were familiar with the rituals of courtship and could themselves become objects of desire. Thus, after noting that little Carrie Coote was "thoroughly efficient, whisking and flirting with all the airs and graces of a full-grown maiden," an *Era* reviewer teasingly added "but Miss Carrie is not in her teens yet, so we warn all the young gentlemen home for the holidays that they must not fall in love at present" (review of *Little Goody*, 24 Dec. 1876, 13). This critic seems more amused than upset by the notion that older boys or men might find this little girl sexy.

What all this suggests is that even in the late 1870s, people were still working out what it meant to conceive of the child as innocent. Far from being idiosyncratic, Blanchard's treatment of young people reflected the fact that juvenile Victorians were continuing to engage in activities that we now decisively categorize as adult. For example, historians of childhood observe that youngsters "commonly were allowed to [drink to inebriation] until the beginning of the [twentieth] century" (Pinchbeck and Hewitt 349). It is therefore unsurprising that Blanchard included drinking jokes in his children's pantomimes. Indeed, this practice continued for quite a long time; the 1904 Drury Lane pantomime *The White Cat* included similar material, prompting one critic to object that drinking scenes were out of place in a show that billed itself as a "Children's Pantomime" (*White Cat* advertisement). Yet even at that late date, "no other journal seemed to notice the 'vulgarity' which the *Daily Mail* so severely denounced," according to A. E. Wilson (213). Still, the fact that this one negative voice had a "disastrous effect on the business of the pantomime" suggests that attitudes were finally changing (213).

As this example indicates, the implementation of the ideology of innocence was a slow, halting process, and the cultists and creators of Golden Age children's theatre were hardly the most fanatical proponents of this new conception of childhood. At times, to be sure, no one could be more stern than they about the necessity of steering clear of anything the least bit coarse, particularly if women or children were involved. Yet, as I have already shown, they also attended "all manner of wicked plays and pantomimes"—as Ruskin cheerfully called them[8]—often exposing their child-friends to shows they knew had drawn strong objections from self-declared defenders of innocence and virtue such as Leigh Hunt and W. Davenport Adams. For example, since

Carroll read and contributed to the *Theatre*, he was almost certainly familiar with attacks on the vogue for child performers that appeared there, including the aforementioned "Children on the Stage," which criticized the all-child pantomimes he so eagerly attended.

These contradictory impulses were also evident in the role Carroll, Burnett, and Barrie played in creation of juvenile drama. One the one hand, they helped precipitate the emergence of children's theatre, a genre whose existence depends on the idea that children are different from adults and therefore ought to have a different kind of drama designed especially for them. (In a clear sign that the birth of this subgenre was inspired by the spread of the ideology of childhood innocence, the most lauded of these new shows were praised for their simplicity, delicacy, and refinement: that is to say, for eschewing the extravagance, vulgarity, and convoluted plotting of pantomime and other preexisting theatrical fare aimed at mixed audiences.)[9] On the other hand, the shows these cultists helped create were shot through with a lingering fondness for the old forms of drama that their contemporaries were so vehemently dismissing as degenerate or simply unsuited to the tastes of juvenile playgoers. Indeed, rather than striving to erect a firm line between child and adult, shows such as *Little Lord Fauntleroy* and *Peter Pan* promoted mingling on multiple levels: they were performed by mixed casts, received by mixed audiences, and often centered around precocious child characters played by precocious child actors.

To begin with Carroll, he firmly informed librettist Henry Savile Clarke in 1886 that he would only allow *Alice* to be adapted for the stage on the understanding that it would contain no "coarseness, or anything suggestive of coarseness" and that for this reason it should "not [be] a Pantomime" (quoted in Lovett 37). But he had not always felt this way. When he first contacted a theatrical producer about dramatizing *Alice* in 1867, Carroll confided to his brother Edwin, "I have vague hopes . . . that it may occur to him to turn it into a pantomime. I fancy it would work well in that form" (*Letters* 1:102). Putting together a team to stage *Alice* took a long time, and over the ensuing years Carroll entertained many different ideas as to what form the show should take: an extravaganza, an all-child production, an operetta. When *Alice in Wonderland* finally opened at Prince of Wales's Theatre in December 1886, it featured a mixed cast of children and adults, and the playbill identified it as "A Musical Dream Play, in Two Acts, for Children and Others" (quoted in Lovett 47). Discussing the wording of this description, Carroll told Clarke, "what you are producing is not in any existing lines at all & cannot fairly be classified into any existing form of drama, & I would say 'for a new *thing* try a new *name*'" (quoted in Lovett 44).

But how new was it? Frankie Morris has persuasively demonstrated that Carroll's fascination with pantomime affected his composition of the *Alice* books, and reviews of the stage version suggest that it, too, had ties to this tradition. Thus, the *Theatre* praised the original production of *Alice* for giving "the little folk this winter a genuine children's pantomime" (E. R. 48). A negative review of the 1898 revival of the show in the *Times* offered a more substantive account of the show's links to this tradition. "It is significant of the limitations of the stage in dealing with Lewis Carroll's wonderful story-book," this critic declared, that the creators of *Alice in Wonderland* felt that "there was nothing better to be done than to bring on the Hatter, the Gryphon, the Mock Turtle, the Cheshire Cat . . . and the other familiar characters in the grotesque masks and costumes of pantomime" and let them each do a number, thus emulating the "incoherency" of traditional Christmas shows (review of *Alice*, 23 Dec. 1898). Indeed, advertisements for this revival included the descriptive phrase "The Children's Pantomime" (see figure 6.2), and the show concluded with a harlequinade by the Leoville Troupe. Moreover, the *Pall Mall Gazette* sniffily objected to the "the cockney element" of pantomime humor that was "perceptible enough" in the performances of some of the adult actors ("Alice in Wonderland").

Whether because it reminded them of pantomime or for some other reason, critics of the original production did not treat *Alice* as a novelty. "It is, of course, eminently a children's play," the *Times* calmly observed, and a similarly matter-of-fact tone marked reviews that appeared in *Punch*, the *Theatre*, and the *Illustrated London News* (review of *Alice, Times,* 24 Dec. 1886). Such nonchalance about the idea of creating a drama "specially intended for children" seems surprising (review of *Alice, Era,* 25 Dec. 1886), considering that roughly a decade later commentators began to hold up *Alice in Wonderland* as the first example of the subgenre of "Children's Plays" (1899), which they tended to exalt as an *antidote* to pantomime's excess. What might this mean? Clearly, the line between children's plays and pantomimes was blurrier than such critics liked to admit. It is also possible that other plays targeted specifically to young people preceded *Alice* but were quickly forgotten. Or, as seems quite likely, perhaps Blanchard and his fellow producers of all-child pantomimes and operet-

FIGURE 6.2 Advertisement for *Alice in Wonderland* (Opera Comique 1898). *Era*, 24 Dec. 1898. British Library.

tas had so effectively popularized the general idea of catering shows to young people that a children's play that featured music and dancing did not seem like a remarkable innovation.

Certainly, *Alice* critics followed in the footsteps of reviewers of Blanchard's shows by placing great importance on the reactions of child audience members. Indeed, the *Era* firmly declared that it could not render judgment on the play because while it was evidently designed for children, the audience for its first performance naturally consisted of adult critics and theatrical insiders: "Until we see, as we may next week, the Prince of Wales's Theatre filled with juveniles, accompanied, of course, by their parents and guardians, but still themselves constituting *the* audience, it will be impossible to say if *Alice in Wonderland* is successful or not" (review of *Alice*, 25 Dec. 1886). A similar desire to attend to the input of children manifested itself in *Punch*'s first brief mention of *Alice*: "Our Child-Critic says that the place to spend a really happy afternoon is at the Prince of Wales's Theatre, where *Alice in Wonderland* is being played. 'They must know the book,' she says, 'and then they'll recognize all Mr. Tenniel's pictures walking about.' The Dormouse is delightful, she adds, and the Oysters charming" ("Christmas Carroll"). Of course, we cannot discount the possibility that this commentary might have been invented by an adult critic; at the very least, it was filtered through and edited by grown-ups. Still, it shows how attentive Victorian critics often were to the issue of audience. Indeed, a few weeks later, in "The Children's Choice," *Punch* revisited *Alice* in order to inform its readers that the show was "crowded every afternoon" with "children [who] could go and see it over and over again, and never be tired." In fact, this critic warns his readers that *Alice* is so child-oriented that it will bore and annoy adult theatregoers! As for the *Era*, the success of the first production of *Alice* was such that it did finally feel comfortable asserting that this "play for the juveniles" had been and would continue to be popular with child-dominated audiences (review of *Alice*, 29 Dec. 1888).

Still, despite the popular success of Blanchard's shows and *Alice*, and despite the fact that the idea of targeting a show specifically to children had ceased to seem new by the late 1880s,[10] children's theatre did not immediately take off as a concept. Thus, in 1899, the *Era* felt compelled to advocate for the existence of this subgenre of dramatic entertainment. In the aforementioned article "Children's Plays," an anonymous critic complained that despite the "enormous vogue" of *Alice in Wonderland*, only a few shows catered specifically to "children between the ages of seven and twelve" followed in its wake, including *The Rose and the Ring* (Prince of Wales's 1890), an omnibus adaptation of some Hans Christian Andersen stories (Terry's 1897), and *The Snow Man* (Lyceum 1899). Sagely noting that "children are not free agents in the choice of their theatrical amusements" since "they have to go where they are taken," this critic claims to have polled his child friends about their preferences and discovered "that the little ones prefer fairy, fanciful, fantastic plays" to "gaudy" pantomimes packed with topical allusions ("Children's Plays").

Of course, we may doubt the accuracy of this generalization, particularly when we recall Mackenzie's and Shepard's accounts of how much they enjoyed pantomime. Rather than providing us with solid evidence about what nineteenth-century child audiences wanted, this article reflects a growing tendency on the part of commentators to conceive of the child as a separate order of being whose theatrical taste differed significantly from that of adults. Given the *Era*'s prominence as a leading source of theatrical gossip and information, it is probably not a coincidence that the sort of "fairy plays" this critic praised soon began appearing in much greater numbers, including *Bluebell in Fairyland* (Vaudeville 1901), which *The Oxford Companion to the Theatre* (mis)identifies as the first play "specially written for children" (Hartnoll 171). Yet as Roger Lancelyn Green has observed, these shows were often greatly influenced by the pantomime tradition and included precisely the sort of material the author of "Children's Plays" dismissed as too adult-oriented.

Of *Bluebell*, for instance, Green notes that "it had much of the spectacle of pantomime still, and its comedy was largely of the heavy-handed and topical variety, with comic business inserted solely as an excuse for laboured puns and quibbles" (*Fifty Years* 29). Clearly, old habits died hard; despite the new impulse to cater shows specifically to children, dramatists and producers clung to the idea of attracting mixed audiences—a rational choice, since attracting the broadest possible audience made commercial sense. Meanwhile, though, critics felt compelled to sort out which of these productions were truly suitable for children. For example, after noting in 1904 that "the children's fairy plays have continued to be a growing class," a reviewer for the *Stage* makes a point of distinguishing those shows that are "unaffectedly for children" from those that seem "less for a child than for the child-like mind knowing something of the sophistication of life" ("Dramatic Year" 17).

Recognizing how slow and unsteady this process of audience differentiation was helps us makes sense of the dramatic career of Frances Hodgson Burnett, whose many plays based on children's stories debuted between 1887 and 1912. By the time she completed her final play, *Racketty-Packetty House* (1912), children's theatre had fully emerged as a recognized phenomenon, as indicated by the fact that this drama was first performed at the Century Theatre's newly established Children's Theatre in New York. *St. Nicholas* magazine, which had published the story the play was based on, confidently declared *Racketty-Packetty House* "the first play for children to be given in a real Children's Theatre and enacted chiefly by real children" (Meadowcroft 352).[11] Located on the roof of the Century, this separate auditorium featured child-sized chairs, and, for this production, "the usherettes were dressed as Little Red Riding Hoods, and the booking office was like a gate-keeper's lodge" (Thwaite 230).

In this last detail, producers were perhaps building on a *Peter Pan* tradition; under Dion Boucicault's direction, the box office where you picked up your tickets became a version of the "Wendy House" that featured in the play itself.[12] Indeed, by this point, children's theatre had become similarly established in England. By 1914, the *Times* regularly subtitled its column on Christmas shows "Children's Plays" or "Plays for Children," while Jean Sterling Mackinlay had begun her long-running series of holiday children's matinées (1914–39) whose existence has prompted some theatre historians to single *her* out as the originator of the British children's theatre movement.[13] In fact, Mrs. Percy (Mabel) Dearmer and Netta Syrett had anticipated Mackinlay in December 1913 by establishing "the Children's Theatre, a scheme for producing simple and beautiful plays to be acted by children for children in one of the London theatres . . . for the express purpose of interesting the children themselves rather than their grown-up relations" ("Children's Theatre").

At this late date, *The Real Little Lord Fauntleroy* (Terry's 1888)[14]—one of Burnett's earliest dramas—was retrospectively dubbed a "children's play," with revivals of it lumped in under this heading with ostentatiously child-oriented shows such as Mrs. Dearmer's play *The Cockyolly Bird* (Court 1914).[15] Yet when it first appeared, *Little Lord Fauntleroy* did not officially present itself as a play for children; according to the *Era*, it was billed merely as "A Play, in Three Acts" (review of *Real Little*, 19 May 1888), and reviewers of the original British production did not dilate on the issue of what effect it might (or did) have on young people. Still, in keeping with the state of affairs just described, many children were taken to see *Little Lord Fauntleroy* anyway, both in England and in the United States.[16] Thus, by the time the show was revived in 1901, the *Illustrated London News* chose to describe it as "a veritable treat for all youngsters" (review of *Little*, 4 Jan. 1902), while an American journalist describing the origins of children's theatre in 1914 confidently recalled that in the nineteenth century, "children had their own books, their own pictures, and their own songs . . . but only once in a while, a very long while, a play of their own, like 'Little Lord Fauntleroy'" (Meadowcroft 351).

Nevertheless, a better category to drop *Little Lord Fauntleroy* into might be the "child drama," the term the Victorians themselves used for it and other similar shows in the 1880s and 1890s.[17] For this was the precise period when, despite the popularity of Blanchard's shows and *Alice*, playwrights and producers nevertheless seemed unwilling or uninterested in the prospect of creating specially sanitized entertainments intended specifically for youth. And Burnett, though often assumed to be complicit in the fetishization of purity through her creation of the infamously adorable Fauntleroy, actively participated in this very trend: that is to say, the creation of shows that centered around child characters and that children went to see but that also roused the wrath of some reviewers precisely because they did not shy away from including racy adult content.

Though a number of Burnett's plays were descried as being unsuited to the blissfully naïve nature of children, *Nixie* (Terry's 1890)—a play based on her children's story *Editha's Burglar* (1880)—engendered the most controversy. Both the *Era* and the *Illustrated London News* noted disapprovingly that Nixie herself was not a truly innocent character but rather an "over-developed and unnaturally clever child" who exhibited a decidedly "precocious" streak (C. S., review of *Nixie*; "'Nixie' at Terry's"). Critics were particularly incensed that Burnett and her husband, Stephen Townsend (who collaborated with her on the script), had introduced a new plotline involving adultery and other subjects that were "not 'spoon meat' for children," as "C. S." put it in the *Illustrated London News* ("Playhouses"). Indeed, this commentator was so horrified by *Nixie* that he vented his disgust in two consecutive columns aimed at exposing "the decadence of the child-drama" ("Playhouses"). His principal complaint against *Nixie* was that such an impure play had been "put forward to attract and interest the same innocent audience of children that delighted in 'Little Lord Fauntleroy'" ("Playhouses"). Comparing *Nixie* to Henrik Ibsen's *A Doll's House*, he demanded, "Does the modern craze for enlightenment extend to plays where children are taught in their infancy what they will most surely know later on by bitter experience and knowledge of the world?" (review of *Nixie*). If so, "I for one most vigorously protest against it in the interests of innocence and purity" ("Playhouses").

But although this critic emphatically warns that child audience members could not be more wrong in "expecting [Nixie to be] the foster-sister of Little Lord Fauntleroy," the two plays actually had a great deal in common (review of *Nixie*). Just as *Nixie* exposes its audience to the sordid tale of a woman who elopes with a married man who means to ruin her, the last two acts of *Little Lord Fauntleroy* revolve around the machinations of a "vulgar," low-class woman named Minna who, in marrying the Earl's oldest son for his money, not only committed bigamy (since her first husband was still alive) but also abandoned her son from that earlier union (Burnett, *Little Lord* [1889] 58). Besides containing risqué content of this sort, *Little Lord Fauntleroy* anticipates *Nixie* because it, too, chronicles the exploits of a highly precocious child character who has been exposed early on to the pleasures and hardships of the adult world. Contemporary commentators picked up on this quality; drama critic Clement Scott described Fauntleroy as "a strange child with an old head on young shoulders" (3), while *Punch* provided an amusingly literal take on this aspect of the boy's character (see figure 6.3).

Just as Nixie protects her mother from coming into contact with a burglar by dealing with him herself, Fauntleroy cares for his mourning mother, treating her more as a companion than a parent, as indicated by his habit of calling her "Dearest," as his father did before his death. Despite his youth, moreover, Fauntleroy's extensive contact with the public sphere has made him familiar with the trials

FIGURE 6.3 "'The *Real* Little Lord Fauntleroy.': (A Very Imaginary Conversation. With Apologies to Mrs. F. Hodgson Burnett.)" This image accompanied a brief, unsigned parody of Burnett's story. *Punch*, 19 May 1888. Journal Collection, University Library System, University of Pittsburgh.

of the laboring classes. Telling his grandfather about the case of a poor man to whom he has given money, the little boy sagely observes that "when a man is ill and has twelve children, you know how it is" (30). His worldly knowledge even extends to politics. Indeed, Fauntleroy's involvement in the hurly-burly of American electioneering is one of first things we learn about him, thanks to his Irish servant Mary's monologue in praise of his "ould-fashioned" ways:

> "Mary," sez he, "I'm very much ent'rusted in the 'lection," sez he, "I'm a 'publican an' so is Dearest. Are you a 'publican, Mary?" Sorra a bit," sez I, "I'm the best o' Demmycrats." An' he looks up at me with a look that wud go to yer heart an' sez he, "Mary," sez he, "the country will go to ruin," an'

> nivver a day since thin has he let go by widout argyin' wid me to change me polytics. (7)

As this speech suggests, the appeal of little Fauntleroy is not based on his status as an untouched, primitive Other who manages to remain detached from contemporary society. Rather, it arises from the frisson of contact, of innocence mingled (and mingling) with experience. As Brian Crozier notes, child-centered dramas from this era generally represent children as enmeshed in close relationships with adults, "typically in family situations and commenting on adult life" (3). And just as the "strange, refined, worldly-wise little [Fauntleroy]" exhibits an attractive mixture of naïveté and knowingness,[18] Vera Beringer—the first child actress to impersonate him—drew praise for combining "the artlessness of the nursery with the skill of the Conservatoire" (review of *Real Little, Times*).

The diametrically different receptions accorded *Little Lord Fauntleroy* and *Nixie*—which appeared within two years of one another—attest more to a profound cultural ambivalence about children acting like adults than to any deep dissimilarity between the two plays. This tension is also evident in the Victorians' use of the term "old-fashioned" to characterize children prematurely exposed to the adult world. In Fauntleroy's case, this adjective functions as a term of praise that evokes the old conception of the child as miniature participant in adult life in a positive way. But in general, the Victorians associated this phrase with the pathetic child heroes of Dickens, for whom such premature competence was damaging, if not deadly. "The old-fashioned child is in fact a development of modern writers, [especially] Dickens" Frederic Adye declared in his 1893 essay "Old-Fashioned Children." Yet Adye also cites real-life examples of this sort of child to support his conclusion that "they do so often die, these old-fashioned children, in real life as in fiction" (286).

Just as Carroll's representation of child actresses as hardy giants in his 1887 letter to the *St. James Gazette* signifies his determination to resist rhetoric that insists on the helpless vulnerability of the young, Burnett's passionate insistence on Fauntleroy's vigor and health amounts to an attack on Dickensian morbidity, criticism of which was already in the air. In 1855, Fitzjames Stephen quipped that a child character introduced in a Dickens novel "runs as much risk as any of the troops that stormed the Redan" (quoted in Lerner 118). A decade later, Henry James mercilessly skewered Jenny Wren and her ilk in his 1865 review of *Our Mutual Friend*: "Like all Mr. Dickens's pathetic characters, she is a little monster; she is deformed, unhealthy, unnatural; she belongs to the troop of hunchbacks, imbeciles and precocious children who have carried on the sentimental business in all Mr. Dickens's novels: the little Nells, the Smikes, the Paul Dombeys" (470–71).

In contrast to the saintly but doomed Paul, who is often described as old-fashioned, Fauntleroy is the picture of health. Burnett repeatedly emphasizes his physical strength; in the first scene of the play, he wins a race and describes his exploits with a baseball, while later ones feature him supporting the gouty Earl like a human cane and earning praise for his ability to ride a horse. As in the case of Sara Crewe, Burnett takes pains to link precocity with power, a move signaled by the fact that both of these child protagonists assume a royal title. Her interest in authoritative children is also manifest in her willingness to allow a child actor to "carry" a production. Her decision to focus not only on the cuteness of children but also on their capacity and clout may help explain why *Little Lord Fauntleroy* was such a smash hit with mixed audiences on both sides of the Atlantic. The much-descried (and undeniable) sentimentality that sets Fauntleroy up as a picturesque object of the adult gaze is balanced by an opposing tendency to portray him as a sturdy, influential agent who acts in accordance with his own principles and desires.[19] He was, as Beverly Lyon Clark notes, "a figure [who] spoke to both adults and children, a figure [who] maintained the conjunction of child and adult audiences" (22).

In general, the content of Burnett's plays indicates that she was not invested in maintaining a strict barrier between innocence and experience, even as the critical reaction to them suggests that the culture around her was becomingly increasingly intent on policing this line. The way London theatre critics responded to Burnett's dramatization of the story of Sara Crewe provides another illustration of this point. The reviewer for the *Times* protested that for "a play designed for children," Burnett's *A Little Un-Fairy Princess* (Shaftesbury 1902) was "excessively concerned with money," a topic he claimed held no interest for children (review of *Little Un-Fairy*). Similarly, both the *Era* and the *Illustrated London News* found this show "too sad and cynical" (*Era*, quoted in Thwaite 131), objecting to the fact that the play dwelt extensively and honestly on Sara's struggles with poverty and abuse, subjects that "should surely be passed over quickly in a play intended for laughter-loving children" (review of *Little Un-Fairy, Illustrated*).

Such reactions were part of a larger trend; right around the turn of the century, commentators repeatedly chastised authors and producers for failing to recognize that children were a special audience with their own unique likes and dislikes, quite different from adults. Two years after the author of "Children's Plays" exhorted dramatists to respect and cater to the interests of children under twelve, a *Times* critic prodded experts in emerging fields such as child psychology to come up with "a formula for juvenile tastes in theatrical entertainment" (review of *Shock*, 17 Dec. 1901). "At what age," this critic inquires, "does the clown's red-hot poker cease to give an aesthetic 'thrill'? Do little playgoers prefer parents and guardians as 'serious interest' or as 'comic relief'?" If a "mere lay observer [can] safely permit himself" one guess, this critic declares, it is that children prefer raucous fun to sappy sentimentality—a notion that seems to have emerged right around this time, since reviewers suddenly began to object to the schmaltziness of revivals of child-centered shows that had not prompted this criticism in their earlier incarnations.[20]

Besides objecting to sentimentality and seriousness, turn-of-the-century reviewers also complained about shows that featured topical jokes and lavish spectacle. Protesting against the "exaggeration" and "excess" infusing "Children's Christmas Amusements" (1905), for example, Edward H. Cooper faulted producers and playwrights for treating child theatregoers as if they were as blasé as their adult counterparts by failing to adhere to "the rule of simplicity" (81). As a culture, he declared, "we are so used to . . . catering for bored, satiated folk who are tired of novelties . . . that we have not only forgotten the vulgarity of the business but cannot immediately remember the existence of a class of person who is not satiated and is very easily satisfied" (79, 80).

To their credit, reviewers did occasionally recognize that their often-repeated calls for simplicity and directness in children's shows were more reflective of their own desires than those of children. Reviewing a 1912 revival of Philip Carr and Nigel Playfair's *Shock-Headed Peter* (Garrick 1900), for instance, one commentator followed up his complaint about the elaborate comic business that interrupted the show's action with the admission that "the examiners must, of course, be the children in the audience; and on Saturday the children laughed so loud that we felt our grown-up hankering after the simplicity, the vigorous spareness of 'Strewwelpeter' to be quite out of place and 'superior'" (review of *Shock*, *Times*, 23 Dec. 1912).

More often, though, early twentieth-century critics were upset when shows that attracted children threatened their cherished stereotypes about the primitive naïveté of the young. Burnett was not the only offender; Barrie, too, was taken to task for refusing to acknowledge the otherness of children. In keeping with the journalistic tradition of demanding that shows aimed at young people should eschew "adult" content, Max Beerbohm insisted in his reviews of multiple productions of *Peter Pan* that although Barrie's show included elements that might appeal to children, its sappiness disqualified it as a children's drama:

> Written ostensibly to amuse children, [*Peter Pan*] was written really to amuse to touch and amuse their elders. If children were people of independent means, accustomed to book seats for themselves, and free to pick and choose just whichever entertainments gave them the greatest pleasure, the Duke of York's Theatre would not, I fancy, be quite so well packed as it now is. . . . If there is one thing which the average child has not, that thing is sentimentality. ("*Peter Pan* Revisited" 335)

Shaw agreed, twice characterizing *Peter Pan* as a phenomenon foisted on children by grown-ups, and declaring that the public was "altogether wrong" in regarding Barrie as "the children's playwright" ("Unhappy" 1481).[21]

If this line of argument sounds familiar, it is because Rose echoes it in *The Case of Peter Pan*. Suspicious of the whole idea of "theatre *for* the child" (94), she contends that the popularity of plays such as *Peter Pan* was due solely to the voyeuristic adult desire to consume "the child as spectacle" (97). One problem with this stance, as I have already suggested, is that these critics' admirable attentiveness to the indisputable power adults wield over children leads them to conceive of young people as primitive beings devoid of agency and intelligence. Indeed, this tendency manifests itself strongly in Beerbohm's reviews of *Peter Pan*. His "evidence" for the claim that the play was not written for children is that youngsters could never appreciate the humor of lines such as Hook's "Split my infinitives!" or the beauty of the more pathetic scenes: "a child is not, like you and me, sensitive to the finer shades of pathos and humour. To move a child's pity, or to move a child's sense of humour, you must proceed on very broad lines" ("Pantomime" 118). Immature spectators, he explains, like horseplay and simple plotlines in which moral matters are portrayed in black-and-white terms: "Savages, they have not acquired the art of being sentimental. They are not in a position to appreciate the central beauties of *Peter Pan*" ("*Peter Pan* Revisited" 336).

Working on the assumption that children are a different order of being from adults, Beerbohm takes it for granted that if *Peter Pan* appeals strongly to grown-ups, it must therefore not be aimed at or appreciated by children. Similarly, referring to *Peter Pan*, *Alice in Wonderland*, and other similar shows, Rose reveals that she views the issue of audience as an either–or question: "Spectacle of childhood for *us*," she asks, "or play for *children*?" (33). She then decisively declares that "children are not the cause of this literature. They are not the group for whom it was created" (102). Yet framing the issue of audience as a stark binary is ahistorical and obfuscatory. Many early dramas based on children's books aimed to attract a *mixed* audience, as pantomimes did throughout the century. Denying the possibility that children formed a crucial target audience for such shows forces us to ignore or misrepresent a large body of evidence to the contrary.

For instance, Rose attempts to cast doubt on the extent to which *Alice* was designed to attract child theatregoers by asserting that the 1898 revival "was put on, not for mother-and-child matinees, but for the general public [in] evening performances" (97). But as the advertisement reproduced in figure 6.2 reveals, matinees *were* offered, and the producers evidently hoped to attract parents and children, as indicated by their choice of subtitle.[22] Similarly, in making the case that *Peter Pan* was not intended for young people, Rose declares that on opening night, "the audience was made up of London's theatregoing élite and there was hardly a child among them" (32). Yet as I have shown, this proves very little, since first night audiences were traditionally dominated by critics and other theatrical insiders; indeed, they were often lured to attend first nights by the offer of free tickets.[23]

Whether we categorize *Peter Pan* as a children's play, a child drama, or a fairy play, there is no doubt that young people formed a key target audience for it from the very beginning, as Barrie's own testimony and virtually every contemporary review attests.[24] Moreover, no other show from this era boasts so much evidence of children responding enthusiastically, from reminiscences by actors and former child audience members to hundreds of fan letters from children who attended early productions.[25] Of course, despite this wealth of evidence, we still cannot generalize about how children as a group responded, as if all young people were alike (and present in the theatre). Pauline Chase, the actress who played Peter from 1906 until 1915, recognized this; in her introduction to *Peter Pan's Postbag* (1909), a collection of fan letters she received from children, she wisely observed that "you never can tell how they will take it" (ix). Still, some common themes do emerge in surviving letters from child audience members that support the accounts penned by Chase and other actors describing how child-dominated audiences tended to react to the show.

To begin with, as in the case of Blanchard's all-child productions, young audience members evidently enjoyed the interactive aspect of *Peter Pan*. In numerous letters, children describe how they waved, clapped, cheered, hissed, yelled out comments, and otherwise involved themselves in the action, behavior that early "Peters" such as Chase and Maud Adams recalled well.[26] Twelve-year-old Lesley provides a vivid sense of how raucous the scene sometimes was: describing her third trip to see *Peter Pan*, she declares, "I was amongst those that made that awfull [*sic*] noise I nearly shouted myself hoarse, I tried to throw a thimble onto the stage I don't know whether it arrived, because there were such a lot of other thimbles thrown" (*Peter Pan's Postbag* 5). (Thimbles come to symbolize kisses in the course of the play.) It also seems worth noting that the letter writers themselves seemed to consider *Peter Pan* a children's play. Thus, after informing Peter that he has seen the show four times and hopes to see it again the following year, a boy named Frank solemnly adds, "I am nine years old, but I don't think that I am too old to see it" (61).

But the most striking aspect of the letters collected by Chase is the nakedness of desire expressed for Peter, particularly in the missives from girls. Several correspondents inform Peter that he has been haunting their dreams, while six-year-old Margery announces, "I still love you, last winter I cried because I loved you so" (10). In 1906, a girl named Nettie wrote to assure Peter that

> If I had been "Wendy" I should never, never have left *you*. I should have stayed with you for ever in your house under the ground. Fancy you not knowing what a kiss was! I think you were made for kissing. No one could help loving you, you dearest and sweetest of girls. If I were a Fairy Prince, you would have to live in Fairyland because I should take you away with me. I should love you more than words can tell. (14–15)

Having recognized that Peter is a girl playing a boy, Nettie imaginatively reenacts such gender-bending in regard to herself: "If I had been Wendy"; "If I were a Fairy Prince." Similarly, a girl named Madge appends the postscript "If I were a man I would marry you" (37).

Such testimony in no way undermines Rose's valuable point that adults' desires (voyeuristic and otherwise) shaped the content of shows such as *Peter Pan* and helped ensure their success. But it does offer a salutary reminder that we cannot therefore assume that children's desires played no role at all in this process. Such a stance is especially unhelpful in considering Golden Age texts, since so many of them were inspired by intense relationships with actual children, and of course *Peter Pan* is no exception. Not only did the original story grow out of games Barrie played with the Llewelyn Davies brothers, the idea of turning this material into a play occurred to him in 1901, after he took the boys to see *Bluebell in Fairyland.* According to Andrew Birkin, *Bluebell* had astonished the London theatrical community by running "for nearly 300 performances, attracting a fanatical audience of children who saw the play again and again" (92). The Llewelyn Davies boys greatly enjoyed it, as did Barrie, who decided to see if he could compose a fairy play that would attract the same sort of audience.

Thus, rather than heeding the pleas of commentators who were attempting to establish a sharp dividing line between plays and pantomimes, children's shows and adult ones, Barrie chose instead to emulate the creators of *Bluebell* by keeping such boundaries blurry. Even though he privately described *Peter Pan* as a "play for children" and delighted in taking his child-friends to see it (quoted in Birkin 103), he had no qualms about including material in it that critics had long complained was unsuitable for the youthful eye and ear. In 1882, W. Davenport Adams had attacked pantomimes for indulging in the "gratuitous exhibition of female anatomy" enabled by cross-dressing: "Why" he demanded, "must the hero always be a woman dressed in tights and tunic?" (89). *Peter Pan* defiantly carried on this tradition; "In so far as [Peter] is dressed at all," Barrie declared in his stage directions, "it is in autumn leaves and cobwebs" (97). We might assume that child audience members were not expected to succumb to Peter's sexual allure, were it not for the fact that Barrie's script chronicles how three young people become violently infatuated with the eternal boy; Wendy and Tinker Bell fight over the right to kiss Peter, and the first production emphasized that Tiger Lily had erotic designs on him as well.

Even as Barrie refused to characterize desire as a purely adult domain, he also included parodic moments whose humor hinged on the assumption of shared cultural knowledge. The first few performances of Peter Pan featured a "front scene" in which the man playing Hook impersonated a series of famous actors such as Sir Henry Irving and Herbert Beerbohm Tree, as well as a tableau based on a well-known paining of Napoleon on the Bellerophon. Then, too, Barrie utterly ignored critical pleas that simplicity should be the hallmark of shows aimed at young people; *Peter Pan* was an extravagant spectacle that featured massive sets, flying actors, and a circus-like variety of animals in its large cast. Finally, there was the sentimentality Beerbohm so strongly objected to, which reached its height in the infamously saccharine "Beautiful Mothers" scene.

Because these elements were not in keeping with new notions about the simplistic otherness of child theatregoers, they engendered a negative critical reaction, and many of them were eventually cut. But their presence in the original production signals Barrie's fond regard for theatrical traditions that were routinely attacked for failing to differentiate between child and adult audience members, including and especially pantomime.[27] The inclusion of this material alongside elements critics deemed more child-oriented caused one reviewer to characterize *Peter Pan* as an "amalgam . . . of the oddest and most contrary ingredients" (quoted in Hanson 45). Perhaps, too, this critic was responding to the paradoxical quality of Barrie's representation of childhood. Along with Dowson, Carroll, and many other late Victorian child-lovers, Barrie exhibited the inconsistency I have singled out as a defining characteristic of the cult of the child: one moment he trumpeted the perfect purity of the young; the next he satirized, discounted, or ignored the implications of this posture.

For instance, in "To the Five," the lengthy dedicatory essay he composed for the published script of *Peter Pan*, Barrie laments how quickly the Llewelyn Davies brothers passed from "the wood of make-believe [to] the tree of knowledge," a formulation that seems to set up innocence and experience as separate states of being (75–76). Yet in the same essay, he makes a point of disagreeing with people who "say we are different people at different periods of our lives": "I don't hold with it; I think one remains the same person throughout, merely passing, as it were, in these lapses of time from one room to another, but all in the same house. If we unlock the rooms of the far past we can peer in and see ourselves, busily occupied in beginning to become you and me" (78). Here, rather than suggesting that a firm barrier divides childhood from adulthood, Barrie instead imagines development as a continuum, characterizing the child as an adult in the making and the adult as a compound being inextricably linked to his younger selves.

The play itself similarly both floats and subverts the idea that children are a race apart. Peter certainly believes that adulthood is an entirely separate state from childhood, and he repeatedly asserts the superiority of innocent juvenility, as when he brags to Hook, "I'm youth, I'm joy, I'm a little bird that has broken out of the egg" (145). Notably, though, when Barrie narrated this scene in *Peter and Wendy*, he followed up this little speech with the sardonic disclaimer "This, of course, was nonsense" (203). While this proviso does not appear in the drama, it is no accident that one of the lost boys is named "Slightly Soiled," since many aspects of the play undermine Peter's conviction that innocence and experience are radically opposed states of being.

Wendy, for example, is both naïve and knowing; she readily believes her father's unlikely story about how willingly he took his medicine as a boy, yet when Peter flies into her bedroom she twice invites him to kiss her, and then spends the rest of the play trying to seduce him into treating her as a lover rather than a mother (the role she happily plays to the other lost boys). Barrie emphasizes her prematurely developed emotional intelligence in his stage directions, as when he prefaces one of her entreaties to Peter with the remark "She is too loving to be ignorant that he is not loving enough, and she hesitates like one who knows the answer to her question" (129).

In other words, Wendy is precocious, both because of her intense interest in the opposite sex and because she functions as a "nice motherly person" who knows "lots of stories" to tell the boys (116, 102), as the sampler curtain that came down between the acts illustrated. Scoffing at the authors identified there as Wendy's favorites, Beerbohm reveals his own investment in the Romantic ideal of childish simplicity, rudely observing that "her bump of precocity must be the size of an orange" because she prefers the "elaborate" writings of authors such as Lamb and Andersen over more "straightforward" tales by the Brothers Grimm ("*Peter Pan* Revisited" 336). Indeed, Wendy's sophisticated literary taste is in line with Barrie's general habit of conceiving of her as a child-woman; in a letter to Maude Adams, he described Wendy as "a dear of a girl with ever so many children long before her hair is up" (quoted in Birkin 103).

Moreover, the theme of children acting like adults and adults acting like children pervades the entire play. One of the first lines uttered by a child character in *Peter Pan* is John's announcement to his mother that "we are doing an act; we are playing at being you and father" (89). The scene that follows, in which he and Wendy pretend to have babies, could certainly be played in such a way as to highlight their adorable naïveté. Yet as the rest of the play unfolds, Barrie repeatedly emphasizes the knowingness of children and the ignorance of adults, thus undermining the idea that these two categories are separate and stable. Thus, act 1, scene 1 also features Mr. Darling throwing a tantrum because he cannot tie his tie and sulkily refusing to take his medicine. He also calls Mrs. Darling a "Cowardy, cowardy custard"; she responds by "pouting" and twice insisting "I'm not," thus proving that she is as childish as he (93). Indeed, the stage directions inform us that of all the Darlings, Wendy is "the one . . . who can be trusted to know or not to know" (96), a point Peter reinforces when he remarks "Children know such a lot now" (100). Once in Neverland, Wendy mothers the boys so successfully that her brothers forget their real parents, while Peter imitates the pirate captain "so perfectly that even the author has a dizzy feeling that at times he was really Hook," to quote another of Barrie's revealing stage directions (120).

The result of all this boundary-blurring and role-playing is that "child" and "adult" start to seem less like binding biological categories and more like parts open to players of all ages—a sensation that must have been enhanced by the fact that many of the child parts were played by adults, a liberty that at least one critic strongly objected to, as Bruce K. Hanson notes (62). In other words, Barrie revels in smudging a line that activists had spent the last century trying hard to assert, even treating child labor as a joke rather than a serious problem. It often goes unmentioned in critical accounts of *Peter Pan* that the Darlings employ a very young, very little maid named Liza. Her early entry into adult activities is treated solely as a subject for humor. She "is so small," Barrie remarks in his stage directions, "that when she says she will never see ten again one can scarcely believe her" (103), a quip that also appears in *Peter and Wendy*: "Such a midget she looked in her long skirt and maid's cap, though she had sworn, when engaged, that she would never see ten again" (72). Barrie also plays with the idea that Liza is sexually precocious; later in the play, she announces, "I am a married woman myself" (147) and claims to be one of the lost boys' mothers (151).

Were audiences meant to laugh at the absurdity of the idea of a young girl having sex or working as a servant? Perhaps, but in 1904, domestic child labor was hardly a relic of the distant past. In 1891, over one hundred thousand girls between the ages of ten and fourteen were still employed as domestic servants in England and Wales (Horn, *Country* 133). Not until 1918 was a law passed that abolished the half-time system and banned the employment of children under fourteen. Similarly, sex and children were often conjoined in the news after a series of scandals about men becoming erotically involved with children erupted in the 1890s.[28] While some commentators characterized these incidents as harrowing tales of innocence lost, others cynically questioned whether working-class youth were really that pure in the first place. For example, Dr. Lawson Tait, who had examined seventy young girls who claimed to have been sexually assaulted, felt that all but six of them were too knowing to be innocent victims:

> There is not a piece of sexual argot that ever had before reached my ears but was used by these children in the descriptions given by them of what had been done to them, and they introduced, in addition, quite a new vocabulary on the subject. The minute and detailed descriptions of the sexual act given by chits of 10 and 11 would do credit to the pages of Mirabeau. (Ellis 226)

Tait's unsympathetic testimony, which recalls accounts of the sexual promiscuity of poor children penned by mid-Victorians such as Doré and Jerrold and William Acton, appeared in the third volume of Havelock Ellis's *Studies in the Psychology of Sex* (1903). It suggests that those who regarded precocity as a "hideous antithesis" still had plenty of cause for concern. Indeed, well into the 1920s, activists such as Margaret McMillan were still fighting to ensure that poor children were given the opportunity to experience childhood as a protected period of dependence and development.

Given that this battle was still being fought, Barrie's decision to make light of Liza's premature competence and revel in the idea of children acting like adults indicates that—like Carroll and Dowson—he was at some level unwilling to align himself with his culture's efforts to shield and segregate children. Indeed, just as his refusal to treat the young as a race apart manifested itself strongly in his decision to include "adult" material in what he himself referred to as a children's play, his mode of addressing his audience in novelized versions of *Peter Pan* betrays a similar desire to deny that any real difference separates children and adults. As Rose brilliantly demonstrates, the narrator of *Peter and Wendy* flouts the convention that the narrator of a children's book "be adult *or* child, one or the other"; he slides from one pronoun position to another, referring to children first as "you" and then as "we," even in the course of a single sentence (69). Moreover, the implied reader's position is equally unstable; in both *Peter and Wendy* and *The Little White Bird*, Barrie sometimes seems to be addressing children and sometimes adults. Thus, although *The Little White Bird* is a novel aimed at adults, the whole middle section of it addresses the reader as if he or she were a child, as when the narrator describes Kensington Gardens by declaring, "we are now in the Broad Walk, and it is as much bigger than the other walks as your father is bigger than you" (111).

In other words, Birkin's observation that the confused content of the play made it "none too clear what sort of an audience Barrie had in mind" also holds true for the novelized versions (104); all three of these texts continually blur the line between child and adult. Why, then, do so many critics assume that Barrie yearned to freeze the child in place as an icon of otherness? Often, it is because they associate him with his main character. For there can be no doubt that Peter Pan himself believes that a radical difference divides children from adults and vows never to cross that line. Rejecting Mrs. Darling's offer to adopt him, he declares, "I don't want to go to school and learn solemn things. No one is going to catch me, lady, and make me a man. I want always to be a little boy and to have fun" (*Peter Pan* 151). His playacting thus differs from Wendy's, in that she is trying on elements of an emergent future self, whereas he—like Wordsworth's six-year-old "little Actor"—is merely flitting from one role to another "As if his whole vocation, / Were endless imitation" ("Ode," lines 104, 108–109).

Indeed, as Coveney notes, Peter "retain[s] many of the attributes of the romantic Child of Nature," including an affiliation with animals—especially birds, just like the Boy of Winander—and a distaste for society (256). But Coveney persists in reading Peter biographically, as stand-in for Barrie, rather than recognizing that this character really does function as a kind of thought experiment based on the Romantic paradigm. What would a child be like if he could completely avoid adult influence, if he could detach himself entirely from family, school, and culture? Peter is that child: "I ran away the day I was born," he explains to Wendy, and he has been on his own ever since, a magically autonomous figure (*Peter Pan* 99).

But rather than slavishly endorsing and sentimentalizing the Child of Nature trope (as Coveney claims), Barrie uses the figure of Peter to explore the tremendous appeal *and* the terrifying drawbacks of this paradigm. In some ways, he does portray perpetual boyhood as a joyous Golden Age, but at the same time he emphasizes that Peter is utterly unmoored: this lost boy is not only incapable of connecting to other people, he cannot even maintain a firm sense of his own identity, as indicated by the fact that when we first meet him, Peter has become detached from his own shadow. In his preface to the play, Barrie provides a clue about how to interpret this odd incident; recounting a childhood memory, he describes his communion with his past self by saying, "I follow like his shadow, as indeed I am, and watch him dig a hole in a field . . . it was ages ago, but I could walk straight to that hole in the field now and delve for the remains" (78–79). The adult Barrie may only be a shadow of his child self, but he is intimately connected with all of his past permutations and can recall minute details that collate into a semicoherent life story. In contrast, Peter cannot remain connected to anything that happens to him; both the play and novelized versions emphasize his amnesiac tendency to forget his adventures soon after they occur, to lose any memory even of people who played a huge part in his past life, such as Hook and Tinker Bell. Peter thus remains a radically innocent figure; whatever experience he gets he cannot retain, displaying the impermeability that Richardson views as characteristic of the prototypical Child of Nature (*Literature* 71–72).

This mode of being, Barrie suggests, is not only cruel to others but also represents a kind of living death for oneself. In every version of the story he wrote, he characterizes Peter as a liminal figure who hovers between the realms of the living and the dead: "when children died he went part of the way with them, so that they should not be frightened" (*Peter and Wendy* 75). As Coveney notes, Peter's costume consists not of greenery but of dead leaves and cobwebs. Other stage directions likewise suggest that he is trapped in static, moribund state. For example, after Peter draws back from Wendy's final effort to entice him into intimacy, Barrie revises his hero's famous remark "To die will be an awfully big adventure" by noting that if Peter could solve the "riddle of his being . . . his cry might become 'To live would be an awfully big adventure!' but he can never quite get the hang of it, and so no one is as gay as he" (125, 153–54).

As the unexpected ending of this line implies, Peter's manic cheerfulness masks a distressing inability to engage with other people. People who love Peter are naturally upset by his unresponsiveness, but Barrie also suggests that Peter himself is not completely content with his condition. Just after Peter declares that he wants to be a boy forever, Barrie's stage directions read "So perhaps he thinks, but it is only his greatest pretend" (151). He builds on this idea in *Peter and Wendy* by informing readers that Peter suffers from "painful" recurrent nightmares: "For hours he could not be separated from these dreams, though he wailed piteously in them. They had to do, I think, with the riddle of his existence" (*Peter and Wendy* 181).

Still, Barrie spends much more time dilating on how the disheartening obliviousness of Peter pains others, which is why *Peter Pan* cannot be regarded as an exercise in nostalgic escapism: every version of this story that Barrie wrote engages extensively with the theme of how agonizing the act of child-loving can be. "Oh Peter," Wendy wails disconsolately, "you forget everything!" (*Peter Pan* 161). One of the strangest aspects of interacting with very young children is that they will often not recall even the most momentous events or people closest to them, once those events are over and the people have gone away. Having loving, detailed memories of someone who does not recognize you is a genuinely sad, eerie experience. "Oh, why can't you remain like this forever?" cries Mrs. Darling to two-year-old Wendy (*Peter and Wendy* 69). Rather than dismissing such sentiments as sappy and self-indulgent, we might note that they highlight something unique about child-loving: unlike intimate relationships with people one's own age, caring for a child involves coping with dramatic alterations in the object of one's affection, changes that utterly transform the child's physical, emotional, and intellectual way of being and relating to others.

Finally, there is the fraught issue of reciprocity. Over and over again, Barrie characterizes children as "heartless" creatures who do not (or cannot) return the love lavished on them by adults (*Peter and Wendy* 226). As the narrator of *Peter and Wendy* puts it, "off we skip like the most heartless things in the world, which is what children are, but so attractive; and we have an entirely selfish time, and then when we have need of special attention we nobly return for it, confident that we shall be rewarded instead of smacked" (166). Aligning himself with children even as he criticizes them, the narrator represents innocence as both appealing and awful, associating it with cocky self-regard and a cruel neglect of the feelings of others. Indeed, Kincaid identifies this tendency to link innocence to callous egocentrism as the major way Barrie departs from a Wordsworthian vision of childhood (*Child-Loving* 281), a position seconded by Glenda A. Hudson. Rather than representing the child as a healer, a bringer of "hope . . . and forward-looking thoughts" (Wordsworth, "Michael," lines 154–55), Barrie suggests that contact with children more often engenders feelings of anger and despair, as indicated by the narrator's resentful remarks, the misery of the deserted Darling parents, and (in the play) the maddened Hook's suicide.

As in the case of *Fauntleroy*, though, it seems plausible to assume that the play's phenomenal popularity with mixed audiences was due to the fact that the child hero functions both as a passive object of desire (as in the scene when Hook gloats over Peter's sleeping body) *and* as an energetic, authoritative agent who "hates lethargy" (*Peter and Wendy* 112). Reading fan letters from child audience members reminds us that despite the deathly tinge to his character, Peter nevertheless can be (and was) perceived as a vibrant, vigorous, even omnipotent figure. In stark opposition to Dickensian waifs buffeted by the cruelty of a world in which they cannot survive without help, "the artful one" runs away and immediately finds a kingdom to rule over (*Peter Pan* 99). His fabulous autonomy manifests itself physically in his ability to fly, a quality mentioned more than any other in surviving letters from child fans.

Yet Barrie never pretends that young people as a group enjoy such enviable independence; rather, he emphasizes how different Peter is from ordinary children like the Darlings, who can only fly with his help and who are deeply dependent on family routines, social norms, and the necessity of eating real—rather than make-believe—food. (The miraculously autonomous Peter can subsist on imagination alone, but the Darlings want their tea.) Indeed, Peter is so different from real children that one of his favorite games is to impersonate a normal child: "doing the sort of thing John and Michael had been doing all their lives" seems to him "such a comic thing to do" (*Peter and Wendy* 137).

Barrie's recognition of the limited power of ordinary children also emerges in "To the Five." On the one hand, he repeatedly represents the creation of *Peter Pan* as a genuine collaboration between himself and the Llewelyn Davies boys. "We had good sport of him before we clipped him small to make him fit the boards," he writes, crediting the boys for their original input into the story: "no doubt I was abetting, but you used to provide corroboration that was never given to you by me" (75). On the other hand, he seems to share Carroll's concern that the difference in status between adult and child ensures that true reciprocity is impossible. Thus, even as he depicts the creation of his most famous character as a joint endeavor, his choice of metaphor suggests that the process was more coercive than collaborative. "We first brought Peter down" with an arrow in Kensington Gardens, he recalls, adding, "I seem to remember that we believed we had killed him . . . and that after a spasm of exultation in our prowess the more soft-hearted among us wept and all of us thought of the police" (75). Here Barrie implies that the birth of this story constituted an act of aggression aimed at a child, a notion that is reinforced by his admission "I suppose I always knew that I made Peter by rubbing the five of you violently together, as savages with two sticks produce a flame" (75). And yet, even here, at the very moment when he finally claims credit for creating *Peter Pan*, Barrie nevertheless refuses to conceive of the child as a helpless, artless naïf: he characterizes *himself* as primitive, reversing the common tendency to cast this aspersion onto children.

Thus, "To the Five" closely resembles Carroll's "All in the Golden Afternoon," since both of these prefatory pieces simultaneously entertain and undermine the idea that the child can function as a genuine collaborator. Like Carroll, Barrie suspects that children often function more like parrots than partners, as indicated by his account in *The Little White Bird* of how he and his child-friend David cocreate the tale of Peter Pan: "the following is our way with a story: First I tell it to him, and then he tells it to me, the understanding being that it is quite a different story; and then I retell it with his additions, and so we go on until no one could say whether it was more his story or mine" (123). The implication here is that the child is not really telling an original story but merely repeating back material composed by the adult after making some minor revisions. Furthermore, the same passage also includes a section in which the narrator describes how he manages to implant memories in David's head: he tells the boy stories about his early childhood that the youngster at first resists but—when pressed—finally internalizes and claims as his own.

By suggesting that adult storytellers employ narrative in order to shape the child's sense of self, Barrie anticipates the central tenet of the colonization paradigm: that "children's fiction builds an image of the child inside the book . . . in order to secure the child who is outside the book, the one who does not come so easily within its grasp" (Rose 2). Indeed, in the dedicatory preface to *Peter Pan*, Barrie acknowledges the possibility that he wrote the play because he realized he was "losing my grip" on the Llewelyn Davies boys (75); even as he characterizes the creation of *Peter Pan* as a mutually entertaining game, he confesses that this singular literary act may have represented "a last desperate throw to retain the five of you for a little longer"—to maintain the intimacy that gave meaning to his life (76).

My contention here has been that many nineteenth-century children's authors shared Barrie's critical self-consciousness; they interrogated Romantic ideas about childhood rather than simply affirming them, and they recognized that the act of writing for children was informed by their own desire to captivate, influence, educate, mold, and manipulate young people. Rather than conceiving of children as a pure point of origin, they acknowledged the primacy and power of adults and the myriad ways children are affected by the literary, social, familial, and cultural milieu they inhabit. Yet their interest in the idea that children could function as precocious actors, authors, editors, and collaborators reflects their hope that the authority of adults does not obviate the possibility that the child can enjoy a measure of agency and creativity: though not entirely autonomous, they can take a hand in their own self-fashioning. To this end, their texts often promote a kind of active literacy aimed at enabling children to become more artful dodgers of adult influence. Perhaps that is why stories like *Alice, Treasure Island, A Little Princess,* and *Peter Pan* remain popular today and have long been celebrated for composing the Golden Age of children's literature.

NOTES

INTRODUCTION

1. See, for example Coveney, Carpenter, Polhemus, Wullschläger, and Honeyman. Even Prickett, who repeatedly emphasizes that we cannot simply assume "that fantasy is always an escape or refuge from a repressive social code" and who lauds Charles Kingsley and George MacDonald for deploying fantasy in sophisticated, self-conscious ways in order to explore pressing "adult" issues (40), ends up dismissing Carroll and Edward Lear as childish "eccentrics" who gave way to their escapist tendencies (137). Similarly, Ann Wilson characterizes Barrie's Neverland as a "world of childish adventure that is an escape from the pressures of real life" (600), even though—as she herself admits—the anxieties about class, gender, and Empire that emerge in the scenes set in England in no way dissipate when the action shifts to Peter's island.

2. Thus, Wullschläger defines the Golden Age as a period when "a handful of men" created "a radical new literature for children" of unparalleled power and allure (4). Similarly, Carpenter's characterization of the Golden Age as a period extending "from Lewis Carroll to A. A. Milne" in his preface reflects his general practice of rating male authors higher than female ones and fantasy over "the detritus of the moralists" and authors who penned realistic fiction (10), a genre he claims "attracted few writers of any quality" (15). In *Ventures into Childland* (1998), Knoepflmacher has moved to redress such sexist accounts by including appreciative readings of the work of influential female authors such as Juliana Ewing, Jean Ingelow, and Christina Rossetti. Yet he, too, focuses solely on fantasy, tracing how female authors responded to fairy tales by Ruskin, Thackeray, and Carroll. Interestingly, the earliest critical account of this period is actually the one that is most open to the idea that nonfantastic texts might have helped to make the Golden Age great. In "The Golden Age of Children's Books" (1962), R. L. Green has some kind words for Charlotte Yonge's domestic stories and historical romances and even proposes

that didactic stories involving dying children by Ewing and Mary Louisa Molesworth "should not be condemned out of hand" (66). Though Green's praise for such work is highly qualified, by mentioning it here and in *Tellers of Tales* (1946) he raises a fascinating question: besides the fact that this era witnessed the arrival of a slew of famous fantasies (written mostly by men), what *else* made it a "Golden Age" for children's literature? To be sure, the term is of Green's own making, a critical construction that some commentators have recently begun to challenge. Yet I have chosen to employ it here not merely because of its pithiness ("mid-nineteenth to early twentieth-century children's literature" is quite a mouthful) but also because I believe that this era did in fact witness an unprecedented explosion of high-quality children's fiction and poetry, not to mention an unparalleled proliferation of children's periodicals and the emergence of children's theatre. Indeed, many new genres and ways of writing for children flourished during this period, including (as I will show) the technique of using a child narrator—a literary mode that female authors of domestic stories played a key role in developing.

3. See, for example, Yonge's fascinating story *Countess Kate* (1862), which exposes its hyperliterate heroine to multiple modes of adult authority. Or consider *Holiday House* itself: the parentless status of the three child protagonists enables Sinclair to weigh competing strategies of child-rearing, including Mrs. Crabtree's old-school reliance on corporal punishment, Uncle David's humorous lenience, and Aunt Harriet's loving yet stern religiosity.

4. For examples of critics who take this line, see chapter 1, note 2.

5. In tracing the tendency of Golden Age authors to conceive of the child as a collaborator, I follow in the footsteps of Knoepflmacher ("Kipling's 'Just-So' Partner"), who explores how Rudyard Kipling makes use of this trope in *Just So Stories for Little Children* (1902).

6. Innumerable scholars have elaborated on the Victorian habit of representing children as victims: see for example Avery and Reynolds, Berry, Lerner, Plotz ("Literary Ways"), Thornton, and Spilka. I do not deny that children's authors participated in this trend; my point is merely that they also resisted it.

7. Let me stress that I do not mean to suggest that all Victorian literature aimed at adults promoted a primitivist paradigm. Banerjee has persuasively countered the popular assumption that Victorian novelists unthinkingly "appropriated and sentimentalized a concept of childhood derived from [Romantic] poetry" (xvii). Similarly, Knoepflmacher traces how Victorian poets, essayists, and novelists simultaneously embraced and contested Romantic figurations of childhood ("Mutations"). In this book, I aim to make the same move in reference to Golden Age children's fiction.

8. Besides Rose, see for example Morgenstern, C. Robson, and Wilkie. Petzold offers a variation on this theme as well. For other essays that trace how various Romantic impulses manifested themselves in Golden Age children's texts, see McGavran's two collections of essays on this subject.

9. "The New Hero" was by Theodore Watts and "The Literary Cult of the Child" was by Louise Betts Edwards. The rest of these essays were anonymously authored.

10. Norval was a character in John Home's play *Douglas* (1756). Professional child prodigies such as Master William Betty frequently tackled this role.

11. Critics who endorse this view include Manlove, Summerfield, Carpenter, von Koppenfels, Polhemus, and Sandner.

12. See particularly chapter 3 of Richardson (*Literature*) and Myers ("Romancing the Moral Tale").

13. Richardson also points out that the Romantic endorsement of fairy tales was linked to a desire to return "the new mass readership to an apolitical" discourse ("Wordsworth" 45). For an account of how Coleridge employs the term "Faerie," see J. Watson.

14. All line numbers refer to the 1805 version of *The Prelude.*

15. Indeed, the same critics who carefully avoid generalizing about the Romantics feel comfortable making blanket claims about the Victorian view of childhood. For example, even as C. Robson makes her compelling, meticulous argument about how Wordsworth's representation of childhood fluctuates from poem to poem, she declares that "in [the Victorian] period, ideal childhood is generally imagined as a wholly separate estate from adulthood, a pitifully brief era of bliss and innocence, which is lost forever at the onset of maturity. The child itself is viewed from the perspective of an adult looking backwards and is therefore an essentially nostalgic construction, associated with the past, often with stasis and sealed perfection, and very frequently with death" (136).

16. See, for example, Ray, Plotz, and Hemmings. Prickett's *Victorian Fantasy* (1979) provides a more complicated case. He, too, observes that children's authors owed a great deal to Romantic literature, criticism, and philosophy, but he adds nuance to this argument by including German Romantic writers in his study and by tracing how Golden Age writers were deeply influenced by another "very different" tradition as well, "an English one of vigorous popular journalism in satire and cartoon" (41). Unfortunately, this aspect of Prickett's argument has been ignored, as indicated by the fact that the Golden Age fantasists whose work was most strongly influenced by this satiric tradition—such as Tom Hood and F. Anstey—have received very little critical attention.

17. See book 2 of *Emile.*

18. This description of Rose is quoted in volume 35 of Ruskin's *Works* (lxxvi). For an account of Ruskin's own precocity as a child, see the introduction to volume 1 of his *Works*, as well as the opening chapter of Hilton.

19. See Cunningham (*Children of the Poor*) and Pinchbeck and Hewitt. I will introduce and discuss further evidence for this claim in chapter 5.

20. See Rose (83) and Richardson (*Literature* 151–53).

21. For the story of how Ruskin tried to censor "The Light Princess," see Knoepflmacher (*Ventures* 138–40). "The Light Princess" first appeared as an interpolated story in *Adela Cathcart* (1864), a novel for adults; it was then reprinted in *Dealings with the Fairies* (1867) and in other editions aimed at children.

22. For example, both Chitty and Colloms declare that *The Water-Babies* became an "instant" children's classic without citing any reviews or other evidence to support this claim (Chitty 216).

23. Alderson provides the most thorough account of early reaction to Kingsley's novel in his introduction to the Oxford World's Classic edition of *The Water-Babies*. He points out that when publisher Alexander Macmillan sent Kingsley "the first puzzled reviews of

the book" he clumsily tried to comfort the author by remarking, " 'Of course it has not and cannot have the general acceptance that a right good human story would have' " (xxvi).

24. To be sure, this criticism of *Peter Pan* appeared not in a review or letter but in Saki's novel *The Unbearable Bassington* (1912), so it may not represent his own view of Barrie's work. Within the context of the novel, however, this attitude is endorsed by another character who adds, "the 'Boy who would not grow up' must have been written by a 'grown-up who could never have been a boy.' Perhaps that is the meaning of the 'Never-never land" (21).

25. See also Hemmings.

26. He was particularly upset by the idea of a mole whitewashing, and by the suspicion that the "foibles" of the animals "doubtless are borrowed from mankind" (362).

27. Grahame himself declared that the story was "clean of the clash of sex" (quoted in Avery, "Introduction" xiii), and many critics have taken his word as law. But this description only fits if we agree to adopt the (deeply heteronormative) view that sex must involve a relationship between two people of the opposite sex. Thus, critics who adopt Grahame's view that there is no sex in the book invariably cite as evidence the fact there are no major female characters. Now, even if we ignore the possibility that loving all-male households might hold some hint of sex, erotic desire is evident elsewhere in the story. Knowing that his male pals are watching him, for example, Toad indulges in masturbatory fantasies about driving a car: "When his violent paroxysms possessed him," he is found "bent forward and staring fixedly ahead, making uncouth and ghastly noises, till the climax was reached, . . . [whereupon] he would lie prostrate . . . apparently completely satisfied for the moment" (70).

28. These words were embossed on a giant sampler, purported to be by "Wendy Moira Angela Darling . . . Age 9," that served as the curtain for a number of early productions of *Peter Pan*. An image of "The Sampler Curtain" is reproduced in R. L. Green (*Fifty* 67) and Hanson (87).

29. See for example Kingsley's *The Water-Babies* (1863), Alcott's *An Old Fashioned Girl* (1870), Ruskin's *Fors Clavigera* (1871–84), Twain's "The Story of the Good Little Boy Who Did Not Prosper" (1870), Anstey's "The Good Little Girl" (1891), Burnett's *The One I Knew the Best of All* (1893), Belloc's *Cautionary Tales for Children* (1908), Nesbit's *Wet Magic* (1913), and so on.

30. In chapter 3 of *Literature, Education and Romanticism*, Richardson helpfully delineates how some early children's literature promoted "passive literacy" (64), as well as outlining how Romantic writers objected to this authoritarian stance.

31. Nodelman helped to popularize this Rosian move in his article "The Other: Orientalism, Colonialism, and Children's Literature" (1992) but also challenged it in "The Case of Children's Fiction: or The Impossibility of Jacqueline Rose" (1985) and "Fear of Children's Literature: What's Left (or Right) after Theory?" (1997). Other critics have enthusiastically embraced Rose's habit of characterizing the adult–child relationship in terms of imperial domination. For an extreme example, see Zornado, who argues that "the relationship between the parent and the child in Victorian England was precisely that of the relationship between colonizer and colonized, precisely that of the relationship between the physically dominant and the physically dominated" (102).

32. As Clark points out in *Kiddie Lit* (2003) and elsewhere, the line between "adult" and "children's" literature was blurrier during this period than it is now, and young people were regularly exposed to weighty tomes by such authors as Scott as Dickens. The fact that children were not an officially designated target audience for Barrie's early versions of *Peter Pan* does not prove that it was impossible for them to gain access to them, nor does it prove that they were incapable of reading and comprehending them. More careful work needs to be done on the reception history of these texts before any definite claims can be made about how and by whom they were read.

33. Rudd's argument differs from mine in that he believes critics such as Lesnik-Oberstein are misreading *The Case of Peter Pan* when they choose to represent real children as devoid of agency. (In contrast, I've tried to demonstrate that they are picking up on the inescapable implications of the dire rhetoric Rose employs.) But he, too, observes that critical discourse that represents the child as a voiceless victim "actually helps [to] construct the child as a helpless, powerless being, and contributes to the culturally hegemonic norm" (31). Similarly, Boone notes that this type of approach "flattens out the history of a text's reception, and fails to register any audience resistance to the author's intent" (7). He points out that when we assume that pro-imperialist fictions achieved their goal of colonizing the hearts and minds of working-class youth, we characterize the poor in precisely the same terms as their snobbish "superiors" did: as intellectually inept beings who mindlessly absorb and parrot back whatever they read.

34. For an example of a critic who makes this argument, see Lurie.

35. Proponents of this view include Honeyman and various children's literature critics associated with the University of Reading's Centre for International Research in Childhood, including Lesnik-Oberstein and Walsh.

36. I concur here with Galbraith and K. Jones, both of whom contend that critics of children's literature and culture should not let their recognition that there is no such thing as an essential, unchanging "child" whose nature can be fully known lead them to insist on the impossibility of knowing anything about the lives, practices, and discourse of individual children in particular times and places. See also Thacker's persuasive argument that literary critics who theorize reading should not ignore children, their reading practices, and the possibility that they can function as "*co-producer[s]* of fictional meaning within a web of social discourse" (9).

37. Here Kincaid quotes from Spilka (162) and Weeks (48).

38. *Child-Loving* and *Erotic Innocence* (1998) identify two interlinked practices that Kincaid finds particularly destructive. First, we insist that children are innocent, and "this hollowing out of children by way of purifying them of any stains (or any substance) also makes them radically different, other. In this empty state, they present themselves as candidates for being filled with, among other things, desire. The asexual child is not . . . any the less erotic but rather more" (*Child-Loving* 175). Then, having eroticized the child, we make a monster of the pedophile in order to assure ourselves that our own ways of loving children are unassailably pure.

39. Two more magazine articles entitled "Precocious Children" that appeared in 1862 and 1888 likewise warned that "too highly cultivated" children ran the risk of having their "health undermined" ("Precocious Children," *British Mothers'* 97). The 1888 piece

quotes from a scientific journal to bring home its point, while the 1862 one urges parents to follow the advice given by a mother whose precocious son has died: " 'If you have among your household treasures one brighter . . . than the rest, guard it from books and lessons and exciting conversations, as you would from fever' " ("Precocious Children," *British Mothers'* 97). As for novels, in *The Mighty Atom* (1896) Marie Corelli followed Dickens in representing precocity as deadly. For more examples of Victorian texts—both fictional and "factual"—that trumpeted the dangers of early intellectual development, see Gargano and Goetsch.

40. I do not mean to suggest that Burnett's stories in no way reflect or support imperialist ideology; the problematic representation of Ram Dass, Mr. Carrisford's Indian servant, illustrates that these novels cannot simply be read as antagonistic to colonialist discourse and practice. But I do want to challenge Hunt and Sands's contention that "the valorization of home" in such stories "was . . . in itself a part of the inescapable matrix of imperialism" (45). As I hope to show through my reading of Ewing's *We and the World* (1877–78) in chapter 1, authors who validated the decision to remain in (or return to) the domestic realm sometimes did so precisely in order to challenge the moral legitimacy of the male-dominated project of empire building.

CHAPTER 1

1. For example, Coveney points out that in creating the character of Jo in *Bleak House*, Dickens recycles "almost verbatim" the testimony of a child laborer interviewed in an 1850 Law Report (124). For Cunningham's point about testimony, see *Children of the Poor* (92).

2. Moss herself makes this move in "Varieties of Children's Metafiction" (1985), asserting that "Nesbit had undoubtedly read Dickens's *A Holiday Romance*, and she adopts his rhetorical device of a child narrator who is also the child author" (90). My contention is not that this statement is untrue—merely that it represents an incomplete genealogy. Similarly abbreviated accounts of the history of the child narrator appear in R. L. Green (*Tellers* 79), Rose (82), Kuznets, and Susina ("Textual").

3. For example, T. S. Eliot insisted that *Huckleberry Finn*, unlike *The Adventures of Tom Sawyer*, "does not fall into the category of juvenile fiction" (quoted in Clark 77). Comments like this one may explain why literary critics have been so uninterested in exploring the question of whether Twain was the first American children's author who chose to employ a child narrator. My hunch is that he was not, although I have not had a chance to investigate this issue.

4. Craik also indicated her interest in this form of writing by editing *Twenty Years Ago: From the Journal of a Girl in Her Teens* (1871). But she was not the first to experiment with the technique of the child narrator, either. English children's authors played with this possibility from very early on: Isaac Watts employs child speakers in numerous poems in *Divine Songs Attempted in Easy Language for the Use of Children* (1715), while Sarah Fielding's *The Governess* (1749)—often identified as the first children's novel—features interpolated confessions in which Mrs. Teachum's little pupils narrate the story

of their own past lives—a technique Charles and Mary Lamb borrow and employ in *Mrs. Leicester's School: or, The History of Several Young Ladies, Related by Themselves* (1809). However, Craik does seem to have been one of the first writers to create a full-length novel ostensibly narrated by a child. See note 11.

5. Wall acknowledges that women writers played a key role in developing the technique of the child narrator but dismisses such early attempts as unworthy of critical attention. In the whole nineteenth century, she declares, "Only Huckleberry Finn and Oswald Bastable stand out" (247).

6. Ewing's influence is also evident in the work of early twentieth-century writers such as L. M. Montgomery, who echoes Ewing's *Mrs. Overtheway's Remembrances* (1866–69) many times in her popular *Anne of Green Gables* series (1908–39).

7. It would take another full chapter to explore these similarities, so I will not attempt to summarize them here, except to say that like Mary and Sara, Eunice Lychett is orphaned by the British Empire—her parents are killed while adventuring abroad. Anticipating Burnett, Craik places a strong emphasis on the rehabilitative power of returning home to England; like Mary, the sickly, spoiled Bion Lychett grows both stronger and nicer after returning from India and living a more active life on the English moors. As I argue later in this chapter, authors who focus on the dangers of life abroad and the advantages of staying home often aim to differentiate themselves from pro-imperialist children's writers, who characterize roving as a profoundly rewarding career and ignore the pleasures of domestic life.

8. Rose articulates this argument in chapters 2 and 3 of *The Case of Peter Pan*.

9. British child psychoanalyst D. W. Winnicott coined the term "potential space" to refer to the intermediate area between internal and external reality, where play and aesthetic experience take place (41). As M. Schwartz has argued, locating literature in this "inclusive realm" allows us to take account of both the instructions and meanings texts issue and the individuality of our own responses to them (60).

10. Ewing also celebrates the pleasure and liberating potential of revision in stories that do *not* feature child narrators. For example, in *The Brownies* (1865), she rewrites the Grimm Brothers' tale "The Elves and the Shoemaker" in order to encourage child readers to appropriate and revise the scripts handed to them by adults. I make this argument at length elsewhere (Gubar, "Revising").

11. *The Little Lychetts* is not the first full-length English children's novel to feature a child narrator; William Howitt's *The Boy's Country-Book: Being the Real Life of a Country Boy, Written by Himself* (1839) precedes it by sixteen years. While the existence of Howitt's story raises the possibility that other early nineteenth-century children's authors experimented with this technique as well, the children's novels penned by his wife, Mary Howitt, suggest that the use of this formula was not widespread during the first half of the century. For although she declared in the preface to one of her books that children's authors ought to "endeavour to enter more fully into the feelings and reasonings of a child . . . [to] look at things as it were from the child's own point of view" (*Children's Year* v), and although many of her children's novels featured titles such as *My Own Story, or, The Autobiography of a Child* (1845), Mary Howitt nevertheless did not employ child narrators in these tales.

12. The only copy of *The Little Lychetts* I could obtain—a microfilm version from the University of Florida—has no page numbers, so I have simply labeled the first page "1" and so forth.

13. Huck's ultimate inability to regard black people as full-fledged human beings is evident in the cruel way he and Tom treat Jim in the final section of the novel, as well as in his response to Aunt Sally when she asks him if anyone was hurt when the boat he was traveling in ran aground: " 'No'm. Killed a nigger' " (279).

14. In *A Literature of Their Own*, Showalter affirms Ellen Moers's claim that nineteenth-century women writers like Craik " 'studied with a special closeness the works written by their own sex'; in terms of influences, borrowings, and affinities, the tradition is strongly marked" (Showalter 11). Moreover, Showalter notes that *Jane Eyre* in particular inspired a host of female writers, including Craik, to create heroes of "the Mr. Rochester stamp" (139).

15. Eunice's expressions of sympathy get more impassioned as the scene goes on. For example, after observing how the keeper "put his foot upon a miserable-looking, blind old lioness, [and] made the leopards leap through hoops, and the tiger perform *poses plastiques* . . . like feline opera-dancers," she not only declares that she "felt downright uncomfortable in my pity for the poor beasts," she also fantasizes that the lion will bite the keeper's head off (62)!

16. For example, Showalter repeatedly dwells on this theme in *A Literature of Their Own*.

17. Bogy is blind because his brother, who had been passionate and quick-tempered as a child, pushed him aside impatiently one day while holding a gun and accidentally shot him.

18. Here Rose builds on the work of Pratt and other postcolonial theorists.

19. Communion between animals and humans is likewise celebrated in this tale. Indeed, in the opening line of this story, the capacious "we" refers not just to the three children but to Perronet as well: "There were four of us, and three of us had godfathers and godmothers" (228).

20. Ewing's Alister does eventually get recognized and promoted, but not as quickly or dramatically as Kingston's boys do.

21. Jack ignores the cautionary tale of his first schoolteacher, Mr. Wood, who explains that he, too, used to chafe at the bit "whenever I heard of manly exploits, and of the delights and dangers that came of seeing the world" (67). Wood returns from his miserable adventures abroad as a "gaunt, white-haired, shattered-looking man" (56). He tries to convince Jack that "tropical loveliness has its drawbacks," a lesson Jack ends up having to learn by experience (64).

22. Loxley insists that Victorian authors who employ the island motif "must" be viewed as adopting a pro-imperialist stance (131).

CHAPTER 2

1. Other critics who read *Treasure Island* as a conservative, pro-imperialist text include K. Blake, D. Jackson, Rose, Loxley, and Boone.

2. H. Watson provides the fullest overview of Stevenson's borrowings, but see also J. Moore and Hardesty and Mann.

3. "How that personage haunted my dreams, I need scarcely tell you. . . . I would see him in a thousand forms, and with a thousand diabolical expressions. Now the leg would be cut off at the knee, now at the hip; now he was a monstrous kind of a creature who had never had but one leg, and that in the middle of his body. To see him leap and run and pursue me over hedge and ditch was the worst of nightmares" (3).

4. After an opening description like this, it seems perverse to describe the treasure as "unsullied" (N. Wood 70) or as "a quick and guiltless fortune" (Loxley 130). A few pages later, Jim does mention that he takes delight in sorting out all the different coins, but his pleasure quickly turns to pain; associating the coins with dead foliage, he concludes, "I am sure they were like autumn leaves, so that my back ached with stooping and my fingers with sorting them out" (187).

5. Boone also notes that *Treasure Island* "offers none of these typical trappings of boys' adventure fictions" but argues that the absence of these elements simply makes more room for "the adult enterprise of imperialism: emptying foreign lands of their riches" (73).

6. In his influential study of Stevenson, Kiely argued that *Treasure Island* should be "placed in the category of . . . boy's daydream" (81). Many critics have since followed in his footsteps by describing Jim as the novel's "perfected dream-hero, the initiator, manipulator and controller of the action" (Loxley 151).

7. An anonymous early reviewer immediately noted this difference, lauding Stevenson for avoiding "that false and specious luxuriance which denaturalizes the action of a story. . . His island is no garden of Eden" (quoted in Maixner 128–29). More recently, Blackburn and N. Wood have both noticed that the portrayal of the island fails to conform to the traditional formula.

8. Readers sometimes assume that "Skeleton Island" is simply another name for "Treasure Island." But in fact the former is an "islet" on the south side of the main island, as Stevenson's map indicates (63). Coupled with the fact that Treasure Island exudes a deadly infection, the presence of this tumorous appendage undermines the idea that Stevenson's island setting functions as an "appropriately diminutive world in which dangers can be experienced within safe boundaries" (Bristow 94).

9. As Maher notes, nineteenth-century admirers of *Robinson Crusoe* tended to "omit mention of Crusoe's introspection" and indecisiveness in order to recast him as a forceful figure associated with "Empire, the outer world of action, power, and expansion" (169).

10. See Paquette for examples of this kind of anti-Spanish rhetoric.

11. See, for instance, Rose (80) and Loxley (132).

12. See also Kucich and Colley.

13. For example, although David H. Jackson acknowledges that Stevenson's later romances make him "the true and central forerunner" of Joseph Conrad, he nevertheless insists that *Treasure Island* promotes a "reactionary ideological agenda perfectly in keeping with the crude pronouncements of Haggard, Hall Caine, and Stevenson's other colleagues in the romance revival" (31). Even critics like Blackburn and Hardesty and Mann, all of whom recognize that Stevenson radically revises the Robinsonade formula,

still contend that the author "enriches and extends the tradition" rather than subverting it (Blackburn 11).

14. Indeed, Bristow identifies the skill of "remembering details that were in themselves useless" as "one of the major defining features of imperial boyhood" (43)!

15. Similarly, when Peterkin, one of the boy castaways in the *The Coral Island*, marvels at his friend Jack's amazing knowledge, Jack accounts for his expertise by explaining, " 'I have been a great reader of books of travel and adventure all my life' " (Ballantyne 39).

16. Hands mentions his spectacular lack of luck three separate times over the course of this scene. He also offers up the hopeful toast " 'Here's luck!' " before he attacks Jim (138), but "the dice [keep] going against him" anyway, as Jim observes (142).

17. Fowler, Hardesty and Mann read *Treasure Island* as a bildungsroman. Sandison also ends up arguing for this claim, though he admits that "there are one or two clues scattered around to suggest that the carapace of adulthood may not . . . be quite complete" (59–60).

18. Nor are these the only clues Jim carelessly disregards; before he enters the stockade, he hears "a flickering or pecking that I could in no way account for," which turns out to be Silver's parrot, Captain Flint, tapping on a piece of bark (147).

19. For example, Kiely declares: "*Treasure Island* is a very simple book . . . There is not a trace of wit or irony in it" (68).

CHAPTER 3

1. All citations to Carroll's poetry and fiction are from the one-volume Penguin edition of *The Complete Works of Lewis Carroll*, unless otherwise noted.

2. As Leach has documented, many early critics and biographers—including Virginia Woolf—insisted that Carroll remained frozen in eternal childhood throughout his life. Though both Leach and Cohen (*Lewis Carroll*) have marshaled compelling evidence against this claim, it continues to be made. For example, describing Carroll, Lear, and Barrie, Wullschläger observes, "Each was a boy who did not want to grow up, who remained in part always a child" (5).

3. Thus, in his guidebook for producing amateur *tableaux vivants*, Harrison declares that "it requires a skilful man to take the management in hand, and to study the various poses which will look the most effective" (113). The anonymous author of *Tableaux, Charades and Conundrums* (1893) goes even further, declaring "The success of this form of evening entertainment, depends entirely upon the ability of the stage-manager; for a vivid tableau cannot be produced unless the grouping is good and the coloring natural" (1).

4. See for example Taylor ("All in the Golden" 101) and Waggoner (159).

5. Holström quotes the relevant section of Madame de Genlis's memoirs in French (217); I am grateful to Elissa Bell for translating it for me.

6. Hovet and Hovet elaborate on this point.

7. In her discussion of a Victorian newspaper illustration of chorus girls on trial, Davis explains that returning the male gaze marks a woman as corrupt: "one girl exchanges looks with two of the [men] seated near her, confirming the implication of sexual complicity and conspiracy" ("Actress" 107). On the street, unaccompanied females

who looked back at male flaneurs were often assumed to be prostitutes. Thus, the *Girl's Own Paper* instructed their readers to avert their eyes to "the opposite side [of the street] when passing any man. Never look at them when near enough to be stared at in any impertinent or abrasive way" (quoted in Walkowitz 51).

8. For example, in an 1864 letter, Carroll thanks Tom Taylor for being kind enough to offer to "entrap [some] victims for me," explaining that he has already secured "many children sitters" already (*Letters* 1:64–5). This may have been a relatively common expression; meeting the Prince of Wales, Carroll asked him "if the Americans had victimised him much as a sitter," and the Prince seems to have been familiar with this phrase (*Letters* 1:45).

9. Their deviance from the ideal of the passive, compliant sitter amused Carroll so much, I believe, that he revisits it in "A Photographer's Day Out"; his description of the shot of the three miserable girls who look as if they have swallowed poison and been tied together by the hair may well have been based on this shot. Moreover, Carroll took a picture of Edith Liddell by herself that also fits this mold; her expression is so sour that when Cohen reproduced it he captioned it "Edith Liddell, apparently not very happy at having to hold a pose for almost a whole minute" (*Reflections* 60).

10. For example, when Carroll invites Margaret and Lillian Brody to pose as classical statues, he inscribes their names in Greek underneath the photograph (see Taylor and Wakeling 178). He often alerts viewers to the source that inspired a particular image by inscribing scraps of poetry or titles next to the print. The "Henry Holiday Album," reproduced by Taylor and Wakeling, offers many examples of this habit.

11. This argument is not new, but it is worth making again because it is still disputed. See for example Susina ("Educating Alice").

12. Similarly, the King of Hearts uses the term "nonsense" to silence the executioner's argument about who can be beheaded (86).

13. Wagner persuasively counters readings that characterize Oz as a pastoral utopia by tracing how contemporary concerns about technology, capitalism, class, and gender shape Baum's representation of this unstable and dangerous land.

14. Noticing this focus on negation, Kincaid interprets Alice's moments of resistance as the means by which she titillates other people; "supremely indifferent to the adult's feelings and desires," she declines to engage and thereby maintains her "erotic Otherness" (*Child-Loving* 275).

15. See for example Polhemus (584–85).

16. As Berman notes, this is a very unsympathetic reading of Wordsworth, since the father himself recognizes that he has dealt with his son in a rough, insensitive way at the end of "Anecdote for Fathers." Clearly, Wordsworth was not incapable of perceiving the boorishness of his own narrators.

CHAPTER 4

1. Sweet is not the first to make this point; Sutphin lists numerous critics who have weighed in on this issue (72), beginning with E. P. Thompson.

2. See my essay "Lewis in Wonderland: The Looking-Glass World of *Sylvie and Bruno*" (2006).

3. Narrative, Sherwood repeatedly emphasizes, offers adults by far the most effective means for indoctrinating children. Thus, the parents of Lucy, Emily, and Henry Fairchild train their children by regaling them with a series of stories, including biblical sagas, autobiographical accounts of their own spiritual struggles, and cautionary tales such as the history of little Augusta, who dies as a result of ignoring her parents' injunction not to play with fire. Naturally, she is burnt to a crisp, and just as naturally the little Fairchilds learn to comply with their parents' slightest wish. After reading this chapter, entitled "Fatal Effects of Disobedience to Parents," child readers are presumably expected to follow suit!

4. A selection of essays about children's literature by these and other writers can be found in the wonderfully titled volume *A Peculiar Gift: Nineteenth–Century Writings on Books for Children* (1976), edited by Lance Salway. I discuss one of Yonge's contributions to this debate later, and an essay by Rands at the beginning of chapter 5.

5. Crouch was so convinced of Nesbit's wide-ranging influence on the genre that he titled his book on post–World War II British children's fiction *The Nesbit Tradition*.

6. In *Knight's Castle* (1956), for example, Eager openly acknowledges Nesbit as in influence by having his child characters discuss her books and use them as inspiration for their games and fantasies. For more on Nesbit's influence on Rowling, see Nel ("Is There a Text" and *J. K. Rowling's Harry Potter,*).

7. The "burglar" caught in *The Story of the Treasure Seekers* turns out to be an honest man, but the children continue to refer to him as "our own robber" throughout the series (*Wouldbegoods* 291).

8. Both Moss ("E. Nesbit's Romantic Child" and "Varieties") and Briggs (*Woman of Passion* and "Women Writers") focus on this aspect of Nesbit's work.

9. As a number of critics have pointed out, Nesbit simultaneously sends up and recycles the benevolent old gentleman theme in *The Story of the Treasure Seekers*; although the Bastables' first attempts to befriend rich old men humorously backfire, their story concludes happily because they touch the heart of their crusty "Indian Uncle," who showers them with wealth and affection.

10. According to her first biographer, Doris Langley Moore, Nesbit "detested plagiarism and thought it a stigma to be accused of it" (148). Briggs stresses the contradiction inherent in Nesbit's vigilant position on this subject; though she herself often drew on the work of authors like Kipling, when she believed that Kipling had revamped one of her stories, she angrily "accused him of pinching her ideas and even her treatment of them" (*Woman of Passion* 253).

11. Indeed, the cycle of exploitation is even more complicated than I have indicated: robbed of his day's wages by a pickpocket, the burglar tries to take advantage of the children, who ultimately take advantage of him—and the whole event is set into motion because the family's servants cheat them by leaving the house unattended.

12. D. Moore reports that Nesbit once explained to a friend: "Sometimes I deliberately introduce a word that [child readers] won't know, so that [they] will ask a grown-up the meaning and learn something by it" (151).

13. Following in the footsteps of Moss ("Story of the Treasure Seekers" 191–93), Briggs observes that Nesbit "sets [Oswald] up as a target for comic irony, the complacent Victorian patriarch in embryo" ("Woman Writers" 245).

14. Nesbit later attempted to make amends for her anti-Semitic portrait of Rosenbaum by featuring a kind and genuinely generous Jewish pawnbroker in *Harding's Luck*. This likable character repeatedly comes to the aid of young Dickie Harding, the hero of the story. During one such intervention, Nesbit soberly informs her readers that the Jewish people's ability to empathize with others and appreciate beauty and greatness "has survived centuries of torment, shame, cruelty, and oppression" (84). She continues to characterize Jewishness as a force for good throughout the story; Dickie's magical adventures begin when he arranges some silvery seeds into the shape of a Jewish star (62).

15. Kutzer claims that Nesbit romanticizes the imperialist project, portraying the process of "removing treasure from the colonies and bringing it home to England as both good and natural" (69). But Nesbit's attitude toward empire-building is—at the very least—ambivalent. Not only does she implicitly equate colonists with greedy, unethical financiers in *The Story of the Treasure Seekers*, she mercilessly and consistently satirizes the paternalist, philanthropic impulse that served as a key justification for imperialism. "Do-gooding" of all kinds gets sent up in her stories; she makes fun not only of the children's efforts to aid the poor but also of adults' attempts to improve children or other adults, including foreigners.

16. Begging continues to be a theme throughout *The Railway Children*. Later in the story, the children offend their friend Perks by asking his neighbors to donate food, clothing, and supplies to his family as a surprise for his birthday; and the novel draws to a happy close because Roberta beseeches the old gentleman to prove their jailed father innocent of treason.

CHAPTER 5

1. *Secret Gardens* is a very confusing book: Carpenter begins by defining Golden Age children's literature as an escapist genre that characterizes childhood as "an Arcadia, a Good Place, a Secret Garden" but goes on to give readings of stories such as *The Water-Babies* and *Alice's Adventures in Wonderland* that fail to support this argument (13). Indeed, he eventually admits that the only text that perfectly fits his paradigm is Grahame's *Wind in the Willows* (155). As he moves rapidly through a roll call of other famous children's authors, chronicling how they "were not really successful" in aligning themselves with the "Arcadian movement" (103, 188), one begins to suspect that it is Carpenter's thesis that is inadequate, not the authors' literary efforts.

2. In their magisterial study *Children in English Society*, Pinchbeck and Hewitt observe that the struggle to pass and enforce child labor laws was "long and bitter" (347), impeded not just by greedy businessmen and indifferent politicians but also by parents and communities who were reconciled by tradition and financial necessity to children's early introduction into the workforce. Thus, although legislation aimed at regulating and reducing child labor was passed throughout the nineteenth century, there was no attempt to outlaw it completely. Loopholes in laws like the 1833 Factory Act and the 1867 Workshops Act, coupled with a lack of local enforcement, meant that many children continued to work. Even the mine work that so horrified the 1842 Royal Commission

on child labor had its defenders: "I went to pit myself when I was five years old," declared one Yorkshire mother, "and two of my daughters go. It does them no harm. It never did me none" (quoted in Pinchbeck and Hewitt 402). As late as 1891, the British government dragged its feet at raising the minimum age for part-time factory work from ten to eleven, even though it had promised to extend it to twelve at an 1890 European congress on child labor (Horn, *Victorian Town* 118). For more on this topic, see Lavalette.

3. Education reform proceeded at a very slow pace. In the early 1860s, the Royal Commission on Popular Education flatly declared that compulsory schooling for all children was "neither obtainable nor desirable" (quoted in Horn, *Victorian Town* 74). If the child's wages are crucial to the family economy, they wrote, "it is far better that it should go to work at the earliest age at which it can bear the physical exertion than that it should remain at school" (74). Shaftesbury himself was opposed to compulsory education laws, on the grounds that they infringed on the rights of the father and encouraged "a dependence on the State instead of a robust development of the virtues of personal initiative and responsibility" (Pinchbeck and Hewitt 358). The 1870 Elementary Education Act called for the creation of a national network of primary schools, but it was not until 1880 that legislation finally passed that unequivocally required children between the ages of five and ten to attend school full-time. Even then, Horn notes, many rural families refused to comply, although an 1891 ruling that abolished most elementary school fees helped to close this breach. A similar system of secondary schooling was not established until 1902.

4. The movement to raise the age of consent met with serious resistance. Even after an 1871 Royal Commission reported that the "traffic in children for infamous purposes is notoriously considerable in London and other large towns" (quoted in Pearsall 290); even after an 1881 House of Lords committee turned up evidence of an international traffic in British girls; even after a scandal erupted over the activities of Mary Jeffries, a brothel-keeper who allegedly supplied girls to "patrons of the highest social order" (quoted in Linnane 199), legislation to raise the age of consent from thirteen to sixteen repeatedly failed to garner enough support to pass through Parliament. Only when W. T. Stead sensationalized and exaggerated the scope of the problem in his series of articles "The Maiden Tribute of Modern Babylon" (1885) did the movement to make this change finally succeed. Even then, it was against the will of some lawmakers who "objected to curtailing male sexual prerogatives to protect girls who, they claimed, were already defiled" by their sordid upbringing (Walkowitz 103). Indeed, rather than responding with outrage to stories about the sexual exploitation of young people, many Victorians maintained a flippant attitude. Thus, as Gorham notes, one lawmaker opposed to the age of consent bill warned his peers to remember their own youthful peccadilloes and refrain from passing a law that might get their sons in trouble (366). Similarly, when charges of indecent assault were brought against James Crumbie for molesting boys, magistrates at two different courts had to rebuke the raucous public for laughing, sternly informing them on both occasions that such behavior was "disgusting" rather than funny (quoted in Pearsall 356).

5. Both of these historians point out that the redefinition of childhood as a prolonged period set aside for education and entertainment was an extremely gradual process: "only in the twentieth century did it become accepted that children in all classes were

an expense rather than an economic asset to their families" (Cunningham, *Children of the Poor* 3).

6. Walkowitz elaborates on this tendency in *City of Dreadful Delight* (1992), as does Cunningham in *The Children of the Poor* (1991).

7. Ward was professionally precocious, too: the same year, one of her pictures was hung in the Royal Academy.

8. See *Time and Tide* (1867), letter 5 (*Works* 17:333–38).

9. I offer more evidence that large numbers of children flocked to see shows featuring precocious child performers in my final chapter. As for women, Crozier supplies proof that many of them attended such shows in chapter 6 of his dissertation on the representation of childhood on the Victorian stage.

10. Steedman also suggests that very few Victorian child actors had the opportunity to play featured or starring roles (143–44).

11. See my discussion of the anonymously authored "Children on the Stage" later in this chapter.

12. Born a slave, the Roman actor Quintus Roscius Gallus had such a triumphant stage career that his name became an honorary epithet applied to other successful actors.

13. See the review of *The Real Little Lord Fauntleroy* that appeared in the *Times*.

14. Rose, Steedman, Lebaille, Danahay, and Foulkes all elaborate on this trend.

15. According to Blainey, Hunt became "so well known" as a drama critic for the *News* that a collection of his reviews was quickly published in book form (31). *Critical Essays on the Performers of the London Theatres* (1807) garnered high praise and "established Hunt as the first modern theatre critic" (Roe 82). Yet almost none of Hunt's impassioned rants against child actors appear in this volume, which may explain why biographers and critics rarely mention his vehement opposition to this vogue.

16. The actual title of this production was *The Country Girl*, which suggests that the company was performing David Garrick's bowdlerized version of Wycherly's play.

17. When a reader wrote in to protest the claim that the parents of these child actors were ruining their characters, Hunt made fun of him by scripting a mock trial in which the father of a child performer fruitlessly tried to defend himself against Hunt's accusations in a "Court of Justice" ("Theatricals," 11 May 1806, 414). Hunt later bragged that the dissolution of the Academic Theatre "was materially owing to the ridicule of the NEWS" (*Critical Essays* 146).

18. Dickens based the childish, irresponsible character of Harold Skimpole in *Bleak House* on Hunt.

19. Hunt's hostility toward infant phenomena might have been connected to his ambivalent feelings about his own prematurely developed talents. A literary prodigy, his first publication was a volume of poetry entitled *Juvenilia: A Collection of Poems, Written between the Ages of Twelve and Sixteen* (1801). According to Blainey, Hunt later regretted his early entry onto the literary scene, blaming *Juvenilia* "for giving him a spurious sense of his own importance [and] for having caused him to waste many years in imitating Pope, Gray and Collins when he should have been studying 'poetical art and nature'" (17).

20. For example, an American critic complained in 1829 that most theatrical prodigies were "taught to repeat certain words like a parrot, and drilled to imitate certain

actions like a monkey, and then . . . stuck upon the stage for 'children of a larger growth' to gape and wonder at, and applauded for no better reason than because it is six years old and two feet odd inches high" (quoted in Young 372). Like Hunt, this critic implies that an admiration for such shows attests to the infantile nature of adult fans rather than the genuine talent of child actors.

21. This quotation comes from the review of Blanchard's *Little Goody Two Shoes* that appeared in the *Era* (12). Many other examples could be cited of commentators who refer to Dickens by name when discussing child performers. For instance, Marcus Tindal declared in 1897 that contemporary "Baby Actors" enjoyed "delightful" working conditions, in sharp contrast to the sad state of child performers "in times gone by, as those who know their Dickens well realise" (678). The tendency to treat Dickens's account as factual rather than fictional, as Tindal does here, is also quite common.

22. See my essay "The Drama of Precocity: Child Performers on the Victorian Stage" (2008).

23. See Morley's three essays on this subject, as well as McLean.

24. Other families of siblings who played featured roles include the Solomons, the Dampiers, the Denins, the Ternans, the Roselles, and the Bottomleys.

25. In *Children and Theatre in Victorian England* (2008), which came out just as this book went to press, Anne Varty seconds Steedman's characterization of the appeal of nineteenth-century child actors, arguing that the work of these performers represented "an enactment of childishness, a public assertion of the categorical difference between children and adults, and the demonstration of the child's kinship with an altogether more atavistic state of being" (16). Varty's goal, as she acknowledges in her introduction, is to carry on "a familiar tradition of analysis concerning the Romantic signification of the child as an embodiment of primal innocence" (18). But the wealth of evidence that she unearths in this valuable study—the first book-length examination of the topic—problematizes this account of the appeal of child performers, since so much of it attests to the professionalism and precocity of successful child actors.

26. This praise was heaped on the six-year-old child prodigy Clara Fisher, for her appearance in an 1817 production of David Garrick's *Gulliver in Lilliput* that served as an afterpiece to a production of *Hamlet* at Drury Lane. According to the *Times*, all of the characters except Gulliver "were performed by children, young ladies between the ages of 6 and 13 years" (review of *Hamlet*). "We felt a little alarm at first for the success of this experiment," this commentator observed, "but the little performers proved to be in perfect training, and the whole went off very well." Indeed, Fisher's impersonations in this piece were so impressive that she earned a second mention in the *Times* in which her acting ability was referred to as "one of the most extraordinary intellectual phenomena that ever puzzled a metaphysician" (review of *John Bull*).

27. Hunt observes that Miss Mudie was billed as the Infant Phenomenon in his "Theatricals" column on August 11, 1805. Perhaps she, as well as Miss Davenport, served as an inspiration for Dickens's character.

28. For a detailed report of this disastrous appearance, see the review of *The Country Girl* that appeared in the *Times*.

29. The *Western Mail*'s account of the touring all-child production of *The Pirates of Penzance* (Theatre Royal, Cardiff 1885) also makes this case at length ("Children's *Pirates*").

30. This quotation comes from the review of Blanchard's *Little Goody Two Shoes* which appeared in the *Era* (12).

31. Because the public loved the idea of seeing children onstage, many performers pretended to be younger than they were. In terms of my argument, the chronological age of "child" actors matters little; the crucial point is that however old they actually were, their appeal to audiences was based on seeming precocious, gifted with "talent very far in advance of [their] years" (review of Baby). That said, most of the child performers I discuss here really were very young when they began acting.

32. According to Crozier, twenty-two dramas with "major child roles" debuted on the London stage during the five-year period 1887–1891, and this total does not include melodramas or pantomimes, which frequently used children in featured parts (266).

33. Similarly, when Dowson fell for Adelaide Foltinowicz, he described her as looking like the child star Minnie Terry (*Letters* 114) and took her to a matinée of *Nixie* (Terry's 1890), a show that featured a precocious child actress—Lucy Webling—playing the role of Nixie, a character the *Era* described as "the most precocious child ever brought into this wicked world" ("'Nixie' at Terry's"). I discuss *Nixie* at greater length in chapter 6.

34. He was for instance very impressed with the piano prodigy Pauline Ellice, who was lauded by critics for displaying great technical ability and "a musical intelligence far in advance of her years, only eleven in number" ("Our Musical-Box" 92). As for child actors, he faulted those whom he felt failed to display the requisite skills, such as the ability to articulate their words clearly and fully inhabit the character they were portraying. The terms of praise he employed likewise reveal an appreciation of the talent and intelligence of child actors; tellingly, the word that recurs most often in his admiring descriptions of child performers is "clever," as when he observes: "Puck was very cleverly acted by little Ellen Terry" (*Diaries* 1:98).

35. Evidence for this claim can be found in Walkowitz's discussion of Josephine Butler and C. Robson's of W. T. Stead.

36. I still have not identified the hostile critic to whom Dowson refers here. It might be Shaw, but if so, Dowson was reacting to an earlier essay than the one cited earlier in which Shaw complains about the "epidemic of child exhibition" ("Van Amburgh" 457), since that piece appeared nine years after Dowson's "The Cult of the Child."

37. Praising Beringer's performance as Little Lord Fauntleroy, for example, the *Illustrated London News* emphasized her naturalness in order to dismiss the possibility that she had been coerced: "It was not acting but nature. As a rule a child is parroted, trained, and taught to death. But this child is a born actress, and seems as accustomed to the stage as if she were born on it" (review of *Real Little*). Critics in the United States were just as anxious to clear child stars of what had evidently become a damaging charge, precisely because it implied that the child had been damaged: the accusation of precocity. Thus, after noting that American child star Elsie Leslie "dominates the scene and carries the entire play [of *Little Lord Fauntleroy*] on her dainty shoulders," the author of "Gotham Gossip" (1888) quickly adds, "She accomplishes her task, not as a marvel

of precocity, but like an artist of rare finish, with reliable resources in reserve. There is nothing of the parrot in her performance. . . . Her self-possession is wonderful. Never for an instant, however, does she appear prematurely mature."

38. Cunningham elaborates on this subject in *The Children of the Poor.*

39. In his wonderfully detailed account of Carroll's theatregoing, Foulkes characterizes such inconsistency as a defining feature of Carroll's attitude toward the stage in general. After noting that "Carroll's attitude towards the theatre was made up of several different attitudes" (50), Foulkes charts how his subject veered back and forth between open-minded liberalism and staid "prissiness" (106).

40. This description of Fauntleroy appeared in the 1886 novel *Little Lord Fauntleroy* that the play was based on (49).

41. While Burnett is now better known for writing *The Secret Garden* and *A Little Princess*, *Little Lord Fauntleroy* was far more acclaimed during her own lifetime.

42. Similarly, in his study of Victorian sexuality, Pearsall includes a brief chapter on "The Cult of the Little Girl."

43. For details about the enthusiastic public response *Fauntleroy* inspired, see Anna Wilson (235) and Clark (18–25).

44. Of all the critics of the cult of the child, Roth comes closest to acknowledging this aspect of it when she notes the way female characters produced by its members, including Barrie's Wendy, "hold two simultaneous images—child and woman, dream and reality, chaste and fallen—in constant tandem" (48). But whereas Roth contends that these female figures "cannot exhibit both paradoxical identities simultaneously in one body" (56), I suggest that their precocity enables them to do precisely that: to embody both sides of these (and other) binaries, and thus to subvert the notion that identity is defined and delimited by such sharp oppositions.

CHAPTER 6

1. A more charitable way to put this point is that eighteenth-century children's writers were attuned to the fact that children are not born readers. Since literacy is an acquired skill, these writers wanted to provide young people with reading material that matched up well with each stage of development. Thus, the brief tales in Maria Edgeworth's *Early Lessons* (1801–2) were geared toward very young readers, while her more involved *Moral Tales for Young People* (1801) were targeted to older youth.

2. For example, when this all-child production of *Pinafore* was revived a year later, the *Era* confidently declared that the show "will be largely patronized, because all the little folks will want to see how children sing and act" ("Children's Pinafore"). Similarly, drama critic C. A. M. predicted that *Bluebell in Fairyland* (Vaudeville 1901) would be a success because "the number of children on the stage will be sure to attract children to the front of the stage" (536).

3. See for example the review of Filippi and Levey's *Little Goody Two Shoes* (Court 1888) that appeared in the *Era*. Besides this production, other all-child shows aimed at children in the 1880s and 1890s included *Dick Whittington and His Cat* (Avenue

1882), *The Belles of the Village* (Avenue 1889), *Cinderella* (Covent Garden 1889), and *The House That Jack Built* (Opera Comique 1894). The producers of this last show, one reviewer explained, believe that "there is always room in London at Christmas for one performance by children for children" (review of *House*). Because these critically ignored productions were designed for and marketed to children, they bolster my claim that the emergence of children's theatre in England occurred in the late nineteenth century.

4. Twain made this remark in a September 1908 letter to Mrs. Hookway. Scholars who agree with his characterization of children's theatre as a twentieth-century phenomenon include England, T. Jackson, McCaslin, Salazar, and W. Ward. Although I quibble with this account, I am indebted to them for their pioneering work on this neglected topic.

5. For more information on the habits of Victorian child playgoers, see Cook's "Survey of Children Audience Members" (1996) and Davis and Emeljanow's *Reflecting the Audience* (2001).

6. Before and after this innovation, evening performances of pantomimes generally began at about 10:00 at night (A. E. Wilson 136), but this late starting time apparently did not prevent many children from attending.

7. This quotation comes from the review of Blanchard's *Little Goody Two Shoes* that appeared in the *Era* (13).

8. See Ruskin's *Works*, 33:xxx.

9. For example, the *Era* praised *Alice in Wonderland* for being "refined and delicate" (review of *Alice*, 25 Dec. 1886) and lauded an all-child production of *Dick Whittington and His Cat* (Avenue 1882) for the "simplicity" of its plotting: "The author has . . . shown his discretion in keeping to the legend so closely, instead of going far away from the text of the familiar narrative, after the manner of many pantomime writers. . . . This] pantomime is not a rough-and-tumble entertainment, with which to catch Boxing Night audiences, but a pleasant rendering of a favourite story" (review of *Dick*).

10. I base this assertion not only on the fact that reviewers did not treat *Alice in Wonderland* as a novelty but also on the critical reaction to Filippi and Levey's musical play *Little Goody Two Shoes*. Most notably, the *Era*'s reviewer declared, "Plays and comic operas have frequently before been acted by children for children of larger or lesser growth" (review of *Little Goody*, 29 Dec. 1888).

11. Similarly, *Current Opinion* christened the Children's Theatre "the first of its kind in the world" ("Century of the Child" 121). Such puffery may not be based in fact, but it supports theatre historians' point that it was only in the early 1900s that children's theatre became firmly established as a recognized phenomenon.

12. This piece of information comes from Angela du Maurier's account of seeing *Peter Pan* multiple times as a child in her autobiography *It's Only the Sister* (15).

13. See W. Ward (21) and Hartnoll (171).

14. Burnett titled her play *The Real Little Lord Fauntleroy* in order to differentiate it from E. V. Seebohm's pirated dramatic adaptation of her book, which had opened three months earlier at the Prince of Wales's Theatre. I will exclude the word "Real," both for convenience and because it was dropped in later productions and in the published script.

15. For an example of this tendency, see "Christmas at the Theatres" (1914).

16. Describing the opening night of the English production of Burnett's *Little Lord Fauntleroy* for readers of *St. Nicholas* magazine, Franklyn observed that "the children who were present were delighted: they wagged their little heads, laughed cheerily, and clapped heartily whenever they saw an opportunity!" (10). Two years later, the drama critic for the *Illustrated London News* noted that a large "audience of children . . . delighted in 'Little Lord Fauntleroy'" during its original run (C. S., "Playhouses"). Carroll took a number of young people to see it, including Lily Morgan, Helen and Maud Dymes, and Isa Bowman. Many American children attended productions of *Little Lord Fauntleroy* as well; Burnett's play opened in Boston, then moved to New York and other cities. According to her son, "Old and young alike went to it in droves to laugh and sigh weep" (V. Burnett 175). Elsie Leslie, the child actress who originated the part in Boston, told one reporter that she especially enjoyed the sight and sound of children in the audience (Lillie 412), while youngsters such as seven-year-old Zoe wrote to *St. Nicholas* to say "last week I went to see 'Little Lord Fauntleroy' played, and as my mamma had read it to me I understood it" ("Letter-Box" 630).

17. Two excellent illustrations of the Victorians' use of this term can be found in the *Era*'s editorial "The Child Drama" (1888) and C. S.'s column "The Playhouses" (1890) in the *Illustrated London News*.

18. This description appeared in a review of Seebohm's dramatic adaptation of *Little Lord Fauntleroy* (*Daily Telegraph*, 24 Feb. 1888).

19. Recognizing this, the author of yet another reflective essay on "The Cult of the Child" (1894), one "E. A. D.," both pokes fun at how "decorative" Fauntleroy is and declares it "cheering" that Burnett renders him "healthy enough to grow up . . . and not die early in an aroma of piety."

20. Reviews of Philip Carr and Nigel Playfair's dramatic adaptation of *Shock-Headed Peter* (Garrick 1900, 1901) bear this out. In 1900, the *Times* had no objection to the coupling of this children's play with *The Man Who Stole the Castle*, a "charming," rather sappy one-act play of the *Fauntleroy* type (review of *Shock*, 27 Dec. 1900). But a year later, a number of critics (including the *Times*'s) objected that the "lachrymose sentimentality" and "precious" use of child actors in this piece made it "better calculated to please foolish mothers than healthy children" (review of *Shock*, *Illustrated*). *Fauntleroy* itself experienced a similar backlash; reviewers of the original British and American productions did not single out the play's schmaltziness as a quality that would displease children, but this criticism did crop up in later years, when the character of Fauntleroy was consigned to "the pantheon of all-time kickable children of literature" (Howard).

21. See his letter to August Strindberg on March 16, 1910 (*Collected Letters* 906–9) and his 1937 obituary for Barrie, entitled "The Unhappy Years of Barrie."

22. Reviews of this show likewise indicate that the producers hoped to lure in this crowd. For instance, the *Era*'s critic pronounced this revival "exactly suited to the juvenile perception" and confidently predicted that "parents will be pestered this Christmas by urgent entreaties from their children to take them to see *Alice in Wonderland*" (review of *Alice*, 24 Dec. 1898).

23. A May 1882 column in the *Theatre* mentions "the free admissions usually . . . offered as a compliment to the critics of the press" on first nights ("Our Omnibus-Box" 306).

24. After he finished drafting *Peter Pan* in April 1904, Barrie announced to Maude Adams in no uncertain terms "I have written a play for children" (quoted in Birkin 103). Reviewers recognized that this was his intent: see for example the *Times*—which described the show as "a play for children and about children" (review of *Peter*)—and the *King* (quoted in Hanson 49). Such articles undermine Rose's claim that "the first reviewers saw the play entirely from the adult's point of view" (99).

25. For extensive lists of such resources, see R. L. Green (*Fifty Years* 244) and Hanson (274–75). For a sampling of fan letters received by British Peters, see *Peter Pan's Postbag* (1909) and *Dear Peter Pan* (1983).

26. Fields reveals that Adams—the first American Peter—received "hundreds of letters" from children (194); during holiday matinees, "children dominated the audiences and outdid their parents in participating in the play's actions: cheers, clapping, hisses, foot stamping, singing aloud with Maude, and responding with loud enthusiasm when Maude asked them if they believed in fairies" (193). For more information on early English productions, see Chase's "My Reminiscences of 'Peter Pan'" (1913) and the collaboratively authored piece "When I Was Peter Pan" (Boucicault et al.1923), in which nine Peters recalled their experiences.

27. R. L. Green has meticulously outlined how indebted early versions of *Peter Pan* were to this genre, so there is no need to belabor that point here (*Fifty Years* 55–69, 82, 99). Rose also makes this point, contending that "*Peter Pan* did not found a new type of drama so much as revivify a number of old ones" (102). White and Tarr offer still more evidence of *Peter Pan*'s links to pantomime in their introduction to *J. M. Barrie's "Peter Pan" In and Out of Time* (2006).

28. See Pearsall (294–96, 353–56), Diamond (142–47), and Sweet (170) for more on these sex scandals.

WORKS CITED

à Beckett, Gilbert. "Theatricals." *Figaro in London* 5 Jan. 1833: 4.

Acton, William. *Prostitution: Considered in its Moral, Social, and Sanitary Aspects in London and Other Large Cities and Garrison Towns, with Proposals for the Control and Prevention of its Attendant Evils.* London: J. Churchill, 1857.

Adams, Jad. *Madder Music, Stronger Wine: The Life of Ernest Dowson, Poet and Decadent.* London: I. B. Tauris, 2000.

Adams, W. Davenport. "The Decline of Pantomime." *Theatre* 1 Feb. 1882. Reprinted in *Theatre* new ser. 5 (Jan.–June 1882): 85–90.

Adye, Frederic. "Old-Fashioned Children." *Macmillan's Magazine* 38 (Aug. 1893): 286–92.

Ainger, Alfred. "The Children's Books of a Hundred Years Ago." Lecture, March 1, 1895, Royal Institution. Reprinted in Salway 62–76.

Alcott, Louisa May. *Jimmy's Cruise in the "Pinafore." St. Nicholas* Oct. 1879. Reprinted in *Jimmy's Cruise in the "Pinafore," &c.* London: Sampson Low, 1879.

Alderson, Brian. Introduction. In *The Water-Babies.* By Charles Kingsley. Oxford: Oxford University Press, 1995: ix–xxix.

Aldington, Richard. *Portrait of a Rebel: The Life and Work of Robert Louis Stevenson.* London: Evans, 1957.

"'Alice in Wonderland,' at the Opera Comique." *Pall Mall Gazette* 23 Dec. 1898: 2.

Altick, Richard D. *The Shows of London.* Cambridge, MA: Harvard University Press, 1978.

Andrews, Malcolm. *Dickens and the Grown-up Child.* Iowa City: University of Iowa Press, 1994.

Armstrong, William A. "The Nineteenth-Century Matinée." *Theatre Notebook* 14.2 (Winter 1959): 56–59.

Auerbach, Nina. *Romantic Imprisonment: Women and Other Glorified Outcasts.* New York: Columbia University Press, 1986.

Austin, Linda M. "Children of Childhood: Nostalgia and the Romantic Legacy." *Studies in Romanticism* 42.1 (Spring 2003): 75–98.

Avery, Gillian. Introduction. In *The Wind in the Willows*. New York: Penguin Classics, 2005.

———. *Mrs. Ewing*. New York: H. Z. Walck, 1964.

Avery, Gillian, and Kimberly Reynolds, eds. *Representations of Childhood Death*. New York: St. Martin's Press, 2000.

"Babyolatry." *Chambers' Edinburgh Journal* 28 Feb. 1846: 129–30.

Bacile di Castiglione, Claudia. "*Holiday Romance*: Children's Dreams of Omnipotence in Dickens's Last Fiction." In *Dickens: The Craft of Fiction and the Challenges of Reading*. Milan: Unicopli, 2000. 153–65.

Ballantyne, Robert Michael. *The Coral Island*. New York: Garland, 1977.

Banerjee, Jacqueline. *Through the Northern Gate: Childhood and Growing Up in British Fiction, 1719–1901*. New York: Peter Lang, 1996.

Barlee, Ellen. *Pantomime Waifs: Or, A Plea for Our City Children*. London: S. W. Partridge, 1884.

Barrie, J. M. *The Little White Bird*. London: Hodder and Stoughton, 1928.

———. *Peter and Wendy*. In *Peter Pan in Kensington Gardens* and *Peter and Wendy*. Ed. Peter Hollindale. Oxford: Oxford University Press, 1991.

———. *Peter Pan and Other Plays*. Ed. Peter Hollindale. Oxford: Oxford University Press, 1995.

———. "To the Five: A Dedication." In Barrie, *Peter Pan* 75–86.

Barthes, Roland. *The Pleasures of the Text*. Trans. Richard Miller. New York: Hill and Wang, 1975.

———. *S/Z: An Essay*. Trans. Richard Miller. New York: Hill and Wang, 1974.

Baum, L. Frank. *The Wonderful Wizard of Oz*. New York: Dover, 1960.

Beatty-Kingston, William. Review of *The Pirates of Penzance*. *Theatre* 2 Feb. 1885. Reprinted in *Theatre* 5 (Jan.–June 1885): 80–82.

Beerbohm, Max. "*Peter Pan* Revisited." *Saturday Review* 28 Dec. 1907. Reprinted in *Last Theatres 1904–1910*. London: Rupert Hart-Davis, 1970: 334–37.

———. "Pantomime for Children." *Saturday Review* 14 Jan. 1905. Reprinted in *Last Theatres 1904–1910*. London: Rupert Hart-Davis, 1970: 116–20.

———. "Two Pantomimes." *Saturday Review* 31 Dec. 1898. Reprinted in *More Theatres 1898–1903*. New York: Taplinger Publishing Company, 1969: 92–96.

Benson, E. F. *As We Were: A Victorian Peep Show*. New York: Blue Ribbon Books, 1930.

Berman, Ruth. "White Knight and Leech Gatherer: The Poet as Boor." *Mythlore* 33 (Autumn 1982): 29–31.

Berry, Laura C. *The Child, The State, and the Victorian Novel*. Charlottesville: University Press of Virginia, 1999.

Birkin, Andrew. *J. M. Barrie and the Lost Boys: The Love Story That Gave Birth to Peter Pan*. New York: Clarkson N. Potter, 1979.

Blackburn, William. "Mirror in the Sea: *Treasure Island* and the Internalization of Juvenile Romance." *Children's Literature Association Quarterly* 8.3 (Fall 1983): 7–12.

Blainey, Ann. *Immortal Boy: A Portrait of Leigh Hunt*. London: Croom Helm, 1985.

Blake, Kathleen. *Play, Games, and Sport: The Literary Works of Lewis Carroll*. Ithaca: Cornell University Press, 1974.

———. "The Sea-Dream: *Peter Pan* and *Treasure Island*." *Children's Literature* 6 (1977): 165–81.

Blake, William. "Auguries of Innocence." In *The Complete Poetry and Prose of William Blake*. Rev. ed. Ed. David V. Erdman. New York: Anchor Books, 1982.

Boas, George. *The Cult of Childhood*. Dallas: Spring, 1966.

Boone, Troy. *Youth of Darkest England: Working-Class Children at the Heart of Victorian Empire*. New York: Routledge, 2005.

Boucicault, Nina, et al. "When I Was Peter Pan." *Strand* Jan. 1923: 32–39.

Brantlinger, Patrick. *Rule of Darkness: British Literature and Imperialism, 1830–1914*. Ithaca: Cornell University Press, 1988.

Briggs, Julia. *A Woman of Passion: The Life of E. Nesbit, 1858–1924*. New York: New Amsterdam Books, 1987.

———. "Woman Writers and Writing for Children: From Sarah Fielding to E. Nesbit." In *Children and Their Books: A Celebration of the Work of Iona and Peter Opie*. Ed. Gillian Avery and Julia Briggs. Oxford: Clarendon Press, 1989: 221–51.

Bristow, Joseph. *Empire Boys: Adventures in a Man's World*. London: HarperCollins, 1991.

Brontë, Charlotte. *Jane Eyre*. Ed. Michael Mason. New York: Penguin Books, 2003.

Brown, Penny. *The Captured World: The Child and Childhood in Nineteenth-Century Women's Writing in England*. New York: St. Martin's, 1993.

Burnett, Frances Hodgson. "How Fauntleroy Occurred: And a Very Real Little Boy Became an Ideal One." In *Piccino and Other Child Stories*. New York: Scribner's, 1894: 147–203. Reprint of "How Fauntleroy Really Occurred: And a Very Real Little Boy Became an Ideal One." *Ladies' Home Journal* Dec. 1893: 1–2; Jan. 1894: 3–4; Feb. 1894: 5–6.

———. *Little Lord Fauntleroy*. Mineola, NY: Dover, 2002.

———. *Little Lord Fauntleroy: A Drama in Three Acts*. Samuel French: New York, 1889.

———. *A Little Princess*. Ed. U. C. Knoepflmacher. New York: Penguin Books, 2002.

———. *The One I Knew Best of All*. New York: Arno Press, 1980.

———. "The Whole of the Story." In Burnett, *A Little Princess* 3–4.

Burnett, Vivian. *The Romantick Lady (Frances Hodgson Burnett): The Life Story of an Imagination*. New York: Scribner's, 1927.

C. A. M. "Players and Playtime." *Idler: An Illustrated Monthly Magazine* Jan. 1902: 535–36.

C. S. "The Playhouses." *Illustrated London News* 19 April 1890: 483.

———. Review of *Nixie*. *Illustrated London News* 12 April 1890: 454.

Carpenter, Humphrey. *Secret Gardens: A Study of the Golden Age of Children's Literature*. Boston: Houghton Mifflin, 1985.

Carroll, Lewis. *The Complete Works of Lewis Carroll*. New York: Penguin Books, 1988.

———. *The Diaries of Lewis Carroll*. Ed. Roger Lancelyn Green. 2 vols. New York: Oxford University Press, 1954.

———. *The Letters of Lewis Carroll*. Ed. Morton N. Cohen. 2 vols. New York: Oxford University Press, 1979.

———. *The Rectory Umbrella* and *Mischmasch*. New York: Dover, 1971.

———. "The Stage and the Spirit of Reverence." *Theatre* June 1888. Reprinted in Lovett, 214–23.

———. "Stage Children." *Theatre* 2 Sept. 1889. Reprinted in Lovett, 223–28.

"The Century of the Child in the Playhouse." *Current Opinion* Feb. 1913: 121–23.

Chambers, Aidan. "The Reader in the Book." In *The Signal Approach to Children's Books*. Ed. Nancy Chambers. Harmondsworth, UK: Kestral Books, 1980: 250–75.

Chapman, Mary. "'Living Pictures': Women and *Tableaux Vivants* in Nineteenth-Century American Fiction and Culture. *Wide Angle* 18.3 (1996): 22–52.

Chase, Pauline. "My Reminiscences of 'Peter Pan.'" *Strand* May 1913: 42–51.

Chesterton, G. K. *Robert Louis Stevenson*. New York: Sheed and Ward, 1955.

"The Child Drama." *Era* 26 May 1888: 13.

"Children on the Stage." *Theatre* 1 Oct. 1878. Reprinted in *Theatre* 1 (Aug. 1878–Jan. 1879): 185–88.

"The Children's Choice" *Punch* 29 Jan. 1887: 60.

"Children's Literature." *Quarterly Review* Jan. 1860. Reprinted in Salway, 299–331.

"A Children's Pantomime." *Era* 7 Jan. 1877: 12.

"The Children's Pinafore." *Era* 26 Dec. 1880: 12.

"The Children's *Pirates of Penzance* at the Theatre Royal, Cardiff." *Western Mail* 17 June 1885: 3.

"Children's Plays." *Era* 16 Dec. 1899: 7.

"The Children's Theatre." *Times* 27 Oct. 1913: 12.

Chitty, Susan. *The Beast and the Monk: A Life of Charles Kingsley*. New York: Mason / Charter, 1975.

"Christmas Amusements." *Times* 21 Dec. 1909: 11.

"Christmas Amusements." *Times* 26 Dec. 1877: 4.

"A Christmas 'Carroll.'" *Punch* 8 Jan. 1887: 17.

"The Christmas Entertainments." *Era* 23 Dec. 1866: 10–11.

"Christmas at the Theatres: Pantomimes and Children's Plays." *Times* 21 Dec. 1914: 11.

Clapp, Henry Austin. *Reminiscences of a Dramatic Critic: With an Essay on the Art of Henry Irving*. Boston: Houghton, Mifflin, 1902.

Clark, Beverly Lyon. *Kiddie Lit: The Cultural Construction of Children's Literature in America*. Baltimore: Johns Hopkins University Press, 2003.

Cohen, Morton N. *Lewis Carroll: A Biography*. London: Macmillan, 1995.

———. "Lewis Carroll and Victorian Morality." In *Sexuality and Victorian Literature*. Ed. Don Richard Cox. Knoxville: University of Tennessee Press, 1984: 3–19.

———. *Reflections in a Looking Glass: A Centennial Celebration of Lewis Carroll, Photographer*. New York: Aperture, 1998.

Coleridge, Hartley. "A Nursery Lecture Delivered by an Old Bachelor." *Essays and Marginalia*. Vol. 1. Plainview, NY: Books for Libraries Press, 1973: 300–307.

Coleridge, Samuel Taylor. *Inquiring Spirit: A New Presentation of Coleridge from His Published and Unpublished Prose Writings*. Ed. Kathleen Coburn. London: Routledge and Kegan Paul, 1951.

Colley, Ann C. *Robert Louis Stevenson and the Colonial Imagination.* Burlington, VT: Ashgate, 2004.

Colloms, Brenda. *Charles Kinsgley: The Lion of Eversley.* London: Constable, 1975.

Cook, Nicholas J. "A Survey of Children Audience Members in English Theatre from the Anglo-Saxon to Victorian Eras." Diss. Claremont Graduate School, 1996.

Cooper, Edward H. "Children's Christmas Amusements." *Nineteenth Century and After, a Monthly Review* Jan. 1905: 78–88.

Coveney, Peter. *The Image of Childhood.* 1957. Rev. ed. Baltimore: Penguin Books, 1967.

Craik, Dinah Maria Mulock. *The Little Lame Prince.* Cleveland: World, 1948.

———. *The Little Lychetts: A Piece of Autobiography.* London: Sampson Low, 1855.

———. *Olive* and *The Half-Caste.* Oxford: Oxford University Press, 1996.

———. *Our Year: A Child's Book, In Prose and Verse.* New York: Harper, 1860.

Crompton, Frances E. *The Gentle Heritage.* New York: Dutton, 1893.

Crouch, Marcus. *The Nesbit Tradition: The Children's Novel in England 1945–1970.* London: Ernest Benn, 1972.

Crozier, Brian. "Notions of Childhood in London Theatre, 1880–1905." Diss. University of Cambridge, 1981.

Cunningham, Hugh. *Children and Childhood in Western Society since 1500.* London: Longman, 1995.

———. *The Children of the Poor: Representations of Childhood since the Seventeenth Century.* Oxford: Blackwell, 1991.

Danahay, Martin. "Sexuality and the Working-Class Child's Body in Music Hall." *Victorian Institute Journal* 29 (2001): 102–31.

Darton, F. J. Harvey. *Children's Books in England: Five Centuries of Social Life.* Third Ed. Rev. by Brian Alderson. Cambridge: Cambridge University Press, 1982.

Davis, Jim and Victor Emeljanow. *Reflecting the Audience: London Theatregoing, 1840–1880.* Iowa City: University of Iowa Press, 2001.

Davis, Tracy C. *Actresses as Working Women: Their Social Identity in Victorian Culture.* London: Routledge, 1991.

———. "The Actress in Victorian Pornography." In *Victorian Scandals: Representations of Gender and Class.* Ed. Kristine Ottesen Garrigan. Athens: Ohio University Press, 1992: 99–133.

Dear Peter Pan . . . Ed. Catherine Haill. London: Victorian and Albert Museum, 1983.

Defoe, Daniel. *Robinson Crusoe.* Ed. Michael Shinagel. New York: Norton, 1975.

Diamond, Michael. *Victorian Sensation: Or, the Spectacular, the Shocking and the Scandalous in Nineteenth-Century Britain.* London: Anthem Press, 2003.

Dickens, Charles. *Bleak House.* New York: Norton, 1977.

———. *Dombey and Son.* New York: Penguin Classics, 1985.

———. "Frauds on the Fairies." *Household Words* 1 Oct. 1853. Reprinted in Salway, 111–18.

———. *Holiday Romance: In Four Parts. All the Year Round* and *Our Young Folks* 1868. Reprinted in *The Works of Charles Dickens.* Vol. 6. London: Chapman and Hall, 1908: 326–61.

———. *Nicholas Nickleby.* New York: Penguin Classics, 1986.

———. *Oliver Twist*. New York: Penguin Classics, 1985.

———. *Our Mutual Friend*. New York: Penguin, 1971.

Dixon, Gerald. "Bashful Fifteen." *Theatre* Sept. 1878. Reprinted in *Theatre* 1 (Aug. 1878–Jan. 1879): 126–33.

Dolman, Frederick. "Stage Children: Leading Little Actors and Actresses of the Day." *English Illustrated Magazine* May 1899: 177–85.

Doré, Gustave, and Blanchard Jerrold. *London: A Pilgrimage*. London: Grant, 1872.

Dowson, Ernest. "The Cult of the Child." *Critic* 17 Aug. 1889. Reprinted in *The Letters of Ernest Dowson* 433–35.

———. *The Letters of Ernest Dowson*. Ed. Desmond Flower and Henry Maas. London: Cassell, 1967.

"The Dramatic Year.—II." *Stage* 29 Dec. 1904: 16–17.

Drotner, Kirsten. *English Children and Their Magazines, 1715–1945*. New Haven: Yale University Press, 1988.

du Maurier, Angela. *It's Only the Sister*. London: P. Davies, 1951.

E. A. D. "The Cult of the Child." *Hearth and Home* 15 Nov. 1894: 22.

E. R. Review of *Alice in Wonderland*. *Theatre* 1 Jan. 1887. Reprinted in *Theatre*, new ser. 9 (Jan.–June 1887): 48–50.

Edmond, Rod. *Representing the South Pacific: Colonial Discourse from Cook to Gauguin*. Cambridge: Cambridge University Press, 1997.

Edwards, Louise Betts. "The Literary Cult of the Child." *Critic* 39.2 (Aug. 1901): 167–70.

Ellis, Havelock. *Studies in the Psychology of Sex*. Vol. 3: *Analysis of the Sexual Impulse* (1903). Rev. ed. Philadelphia: F. A. Davis, 1913.

England, Alan. *Theatre for the Young*. New York: St. Martin's Press, 1990.

Ewing, Juliana Horatia. *A Great Emergency and Other Tales*. London: G. Bell, 1911.

———. "A Happy Family." In *Melchior's Dream and Other Tales*. London: G. Bell, 1929: 197–209.

———. *Mary's Meadow and Letters from a Little Garden*. London: S.P.C.K., 1886.

———. "Our Field." In *The Brownies and Other Stories*. London: Dent, 1954. 228–40.

———. *We and the World: A Book for Boys*. Boston: Roberts, 1894.

Fielding, Sarah. *The Governess; or, The Little Female Academy*. Ed. Candace Ward. Toronto: Broadview, 2005.

Fields, Armond. *Maude Adams: Idol of American Theater, 1872–1953*. Jefferson, N.C.: McFarland, 2004.

Filon, Augustin. "Child-Worship." *East and West* 1.1 (Nov. 1901): 39–44. Reprinted on pt. 1, reel 6 of *The Empire Writes Back: Indian Views on Britain and Empire, 1810–1915, from the British Library, London*. Microform. Marlborough: Adam Matthew, 2003.

Foulkes, Richard. *Lewis Carroll and the Victorian Stage: Theatricals in a Quiet Life*. Burlington, VT: Ashgate, 2005.

Fowler, Alastair. "Parables of Adventure: The Debatable Novels of Robert Louis Stevenson." In *Nineteenth-Century Scottish Fiction: Critical Essays*. Ed. Ian Campbell. Manchester: Carcanet New Press, 1979.

Franklyn, Cecil W. "'Little Lord Fauntleroy' as a Play, in London." *St. Nicholas* 16.1 (Nov. 1888): 8–10.

Galbraith, Mary. "Hear My Cry: A Manifesto for an Emancipatory Childhood Studies Approach to Children's Literature." *Lion and the Unicorn* 25.2 (April 2001): 187–205.

Gargano, Elizabeth. "Death by Learning: Zymosis and the Perils of School in E. J. May's *Dashwood Priory*." *Children's Literature* 33 (2005): 1–19.

Gatty, Horatia K. F. *Juliana Horatia Ewing and Her Books*. London: Society for Promoting Christian Knowledge, 1887.

Gérin, Winifred. *Anne Thackeray Ritchie: A Biography*. Oxford: Oxford University Press, 1981.

Gielgud, Kate Terry. *Kate Terry Gielgud: An Autobiography*. London: M. Reinhardt, 1953.

Gilbert, Sandra M., and Susan Gubar. *The Madwoman in the Attic: The Woman Writer and the Nineteenth-Century Literary Imagination*. 1979. New Haven: Yale University Press, 1984.

Gillies, Midge. *Marie Lloyd: The One and Only*. London: Victor Gollancz, 1999.

Gillis, John R. *Youth and History: Tradition and Change in European Age Relations, 1770–Present*. Rev. ed. New York: Academic Press, 1981.

Goetsch, Paul. "Old-Fashioned Children: From Dickens to Hardy and James." *Anglia: Zeitschrift für Englische Philologie* 123.1 (2005): 45–69.

Gorham, Deborah. "The 'Maiden Tribute of Modern Babylon' Re-Examined: Child Prostitution and the Idea of Childhood in Late-Victorian England." *Victorian Studies* 21.3 (Spring 1978): 353–79.

"Gotham Gossip." *New Orleans Daily Picayune* 20 Dec. 1888: 2.

Grahame, Kenneth. *The Golden Age*. London: Thomas Nelson, n.d.

———. *The Wind in the Willows*. New York: Penguin Classics, 2005.

Green, Martin. *Dreams of Adventure, Deeds of Empire*. New York: Basic Books, 1979.

———. "The Robinson Crusoe Story." In *Imperialism and Juvenile Literature*. Ed. Jeffrey Richards. Manchester: Manchester University Press, 1989: 34–52.

Green, Peter. *Kenneth Grahame, 1859–1932: A Study of His Life, Work, and Times*. London: John Murray, 1959.

Green, Roger Lancelyn. *Fifty Years of Peter Pan*. London: Davies, 1954.

———. "The Golden Age of Children's Books." *Essays and Studies* 15 (1962): 59–73.

———. *Tellers of Tales*. 1946. Rev. ed. Leicester, UK: E. Ward, 1953.

Gubar, Marah. "The Drama of Precocity: Child Performers on the Victorian Stage." In *The Nineteenth-Century Child and Consumer Culture*. Ed. Dennis Dennisoff. Burlington, VT: Ashgate, 2008: 64–78.

———. "Lewis in Wonderland: The Looking-Glass World of *Sylvie and Bruno*." *Texas Studies in Literature and Language* 48.4 (Winter 2006): 372–94.

———. "Revising the Seduction Paradigm: The Case of Ewing's *The Brownies*." *Children's Literature* 30 (2002): 42–66.

Hall, Donald E. "'We and the World': Juliana Horatia Ewing and Victorian Colonialism for Children." *Children's Literature Association Quarterly* 16.2 (Summer 1991): 51–55.

Hanson, Bruce K. *The Peter Pan Chronicles: The Nearly 100 Year History of "The Boy Who Wouldn't Grow Up."* New York: Birch Lane Press, 1993.

Hardesty, William H., and David D. Mann. "Stevenson's Method in *Treasure Island*: The Old Romance, Retold." *Essays in Literature* 9.2 (Fall 1982): 180–93.

Harrison, Charles. *Theatricals and Tableaux Vivants for Amateurs*. London: L. Upcott Gill, 1882.

Hartnoll, Phyllis, ed. *The Oxford Companion to the Theatre*. 3rd ed. London: Oxford University Press, 1967.

Hemans, Felicia. "Casabianca." In *British Literature 1780–1830*. Ed. Anne K. Mellor and Richard E. Matlak. New York: Harcourt Brace, 1996: 1227.

Hemmings, Robert. "A Taste of Nostalgia: Children's Books from the Golden Age—Carroll, Grahame, and Milne." *Children's Literature* 35 (2007): 54–79.

Henkle, Roger B. "The Mad Hatter's World." *Virginia Quarterly Review* 49 (1973): 99–117.

Higgonet, Anne. *Pictures of Innocence: The History and Crisis of Ideal Childhood*. New York: Thames and Hudson, 1998.

Hilton, Tim. *John Ruskin: The Early Years 1819–1859*. New Haven: Yale University Press, 1985.

Holström, Kirsten Gram. *Monodrama Attitudes Tableaux Vivants: Studies on Some Trends of Theatrical Fashion 1770–1815*. Stockholm: Almquist & Wiksell, 1967.

Honeyman, Susan. *Elusive Childhood: Impossible Representations in Modern Fiction*. Columbus: Ohio State University Press, 2005.

Hood, Thomas. *Fairy Realm: A Collection of the Famous Old Tales*. London: Cassell, Pelter, and Galpin, 1865.

———. *From Nowhere to the North Pole*. London: Chatto and Windus, 1875.

———. *Petsetilla's Posy: A Fairy Tale For Young and Old*. London: Routledge, n.d..

Horn, Pamela. *The Victorian Country Child*. 1974. Stroud, UK: Sutton, 1997.

———. *The Victorian Town Child*. New York: New York University Press, 1997.

Hovet, Grace Ann and Theodore R. "*Tableaux Vivants*: Masculine Vision and Feminine Reflections in Novels by Warner, Alcott, Stowe, and Wharton." *American Transcendental Quarterly* 7.4 (Dec. 1993): 335–56.

Howard, Philip. "Fond Salute to Little Lord Fauntleroy." *Times* 25 May 1974: 3.

Howitt, Mary. *The Children's Year*. London: Longman, Brown, Green, and Longmans, 1847.

Hudson, Glenda A. "Two Is the Beginning of the End: *Peter Pan* and the Doctrine of Reminiscence." *Children's Literature in Education* 37.4 (Dec. 2006): 313–24.

Hughes, Felicity A. "Children's Literature: Theory and Practice." *English Literary History* 45.3 (Autumn 1978): 542–61.

Hughes, M. V. *A London Child of the 1870s*. Oxford: Oxford University Press, 1934.

Hunt, Leigh. "Abstract of Objections to Rosciuscism." *News* 1 Dec. 1805: 232.

———. "Academic Theatre." *News* 4 May 1806: 406.

———. "Academical Theatre." *News* 16 March 1806: 352.

———. "An Accurate List of All the Infant Prodigies of the Dramatic Art, as They Appear at Present before the Public." *News* 19 May 1805: 6.

———. *Critical Essays on the Performers of the London Stage Including General Observations on the Practise and Genius of the Stage*. London: John Hunt, 1807.

———. Review of *The Country Girl*. *News* 24 Nov. 1805: 223.

———. Review of *Roxalana*. *News* 13 April 1806: 381.

———. "Some Remarks on the Merits and Reputation of the Young Roscius." *News* 26 May 1805: 14.

———. "Theatricals." *News* 11 Aug. 1805: 102.

———. "Theatricals." *News* 11 May 1806: 414–15.

Hunt, Peter and Karen Sands. "The View from the Center: British Empire and Post-Empire Children's Literature." In *Voices of the Other: Children's Literature and the Postcolonial Context*. Ed. Roderick McGillis. New York: Garland, 2000: 39–53.

Jackson, David H. "*Treasure Island* as a Late-Victorian Adults' Novel." *Victorian Newsletter* 72 (Fall 1987): 28–32.

Jackson, Tony. "Great Britain." In *International Guide to Children's Theatre and Educational Theatre: A Historical and Geographical Source Book*. Ed. Lowell Swortzell. New York: Greenwood Press, 1990: 113–131.

James, Henry. Review of *Our Mutual Friend. Nation*, 1865. Reprinted in *Dickens: The Critical Heritage*. Ed. Philip Collins. New York: Barnes and Noble, 1971: 469–73.

———."Robert Louis Stevenson." *Century Magazine* Apr. 1888. Reprinted in J. Smith, 123–60.

Jolly, Roslyn. Introduction. In *South Sea Tales*. By Robert Louis Stevenson. Oxford: Oxford University Press, 1996: ix–xxxiii.

Jones, Katharine. "Getting Rid of Children's Literature." *Lion and the Unicorn* 30.3 (Sept. 2006): 287–315.

Jones, Raymond E. Introduction. In *E. Nesbit's Psammead Trilogy: A Children's Classic at 100*. Ed. R. Jones. Lanham, MD: Scarecrow Press, 2006: vii–xxv.

Kiely, Robert. *Robert Louis Stevenson and the Fiction of Adventure*. Cambridge, MA: Harvard University Press, 1964.

Kincaid. James R. *Child-Loving: The Erotic Child and Victorian Culture*. New York: Routledge, 1992.

———. "Dickens and the Construction of the Child." In *Dickens and the Children of Empire*. Ed. Wendy S. Jacobson. New York: Palgrave, 2000. 29–42.

———. *Erotic Innocence: The Culture of Child Molesting*. Durham, NC: Duke University Press, 1998.

Kingsford, Maurice Rooke. *The Life, Work, and Influence of William Henry Giles Kingston*. Toronto: Ryerson Press, 1947.

Kingston, W. H. G. *The Three Midshipmen*. London: Oxford University Press, 1930.

Knoepflmacher, U. C. "Kipling's 'Just-So' Partner: The Dead Child as Collaborator and Muse." *Children's Literature* 25 (1997): 24–49.

———. "Mutations of the Wordsworthian Child of Nature." *Nature and the Victorian Imagination*. Ed. Knoepflmacher and G. B. Tennyson. Berkeley: University of California Press, 1977. 391–425.

———. *Ventures into Childland: Victorians, Fairy Tales, and Femininity*. Chicago: Chicago Press, 1998.

Kucich, John. "Melancholy Magic: Masochism, Stevenson, Anti-Imperialism." *Nineteenth-Century Literature* 56.3 (Dec. 2001): 364–400.

Kutzer, M. Daphne. *Empire's Children: Empire and Imperialism in Classic British Children's Fiction*. New York: Garland, 2000.

Kuznets, Lois R. "Henry James and the Storyteller: The Development of a Central Consciousness in Realistic Fiction for Children." In *The Voice of the Narrator in Children's Literature*. Ed. Charlotte F. Otten and Gary D. Schmidt. New York: Greenwood Press, 1989: 187–98.

Lamb, Charles and Mary Anne. *The Letters of Charles and Mary Anne Lamb*. Ed. Edwin W. Marrs Jr. Vol. 2. Ithaca, NY: Cornell University Press, 1976.

Laski, Marghanita. *Mrs. Ewing, Mrs. Molesworth and Mrs. Hodgson Burnett*. London: Arthur Barker, 1950.

Lavalette, Michael, ed. *A Thing of the Past? Child Labour in Britain in the Nineteenth and Twentieth Centuries*. New York: St. Martin's Press, 1999.

Leach, Karoline. *In the Shadow of the Dreamchild: A New Understanding of Lewis Carroll*. London: Peter Owen, 1999.

Lebailly, Hugues. "C. L. Dodgson and the Victorian Cult of the Child." *Carrollian* 4 (1999): 3–31.

Leech, John. *Picture of Life and Character*. London: Bradbury and Evans, 1854.

Lerner, Laurence. *Angels and Absences: Child Deaths in the Nineteenth Century*. Nashville: Vanderbuilt University Press, 1997.

Lesnik-Oberstein, Karín. *Children's Literature: Criticism and the Fictional Child*. New York: Oxford University Press, 1994.

———. "Children's Literature: New Approaches." Introduction. In *Children's Literature: New Approaches*. Ed. Lesnik-Oberstein. New York: Palgrave Macmillan, 2004: 1–24.

Letley, Emma. Introduction. In *Treasure Island*. By Robert Louis Stevenson. Oxford: Oxford University Press, 1985: vii–xxiii.

"The Letter-Box." *St. Nicholas* 17.2 (May 1890–Oct. 1890): 628–30.

Lillie, Lucy C. "'Fauntleroy' and Elsie Leslie Lyde." *St. Nicholas* 16.6 (April 1889): 402–13.

Linehan, Katherine Bailey. "Taking Up with Kanakas: Stevenson's Complex Social Criticism in 'The Beach of Falesá.'" *English Literature in Transition, 1880–1920* 33.4 (1990): 407–22.

Linnane, Fergus. *Madams: Bawds and Brother-Keepers of London*. Stroud, UK: Sutton, 2005.

Lodge, David. "Fire and Eyre: Charlotte Brontë's War of Earthly Elements." In *Language of Fiction: Essays in Criticism and Verbal Analysis of the English Novel*. 1966. New York: Routledge, 2002: 120–152.

Lovett, Charles C. *Alice on Stage: A History of the Early Theatrical Productions of Alice in Wonderland*. Westport, CT: Meckler, 1990.

Loxley, Diana. *Problematic Shores: The Literature of Islands*. New York: St. Martin's Press, 1990.

Lucas, E. V. Review of *The Wind in the Willows*. *Times Literary Supplement* 354 (22 Oct. 1908): 362.

Lurie, Alison. *Don't Tell the Grown-Ups: Why Kids Love the Books They Do*. New York: Avon Books, 1990.

Mackenzie, Compton. *My Life and Times: Octave Two 1891–1900*. London: Chatto and Windus, 1963.

Maher, Susan Naramore. "Recasting Crusoe: Frederick Marryat, R. M. Ballantyne and the Nineteenth-Century Robinsonade." *Children's Literature Association Quarterly* 13.4 (Winter 1988): 169–75.

Maixner, Paul, ed. *Robert Louis Stevenson: The Critical Heritage*. London: Routledge and Kegan Paul, 1981.

Manlove, Colin. *The Impulse of Fantasy Literature*. Kent, OH: Kent State University Press, 1983.

Marryat, Frederick. *Masterman Ready, or, The Wreck of the Pacific. The Complete Works of Captain Frederick Marryat*. Boston: Aldine, 1912.

Mavor, Carol. *Pleasures Taken: Performances of Sexuality and Loss in Victorian Photographs*. Durham, NC: Duke University Press, 1995.

Maxwell, Christabel. *Mrs. Gatty and Mrs. Ewing*. London: Constable, 1949.

May, Margaret. "Innocence and Experience: The Evolution of the Concept of Juvenile Delinquency in the Mid–nineteenth Century." *Victorian Studies* 18.1 (Sept. 1973): 7–29.

Mayhew, Henry. *London Labour and the London Poor*. Ed. Victor Neuburg. New York: Penguin, 1985.

McCaslin, Nellie. *Theatre for Children in the United States: A History*. Norman: University of Oklahoma Press, 1971.

McGavran, James Holt, ed. *Literature and the Child: Romantic Continuations, Postmodern Contestations*. Iowa City: University of Iowa Press, 1999.

———. *Romanticism and Children's Literature in Nineteenth-Century England*. Athens: University of Georgia Press, 1991.

McGillis, Roderick. *A Little Princess: Gender and Empire*. New York: Twayne, 1996.

McLean, Robert Simpson. "How 'The Infant Phenomenon' Began the World: The Managing of Jean Margaret Davenport (182?–1903)." *Dickensian* 88.3 (1992): 133–53.

Meadowcroft, Clara. "At the Children's Matinée." *St. Nicholas* Feb. 1914: 351–57.

Meredith, George. *Letters of George Meredith*. Vol. 2. Ed. C. L. Cline. Oxford: Oxford University Press, 1970.

Millais, John Everett. *The Life and Letters of Sir John Everett Millais*. London: Methuen, 1899.

Molesworth, Mary Louisa. *The Boys and I: A Child's Story for Children*. London: Routledge, 1883.

———. *The Girls and I: A Veracious History*. London: Macmillan, 1892.

Moore, Doris Langley. *E. Nesbit: A Biography*. London: Ernest Benn, 1933. Rev. ed. Philadelphia: Chilton, 1966.

Moore, John Robert. "Defoe, Stevenson, and the Pirates." *English Literary History* 10.1 (March 1943): 35–60.

Morgenstern, John. "The Rise of Children's Literature Reconsidered." *Children's Literature Association Quarterly* 26.2 (Summer 2001): 64–73.

Morley, Malcolm. "Dickens Goes to the Theatre." *Dickensian* 59 (1963): 165–71.

———. "More about Crummles." *Dickensian* 59 (1963): 51–56.

———. "Where Crummles Played." *Dickensian* 58 (1962): 23–9.

Morris, Frankie. "Alice and King Chess." *Jabberwocky* 12.4: 75–90.

Mortimer, Favell Lee. *The Peep of Day: A Series of the Earliest Religious Instruction the Infant Mind is Capable of Receiving*. 1833. London: T. Nelson and Sons, 1893.

Moss, Anita. "E. Nesbit's Romantic Child in Modern Dress." In McGavran, ed., *Romanticism*, 225–47.

———. "The Story of the Treasure Seekers: The Idiom of Childhood." *Touchstones Reflections on the Best in Children's Literature.* Ed. Perry Nodelman. Vol. 1. West Lafayette, IN: ChLA, 1985: 188–97.

———. "Varieties of Children's Metafiction." *Studies in the Literary Imagination* 18.2 (Fall 1985): 79–92.

Mulvey, Laura. "Visual Pleasure and Narrative Cinema." *Screen* 1975. Reprinted in *The Feminism and Visual Culture Reader.* Ed. Amelia Jones. London: Routledge, 2003: 44–53.

"Music and the Drama." *Appletons' Journal of Literature, Science and Art* 5 June 1875: 729–31.

Myers, Mitzi. "Reading Children and Homeopathic Romanticism: Paradigm Lost, Revisionary Gleam, or 'Plus Ça Change, Plus C'est la Même Chose'?" In McGavran, *Literature* 44–84.

———. "Romancing the Moral Tale: Maria Edgeworth and the Problematics of Pedagogy." In McGavran, *Romanticism*, 96–128.

Nel, Philip. "Is There a Text in This Advertising Campaign? Literature, Marketing, and Harry Potter." *Lion and the Unicorn* 29.2 (April 2005): 236–67.

———. *J. K. Rowling's Harry Potter Novels: A Reader's Guide.* New York: Continuum, 2001.

Nesbit, E. *The Enchanted Castle.* New York: Puffin Books, 1994

———. *Five Children and It.* New York: Puffin Books, 1996.

———. *Harding's Luck.* New York: Books of Wonder, 1998.

———. *The House of Arden.* New York: Books of Wonder, 1997.

———. *New Treasure Seekers.* New York: Puffin Books, 1996.

———. *Oswald Bastable and Others.* London: Ernest Benn, 1960.

———. *The Phoenix and the Carpet.* New York: Puffin Books, 1994.

———. *The Railway Children.* New York: Puffin Books, 1994.

———. *The Story of the Treasure Seekers.* New York: Puffin Books, 1994.

———. *The Wouldbegoods.* New York: Puffin Books, 1995.

Nickel, Douglas R. *Dreaming in Pictures: The Photography of Lewis Carroll.* New Haven: Yale University Press, 2002.

Nicoll, Allardyce. *A History of English Drama 1660–1900.* Vol. 4. Cambridge: Cambridge University Press, 1955.

"'Nixie' at Terry's." *Era* 12 April 1890: 8.

Nodelman, Perry. "The Case of Children's Fiction: Or The Impossibility of Jacqueline Rose." *Children's Literature Association Quarterly* 10.3 (Fall 1985): 98–100.

———. "Fear of Children's Literature: What's Left (or Right) after Theory?" In *Reflections of Change: Children's Literature Since 1945.* Ed. Sandra L. Beckett. Westport, CT: Greenwood Press, 1997: 3–14.

———. "The Other: Orientalism, Colonialism, and Children's Literature." *Children's Literature Association Quarterly* 17.1 (Spring 1992): 29–35.

———. "The Precarious Life of Children's Literature Criticism." *Canadian Children's Literature* 33.2 (2007): 1–16.

"An Old Fairy Tale." *Nation* 18 Oct. 1866: 307–9.

"Our Musical-Box." *Theatre* 1 Aug. 1887. Reprinted in *Theatre* 10 (July-Dec. 1887): 88–94.

"Our Omnibus-Box." *Theatre* 1 May 1882. Reprinted in *Theatre* 5, new ser. (Jan.–June 1882): 306–20.

"Our Representative at the Summer Theatres." *Punch* 25 Aug 1877: 83–84.

Paquette, Gabriel B. "The Image of Imperial Spain in British Political Thought, 1750–1800." *Bulletin of Spanish Studies* 81.2 (2004): 187–214.

Pearsall, Ronald. *The Worm in the Bud: The World of Victorian Sexuality*. Stroud, UK: Sutton, 2003.

Peter Pan's Postbag: Letters to Pauline Chase. London: Heinemann, 1909.

Petzold, Dieter. "A Race Apart: Children in Late Victorian and Edwardian Children's Books." *Children's Literature Association Quarterly* 17.3 (Fall 1992): 33–36.

Pinchbeck, Ivy, and Margaret Hewitt. *Children in English Society*. Two Vols. London: Routledge and Kegan Paul, 1973.

Plotz, Judith. "Literary Ways of Killing a Child: The Nineteenth-Century Practice." In *Aspects and Issues in the History of Children's Literature*. Ed. Maria Nikolajeva. Westport, CT: Greenwood Press, 1995: 1–24.

———. *Romanticism and the Vocation of Childhood*. New York: Palgrave, 2001.

Polhemus, Robert M. "Lewis Carroll and the Child in Victorian Fiction." In *The Columbia History of the British Novel*. Ed. John Richetti. New York: Columbia University Press, 1994: 579–607.

Poss, Geraldine D. "An Epic in Arcadia: The Pastoral World of *The Wind in the Willows*." *Children's Literature* 4 (1975): 80–90.

Pratt, Mary Louise. *Imperial Eyes: Travel Writing and Transculturation*. New York: Routledge, 1992.

"Precocious Children." *British Mothers' Journal and Domestic Magazine* 77 (1 May 1862): 97–99.

"Precocious Children." *Lady's Newspaper* 21 June 1856: 2.

"Precocious Children." *Young Folks Paper* 21 Jan. 1888: 38.

Prickett, Stephen. *Victorian Fantasy*. 1979. 2nd rev. Ed. Waco, TX: Baylor University Press, 2005.

Rands, William Brighty. "Children and Children's Books." *Argosy* 2.12 (Nov. 1866): 464–69.

———. *Lilliput Levee: Poems of Childhood Child-Fancy and Child-Like Moods*. New York: Wynkoop and Sherwood, 1868.

Ransome, Arthur. "Betwixt and Between." *Bookman* (UK) Jan. 1909: 190–91.

Ray, Laura Krugman. "Kenneth Grahame and the Literature of Childhood." *English Literature in Transition, 1880–1920* 20.1 (1977): 3–12.

Reid, Julia. "Robert Louis Stevenson and the 'Romance of Anthropology.'" *Journal of Victorian Culture* 10.1 (Spring 2005): 46–71.

Reimer, Mavis. "Treasure Seekers and Invaders: E. Nesbit's Cross-writing of the Bastables." *Children's Literature* 25 (1997): 50–59.

Remnits, Virginia Yeaman. Review of *The Golden Age*. *Bookman* (U.S.) Aug.–Sept. 1895: 48–50.

Review of *Alice in Wonderland*. *Era* 25 Dec. 1886: 9

Review of *Alice in Wonderland*. *Era* 29 Dec. 1888: 18.

Review of *Alice in Wonderland*. *Era* 24 Dec. 1898: 12.

Review of *Alice in Wonderland*. *Times* 24 Dec. 1886: 4.
Review of *Alice in Wonderland*. *Times* 23 Dec. 1898: 4.
Review of Baby Benson. *Era* 24 Dec. 1876: 12.
Review of *The Children's Pinafore*. *Era* 14 Dec. 1879: 7.
Review of *The Children's Pinafore*. *Theatre* 1 Jan. 1880. Reprinted in *Theatre* new ser. 4 (Jan.–June 1880): 38–39.
Review of "The Children's *Pirates of Penzance*." *Era* 27 Dec. 1884: 15.
Review of *The Country Girl*. *Times* 25. Nov. 1805: 4.
Review of *Dick Whittington and His Cat*. *Era* 30 Dec. 1882: 4–5.
Review of *The Forty Thieves, and Their Wonderful Cave*. *Times* 28 Dec. 1888: 4.
Review of *The Golden Age*. *Spectator* 25 Jan. 1896: 140–41.
Review of *Hamlet*. *Times* 11 Dec. 1817: 2.
Review of *The House that Jack Built*. *Era* 29 Dec. 1894: 7.
Review of *John Bull*. *Times* 22 Dec. 1817: 3.
Review of *Little Goody Two Shoes*, by E. L. Blanchard. *Era* 24 Dec. 1876: 12–13.
Review of *Little Goody Two Shoes*, by Rosina Filippi and Andrew Levey. *Era* 29 Dec. 1888: 8.
Review of *Little Lord Fauntleroy*, by F. H. Burnett. *Illustrated London News* 4 Jan. 1902: 2.
Review of *Little Lord Fauntleroy*, by E. V. Seebohm. *Daily Telegraph* 24 Feb. 1888: 3.
Review of *Little Lord Fauntleroy*, by E. V. Seebohm. *Illustrated London News* 3 Mar. 1888: 26.
Review of *A Little Un-Fairy Princess*. *Illustrated London News* 27 Dec. 1902: 979.
Review of *A Little Un-Fairy Princess*. *Times* 22 Dec. 1902: 11.
Review of Living Miniatures. *Era* 30 Dec. 1866: 10–11.
Review of Living Miniatures. *Times* 15 Jan. 1867: 7.
Review of *Peter Pan*. *Times* 28 Dec. 1904: 4.
Review of *The Prince and the Pauper*. *Era* 19 Apr. 1890: 8.
Review of *The Real Little Lord Fauntleroy*. *Era* 19 May 1888: 9.
Review of *The Real Little Lord Fauntleroy*. *Illustrated London News* 19 May 1888: 533.
Review of *The Real Little Lord Fauntleroy*. *Times* 15 May 1888: 10.
Review of *Robin Hood and His Merry Little Men*. *Era* 30 Dec. 1877: 13.
Review of *Robin Hood and His Merry Little Men*. *Times* 27 Dec. 1877: 8
Review of *Shock-Headed Peter*. *Illustrated London News* 21 Dec. 1901: 952.
Review of *Shock-Headed Peter*. *Times* 27 Dec. 1900: 8.
Review of *Shock-Headed Peter*. *Times* 17 Dec. 1901: 13.
Review of *Shock-Headed Peter*. *Times* 23 Dec. 1912: 8.
Review of *The Water-Babies*. *Dublin Review* 1.1 (July 1863): 257–58.
Review of *The Wind in the Willows*. *Punch* 11 Nov. 1908: 360.
Richards, Jeffrey, ed. *Imperialism and Juvenile Literature*. Manchester: Manchester University Press, 1989.
Richardson, Alan. *Literature, Education, and Romanticism: Reading as Social Practice 1780–1832*. Cambridge: Cambridge University Press, 1994.
———. "Wordsworth, Fairy Tales, and the Politics of Children's Reading." In McGavran, *Romanticism* 34–53.

Rigby, Elizabeth. "Children's Books." *Quarterly Review* 74 (June and Oct. 1844): 1–26.

———. Review of *Vanity Fair* and *Jane Eyre*. *Quarterly Review* 84 (Dec. 1848 and Mar. 1849): 153–85.

Robson, Catherine. *Men in Wonderland: The Lost Girlhood of the Victorian Gentleman*. Princeton: Princeton University Press, 2001.

Robson, W. W. "E. Nesbit and *The Book of Dragons*." In *Children and Their Books: A Celebration of the Work of Iona and Peter Opie*. Ed. Gillian Avery and Julia Briggs. Oxford: Clarendon Press, 1989: 251–70.

Roe, Nicholas. *Fiery Heart: The First Life of Leigh Hunt*. London: Pimlico 2005.

Roscoe, William Caldwell. "Fictions for Children." *Prospective Review* Feb. 1855. Reprinted in Salway, 23–45.

Rose, Jacqueline. *The Case of Peter Pan: or, The Impossibility of Children's Fiction*. 1984 Rev. ed. Philadelphia: University of Pennsylvania Press, 1992.

Roth, Christine. "Babes in Boy-Land J. M. Barrie and the Edwardian Girl." In *J. M. Barrie's "Peter Pan" In and Out of Time: A Children's Classic at 100*. Ed. Donna R. White and C. Anita Tarr. Lanham, MD: Scarecrow Press, 2006: 47–67.

Rothstein, Jamie. "Robert Louis Stevenson's Anti-Imperialism." Diss. Northern Illinois University, 1995.

Rothwell, Erika. "'You Catch It If You Try to Do Otherwise': The Limitations of E. Nesbit's Cross-Written Vision of the Child." *Children's Literature* 25 (1997): 60–70.

Rousseau, Jean-Jacques. *Emile: or, On Education*. Trans. Allan Bloom. New York: Basic Books, 1979.

Rudd, David. "Theorising and Theories: The Conditions of Possibility of Children's Literature." *International Companion Encyclopedia of Children's Literature*. Ed. Peter Hunt. 2nd ed. London: Routledge, 2004: 29–43.

Ruskin, John. "Fairy Stories." Introduction. In *German Popular Stories*. By the Brothers Grimm. Ed. Edgar Taylor. London: John Camden Hotten, 1868. Reprinted in Salway, 127–32.

———. *The Gulf of Years: Letters from John Ruskin to Kathleen Olander*. Ed. Rayner Unwin. London: Allen and Unwin, 1953.

———. *The Winnington Letters: John Ruskin's Correspondence with Margaret Alexis Bell and the Children at Winnington Hall*. Ed. Van Akin Burd. Cambridge, MA: Harvard University Press, 1969.

———. *The Works of John Ruskin*. 39 vols. Ed. E. T. Cook and Alexander Wedderburn. London: George Allen, 1903–12.

Saki. (H. H. Munro). *The Unbearable Bassington*. New York: Viking Press, 1929.

Salazar, Laura Gardner. "The Emergence of Children's Theatre, A Study in America's Changing Values and the Stage, 1900 to 1910." *Theatre History Studies* 7 (1987): 73–83.

Salmon, Edward. *Juvenile Literature as It Is*. London: Henry J. Drane, 1888.

———. "Literature for the Little Ones." *Nineteenth Century* 128 (Oct. 1887): 563–80.

———. "Should Children Have a Special Literature?" *Parent's Review* 1890. Reprinted in Salway, 332–39.

Salway, Lance, ed. *A Peculiar Gift: Nineteenth–Century Writings on Books for Children*. Harmondsworth, UK: Kestrel Books, 1976.

Sandison, Alan. *Robert Louis Stevenson and the Appearance of Modernism: A Future Feeling*. London: Macmillan, 1996.

Sandner, David. *Romanticism and Transcendence in Nineteenth-Century Children's Fantasy Literature*. Westport, CT: Greenwood, 1996.

Schwartz, Lynne Sharon. Afterword. *A Little Princess*. New York: Signet Classic, 1990: 223–35.

Schwartz, Murray M. "Where Is Literature?" In *Transitional Objects and Potential Spaces: Literary Uses of D. W. Winnicott*. Ed. Peter L. Rudnytsky. New York: Columbia University Press, 1993: 50–62.

Scott, Clement. Review of *Little Lord Fauntleroy*, by E. V. Seebohm. *Daily Telegraph* 24 Feb. 1888: 3.

Shand, Alexander Innes. "Children Yesterday and Today." *Quarterly Review* Apr. 1896. Reprinted in Salway, 77–91.

Shaw, Bernard. *Collected Letters 1898–1910*. Ed. Dan H. Lawrence. London: Max Reinhardt, 1972.

———. "The Unhappy Years of Barrie." *Sunday Graphic and Sunday News* 20 June 1937. Reprinted in *The Drama Observed*. Vol. 4: 1911–1950. Ed. Bernard F. Dukore. University Park: Pennsylvania State University Press, 1993: 1479–81.

———. "Van Amburgh Revived." *Dramatic Opinions and Essays, with an Apology*. Vol. 2. New York: Brentano's, 1928: 455–62.

Shepard, Ernest H. *Drawn from Memory*. New York: Lippincott, 1957.

Sherwood, Mary Martha. *The History of the Fairchild Family; or, The Child's Manual; Being a Collection of Stories Calculated to Show the Importance and Effects of a Religious Education*. Part 1. 20th ed. London: T. Hatchard, 1854.

Showalter, Elaine. *A Literature of Their Own: British Women Novelists from Brontë to Lessing*. Rev. ed. Princeton: Princeton University Press, 1999.

Smith, Janet Adam, ed. *Henry James and Robert Louis Stevenson: A Record of Friendship and Criticism*. London: Rupert Hart-Davis, 1948.

Smith, Lindsay. *The Politics of Focus: Women, Children, and Nineteenth-Century Photography*. New York: Manchester University Press, 1998.

Spilka, Mark. "On the Enrichment of Poor Monkeys by Myth and Dream; or, How Dickens Rousseauisticized and Pre-Freudianized Victorian Views of Childhood." In *Sexuality and Victorian Literature*. Ed. Don Richard Cox. Knoxville: University of Tennessee Press, 1984: 161–79.

Steedman, Carolyn. *Strange Dislocations: Childhood and the Idea of Human Interiority 1780–1930*. Cambridge, MA: Harvard University Press, 1994.

Stephens, John. *Language and Ideology in Children's Fiction*. New York: Longman, 1992.

Stevenson, Robert Louis. "A Gossip on Romance." In *The Lantern-Bearers and Other Essays*. Ed. Jeremy Treglown. New York: Cooper Square Press, 1988: 172–82.

———. "A Humble Remonstrance." In *The Lantern-Bearers and Other Essays*. Ed. Jeremy Treglown. New York: Cooper Square Press, 1988: 192–201.

———. *The Letters of Robert Louis Stevenson*. Ed. Bradford A. Booth and Ernest Mehew. 7 vols. New Haven: Yale University Press, 1994–95.

———. *Treasure Island*. Ed. Emma Letley. Oxford: Oxford University Press, 1985.

Streatfeild, Noel. *Ballet Shoes, A Story of Three Children on the Stage*. London: Dent, 1936.

Stretton, Hesba. *Max Krömer: A Story of the Siege of Strasbourg*. London: Religious Tract Society, n.d.

Sully, J. "The Child in Recent English Literature." *Fortnightly Review* new ser. 61 (Jan.–June 1897): 218–28.

Summerfield, Geoffrey. *Fantasy and Reason: Children's Literature in the Eighteenth Century*. Athens: University of Georgia Press, 1984.

Susina, Jan. "Educating Alice: The Lessons of *Wonderland*." *Jabberwocky* 18 (Winter–Spring 1989): 3–9.

———. "Textual Building Blocks: Charles Dickens and E. Nesbit's Literary Borrowings in *Five Children and It*." In *E. Nesbit's Psammead Trilogy: A Children's Classic at 100*. Ed. Raymond E. Jones. Lanham, MD: Scarecrow Press, 2006: 151–68.

Sutphin, Christine. "Victorian Childhood. Reading beyond the 'Innocent Title': *Home Thoughts and Home Scenes*." In *Children's Literature: New Approaches*. Ed. Karín Lesnik-Oberstein. New York: Palgrave, 2004: 51–77.

Sweet, Matthew. *Inventing the Victorians*. London: Faber and Faber, 2001.

Tableaux, Charades, and Conundrums. Metropolitan pamphlet ser. 6.4. London: Butterick, 1893.

Taylor, Roger. "'All in the Golden Afternoon': The Photographs of Charles Lutwidge Dodgson." In Taylor and Wakeling, *Lewis Carroll*, 1–120.

Taylor, Roger, and Edward Wakeling. *Lewis Carroll, Photographer: The Princeton University Library Albums*. Princeton: Princeton University Press, 2002.

Tennyson, Alfred. *The Poems of Tennyson*. Ed. Christopher Ricks. London: Longman, 1969.

Thacker, Deborah. "Disdain or Ignorance? Literary Theory and the Absence of Children's Literature." *Lion and the Unicorn* 24.1 (Jan. 2000): 1–17.

Thackeray, W. M. *The Letters and Private Papers of William Makepeace Thackeray*. Ed. Gordon N. Ray. 4 vols. Cambridge, MA: Harvard University Press, 1945–46.

———. *The Rose and the Ring*. Facsimile ed. New York: Pierpont Morgan Library, 1947.

———. *Vanity Fair*. Ed. J. I. M. Stewart. New York: Penguin Classics, 1985.

Thornton, Sara. "The Vanity of Childhood: Constructing, Deconstructing, and Destroying the Child in the Novel of the 1840s." In *Children in Culture: Approaches to Childhood*. Ed. Karín Lesnik-Oberstein. New York: St. Martin's Press, 1998: 122–50.

Thwaite, Ann. *Waiting for the Party: The Life of Frances Hodgson Burnett 1849–1924*. New York: Scribner's, 1974.

Tindal, Marcus. "Baby Actors." *Pearson's Magazine* 3 (June 1897): 678–83.

Tosh, John. *A Man's Place: Masculinity and the Middle-Class Home in Victorian England*. New Haven: Yale University Press, 2007.

Townsend, John Rowe. *Written for Children: An Outline of English Children's Literature*. London: Miller, 1965.

Twain, Mark. *Adventures of Huckleberry Finn*. Berkeley: University of California Press, 1985.

Varty, Anne. *Children and Theatre in Victorian Britain: "All Work, No Play."* New York: Palgrave Macmillan, 2008.

von Koppenfels, Werner. "Vision and Wonderland: Romantic Perspectives in the Golden Age of Children's Fiction." In *Beyond the Suburbs of the Mind: Exploring English Romanticism*. Ed. Michael Gassenmeier and Norbert H. Platz. Essen: Verlag Die Blaue Eule, 1987: 55–78.

Voskuil, Lynn M. *Acting Naturally: Victorian Theatricality and Authenticity*. Charlottesville: University of Virginia Press, 2004.

Waggoner, Diane. "Photographing Childhood: Lewis Carroll and Alice." In *Picturing Children: Constructions of Childhood Between Rousseau and Freud*. Ed. Marilyn R. Brown. Burlington, VT: Ashgate, 2002: 149–66.

Wagner, Vivian. "Unsettling Oz: Technological Anxieties in the Novels of L. Frank Baum." *Lion and the Unicorn* 30.1 (Jan. 2006): 25–53.

Walkowitz, Judith R. *City of Dreadful Delight: Narratives of Sexual Danger in Late-Victorian London*. Chicago: University of Chicago Press, 1992.

Wall, Barbara. *The Narrator's Voice: The Dilemma of Children's Fiction*. London: Macmillan, 1991.

Walsh, Sue. "Child / Animal: It's the 'Real' Thing." *Yearbook of English Studies* 32 (2002): 151–62.

Walton, Mrs. O. F. *A Peep Behind the Scenes*. London: Religious Tract Society, n.d.

Ward, Hayden W. " 'The Pleasure of Your Heart': *Treasure Island* and the Appeal of Boys' Adventure Fiction." *Studies in the Novel* 6.3 (Fall 1974): 304–17.

Ward, Winifred. *Theatre for Children*. Anchorage, KY: Children's Theatre Press, 1958.

Waters, Hazel. " 'That Astonishing Clever Child': Performers and Prodigies in the Early and Mid-Victorian Theatre." *Theatre Notebook* 50.2 (1996): 78–94.

Watson, Harold Francis. *Coasts of Treasure Island: A Study of the Backgrounds and Sources for Robert Louis Stevenson's Romance of the Sea*. San Antonio, TX: Company, 1969.

Watson, Jeanie. "*The Raven: A Christmas Poem*: Coleridge and the Fairy Tale Controversy." In McGavran, *Romanticism* 14–33.

Watts, Theodore. "The New Hero." *English Illustrated Magazine* 3 (Dec. 1883): 181–190.

Wedmore, Frederick. Review of *Little Lord Fauntleroy*, by F. H. Burnett. *Academy* 22 Sept. 1888: 195.

Weeks, Jeffrey. *Sex, Politics and Society: The Regulation of Sexuality since 1800*. London: Longman, 1981.

Wertheim, Albert. "Childhood in John Leech's *Pictures of Life and Character*." *Victorian Studies* 17.1 (Sept. 1973): 75–87.

West, Philip. "Are Children Happier Than They Were?" *Quiver* 43 (Nov. 1908): 1154–56.

"What Children Like to Read." *Pall Mall Gazette* 24 June 1898: 1–2.

The White Cat. Advertisement. *Times* 30 Dec. 1904: 5.

White, Donna R., and C. Anita Tarr. Introduction. In *J. M. Barrie's "Peter Pan" In and Out of Time: A Children's Classic at 100*. Lanham, MD: Scarecrow Press, 2006: vii–xxvi.

Wilkie, Christine. "Digging Up *The Secret Garden*: Noble Innocents or Little Savages?" *Children's Literature in Education* 28.2 (1997): 73–83.

Williams, David. *Genesis and Exodus: A Portrait of the Benson Family*. London: Hamish Hamilton, 1979.

Wilson, A. E. *King Panto: The Story of Pantomime*. New York: Dutton, 1935.

Wilson, Ann. "Hauntings: Anxiety, Technology, and Gender in *Peter Pan*." *Modern Drama* 43.4 (Winter 2000): 595–610.

Wilson, Anna. "Little Lord Fauntleroy: The Darling of Mothers and the Abomination of a Generation." *American Literary History* 8.2 (Summer 1996): 232–58.

Winnicott, D. W. *Playing and Reality*. 1971. Routledge: New York, 1997.

Wood, Mrs. Henry. *East Lynn*. Ed. Norman Page and Kamal Al-Solaylee. London: Dent, 1994.

Wood, Naomi J. "Gold Standards and Silver Subversions: *Treasure Island* and the Romance of Money." *Children's Literature* 26 (1998): 61–85.

Woolf, Virginia. "Lewis Carroll." 1939. Reprinted in *The Moment and Other Essays*. New York: Harcourt, Brace, 1948: 81–83.

Wordsworth, William. "Anecdote for Fathers." Reprinted in *William Wordsworth*. Ed. Stephen Gill. Oxford: Oxford University Press, 1984: 81–83.

———. "Michael: A Pastoral Poem." Reprinted in *William Wordsworth*. Ed. Stephen Gill. Oxford: Oxford University Press, 1984: 224–36.

———. "Ode: Intimations of Immortality from Recollections of Early Childhood." Reprinted in *The Norton Anthology of Poetry*. 3rd edition. Ed. Alexander W. Allison, et al. New York: Norton, 1983: 551–55.

———. *The Prelude 1799, 1805, 1850*. New York: Norton, 1979.

"The Worship of Children." *Spectator* 6 Nov. 1869: 1298–1300.

"Writers for the Young." *Chambers's Journal* 1.45 (Oct. 1898): 716–20.

Wullschläger, Jackie. *Inventing Wonderland: The Lives and Fantasies of Lewis Carroll, Edward Lear, J. M. Barrie, Kenneth Grahame and A. A. Milne*. New York: Free Press, 1995.

Wyss, J. D. *The Swiss Family Robinson*. Trans. William H. G. Kingston. New York: Puffin, 1994.

Yonge, Charlotte. "Children's Literature of the Last Century." *Macmillan's Magazine* 20 (May–Oct. 1869): 229–37; 302–30; 448–56.

Young, William C. *Famous Actors and Actresses on the American Stage*. Vol. 1. New York: Bowker, 1975.

Zelizer, Viviana A. *Pricing the Priceless Child: The Changing Social Value of Children*. New York: Basic Books, 1985 [Princeton: Princeton University Press, 1994].

Zipes, Jack, Lissa Paul, Lynne Vallone, Peter Hunt, and Gillian Avery, eds. *The Norton Anthology of Children's Literature: The Traditions in English*. New York: Norton, 2005.

Zornado, Joseph L. *Inventing the Child: Culture, Ideology, and the Story of Childhood*. New York: Garland, 2001.

INDEX

à Beckett, Gilbert, 166–67
Academic Theatre, 159, 225n.17
Acting Naturally (Voskuil), 172
active literacy: Burnett's promotion of, 35–38; Carroll's promotion of, 92, 110–24; children's literature and, 28–29, 38, 42, 127–48, 180–81, 209, 214n.30, 228n.1; Nesbit's promotion of, 129–48; Stevenson's promotion of, 71, 91
Acton, William, 204
Actress of All Work, An (play), 161
Adams, Jad, 154
Adams, Maude, 200–201, 203, 231nn.24, 26
Adams, W. Davenport, 185, 188, 201
Adela Cathcart (Ruskin), 213n.21
adolescence, emergence of concept of, 152
adult–child collaboration: in Carroll's work, 95–98, 101, 112–24; child performers and, 158–59; emergence of, 6–10, 212n.5; in stories featuring child narrators, 49–53, 58–61, 76; in *Treasure Island,* 81–92; as trope in children's literature, 6–10, 42, 212n.5
Adventures of Huckleberry Finn (Twain), 40, 44–45, 216n.3, 217n.5, 218n.13
Adventures of Tom Sawyer, The (Twain), 28
adventure stories: boys as heroes of, 69; Ewing's treatment of, 63–68; imperialist and anti-imperialist ideology in, 70–92
Adye, Frederic, 196
age categories, child performers and, 174, 227n.31
age of consent laws, 152, 224n.4
"Age of Innocence. From the picture in the Vernon Gallery" (Carroll cartoon), 93–95, 99
Age of Innocence, The (Reynolds painting), 93–95, 99, 102
Aiken, Lucy, 150
Ainger, Alfred, 21
Alcott, Louisa May, 5, 126, 164–65
Aldington, Richard, 80
Alice's Adventures in Wonderland (Carroll), 9, 21, 93–98, 110–24, 223n.1; identity in, 5–6; prefatory poem in, 96–98; self-reflexivity in, 92, 126–27; theatrical versions of, 170, 183, 186, 189–91, 193, 199, 229nn.9–10, 230n.22
Allen, William, 152
"All in the Golden Afternoon" (Carroll), 96–98, 208–9
Altick, Richard D., 103
Andersen, Hans Christian, 37, 191, 203
"Anecdote for Fathers" (Wordsworth), 122–23, 221n.16
Anne of Green Gables (Montgomery), 28, 217n.6
Anstey, F., 135, 213n.16
anti–adventure stories: Ewing's works as examples of, 63–68; Stevenson's works as example of, 70–92
anti-imperialist ideology in children's literature, 59–62, 216nn.40, 42, 217n.7, 218n.21
anti-Semitism, in Nesbit's fiction, 145–46, 223n.14
Arabian Nights, 37, 59, 132, 135
Ariès, Philippe, 34
Artful Dodger (Dickens character), 3, 153, x
At the Back of the North Wind (MacDonald), 21
Auerbach, Nina, 95, 97, 105, 111
"Auguries of Innocence" (Blake), 26
Aunt Judy's Magazine, 12
Austin, Linda M., 174
Austin, Stella, 179
Avery, Gillian, 214nn.27,40, 216n.6

"Babyolatry" (anon.), 10–11, 167, 177, 180
Bacile di Castiglione, Claudia, 52
Baden-Powell, Robert (Lord), 40

"Bad Habit, A" (Ewing), 40
Ballantyne, R. M., 64–66, 77, 85, 90
Ballet Shoes (Streatfeild), 164
Banerjee, Jacqueline, 212n.7
Barlee, Ellen, 9, 165–66, 171–72, 184
Barrie, J. M., 4–7, 86, 211n.1, 220n.2; children's theatre and, 175, 183, 189, 198–209; criticism of, 125–26, 198–99, 202, 204; cult of the child and, 9, 14, 149, 156, 174–79; Llewelyn Davies family and, 175–76, 201–2, 208–9; on performers, 168–79
Barthes, Roland, 117
Bathers, The (Tuke painting), 177
Baum, L. Frank, 64
"Beach of Falesá, The" (Stevenson), 78–79
Beerbohm, Max, 125, 167–68, 198–99, 203
"Beggar-Maid, The" (Carroll photograph), 104–5
"Beggar-Maid, The" (Tennyson), 101, 104–5
beggars, in Nesbit's fiction, 146–48, 223n.16
Belles of the Village, The (play), 228n.3
"Benevolent Bar, The" (Nesbit), 141
Benson, Baby, 158, 163
Benson, Edward White, 155–56
Beringer, Vera, 158, 163, 174, 196, 227n.37
Berman, Ruth, 122–23, 221n.16
Betham-Edwards, Matilda, 128
Betty, William Henry West, 159–60
bildungsroman, *Treasure Island* as, 88–89, 220n.17
Birkin, Andrew, 176, 201, 203, 205, 231n.24
Blackburn, William, 219nn.7,13
Blainey, Ann, 225n.19
Blake, Kathleen, 74, 80, 97, 112
Blake, William, 14, 26
Blanchard, E. L., 169, 184–88, 191, 193, 226n.21, 227n.30
Bleak House (Dickens), 152
Bluebell in Fairyland (play), 192, 201, 228n.2
Boas, George, 9–11, 149, x–xi
Bookman (journal), 26
Boone, Troy, 215n.33, 219n.5
Boucicault, Dion, 193
Bourdieu, Pierre, 41
Bowman, Isa, 169–70, 230n.16
Boys and I, The (Molesworth), 40, 52–53
Boy's Country-Book: Being the Real Life of a Country Boy, Written by Himself, The (Howitt), 217n.11
Brantlinger, Patrick, 79
Brass Bottle, The (Anstey), 135
Briggs, Julia, 43, 132, 140, 142, 146, 222nn.8, 13
Bristow, Joseph, 69–70, 220n.14
British Mothers (journal), 215n.39
Brody, Margaret and Lillian, 221n.10
Brontë, Charlotte, 20, 45–50
Brooks, Van Wyck, 125–26
Brown, Penny, 41
Brownies, The (Ewing), 40, 217n.10
Bubbles (Millais), 177
Burnett, Frances Hodgson, 9, 35–38, 127–28, 132–33, 216n.40 217n.7; cult of the child and, 175–79, 228n.41, 230n.19; theatrical versions of works by, 158, 163, 175, 183, 189, 192–97, 227n.37, 229n.14, 230n.16
Burnett, Vivian, 174–79, 230n.16
Butler, Josephine, 152, 227n.35

Cameron, Julia Margaret, 154
Carpenter, Humphrey, 126, 142, 149, 223n.1
Carpenter, Mary, 9, 17, 152, 211n.2
Carr, Philip, 198, 230n.20
Carroll, Lewis, 4–7, 29, 91–124, 130, 211nn.1–2; criticism of, 4, 14, 21, 24, 98, 104, 109, 125–26, 181, 220n.2, ix; cult of the child and, 9–11, 14, 95, 149–79, 154, 156–57, 177–78, 202, 205, 208; photography of, 95, 99–110; preoccupation with child performers, 168–75, 188–89, 196, 227n.34, 228n.39; Ruskin's critique of, 16, 111; theatrical versions of works by, 158, 183, 189–91
cartoon images of children, 17–21
"Casabianca" (Hemans), 137
Case of Peter Pan: Or, The Impossibility of Children's Fiction, The (Rose), 4, 29–32, 134, 199, 215n.33
Chambers, Aidan, 43
Chapman, Mary, 101, 104
Charles I (play), 184
Chase, Pauline, 200–201
Cherry Ripe (Millais), 177
Chesterton, G. K., 125
child audience members, 33–34, 184–86, 193, 229n.5; *Alice in Wonderland* and, 191, 199, 230n.22; *Little Lord Fauntleroy* and, 193–94, 230n.16; *Peter Pan* and, 198–201, 231n.26; reviewers' accounts of, 186–87, 191, 197–98, 230n.16

"Child in Recent English Literature, The," 27
child labor laws, 152–53, 204, 223n.2; child performers and, 166
Child-Loving: The Erotic Child and Victorian Culture (Kincaid), 34–35, 97, 207, 215n.38
child narrators: Craik's use of, 44–51; Crompton's use of, 55–56; Dickens's use of, 51–52; emergence of, 7–8, 39–43, 212n.2, 216n.4, 217n.11; Ewing's use of, 43–44, 53, 56–68; Molesworth's use of, 52–53; Nesbit's use of, 133–48; Stevenson's use of, 81–92; Stretton's use of, 54–55
Child of Nature paradigm, 5–6, 15, 42, 119–20, 174, 205–6. *See also* primitivism and Romantic ideal of childhood innocence
child performers: ages of, 174, 227n.31; American view of, 161, 225n.20, 227n.37; Carroll's commentary on, 95, 169–71, 173; children's theatre and, 181–89, 192–93, 196–97; cult of the child and, 156–74, 225n.9; families and siblings as, 161–62, 226n.24; Hunt's criticism of, 159–61; opposition to, 159–79; precocity of, 11, 33–34, 156–75, 182, 196, 209, 226n.25, 227n.31–34
child playgoers. *See* child audience members
child readers, 28–29; authors' concerns over, 67–68, 71, 91–92, 113–19, 123–24, 126–29; as characters in children's literature, 4, 6, 16, 21–26, 28–29, 62, 110, 129–30, 132–48; as victimized Others, critical discourse on, 31–33, 214n.31, 215n.33
"Children and Children's Books" (Rands), 150
Children and Theatre in Victorian England (Varty), 226n.25
Children in English Society (Pinchbeck and Hewitt), 223n.2
Children of the Poor (Cunningham), 152, 225n.6, 228n.38
"Children on the Stage," 165, 187, 189
"Children's Books" (Rigby), 128–29
children's literature. *See also* Golden Age of children's literature: as colonization, 30–33, 214n.31
"Children's Literature of the Last Century" (Yonge), 129
Children's Pinafore, The, 157, 162–65, 169, 172, 182, 187, 228n.2
"Children's Plays" (anon.), 190–92, 197
children's theatre, 33–34, 175, 180–209, 215n.36; in America, 182–83, 192–93, 197; emergence of, 11, 175
"Children Yesterday and Today" (Shand), 24–25
Child's Garden of Verses, A (Stevenson), 21
"Child-Worship" (Filon), 10, 177, 180–81
Christianity, Stevenson's treatment of, 77–78
Cinderella (pantomime), 228n.3
Clapp, Henry A., 157
Clark, Beverly Lyon, 40, 125–26, 197 215n.32, 228n.43
Clarke, Henry Savile, 183, 189
class politics: in Burnett's work, 37, 194–97; child playgoers and, 184; cult of the child and, 152–53, 155, 173; sexuality of children and, 152–53, 204–5; in stories with child narrators, 43–45, 54–55, 60
Cockyolly Bird, The (Dearmer), 193
Cohen, Morton N., 95, 154, 220n.2, 221n.9
Coleman, John, 165
Coleridge, Hartley, 23
Coleridge, Samuel Taylor, 12–13
collaboration. *See* adult-child collaboration
colonization paradigm in children's literature, 30–33, 41, 214n.31; in Nesbit's work, 148; *Treasure Island* and, 71–92
Colvin, Sidney, 78
Conan Doyle, Arthur, 132
Conrad, Joseph, 66–67, 79, 219n.13
"Conscience-Pudding, The" (Nesbit), 141
Cooper, Edward H., 198
Coral Island, The (Ballantyne), 64–66, 70–72, 75, 77, 90, 220n.15
Corelli, Marie, 215n.39
Countess Kate (Yonge), 212n.3
Country Girl The (play), 159, 225n.16, 226n.28
Country Wife, The (Wycherly), 160, 225n.16
Coveney, Peter, 3, 14, 39, 126, 149, 177, 205–6, 216n.1
Craik, Dinah Maria Mulock, 5, 29, 38, 216n.4, 217n.7, 218n.14; use of child narrator by, 7, 40–51, 71, 127, 217n.7, 218n.14
Criminal Law Amendment Act (1885), 153

Critical Essays on the Performers of the London Theatres (Hunt), 225n.15
Critic (journal), 10
Crockett, S. R., 28
Crompton, Frances E., 40, 55–56
Crouch, Marcus, 130, 222n.5
Crozier, Brian, 227n.32
Crumbie, James, 224n.4
Cub Scouts, 40
Cult of Childhood, The (Boas), 149
cult of the child, 4, 9–12, 35, 95, 149–80, 188, 202, x–xii; child performers and, 156–79; Victorian discourse about, 10–12, 149–50, 167–68, 180, xi
"Cult of the Child, The" (Dowson), 10, 153, 171–72, xi
"Cult of the Child, The" (E. A. D.), 230n.19
"Cult of the Little Girl," 177, 228n.42
Cumberland, Duke of, 79
Cunningham, Hugh, 3, 17, 39, 152, 213n.19, 224n.5, 225n.6, 228n.38
Current Opinion (journal), 229n.11
Cymbeline (Shakespeare), 184

Daisy Chain: or, Aspirations, a Family Chronicle, The (Yonge), 5
Darton, F. J. Harvey, 186
Davenport, Jean, 161
David Copperfield (Dickens), 28, 39
Davis, Tracy C., 105–6, 220n.7
Day, Thomas, 22
Dead Heart, The (play), 184
Dealings with the Fairies (Ruskin), 213n.21
Defoe, Daniel, 58, 68, 78–79
de Genlis, Madame, 101
De Quincey, Thomas, 13
desert island romance: *Coral Island* as example of, 71–72; deromanticization of, in *Treasure Island*, 72–92
Dickens, Charles: child actors criticized by, 160–61, 163–65, 167, 171–72, 226n.21; child characters of, 3, 8–9, 35–36, 152–53, 161, 196, 215n.39, 226n.27; child labor campaigns and, 17, 153; children as readers of, 215n.32; children's testimony in work of, 216n.1; Nesbit's treatment of, 28, 129, 132, 147; use of child narrators by, 7, 39–40, 51–53, 59, 150, 216n.2
Dick Whittington and His Cat (pantomime), 228n.3, 229n.9
didacticism: Carroll's treatment of, 110–24; Ewing's use of, 61–62; Golden Age children's literature and, 29, 55–56, 84–85, 91–92, 113–14, 118–19, 127–29, 211n.2
Divine Songs Attempted in Easy Language for the Use of Children (Watts), 216n.4
Dixon, Gerald, 165–66
Dodgson, Charles Lutwidge. *See* Carroll, Lewis
Doll's House, A (Ibsen), 194
Donkin, Alice Jane, 105–6, 155
Doré, Gustave, 184, 204
Douglas (Home), 212n.10
Dowson, Ernest, 10, 153–54, 156, 168–79, 202, 205, 227nn.33, 36
"Dream-Children" (Lamb), 178
Dreams of Adventure, Deeds of Empire (Green), 64
Dryden, John, 150
Dubourg, Evelyn, 106–7
du Maurier, Angela, 229n.12
Dunraven, Lord, 165

Eager, Edward, 130–31, 222n.6
East Lynne (Wood), 8, 36
Ebb-Tide, The (Stevenson), 79
Edgeworth, Maria, 12, 132
Editha's Burglar (Burnett), 9, 133, 194
editors, in Nesbit's work, 129–30, 138–39
Edmond, Rod, 79
education reform, 152, 224n.3
Elementary Education Act, 224n.3
Ellice, Pauline, 170, 227n.34
Ellis, Havelock, 204
"Elopement, The" (Carroll photograph), 105–6, 110
Emile; or, On Education (Rousseau), 12–15
Eminent Victorians (Strachey), 125
Enchanted Castle, The (Nesbit), 141–43
England, Edward, 79, 229n.4
English Illustrated Magazine, 158
Era (journal), 163–64, 182, 185, 190–92, 194, 197, 228nn.2–3, 229n.10, 230nn.17, 22
Erotic Innocence (Kincaid), 215n.38
Ewing, Juliana, 5, 7, 28–29, 211n.2, 216n.40, 217n.10; influence on children's literature of, 40–43, 181, 217n.6; Nesbit influenced by, 132; power relationships discussed by, 127; use of child narrators by, 52, 56–68

Factory Act of 1833, 223n.2
Fairy Realm: A Collection of the Famous Old Tales (Hood), 23–24
"Fairy Stories" (Ruskin), 16, 111
fairy tales, role in children's literature of, 12
family story genre, 5
fantasy: Nesbit's use of, 130–31; non-escapist aspects of, 4–7, 14–26, 119, 207, 209, 211n.1, 223n.1; as refuge from modern life, 4, 14, 149, 211n.1; role in children's literature of, 12, 211n.2
Farjeon, Eleanor, 184
"Fictions for Children," 15–16, 18
Fielding, Sarah, 127, 216n.4
Figaro in London, 155
Filon, Augustin, 10, 180
Finley, Martha, 179
Fisher, Clara, 226n.26
Five Children and It (Nesbit), 134, 140
Flaxman's Illustrations of the Iliad of Homer, 49
Foltinowicz, Adelaide, 153–54, 227n.33
Foulkes, Richard, 156, 228n.39
Fouqué, de la Motte, 132
Fowler, Alastair, 80
From Nowhere to the North Pole (Hood), 22

Galbraith, Mary, 215n.36
Garrick, David, 225n.16, 226n.26
Gatty, Horatia, 64
Gatty, Margaret, 12, 150
General History of the Robberies and Murders of the Most Notorious Pirates, A (Defoe), 79
Gentle Heritage, The (Crompton), 40, 55–56, 218n.17
German Popular Stories (Grimm), 16
Gielgud, Kate Terry, 157
Gilbert, Sandra M., 46
Gilbert and Sullivan operettas, all-child productions of, 157, 162–65, 169, 172, 182, 227n.29
Gillis, John R., 152
Girl Guide movement, 40
Girls and I, The (Molesworth), 40, 52–53
Girl's Own Paper, 221n.7
Golden Age, The (Grahame), 26–28, 147–48
Golden Age of children's literature, 4–8, 14–15, 21–29, 37–38, 126–28, 149–51, 158, 180–83, 209, ix–x; critical denigration of, 125–26; as critical term, 211n.2; didacticism and, 29, 55–56, 61–62, 84–85, 91–92, 113–14, 118–19, 127–29, 211n.2; as form of escapism, 4, 14, 211n.1, 223n.1, ix; nineteenth-century discussions of, 14–17, 21, 24–26, 125–29, 150, 222n.4
Good Words for the Young (children's periodical), 12
Gorham, Deborah, 152, 224n.4
"Gossip on Romance, A" (Stevenson), 80–81
Governess, The (Fielding), 127, 216n.4
Grahame, Kenneth, 25–27, 126, 132, 147–48, 162, 181, 214n.27
Grattan, Harry, 158, 178
Great Emergency, A (Ewing), 40, 60–63
Green, Martin, 63–64, 75
Green, Peter, 27, 170
Green, Roger Lancelyn, 192, 211n.2, 216n.2, 231n.27
Gubar, Susan, 46
Gulliver in Lilliput (play), 226n.26

H. M. S. Pinafore (Gilbert and Sullivan), all-child productions of, 157, 162–65, 169, 172, 182, 227n.29, 228n.2
Hall, Donald E., 58, 62–63
Hanson, Bruce K., 202, 204, 214n.28, 231n.24
Hans the Boatman (play), 184
"Happy Family, A" (Ewing), 40, 43–44
Hardesty, William, 77, 219nn.2, 13, 220n.17
Harding's Luck (Nesbit), 142, 147, 223n.14
Harlequin Hudibras (pantomime), 184
Harrison, Frederic, 155, 220n.3
Hemans, Felicia, 137
Henkle, Roger, 112
"Henry Holiday Album," 221n.10
Hewitt, Margaret, 188, 223n.2, 224n.3
"Hiawatha's Photography" (Carroll), 107–8
Higonnet, Anne, 93, 99
History of English Drama (Nicoll), 158
History of the Fairchild Family, The (Sherwood), 127, 222n.3
Holiday House (Sinclair), 5, 16, 212n.3
Holiday Romance: In Four Parts (Dickens), 8, 39, 51–53, 59, 150
Home, John, 212n.10
Honeyman, Susan, 211n.1, 215n.35
Hood, Tom, 6, 21–24, 181, 213n.16
Horn, Pamela, 204, 224nn.2–3
House of Arden, The (Nesbit), 142, 147
House That Jack Built, The (play), 228n.3

Howard, Lydia, 158, 168
"How Doth the Little Busy Bee" (Watts), 111
"How Fauntleroy Occurred" (Burnett), 175–79
Howitt, Mary, 5, 217n.11
Howitt, William, 217n.11
Hudson, Glenda A., 207
Hughes, Felicity A., 126
Hughes, M. V., 114
"*Humble Remonstrance, A*" (Stevenson), 80
Humpty Dumpty (pantomime), 184–85
Hunt, Leigh, 159–63, 165, 169, 188, 225nn.15, 17–19, 226n.27
Hunt, Peter, 216n.40
Hunting of the Snark, The, 24

Ibsen, Henrik, 194
Iliad (Homer), 49
Illustrated London News, 190, 193–94, 197, 227n.37
Image of Childhood, The (Coveny), 14
imperialist ideology. *See also* colonization paradigm in children's literature:
in children's literature, 37, 42, 58–68, 214n.31, 216n.40, 217n.7, 218n.22;
in Nesbit's work, 223n.15; in *Treasure Island,* 69–92
"Infant Phenomenon, The" (Dickens' character), 161, 163–64, 226nn.22–23, 27
"Infant Phenomenon, The" (Miss Mudie), 162–63, 226n.27
Ingelow, Jean, 211n.2
Ingoldsby Legends (Barham), 135
innocence. *See also* Romantic ideal of childhood innocence: Carroll's subversion of ideal of, 93–111; children's theatre and concepts of, 11, 175, 183, 187–209; cult of the child and, 9–11, 35, 95, 149–79, x–xi; Golden Age children's authors' view of, 4–10, 12–38, ix, xi; Victorian culture and, 151–79, 183, x–xi
Inventing the Victorians (Sweet), 125
Inventing Wonderland (Wullschläger), 126
Irving, Henry, 184, 201

"Jabberwocky" (Carroll), 114–18
Jackanapes (Ewing), 40
Jackson, David H., 80, 219n.13
Jackson, Tony, 229n.4
James, G. P. R., 16
James, Henry, 40, 81, 87, 126, 156, 196
Jane Eyre (Brontë), 39, 42, 45–50, 218n.14
Jeffries, Mary, 224n.4
Jerrold, Blanchard, 184, 204
Jeune, Lady Mary, 165
Jimmy's Cruise on the "Pinafore" (Alcott), 164–65
Johnston, Annie Fellows, 179
Jolly, Rosalyn, 78–79
Jones, Katharine, 215n.36
Jungle Books, The (Kipling), 28, 40, 44, 141
Just So Stories for Little Children (Kipling), 212n.5
Juvenile Literature as It Is (Salmon), 69
Juvenilia: A Collection of Poems, Written between the Ages of Twelve and Sixteen (Hunt), 225n.19

Kiddie Lit (Clark), 215n.32
Kiely, Robert, 80, 219n.6, 220n.19
Kincaid, James R., 34–35, 97–98, 112, 151, 178–79, 207, 215n.38, 221n.14, xi
King of the Golden River, The (Ruskin), 15–16
Kingsford, Maurice Rooke, 77
Kingsley, Charles, 6, 21–22, 29, 150, 181, 211n.1, 213n.23
Kingston, W. H. G., 42, 64–68, 218n.21
Kipling, Rudyard, 28, 40, 132, 141, 212n.5, 222n.10
Kitchin, Alexandra (Xie), 100–101, 105–6, 109
Knight's Castle (Eager), 222n.6
Knoepflmacher, U. C., 16, 122, 211n.2, 212nn.5, 7
Kutzer, Daphne, 42, 223n.15

Lady's Newspaper, 36
Lamb, Charles, 12–13, 178, 203, 216n.4
Lamb, Mary, 216n.4
La Touche, Rose, 15, 156, 172–73, 179
Leach, Karoline, 103, 154, 179, 220n.2
Lear, Edward, 126, 211n.1, 220n.2
Lebailly, Hugues, 157, 225n.14
Leech, John, 17–21, 27
legal rights of children, 152, 224n.5; child performers and actors and, 170–79
Leslie, Elsie, 10, 227n.37, 230n.16
Lesnik-Oberstein, Karín, 215nn.33, 35
Letley, Emma, 79
Liddell, Alice, 104–5, 178
Liddell, Edith, 221n.9
Liddell family, 96, 101–2, 108–9
"Light Princess, The" (MacDonald), 21, 213n.21

Lila Field's Little Wonders, 164
Lilliput Levee (Rands), 150–51
Linehan, Katherine, 79
literacy. *See* active literacy; passive literacy
"Literary Cult of the Child, The" (Edwards), 10
"Literature for the Little Ones" (Salmon), 21
Literature of Their Own, A (Showalter), 218n.14
Little Goody Two Shoes (Blanchard pantomime), 162, 164, 185–88, 226n.21, 227n.30, 228n.3, 229n.10
"Little Grattans" (family act), 162
Little Lame Prince, The (Craik), 38
Little Lord Fauntleroy (Burnett), 158, 163, 175–79, 183, 189, 193–97, 207–8, 227n.37, 228nn.40–41, 229n.14, 230nn.16,19–20
Little Lychetts: A Piece of Autobiography, The (Craik), 40, 44–50, 52–53, 217n.7, 218nn.12,14–15
Little Men (Alcott), 165
"Little Mermaid, The" (Andersen), 37
Little Princess, A (Burnett), 9, 35–38, 40, 181–82, 196–97
"Little Red Riding Hood" (Carroll photograph), 107–8
Little Red Riding Hood (pantomime), 186–87
Little Un-Fairy Princess, A (Burnett), 197
Little White Bird, The (Barrie), 126, 205, 209
Little Women (Alcott), 5, 28, 165
"Living Miniatures" (child acting troupe), 163, 169
Llewelyn Davies family, 175–76, 179, 201–2, 208–9
Lloyd, Marie, 184
Lodge, David, 49
London Child of the 1870s, A (Hughes), 114
London Entr'acte (journal), 185
London Labour and the London Poor (Mayhew), 153
Loxley, Diana, 75, 77, 219n.4
Lucas, E. V., 26
Lurie, Alison, 215n.34

MacDonald, George, 12, 16, 128, 150, 181, 211n.1
MacDonald, Irene, 102–3
Mackenzie, Compton, 184, 192
Macmillan, Alexander, 213n.23
Maher, Susan N., 219n.9
"Maiden Tribute of Modern Babylon, The" (Stead), 155, 224n.4
male gaze: Carroll's photographs and, 99–100, 104–10; Victorian *tableaux vivants* and, 103–10, 220n.7
Manager's Daughter, The (play), 161
Manchester Mighty Mites, The, 164
Mann, David, 77, 219nn.2,13, 220n.17
Man Who Stole the Castle, The (play), 230n.20
March of Intellect, The (play), 161
marriage age requirements, 155
Marryat, Frederick, 85, 87, 132
Mary's Meadow (Ewing), 40, 56–64
mass culture, cult of the child as, 179
Masterman Ready (Marryat), 84–85, 87
Mavor, Carol, 102, 107–8
Max Krömer: A Story of the Siege of Strasbourg (Stretton), 40, 54–55
Mayhew, Henry, 153, 184
"May Queen, The" (Tennyson), 101
McCaslin, Nellie, 229n.4
McGillis, Roderick, 37
McMillan, Margaret, 204–5
Mighty Atom, The (Corelli), 215n.39
Millais, John Everett, 177
Mill on the Floss, The (Eliot), 39
Ministering Children (Charlesworth), 44, 134, 141
Moers, Ellen, 218n.12
Molesworth, Mary Louisa, 5, 40, 42, 52–53, 127–28, 211n.2
Montgomery, L. M., 28, 217n.6
Moore, Arthur, 153, 168
Moore, Doris Langley, 222nn. 10,12
Morley, Malcolm, 161
Morris, Frankie, 189–90
Mortality Ode. *See* "Ode: Intimations of Immortality from Recollections of Early Childhood"
Mortimer, Favell Lee, 114, 119
Moss, Anita, 39–40, 140, 216n.2, 222nn.8, 13
Mozley, Harriet, 5
Mrs. Leicester's School: or, The History of Several Young Ladies, Related by Themselves (Lamb), 216n.4
Mrs. Overtheway's Remembrances (Ewing), 217n.6
Mudie, Miss (child prodigy), 162–63, 226n.27
Mulready, William, 101
Mulvey, Laura, 99

Munro, H. H. (Saki), 25, 214n.24
Myers, Mitzi, 12, 32, 232n.12
My Own Story, or, The Autobiography of a Child (Howitt), 217n.11

Nabokov, Vladimir, 109
Nation (journal), 24
Nel, Philip, 222n.6
Nesbit, E., 7, 25, 53, 125–48, 216n.1; child narrators in work of, 39–45, 56, 133–48; Ewing's influence on, 43–44, 60; promotion of active literacy by, 28–29, 129–48, 181
Nesbit Tradition, The (Crouch), 222n.5
"New Hero, The" (Watts), 10
Newton, Edward, 154
New Treasure Seekers, The (Nesbit), 132–33
Nicholas Nickleby (Dickens), 36, 161
Nickel, Douglas R., 95, 154
Nicoll, Allardyce, 158
Nixie (Burnett/Townsend play), 194–96, 227n.33
Nodelman, Perry, 31–33, 214n.31
Norton Anthology of Children's Literature, 182

"Ode: Intimations of Immortality from Recollections of Early Childhood" (Wordsworth), 11, 14, 205
"Of Queens' Gardens" (Ruskin), 15
Olander, Kathleen, 174
Old Curiosity Shop, The (Dickens), 8
"Old-Fashioned Children" (Adye), 196
Oliver Twist (Dickens), 3, 8, 39, 147, 153
One I Knew Best of All, The (Burnett), 37, 214n.29
Open Your Mouth and Shut Your Eyes (Mulready painting), 101
original sin, cult of the child and, 174
"Other: Orientalism, Colonialism, and Children's Literature, The" (Nodelman), 214n.31
"Our Field" (Ewing), 40, 52–53, 55–64
Our Mutual Friend (Dickens), 3, 153, 196
Our Year: A Child's Book, In Prose and Verse (Craik), 40, 50–52
Oxford Companion to the Theatre, The, 192

Pall Mall Gazette, 128, 190
pantomimes: *Alice in Wonderland*, relationship to, 189–91, 229n.9; child performers in, 157, 161–66, 168–74, 185, 227n.32; child playgoers and, 166–68, 184–87, 229nn.5–6; children's theatre and emergence of, 183–209; *Peter Pan* relationship to, 201–2
Pantomime Waifs: or, A Plea for Our City Children (Barlee), 165–66
Paradisi in sole Paradisus terrestris (Parkinson), 56–56
Parkinson, John, 56–57
passive literacy, 29, 114, 118–19, 127–28, 181, 214n.30, 222n.3
Pearsall, Ronald, 155, 224n.4, 228n42, 231n.8
Peculiar Gift: Nineteenth-Century Writings on Books for Children, A, 222n.4
Peep Behind the Scenes, A (Walton), 164
Peep of Day, The (Mortimer), 114
Penelope Boothby (Reynolds painting), 99–101, 105–6
Peter and Wendy (Barrie), 25, 32, 202, 204–8
Peter Pan (Barrie play), 5–6, 25, 119, 193, 198–209, 214n.24, 229n.12, 231nn.24–27; cult of the child and, 175–79; relationship to children's theatre, 175, 183, 189, 199–202; reviews of, 125, 198–200, 202, 231n.24; Rose's claims about, 31–32, 199–201, 215n.32, 231nn.23–26
Peter Pan's Postbag (Chase), 200, 231n.25
Petsetilla's Posy: A Fairy Tale for Young and Old (Hood), 22
Phoenix and the Carpet, The (Nesbit), 131, 134–37, 222nn.10–11
"Photographer's Day Out, A" (Carroll), 98–99, 106–10, 221n.9
Pinchbeck, Ivy, 188, 223n.2, 224n.3
Pirates of Penzance, The, all-child production of, 169, 182, 227n.29
plagiarism, Nesbit's views on, 132–36, 222n.10
Playfair, Nigel, 198, 230n.20
Plotz, Judith, 3–4, 14, 119–20
Poetry for Children (Aiken), 150
Pope, Alexander, 132, 150
power imbalance in children's literature: Carroll's recognition of, 91–92, 96–98, 110–24; critical discussions of, 29–34, 214n.31, 215nn.33–36; Golden Age authors' recognition of, 29–32, 41–62, 126–27, 150, 181–82, 208–9; Nesbit's recognition of, 129–48; Stevenson's recognition of, 70–71, 91–92

precocity: in child-centered plays, 11, 175, 189, 194–97, 203–5; of child performers, 11, 33, 156–75; critical discussions of, 29–34, 214n.31, 215nn.33–36; cult of the child and, 9–11, 15, 95, 153–80, 228n.44, xi; in Dickens's work, 3–4, 8–9, 17, 152–53, 196; Golden Age authors' recognition of, 29–32, 41–62, 126–27, 150, 181–82, 208–9; Romantic and Victorian anxiety about, 3–4, 13, 16–19, 27, 152–53, 156–57, 159–68, 172–73, 196, 215n.39, 227n.37; sexuality of children and, 154–56, 160, 165–66, 179, 204–5
Prelude, The (Wordsworth), 13
Prickett, Stephen, 15, 211n.1, 213n.16
primitivism: Carroll's view of, 93–124; child performers and, 162–63, 167–68, 174, 226n.25; children's literature and, 3–38, 42, 149–51, 205–8; cult of the child and, 3–4, 9–12, 149–79, 212n.7, x–xi; in reviews and criticism, 31–33, 198–99
Prince and the Pauper, The (play), 186
problem of address. *See* power imbalance in children's literature
prodigies. *See* child performers, precocity of
Punch (journal), 17, 25, 190–91, 194–95

racism, Stevenson's treatment of, 77–78
Rackety-Packety House (Burnett), 192
Railway Children, The (Nesbit), 146–48, 223n.16
Rands, William Brighty, 128, 150–51, 181
Ransome, Arthur, 26, 32
Real Little Lord Fauntleroy, The (Burnett). *See Little Lord Fauntleroy*
reciprocity. *See also* adult-child collaboration: in Barrie's work, 7–8, 207–9; in Carroll's *Alice books,* 7–8, 96–98, 111–24; in Nesbit's work, 131–48
Reid, Julia, 79–80
Reimer, Mavis, 41, 132
Remnits, Virginia Yeaman, 27
"Resolution and Independence" (Wordsworth), 122–23
Reynolds, Joshua, 93–95, 99, 105–6, 110
Richards Jeffrey, 58, 69
Richardson, Alan, 12–14, 21, 213n.13, 214n.30
Rigby, Elizabeth, 45–46, 128–29
Rip Van Winkle (play), 184
"Robert Louis Stevenson" (James), 81, 87
Robin Hood and His Merry Little Men (Blanchard pantomime), 186–88
Robinson Crusoe (Defoe), 58, 68–69, 74–78, 219n.9
Robson, Catherine, 14, 149, 171, 213n.15, 227n.35
Robson, W. W., 143
Romantic ideal: Carroll's subversion of, 93–11, 119–24; of childhood innocence, 3–4, 12–14, 27–28, 93–95, 173, 203, 212n.7, x–xi; child mortality and, 13–14; child performers and, 162–63, 167–68, 174, 226n.25; children's theatre and, 11, 175, 183, 187–209; cult of the child and, 3–4, 9–12, 35, 95, 149–79, 226n.25, x–xi; fantasy and fairy tales and, 12, 16, 26, 213n.13; Golden Age and, 4–10, 12–38, 149–51, 205–9, 212n.8, ix, xi; in reviews and criticism of children's literature, 31–33, 198–99; Victorian culture and, 151–79, 183, x–xi
Romanticism and the Vocation of Childhood (Plotz), 119–20
Roscoe, William Caldwell, 15–16, 18–19, 21
Rose, Jacqueline, 4, 21, 23, 29–33, 134, 139, 147–48, 214n.31, 215n.33; on child narrators, 41–43, 58, 68–69, 88, 143, 218n.18; on child performers, 32, 171; on children's theatre, 182, 186, 199–201, 205, 209, 231n.24; on *Treasure Island,* 41, 77
Rose and the Ring, The (Thackeray), 16–17, 21, 28, 63, 191
Rossetti, Christina, 211n.2
Roth, Christine, 177, 228n.44
Rothwell, Erika, 130, 132, 139
Rousseau, Jean-Jacques, 12–15, 22, 25, 76
Rowling, J. K., 130–31, 222n.6
Royal Commission on Popular Education, 224n.3
Ruby, Gold, and Malachite (Tuke painting), 177
Rudd, David, 32, 215n.33
Ruskin, John, 15–16, 211n.2, 213n.18; on child performers, 157–59, 170; on children's literature, 16, 111; cult of the child and, 10, 15–16, 149–50, 154–57, 172–73; on Ewing's work, 40; MacDonald's work criticized by, 21, 213n.21; on pantomimes, 188; precocity of children and, 156, 172–73
rusticity, cult of, 12–13

Safe Compass, The, 114
St. James Gazette, 196
St. Nicholas (journal), 192–93
Saki. *See* Munro, H. H.
Salazar, Laura Gardner, 229n.4
Salmon, Edward, 21–22, 69, 128
Sandison, Alan, 79–81, 220n.17
Sands, Karen, 216n.40
Santayana, George, 69
school story, genre of, 5
Schwartz, Lynne Sharon, 38
Schwartz, Murray, 217n.9
Scott, Clement, 194
Scott, Walter, 128, 150, 215n.32
"Sea-Dream, The" (Blake), 80
Secret Garden, The (Burnett), 37, 40, 217n.7, 228n.41
Secret Gardens: The Golden Age of Children's Literature (Carpenter), 126, 142, 223n.1
Seebohm, E. V., 229n.14
sexism: of boy narrators created by women writers, 43–44, 60–64; in critical accounts of Golden Age, 5, 211n.2
sexuality of children: age of consent laws and, 152–53, 204, 224n.4; child performers and, 165–66; class politics and, 152–55, 173–74; cult of the child and, 151–79, 225n.14, 228n.44; in Grahame's *Golden Age,* 26–28; *Peter Pan* and, 200–205; in Victorian culture, 34–35, 103–10, 151–79, 215n.38, 220n.7; in *Wind in the Willows,* 26, 214nn.26–27
Shaftesbury (Lord Ashley; Anthony Ashley-Cooper), 17, 153, 224n.3
Shakespeare, William, 16–18, 49, 101, 128
Shand, Alexander Innes, 24–25
Shaw, George Bernard, 171–72, 198–99, 227n.36, 230n.21
Shepard, Ernest H., 184–85, 192
Shepard, Odell, 126
Sherwood, Mary Martha, 127, 222n.3
Shock-Headed Peter (Carr/Playfair play), 198, 230n.20
"Should Children Have a Special Literature?" (Salmon), 128
Showalter, Elaine, 48, 218nn.14,16
Shows of London, The (Altick), 103
Sidgwick, Mary ("Minnie"), 156
Silas Marner (Eliot), 8
Sinclair, Catherine, 5, 16, 212n.2
Sir Toady Lion (Crockett), 28
Six to Sixteen (Ewing), 40
size motif in Carroll's works, 112–24
Smith, Janet Adam, 81
Smith, Lindsay, 101, 112
Smith, Sarah. *See* Stretton, Hesba
Snow Man, The (play), 191
Social Purity campaign (1890s), 103
Southey, Robert, 114
Spectator (journal), 11, 150
"Stage Children" (Carroll), 173
Stead, W. T., 152, 154–55, 224n.4, 227n.35
Steedman, Carolyn, 162, 171, 225nn.10, 14, 226n.25
Steer, Philip Wilson, 155
Stephens, John, 139
Stevenson, Robert Louis, 5, 21, 29, 69–92, 130, 181
Story of a Bad Boy, The (Aldrich), 28
Story of the Treasure Seekers, The (Nesbit), 7, 39–40, 43–45, 131–48, 217n.5, 222nn.7,9, 13
storytelling. *See also* active literacy; adult-child collaboration; child narrators: in *Alice in Wonderland,* 96–98, 110–24; in early children's literature, 127–28; in *Treasure Island,* 84–85
Strachey, Lytton, 125
Strand (journal), 138
Strange Dislocations (Steedman), 162
Streatfeild, Noel, 164
Stretton, Hesba, 28, 40, 54–55
Strindberg, August, 230n.21
Studies in the Psychology of Sex (Ellis), 204
Sully, J., 27
Susina, Jan, 216n.2, 221n.11
Sutphin, Christine, 221n.1
Sweet, Matthew, 125, 152, 221n.1, 231n.28
Swinburne, Algernon, 177–78
Swiss Family Robinson, The (Wyss), 84–85
Sylvie and Bruno (Carroll), 126, 178

Tableaux, Charades and Conundrums, 103–4, 107, 220n.3
tableaux vivants, 101–7, 220n.3
Tait, Lawson (Dr.), 204
Tarr, C. Anita, 231n.27
Taylor, Roger, 108, 110, 220n.4, 221n.10
Taylor, Tom, 221n.9
Tellers of Tales (Green), 211n.2, 216n.2
Tenniel, John, 119
Tennyson, Alfred, 20, 101, 104–5
Terry, Ellen, 162, 184
Terry, Kate, 161–62
Terry, Minnie, 227n.33

Thacker, Deborah, 215n.36
Thackeray, William Makepeace, 6, 16, 18–21, 63, 181, 211n.2
Theatre, The (journal), 158, 165–66, 189–90
theft metaphor, Nesbit's use of, 130–48
Thompson, E. P., 221n.1
Three Lieutenants, The (Kingston), 67
Three Midshipmen, The (Kingston), 64–67, 218n.20
Through the Looking-Glass (Carroll), 114–24
Times of London, 190
Tindal, Marcus, 226n.21
"To the Five" (Barrie), 175–76, 202, 208–9
"To the Hesitating Purchaser" (Stevenson), 70–71
Tour Round My Garden, A, 56
Townsend, John Rowe, 77
Townsend, Stephen, 194
Treasure Island (Stevenson), 41, 68; imperialist ideology and, 69–92; self-reflexivity in, 126–27
Tree, Herbert Beerbohm, 201
Tuke, Henry Scott, 177
Turn of the Screw, The (James), 156
Twain, Mark, 28, 40, 44, 126, 216n.3, 217n.5; children's theatre and, 158, 182, 229n.4
Twenty Years Ago: From the Journal of a Girl in Her Teens (Craik), 216n.4

Unbearable Bassington, The (Munroe), 214n.24
Uncle Tom's Cabin (play), 184

Vanity Fair (Thackeray), 16, 19
Varty, Anne, 226n.25
Ventures into Childland (Knoepflmacher), 211n.2
Very Ill-Tempered Family, A (Ewing), 40
victims, images of children as, 8, 212n.6
Victorian era: age of consent laws and culture of, 224n.4; hierarchies of in Carroll's work, 97; mythical anecdotes concerning, 125–26; precocity of children during, 11, 15, 17–21, 22n.25, 33, 149–79, 213n.18, 225nn.7, 19; view of childhood in, 14–20, 34–35, 39, 128, 149–80, 188–89, 196–98, 204–5, 213n.15, 223n.2, 224nn.3–5; visual images of children during, 17–20, 101–10
Victorian Fantasy (Prickett), 213n.16
Voskuil, Lynn M., 172

Waggoner, Diane, 109
Wagner, Vivian, 221n.13
Wakeling, Edward, 108, 110, 221n.10
Walkowitz, Judith, 105, 220n.7, 224n.4, 225n.6, 227n.35
Wall, Barbara, 115, 139, 217n.5
Walton, Mrs. O. F., 164
war, in children's literature, 54
Ward, Hayden W., 82
Ward, Henrietta, 155, 225n.7
Ward, Winifred, 229n.4
Water-Babies, The (Kingsley), 21–22, 213nn.22–23, 223n.1
Watson, Harold Frances, 72, 75, 219n.2
Watts, Isaac, 111, 113–14, 118–19, 216n.4
We and the World: A Book for Boys (Ewing), 40, 60, 63–68, 216n.40, 218nn.20–21
"'We and the World': Juliana Horatia Ewing and Victorian Colonialism for Children" (Hall), 58
Webling, Lucy, 227n.33
Wedmore, Frederick, 163
Weeks, Jeffrey, 151, 215n.37
Weld, Agnes, 107–8
Welsh Family Crusoes, The, 75
Wertheim, Albert, 17
"What Children Like to Read" (anon.), 128
What Katy Did (Coolidge), 28, 134
What Maisie Knew (James), 39
Whirligig Hall (play), 161
White, Donna R., 231n.27
White Cat, The (pantomime), 188
"Whole of the Story, The" (Burnett), 38
Wilde, Oscar, 155
Wilson, A. E., 185, 188, 229n.6
Wilson, Ann, 211n.1
Wilson, Anna, 228n.43
Wind in the Willows, The (Grahame), 24–26, 32, 214nn.26–27, 223n.1
Winnicott, D. W., 217n.9
Winnie the Pooh books, 184
Wizard of Oz (Baum), 64, 119, 221n.13
Woman of Passion (Briggs), 43, 142, 146
women writers of children's literature: child narrator technique and, 40, 211n.2, 217n.5, 218n.14; cult of the child and, 157, 175–79, 193–97; trope of collaboration used by, 7–8, 42–68, 126–27, 129–48
Wood, Mrs. Henry, 36

Wood, Naomi J., 78–79, 219nn.4,7
Woolf, Virginia, 125, 220n.2
Wordsworth, William, 11–14, 95, 122, 205, 207, 213n.15, 221n.16
Workshops Act of 1867, 223n.2
"Worship of Children, The" (anon.), 10–12, 149–50, 167
Wouldbegoods, The (Nesbit), 44, 129, 139, 141
"Writers for the Young" (anon.), 128, 151
Wullschläger, Jackie, 4, 95, 126, 177, 211nn.1–2, 220n.2
Wycherly, William, 160, 225n.16
Wyss, Johann, 84–85, 87

Yonge, Charlotte, 5, 128, 181, 211n.2, 212n.3
Young Folks (journal), 80

Zelizer, Viviana, 152, 224n.5
Zornaldo, Joseph L., 214n.31